Operations, Strategy, and Technology

Pursuing the Competitive Edge

Operations, Strategy, and Technology

Pursuing the Competitive Edge

Robert Hayes
Harvard University

Gary Pisano
Harvard University

David Upton
Harvard University

Steven Wheelwright
Harvard University

WILEY

Operations, Strategy and Technology
Pursuing The Competitive Edge

Authorized reprint by Wiley India Pvt. Ltd., 4435-36/7, Ansari Road, Daryaganj, New Delhi – 110002.

Reprint: 2016

Printed at: Satyam Enterprises, Delhi

ISBN: 978-81-265-3115-8

We would like to dedicate this book to our wives:
Priscilla,
Ingrid,
Nancy,
and Margaret.

We would like to dedicate this book to our wives:

Priscilla,

Ingrid,

Nancy

and Margaret

Preface

The world is a very different place than it was when two of the current co-authors wrote an earlier book on managing operations and technology, titled *Restoring Our Competitive Edge.* The kinds of challenges facing managers are very different, and in many ways more complex, and new technologies have arisen to help them deal with those challenges. While drawing from some of the same concepts and philosophies of *ROCE,* this is a substantially different book. It also boasts two more authors, Professors Gary Pisano and David Upton, who are experts in technology development and information technology. A quick review of the environment in which we wrote *ROCE* will illustrate how much has changed since then, and why we needed to write a new book.

THAT WAS THEN

In the early 1980s, U.S. industry had just begun to accept that it might be vulnerable to foreign competitors. The U.S. merchandise balance of trade had gone negative for the first time in a century as several of its critical industries were successfully attacked by imported products. Previously, each competitive failure had been dismissed individually as either unimportant in the context of the economy as a whole or the result of special conditions, such as low wages, "unfair" trade practices that were unsustainable in the long run, and "cherry picking" of particularly vulnerable industries and companies.

But in the early 1980s, these explanations were revealed to be largely wishful thinking. First automobiles—the largest U.S. industry and the symbol of its collective industrial might—then machine tools, computer peripherals, office machines, and integrated circuits—the pride of American technology—all rapidly lost share to foreign imports. The U.S. merchandise trade deficit soared, and within a few years the United States went from being the world's biggest creditor nation to being its biggest debtor. And the reasons for this decline sounded a common refrain: imported products provided, *in the eyes of customers,* higher quality, better reliability and lower lifetime costs, better value for the money, and greater responsiveness to customers' demands for greater product variety. In short, the common weapon that their foreign competitors were using to attack U.S. producers was sheer manufacturing and engineering prowess.

U.S. managers began to realize that they had fallen behind their foreign competitors on practically every competitive dimension. Their products cost more, had higher defect rates and looser tolerances, took longer to deliver, and were less innovative. So that first book focused on the basic levers for improving manufacturing competitiveness: facilities, production processes, and sourcing, emphasizing the importance of adopting a long-term, strategic perspective on competitiveness, and of learning as much as possible from observing the manufacturing practices of America's two fiercest competitor nations: Germany and Japan.

Heeding that call—one small voice in the chorus of warnings, recriminations, and prescriptions that arose from all directions—U.S. industry embarked on a flurry of manufacturing improvement programs during the 1980s. Every self-respecting company wanted to become *world class* by initiating *lean manufacturing* activities, including Total Quality Management, Just-In-Time production control, and Quick Product Development. They began *benchmarking* their performance of common activities against those of other companies that were recognized as leaders, and sent study teams to Japan and Europe to investigate best practices wherever they could be found. If attempts to make incremental improvements in existing processes were found to be insufficient, some companies began experimenting with *reengineering*—radically restructuring those processes.

Encouragingly, over the next decade or so many of them apparently succeeded: their competitive situation began to improve, although sometimes not for the intended reasons. The defect levels of U.S.-made products went down, sometimes to near-Japanese levels. Companies cut costs, largely by downsizing, slashing overhead, outsourcing, and rationalizing facilities. Inventory levels and delivery times decreased. Key suppliers were integrated more tightly into both production scheduling and product development. A combination of productivity improvement and a weakening U.S. dollar buttressed the cost competitiveness of U.S. goods. New products were introduced at an increasing rate. As a result, U.S. industry began regaining market share in such key industries as autos, integrated circuits, and construction machinery. Clearly, many U.S. companies had relearned "the basics" to the point where they were back to rough competitive parity with foreign producers.

THIS IS NOW

Yet, despite all these improvements, by the early years of the twenty-first century America's merchandise trade balance had risen back to more than $400 billion a year, despite a weakening U.S. dollar. Even the fact that some U.S. producers had been able to regain world leadership did not necessarily indicate that they had become net exporters. Personal computers provide an interesting case in point. Even though the U.S. industry's percentage of global shipments of PC-based systems rose between 1985 and 2000, it still ran a huge trade deficit because these systems were composed largely of imported components and peripheral devices. As they increasingly moved toward global outsourcing, U.S. companies gradually restricted their role to design, assembly, and marketing. Even more disturbing, the growing trade deficit increasingly reflected the growing import/outsourcing of *services*—even high-tech services such as software development, design, and engineering.

Clearly, the new approaches to improving cost, quality, flexibility, and responsiveness had not proven sufficient. In fact, study after study indicated that only about a third of all the operating improvement programs undertaken were regarded as successful. For a time the realization that all was not well was hidden by the enormous, widespread economic boom of the 1990s, which lifted profits and asset values far above their long-term levels. Starting in the late 1990s, however, with the currency devaluations and bank failures in Asia, then the stock market crash in the United States, and finally worldwide recession, managers' sense that they were on the right path to sustained profitability and growth wavered and died. It was time, once again, to give fresh thought to the foundations of competitive success, and the role that operations can play in that success.

Now, however, the "problem" was no longer confined to the United States and a few European countries; it had become worldwide and even more complex. Germany and Japan had entered a long period of economic stagnation, accompanied by increasing unemployment, stock market declines, and the specter of deflation. Other European countries, as well as the "little dragons" of East Asia (including Korea, Malaysia, Singapore, Taiwan, and Thailand) were wrestling with stubborn problems of their own. The increasing power of information technology, and particularly the World Wide Web, had introduced a new dynamic into world competition, allowing companies to both coordinate their internal operations more effectively and communicate directly with external customers and suppliers.

Moreover, it encouraged both more outsourcing and the redefinition of long-accepted corporate boundaries, which led to experiments with new ways of organizing internally as well as externally. Corporate networks—so-called *virtual organizations*—emerged and sometimes were able to restructure markets and modes of competition. The cost structures associated with this New Global Economy were often much different from those of traditional old economy companies, necessitating a fresh look at priorities and performance measures. In short, corporate success in this new world economy demanded a fresh look at strategies, and particularly at strategies for managing operations.

As a result, this book bears only a superficial resemblance to the previous book. It addresses a number of topics that were not covered there, including corporate networks, information technology, process development, project management, and different ways of managing operating improvement. Finally, it updates the previous book's coverage of operations strategy, capacity planning, and outsourcing/vertical integration, based on the latest academic research and corporate experience.

This book drew both inspiration and insight from all that we learned from our colleagues, the business managers we worked with, and other informed observers. We also want to acknowledge the extent to which we benefited from the insight and perspectives of the many MBA and executive students whom we have taught over the years. Most of them took our courses because they thought they would learn something from us; what we tried to hide from them was that often we were learning more from them.

Where possible we try to indicate clearly who was the source of certain ideas or data, but often it is unclear to us exactly where we got a particular insight. We would be remiss, however, if we did not acknowledge our debt to such colleagues and co-investigators as Professors (now Dean) Kim Clark, Amy Edmondson, Takahiro Fujimoto, Andrew McAfee, Stefan Thomke, and—above all—Wickham Skinner, who was the first to articulate and propound the concept of manufacturing strategy. For many years he waged a rather lonely battle to get American managers to understand the problems they were creating for themselves because of their unwillingness to develop and exploit their operating capabilities. Some of his articles, written more than three decades ago, are amazingly prescient; one squirms as one compares the difficulties facing many companies today with those Skinner predicted would occur if the necessary steps were not taken. They weren't, and he was right. We are proud to be his students.

We are particularly indebted to the Harvard Business School's Division of Research, which funded most of the research and course development that provided the foundation for this book. Any errors or omissions, of course, remain our responsibility—as does the delayed embarrassment that we will feel 10 years from now as we look back on what we have written here and realize, from that perspective, how little we still know about the strategic management of operations and technology.

About the Authors

Robert Hayes is the Philip Caldwell Professor of Business Administration, Emeritus, at the Harvard Business School. Prior to his appointment to the Harvard Faculty in 1966, he worked for I.B.M. and McKinsey & Company. He received his Ph.D. degree from Stanford University.

He has published widely. Three of his articles won McKinsey Awards for the best articles published in the *Harvard Business Review* during various years. Representative recent articles include "Operations-Based Strategy," coauthored with David Upton, and "Beyond World-Class: The New Manufacturing Strategy," coauthored with Gary Pisano. He has co-authored seven books, one of which, *Restoring our Competitive Edge: Competing Through Manufacturing* (with Professor Steven C. Wheelwright), won the Association of American Publishers' Award for the best book on business, management, and economics published in 1984. Other books include *Dynamic Manufacturing: Creating the Learning Organization* (with Steven Wheelwright and Kim Clark), and *Strategic Operations: Competing Through Capabilities* (with Gary Pisano and David Upton).

Hayes has held a number of administrative positions at HBS, including Area Head, Program Head, and Senior Associate Dean for Faculty Planning and Development. He has lived and conducted research in Europe and Hong Kong, and in 1998 coordinated the opening of HBS's research office in Hong Kong. He is past president of the Production & Operations Management Society, and serves on the Boards of Directors of the American Productivity & Quality Center, Applera Corporation, and Helix Technology, Inc. He has been selected for listing in *Who's Who in America.*

Gary Pisano is the Harry E. Figgie, Jr. Professor of Business Administration at the Harvard Business School. Since joining the Harvard faculty in 1988, he has taught both MBA and executive-level courses on technology and operations management, operations strategy, competitive strategy, product development, the management of innovation, and health care. He currently serves as a director of the Harvard Business School's Division of Research and Faculty Development. Pisano holds a Ph.D. from the University of California, Berkeley and B.A. in economics from Yale University.

Pisano's research has examined technology strategy, the management of product and process development, organizational learning, and vertical integration and outsourcing strategies. For the past fifteen years, his research has focused heavily on organizations in biotechnology, pharmaceuticals, and health care. His research has led to insights about appropriate licensing, manufacturing, and R&D strategies for biotechnology and pharmaceutical companies. Pisano is a widely published author with over twenty-five research papers published in such journals as *Management Science, Administrative Science Quarterly, Decision Sciences, Strategic*

Management Review, and *Harvard Business Review.* He has also written case studies on such companies as BMW, Flextronics, ITT-Automotive, Intel, Merck, and Eli Lilly. He is the author of *The Development Factory,* a book investigating the strategies and practices leading to superior development performance in biotechnology and pharmaceuticals. He is also co-author (along with Robert Hayes and David Upton) of *Strategic Operations: Competing Through Capabilities.* Pisano's recent research on cardiac surgery teams (in collaboration with colleagues Richard Bohmer and Amy Edmondson) has uncovered new findings about how organizations can accelerate the pace of team learning.

Pisano has served as an advisor to senior managers at a number of corporations in the pharmaceutical, biotechnology, and electronics industries. In addition, he has served on the Board of Directors and Advisory Boards of a number of start-up companies.

David Upton is the Albert J. Weatherhead III Professor of Business Administration and has been on the faculty of the Harvard Business School since 1989. He is currently course head for the required first-year MBA course in Technology and Operations Management and has taught second-year elective courses in Operations Strategy and Operations Improvement. He is faculty chair of Harvard's executive course on Operations, and has taught in the Advanced Management Program for senior managers as well as Harvard's China-based executive courses. He co-leads Delivering Information Services, a course for senior Information Systems managers, as well as the WPO/CEO program for company presidents and CEOs.

Upton graduated with honors in Engineering from King's College, Cambridge University and holds a Master's degree in Manufacturing from the same institution. He completed his Ph.D. in Engineering at Purdue University, with a doctoral dissertation on the application of Artificial Intelligence in Computer Integrated Manufacturing (CIM) systems. His current research project involves operations from around the world, and focuses on operations improvement and information technology in operations. He has written numerous journal and book publications on Operations, most recently in *Management Science, Harvard Business Review, California Management Review,* and *Journal of Manufacturing Systems.*

He is a Chartered Mechanical Engineer, a registered European Professional Engineer, and holds professional qualifications in Accounting and Finance. He was the winner of the British Robot Association Research Prize, the Magoon Award for Excellence in Teaching in Engineering at Purdue University, and the Apgar Award for Innovation in Teaching at Harvard Business School. From 1979–84, he worked in Engineering, Sales, and Production at Tube Investments Ltd., and from 1984–86 he worked in research on robot control and manufacturing systems with Cambridge University's Manufacturing Systems Research Group. He also ran a consulting business developing microcomputer network operating systems. Upton has worked and consulted for numerous corporations including Deloitte and Touche Solutions, IBM Corporation, Unilever, Wells-Fargo, and Novartis, providing advice in areas such as information systems strategy and operations improvement. He serves on the board of Tech Data Corporation, a $16 billion international distributor of information technology products.

Steven Wheelwright rejoined the HBS faculty as a Baker Foundation Professor in 2003, after retiring in 2000 as the Edsel Bryant Ford Professor of Business Administration. From 2000–2003 he and his wife fulfilled a full-time voluntary assignment as the President of the London, England Mission for the Church of Jesus Christ of Latter-day Saints. From 1995 to 1999, Professor Wheelwright served as Senior Associate Dean responsible for the MBA Program. He then served as Senior Associate Dean and Director of Faculty Hiring and Planning and had oversight responsibility for distance learning. Professor Wheelwright currently teaches the required first-year course in Technology and Operations Management and in a number of HBS Executive Education Programs.

Professor Wheelwright first taught at Harvard from 1971–79 and was the Thomas Henry Carroll-Ford Foundation Visiting Professor from 1985–86. He rejoined the Harvard faculty in 1988. In his years away from Harvard, he was the Kleiner, Perkins, Caufield and Byers Professor of Management at Stanford University Graduate School of Business. In his position at Stanford, he directed the strategic management program and was instrumental in initiating its manufacturing strategy program. In his research, Professor Wheelwright examines product and process development and their connection with competitive advantage and operations excellence. Working with HBS colleague, Clayton Christensen and Stanford colleague, Robert Burgelman, they have recently published, *Strategic Management of Technology and Innovation, 4th ed.*

Wheelwright has also co-authored (joined by HBS colleague Kim Clark), *Dynamic Manufacturing: Creating the Learning Organization* and *Leading Product Development: The Senior Manager's Guide to Creating and Shaping the Enterprise,* and is the author or co-author of more than a dozen other books.

Wheelwright has a B.S. degree in Mathematics from the University of Utah and an M.B.A. and Ph.D. from Stanford University's Graduate School of Business. In addition to his Harvard and Stanford positions, he served on the faculty of INSEAD (European Institute of Management) in Fountainebleau, France. He was Vice President of Sales in a family-owned printing company and has consulted in the areas of business/operations strategy and improving product development capabilities. Professor Wheelwright currently serves as Chairman of the Board of HBS Publishing, and as a Board member at O.C. Tanner Company.

Contents

Appendix

Chapter 1

Operations Management Confronts a New Millennium

About the time we can make the ends meet, somebody moves the ends.

—Herbert Hoover

The trouble with our times is that the future is not what it used to be.

—Paul Valery (French academic and patriot)

1.1 INTRODUCTION

As they confronted the twenty-first century, managers around the world experienced mixed emotions: a sense of real accomplishment accompanied by frustration and uncertainty. The famous Lewis and Clark expedition, which two hundred years earlier had been sent by President Thomas Jefferson to explore the Missouri River to its headwaters and then continue on to the Pacific Ocean, provided an appropriate historical analogy. After months of backbreaking labor, during which their very survival was often in question, the expedition finally reached the source of the Missouri. On the other side of the ridge ahead of them they expected to discover the beginning of the Columbia River, down which they could float in relative ease to the Pacific. Instead, when they reached the top they looked out upon the lofty peaks of the Bitterroot Mountains—the most formidable they had yet encountered—stretching into the distance as far as they could see.[1]

Not only were these mountains unexpected, they were largely uncharted—like many of the challenges facing operations managers today. At the same time they were attempting to deal with a sudden and unexpected transition from economic plenty to deflationary decline, and from cold war stability to global insecurity and uncertainty, they were losing confidence in many of the highly touted new approaches to operations that had promised to improve their ability to deal with instability and intensified competition. They found these new approaches not only more difficult and time-consuming to implement on a sustained basis than they expected, but they were often inappropriate in certain situations.

Nor had their previous experience prepared them to deal effectively with the challenges posed by a dizzying series of advances in information technology, including the advent and growing power of the Internet. These created the basis for industries whose operating characteristics were substantially different from those of more traditional ones, and which collectively came to be called "The New World Economy." Exact definitions of this term differ, but most included a combination of three factors:

1. Globalization
2. Advanced technology (generally information-related)
3. Network partnerships, where key outputs and productive assets are primarily intellectual—information and "knowledge"—rather than physical

Although most popular attention has focused on the Internet-related dot-coms, the information-intensive New World Economy is actually much broader. It encompasses software development, telecommunications, and much of the media/entertainment industries, as well as Internet services. Several of its differentiating characteristics (to be discussed later) are also found in such related hardware industries as I.C.s (integrated circuits), computers, and computer gaming devices, and even in biotechnology and pharmaceuticals.

During the 1990s, these new information-intensive industries rapidly became a major force in the world economy. Efforts to ascertain their growing impact suggested that about a third of the U.S. GDP growth between 1995 and 2000 was attributable to information technology (IT) alone, as well as half the growth in its Total Factor Productivity.[2] Sophisticated observers believe that the forces driving these industries are fundamentally reshaping the way the world's economy operates, permitting higher sustained rates of growth, productivity, and employment than ever before possible. Corporate success in this new world economy demanded a fresh look at strategy, and particularly strategies for managing operations. Complicating the picture further, these new technologies were challenging many of operations management's traditional practices—and even some of its conceptual foundations. At the same time, they offered enormous potential for improving operating effectiveness and enabling the operations function to play an even more prominent role in corporate success.

During the closing years of the twentieth century, companies around the world experienced a roller coaster of emotions. First they enjoyed a long period of growth and prosperity, fostering expectations of an almost limitless future. This was followed by profound, almost demoralizing disappointment as the twenty-first century ushered in a deep global economic slowdown—exacerbated by the threat of terrorist acts on such a scale that people's confidence in their institutions and governments was shaken. Corporate scandals further rocked investor confidence and wiped out billions of dollars in paper wealth. Business became much more difficult than it had been in the 1990s, and quick fixes, strategic breakthroughs, and charismatic leaders no longer seemed to be as effective in dealing with these new challenges. The key to enduring success was increasingly recognized to be operational excellence, and such excellence required a firm foundation in a coherent and consistent strategy for operations and technology.

This book seeks to provide insight into the building blocks of such a foundation. We discuss how to construct an operations strategy, the issues that need to be addressed in giving it form and substance, why many of the traditional approaches for dealing with those issues are no longer appropriate, and how new approaches and technologies can be marshaled to the task. We end by providing guidance into how an operations organization can be set on a path of continual improvement, and how to avoid the frequent pressures to deviate from that path. But first, in this introductory chapter, we review how the business environment and competitive priorities have changed over the past two decades, and why many managers have lost confidence in some of the new approaches to operations that had appeared to be so effective earlier in that period. Then we discuss the tremendous impact that advances in information technology are having on business, and particularly on operations, today. Finally, we provide an overview of the remainder of this book, describing how each chapter addresses pieces of this new, and evolving puzzle.

1.1.1 The World Business Context

The United States: Dashed Expectations for Limitless Growth

U.S. operations managers had spent much of the 1980s and 1990s responding to the assaults of Japanese and other Asian competitors. This had forced them to embark on a variety of improvement activities, many of which finally appeared to be bearing fruit. They had downsized (or, more euphemistically, *right-sized*) and delayered their organizations, benchmarked the *best in class,* reengineered their business processes into a semblance of *lean manufacturing,* outsourced noncore activities, and gotten closer to their customers. Finally (and apparently as a result), they appeared to have regained their competitiveness: their quality, responsiveness, and productivity all improved. Business boomed. New technologies and markets opened up, creating a plethora of attractive opportunities. The U.S. economy grew at rates not seen since the mid-1960s, and even the huge federal budget deficit, which had long acted as an anchor on business investment and prosperity, suddenly shifted into surplus.

Even better, stimulated by many years of apparently profitless investment in information technologies, the nation's aggregate annual rate of productivity growth (which had languished at less than about 1.5 percent percent during the 1970s and 1980s) slowly rose to more than 2.5 percent by the year 2000. This allowed companies to increase wages without causing inflation. In an environment of rapid growth in sales and profits, nearly full employment, and low rates of inflation, stock prices soared to unprecedented levels. The NASDAQ index, which tended to track high-technology stocks, rose more than threefold in the course of just three years, and U.S. stock markets as a whole came to be valued at more than the combined GDP of the rest of the world!

But dark clouds threatened this sunny landscape. The very attractiveness of the United States as a place to invest caused the dollar to soar relative to most other currencies, making American products more expensive to sell and foreign products more attractive to buy. The nation's overall trade deficit, which had doubled to more than $100 billion a year between 1991 and 1998, averaged more than $100 billion a *quarter* in the early years of the new millennium, and its current-account deficit rose to 5 percent of GDP. This threatened a return to the dark days of the mid-1980s, despite earlier assurances from economists that reducing the budget deficit would reduce the trade deficit.[3] At the same time, the nation's savings rate dropped from about 7 percent in the 1980s to near 0 percent in the late 1990s, and household debt approached 100 percent of total disposable annual income.[4] The nation's prosperity, therefore, was at least partly due to people buying things faster than they could earn the money to pay for them—essentially borrowing against the future—and hence was unsustainable in the long term.

Moreover, the situation facing many American Old Economy companies was getting steadily bleaker. Because of worldwide gluts in capacity in a number of traditional industries, their profit margins were under pressure. In addition, they were experiencing troubling plateaus in key measures of their operating effectiveness. As a result, they were constrained from increasing the wages of their less-skilled workers—who, in effect, were competing with the lesser-skilled and lower-paid workers in developing countries. Redoubling their effort to do more of the same things seemed increasingly unlikely to generate improvements at a rate any better than (if as good as) before.

Then the dark clouds intensified, bringing a deluge of bad news that washed away much of the gains made in the 1990s. Consumer demand began tapering off around the world, corporate profits fell, and the new dot-com startups rapidly ran through their cash reserves. Just when the downturn began to level out, the horrific events of September 11, 2001, and the war on terrorism (as well as on the "axis of evil") that followed, gave promise that the twenty-first century was likely to be a much less welcoming world than had previously been assumed. Finally, accounting scandals and increasing evidence of corporate fraud undermined investor confidence. Analyzing the 1990s with the benefit of hindsight revealed that much of its apparent growth had been transient and illusory. Not only had it been fueled by massive overinvestment in computers and telecommunications, but the corporate earnings reported at the time were later revised downward by a deluge of earnings restatements at a number of major companies—including Enron, Tyco, WorldCom, and Xerox, as well as by a delayed recognition of the real impact of stock options on profits. As a result, the "irrational exuberance" of the 1990s evaporated, and global stock markets plummeted. The NASDAQ, which peaked at more than 5,000 in early 2000, fell to below 1,100 during the following two-and-a half years, and even broader averages like the S&P 500 fell over a third. Major sectors of the economy—including airlines, telecommunications, and steel, plagued by overcapacity[5] and weakening demand, hovered near bankruptcy.

The Fading Threat of the "Asian Century"

Unlike the United States, the 1990s had not been good years for Japan and much of the rest of Asia. Near the beginning of that decade, in the midst of near euphoric predictions that the twenty-first century would be the "Asian century," Japan, the region's economic driver, saw its exuberant *bubble economy*[6] (based on inflated stock and real estate values) collapse. Thereafter, it grew sluggishly (only about 1 percent annually in real terms) despite more than $500 billion in government funding of several major attempts at fiscal stimulation. As a result, the confidence generated by four decades of rapid growth and the apparent invincibility of Japanese manufacturing companies in a number of major export industries slowly evaporated, and the limitations of Japan's traditional governmental, economic, and industrial structures and systems became ever more apparent.

As Japan's unemployment rate rose to a postwar high of more than 5 percent, the collective return on equity of Japanese companies dropped nearly to zero, and the inefficiencies, rigidities, and weaknesses of much of its service and industrial sectors (except for a few of its elite export industries) became painfully apparent. At the same time, some of the bedrock principles of the Japanese approach to manufacturing—including lifetime employment, just-in-time production scheduling, uncompromising efforts to eliminate all defects, and ever faster rates of new product development—came into question (see Section 1.2.2). Japan found itself attacked by low-cost imitators such as China and Korea on one side, and by innovators like the United States on the other. Meanwhile, starting around 1990, its national multifactor productivity, which had been steadily approaching those of the United States and Germany, began to stall, and the gap widened again.[7] The Nikkei stock price average plummeted from almost ¥40,000 in late 1989 to under ¥8,000 in early 2003—its lowest level in over two decades. Emblematic of the weakness of Japan's traditional industries, in early 2000 the market capitalization of Mitsubishi Heavy Industries, one of the country's bedrock companies, sank to a fifteenth of that of Sony!

In early 2003, teetering on the edge of its fourth "official" recession in ten years, Japan's gross national debt rose to more than 150 percent of GDP,[8] and more than 60 percent of its central government's discretionary spending was devoted to paying interest on that debt. Its attempts to stimulate growth, in turn, drove interest rates so low (close to 0 percent at times) that Japanese banks and finance companies, looking for higher rates of return, dramatically increased their lending to companies in other Asian countries. These loans approached $300 billion by 1997, and when those borrowing countries' currencies were suddenly devalued in late 1997, many of the companies that had lent them money experienced financial crises. Coupled with its problem loans to domestic companies, Japan's banking system was essentially paralyzed by between $1 and $2 trillion in nonperforming loans, unable either to borrow or to lend. In early 2002, citing Japan's soaring national debt, persistent deflation, and unstable banking system, Standard & Poor's and Moody's Investor Services lowered its credit ratings for its government debt offerings to the lowest investment grade—approaching that of such poor, developing countries as Botswana![9]

The rest of East Asia, long used to double-digit growth rates, also experienced a dramatic slowdown in growth and a loss of confidence in traditional economic, political, and corporate policies. Asian managers, who had struggled for forty years to overcome their countries' lack of natural resources, investment capital, physical infrastructures, and low income levels (which had impeded the growth of domestic demand), had finally managed to fight their way to prosperity and world admiration.

During 1997 and 1998, however, most East Asian countries entered a period of sudden and severe financial instability, which in some countries approached economic meltdown. Rampant over-expansion had resulted in massive excess capacity in a number of major industries.

Between 1999 and 2001, the value of nonperforming loans in all of Asia rose 33 percent to more than $2 trillion, nearly a third of the region's GDP.[10] Even China, which grew steadily during this period and was emerging as the new Asian powerhouse, began experiencing difficulties. By 2002, Chinese banks, all owned by the government, held more than $500 million in uncollectible debt, equal to roughly half of China's GDP. Adding this debt to its existing national debt and pension liabilities increased its total national indebtedness to more than 100 percent of its GDP. Hong Kong, the prize colony that it took back in 1997, was proving to be more of an anchor that an engine of growth; its unemployment level rose to more than 8 percent, and its rate of deflation rivaled Japan's.

Bad loans, the collapse of inflated real estate and other asset prices, and excessive borrowing (much of it in foreign currencies) threatened the very survival of many of Asia's financial institutions. And the resulting devalued currencies, economic contractions, and layoffs, together with revelations of cozy, self serving business-government relationships and massive political corruption, threatened their political and social stability. In short, these managers' reward for all those years of hard work, sacrifice, and continual improvement turned out to be the obligation to do it all over again!

The Fading Promise of the European Union

European companies, which had experienced stubborn economic stagnation during most of the 1990s, confronted even starker choices. Worldwide excess capacity in many of their traditional industries—including automobiles, chemicals, shipbuilding, and steel—had forced their managers to deal with the same price pressures as their American counterparts, but without the support of the United States' rapid economic growth and flexible workforce. They wrestled against high labor costs and taxes, uncooperative labor unions, costly and rigid social policies, and the reverberations of the collapse of the eastern bloc countries. After more than a decade of costly, painful, and ultimately insufficient efforts to rationalize, downsize, and automate their European operations, they grudgingly began to move production to Asia, Eastern Europe, and the Americas—which only aggravated national jobless rates, budget deficits, and political turmoil.

The most promising path to future prosperity appeared to lie in economic and monetary union, with the hope that a single currency (the euro), common standards, and a reduction in trade barriers would trigger a new era of growth and opportunity. But true union continually receded before them; foreign competitors moved to establish operations on European soil and capital continued to flow out of Europe. If economic union proved unable to deliver the growth in employment and profitability it promised,[11] and European managers were unable to develop new approaches that would allow them to regain their international competitiveness, there was concern that political and social pressures might force a retreat to a *fortress Europe.* Such a retreat, however, threatened to set into motion the same slow deterioration in living standards, innovation, and international competitiveness that had forced most closed societies around the world to open up their economies during the previous decade.

The problems faced by Germany—Europe's largest economy, accounting for a third of the euro region's GDP—were emblematic of this decline in economic vigor and optimism. At the end of 2002, the German economy had grown only 1.3 percent per year over the previous decade. Its labor costs were the highest in the world and its labor productivity, which had approached that of the United States in the early 1990s, fell to 85 percent of the U.S. level. Coupled with inflexible labor market regulations and powerful unions, this caused German companies to avoid hiring new workers, even during periods of economic growth, and move operations to other countries. As a result, Germany's unemployment level rose to more than 10 percent, of which half consisted of people who had been unemployed for over a year. Domestic investment declined for the third year in a row and deflation also threatened its economy. An inconclusive election in 2002 cast doubt that there would be any bold initiatives to reform the economy, and German stocks fell further in percentage terms that year than did U.S. stocks.[12]

In short, the competitive world that managers confronted in the early twenty-first century had turned out to be much more complex and unforgiving than ever before. Making it even more difficult for operations managers, many of the issues they thought they understood and had surmounted had been reopened to renewed questioning. Indeed, in some respects the solutions seemed to have come full circle.

1.1.2 The Evolving Bases of Competition

The same "full circle" was observable in the way the terms of competition in many industries had evolved over the previous twenty-five years. Although this evolution followed different timetables in different countries, we will use the U.S. experience as our example. In the early 1970s, most competition in the U.S. was price-based. Within a given industry, defect levels, breadth of product line, delivery times, and the rate of new product introductions tended to be roughly similar across companies, thus, rendering them "neutral" as far as competitive differentiation was concerned. Occasional slip-ups—such as surface blemishes or other non-performance-related defects—were dismissed as inconsequential. "The American consumer will not pay for better quality," confidently stated one top auto industry executive to a class of Harvard MBA students back in the mid-1970s.

This, of course, was about the time many Japanese companies were beginning to mount attacks on U.S. markets based on their products' superior performance, fit, and finish, as well as defect rates that were one-hundredth or less of the levels that had been acceptable before. And European luxury cars began flooding U.S. markets in response to an exploding demand for clearly superior—and vastly more expensive—performance and appearance. In the 1980s, as a result, *quality* became "Job #1" at Ford and many other companies as they strove to catch up with foreign competitors. One very senior U.S. auto executive lamented in early 1988—again, ironically, in front of a group of Harvard MBA students—that, given the choice between identical mid-sized vehicles built in the United States and Japan, American consumers were then willing to pay up to $2,000 more for the Japanese car because of their perception that it was of higher quality! Over those fifteen years, foreign producers had grabbed almost a third of the U.S. passenger car market. Clearly, a fundamental shift in consumer preferences had occurred: quality had moved from being a neutral basis of competition to being a powerful source of competitive differentiation.

The resulting, somewhat frantic, efforts by U.S. companies over the next decade to reduce costs and improve quality (whether defined in terms of defect rates, tolerances, reliability, or lifetime operating costs) succeeded in narrowing the gap between U.S. and Japanese products in many industries—to the point where often those attributes no longer served as effective bases for competitive differentiation. This kind of competitive stalemate usually presages a new assault from a different direction (one must be careful not to prepare oneself to fight the previous war, as Marshall Foch vainly warned France in the 1930s). Indeed, even as companies belatedly recognized and grudgingly responded to *the quality revolution,* another competitive battleground began to emerge: *flexibility* and product variety.

Capitalizing on the fragmentation of consumer preferences in the developed countries, foreign competitors sought toeholds in markets that already were approaching saturation by offering specialized (and/or attractive variations of existing) products. Market niches that once were relatively free of competitive pressure no longer offered protection, and companies began to seek out *micro*-niches. The flexibility to respond to customer requests for customized products or services became a new source of competition differentiation in the mid-1980s. This resulted in a substantial broadening of product offerings, to the point where companies in the late 1990s typically offered a much greater variety of products, each at lower volumes than they had a decade earlier.

A compelling illustration of this phenomenon can be found again in the automobile industry. In the early 1970s, U.S. producers offered only five basic engine-drivetrain combinations, and about 80 percent of their customers selected the same one: a front-mounted V-8 engine operating through an automatic transmission that delivered power to the rear wheels. The largest-selling automobile in the U.S. market, the Chevrolet Impala, sold about 1.5 million units. Over the next twenty-five years, the number of engine-drivetrain combinations expanded to more than forty, and the former favorite slipped to less than 25 percent of the market. By the year 2000, U.S. consumers were able to choose from over 600 different kinds of vehicles, carrying more than thirty brand names, and the largest-selling model in the U.S. (usually either a Ford Taurus, a Honda Accord, or a Toyota Camry) accounted for only about 400,000 units—less than a third as much as the leader twenty-five years previously—despite the growth in the total market during those years. The same phenomenon operated even more ferociously in small consumer products such as watches. As a result, Seiko Watch developed the capability to introduce a new model of watch every working day, and to change its assembly line from one model to another in a few seconds. In attempting to respond to this new source of pressure, companies were forced to embark on a series of new programs: simplifying and compressing manufacturing processes, modularizing product designs, implementing mixed-model assembly systems, and establishing just-in-time relationships with suppliers and customers, as they pursued the goals of make-to-order and *mass customization.*

Yet even as companies slimmed down and realigned their organizations to pursue this new competitive goal, the terms of competition began changing once again. The best companies in many industries were able to cut their product development times by half or more and began *speeding up* the rate of new product introduction. In addition, new computerized technologies, such as computer-aided design and engineering, flexible manufacturing systems, and robotic assembly, vastly reduced the time required to produce modifications of existing products. A company that can develop new products twice as fast as its competitors has the luxury of using that advantage in one of two ways. It either can wait longer before initiating the development of a new product, and thereby begin the project with a clearer understanding of where markets and technologies are moving, or it can flood the market with wave after wave of new products. Even if its cost and quality are comparable to its competitors', and it is equally responsive in delivery, a company will get into deep trouble if its customers consider its products to be outdated at the moment they are first introduced.

By the end of the twentieth century, many companies had narrowed the quality, flexibility, and speed gaps between themselves and their competitors. And so—in a world where prices were under pressure and the vast, newly accessible pools of low-cost labor in China, Eastern Europe, India, and Latin America were providing new ways to reduce costs—low cost reemerged in many industries as the primary basis of competition. Like the Bitterroot Mountains that Lewis and Clark looked out upon, however, the challenges in front of operations managers now appeared even more formidable than those just surmounted. Ever-higher standards of quality, speed, and responsiveness had to be met and surpassed. Strong competitors faced them all around the world. New products and services were destabilizing markets and opening up opportunities for competitors faster than ever before. Meanwhile, the proliferation of product lines and the rush to establish beachheads in emerging markets, coupled with a worldwide slowdown in demand growth, had left many industries with a ruinous amount of excess capacity and shrinking profit margins. The world auto industry, for example, was operating at less than 75 percent of capacity, even as it added new capacity in Latin America and China.

1.2 GROWING DISILLUSIONMENT WITH THE NEW APPROACHES TO OPERATIONS

Like the roller coaster experiences of their regional economies during the final years of the twentieth century, operations managers had encountered a similar cycle of extravagant—and then dashed—expectations as they attempted to implement a number of "new approaches to operations" (NAOs). Throughout the 1980s and 1990s, Western manufacturers had pursued world-class manufacturing status through a shotgun blast of three-letter acronyms: TQM (total-quality management), JIT (just-in-time production scheduling), DFM (design for manufacturability), QFD (quality function deployment), QPD (quick product/process development), and CIM (computer integrated manufacturing). The power of these NAOs in improving quality, production scheduling, product development, and supplier management had been forcefully demonstrated in the early 1980s by a number of leading companies, such as AT&T, Hewlett-Packard, Motorola, and Xerox, leading hundreds of others to strive to emulate them and their Japanese role models.

Despite many remarkable successes, depicted in glowing accounts in the business media, a number of subsequent studies revealed a disturbing pattern of failure. Even efforts initially labeled as "successes" often turned out to be so only up to a point—after which, improvements stagnated or even regressed. For example, Ford Motor Company, which had led the quality improvement drive in the U.S. auto industry in the 1980s (and which trumpeted that "Quality is Job #1" slogan), later lost its quality leadership and in 2002 had the highest number of consumer-reported problems per vehicle of the top seven auto producers. The "Big Three" U.S. producers as a whole had quality records that were below the average, and they were losing market share in all vehicle categories.[13]

The conclusion of most large studies has been that only about a third of the companies that attempted to implement the most popular NAOs achieved the results expected—by the companies' own admissions. In the few studies that asked customers and suppliers, rather than the companies themselves, to evaluate the overall effectiveness of such programs, the success rate was even lower. For example, an extensive study of 584 companies in Canada, Europe, Japan, and the U.S. conducted jointly by Ernst & Young and the American Quality Foundation found that most TQM programs had achieved "shoddy results." Other studies [14] suggested that only a third or less of those same programs had had a significant effect on their companies' market success. Similarly, a Bain & Co. survey of managers' evaluations of a variety of new management tools—involving operations as well as other functions—found that 81 percent of the respondents felt that most tools "promise more than they deliver." As a result of (and possibly contributing to) such dissatisfaction, the survey found that the average company had tried ten different management tools.[15]

Finally, a number of attempts to link TQM activities with corporate financial success have produced troublingly ambiguous results—although these may be due largely to the thorny methodological problems encountered.[16] For example, although one might reasonably assume that a company that successfully implemented NAOs faster than its competitors would achieve superior financial results, it would be difficult to measure any individual economic benefit if all the companies in its industry were making similar improvements. As a result, it is difficult to find evidence that the widespread adoption of the NAOs has been somehow superior to the steady operating improvements that U.S. companies have been making ever since aggregate productivity first began to be measured more than fifty years ago.

Such findings have resulted in a growing cynicism among top managers, to the point where the chairman of one consulting company, who had been CEO of two *Fortune* 500 companies and a member of several corporate boards, has called "the steady coming and going of popular management programs ... T.Q.M. and reengineering and others like them ... another sign [of an underperforming CEO]."[17]

How can one reconcile these disappointing findings with all the anecdotes about companies that became "lean and mean" through *right*-sizing, delayering, and reengineering; and "closer to their customers" through attention to quality, response time, and faster product development? One explanation is that the business press tends to focus on the few shining (apparent) successes, and pays little heed to the much larger number of dissatisfied adopters.

A second is that NAOs may be more effective in manufacturing industries than in the much larger service sector. Although it is not altogether clear why this would be the case, several factors may be responsible. First, the "output" (and therefore the productivity) and "quality" of service companies are more subjective and difficult to measure and evaluate. For example, a highly publicized attempt to stimulate improved effectiveness of the care provided by thirty hospitals near Cleveland, Ohio, by gathering and publicizing data comparing their performance, died after a decade despite some evidence that it had had a positive impact. Many of the hospitals that were found to perform poorly in these "benchmarking" ratings objected strenuously to their accuracy, claiming that the differences were due primarily to variation in the severity of the problems of their incoming patients.[18]

Another explanation for lower productivity in service operations is that their direct output is accompanied by attributes that standard productivity statistics don't measure. These include improvements in quality, response time, and innovativeness, which cannot be observed in financial data unless they have been reflected in appropriate price changes. Standard productivity statistics do not reflect the convenience of automatic teller machines (compared with standing in line in front of a live teller), for example, and they treat the higher fees paid for revolutionary new kinds of heart surgery as "price increases."

Although controversial, the findings of these studies square with our own observations. We must acknowledge that we have long been advocates of many of these NAOs. Indeed, we have argued in books and articles over the past twenty years that U.S. companies needed to study and emulate "best practice" in the attempt to improve their productivity, quality, and response times. Yet in company after company—many of which had proclaimed their improvement efforts to be highly successful, and in some cases had even invited us in to see what they had accomplished—we found contradictory evidence and deep cynicism down in the ranks. Most employees felt, instead, that they had been fragmenting their time trying to implement a "blizzard of buzzwords," expanded each time one of their senior managers attended a conference, read the latest "secrets of success" management book, or hired a consultant.[19]

1.2.1 The Limits of the NAOs

Why has the success rate of programs to implement these NAOs, despite their great promise, been so low? The standard explanation is that unsuccessful programs suffered from a lack of commitment on the part of top management, which is accused of not providing sufficient resources or moral support as its attention shifted from cutting costs and improving quality to exploiting the myriad market opportunities that arose out of the long economic boom of the 1990s. Just as important, in our view, is a lack of enthusiasm and poor implementation by lower-level managers and workers.

Sometimes people at the operating level simply do not understand the basic philosophies of different operating approaches, how their various components mesh, or how they would strengthen the company's competitiveness. Indeed, these NAOs often were selected and forced on an organization, even though the improvements promised by them were incompatible with its traditional strategic priorities. A related problem is that such initiatives often turned out to be in conflict with one another—either because they adopted inconsistent goals or methods, or because they fought for common resources. For example, both just-in-time production scheduling (which advocates a "pull" system that drastically reduces the inventories between sequential stages of an operation, and thereby links them more tightly together) and total quality management programs (which emphasize the importance of identifying, through experimentation, the best way to operate a process, and then documenting and diffusing such best practices throughout the organization) reduce worker autonomy—which is directly contrary to the goals of employee empowerment. Moreover, some "enlightened" practices, such as worker flexibility, were found to have deleterious side effects that were not recognized initially.[20]

Finally, serious questions can be raised about some of the basic premises underlying these new approaches. It has become clear that no NAO is appropriate in every situation. This is not necessarily because of basic flaws, but rather that each either is based on assumptions that are not valid in certain situations or with certain types of people, or it contains inherent and initially unappreciated limits, beyond which its effectiveness is diminished. For example, one of the leading—but eventually somewhat chastened—U.S. advocates of TQM came to believe that it is *not* appropriate for problems that are both complex technically and cut across organizational boundaries.[21]

Even in Japan, which generally is given credit for the origin of the lean manufacturing philosophy and practices (although its roots lay in Henry Ford's pioneering efforts to eliminate wasted resources and idle time in auto assembly[22]), not all industries have found it appropriate. Its success varies even within the Japanese auto industry. Although lean manufacturing clearly has been one of the engines driving Toyota's surge to dominance in that industry—indeed, it is the essence of what Toyota calls the "Toyota Production System"—no other auto company has been able to apply it as successfully. Nissan, Japan's second largest auto company, has struggled for years to make it work, and Mazda has found it largely inappropriate for its niche market strategy. Even Toyota abandoned two of lean manufacturing's key features—the Kanban system and mixed model assembly—in one of its newest factories[23] and designed it instead to be "worker-friendly." We return to these issues in the next chapter.

1.2.2 The Limits of Process Reengineering

At the heart of the lean manufacturing paradigm is the concept of continuous improvement. Even though the operating system that results may be vastly different from that embodying the older mass production paradigm (see Chapter 2), the process of getting from the latter to the former generally requires a myriad of incremental improvements, each resulting in less waste, greater speed/responsiveness, and fewer potential problems to deal with in the future. In direct contrast to this approach, the idea of *business process reengineering* (BPR) swept through U.S.

industry during the early 1990s. Hundreds of companies that had been impressed by the performance improvements achieved through the introduction of *cellular manufacturing* were persuaded by the writings[24] and proselytizing of various consulting firms to pursue major breakthroughs in their operating performance by totally reconceptualizing and restructuring their business processes.

At the most basic level, BPR involved transforming processes that had been organized by process stages into direct-line flows. This required that narrow jobs carried out under close supervision in a hierarchical organization be replaced by broader jobs performed by teams of multiskilled people in a more horizontal organization. The resulting structure bore great resemblance to the lean manufacturing ideal, but the approach to getting there was totally different. Rather than a continuous series of small steps, initiated by people at all levels of the organization over a long period of time, reengineering was driven from the top, often with outsiders bearing major responsibility. In the words of one of its foremost proponents, "business reengineering means starting all over, starting from scratch."[25]

Unfortunately, studies of the effectiveness of process reengineering efforts have revealed a lack of success similar to that of NAO implementations.[26] A number of possible explanations have been proposed. Most of the criticism directed at process reengineering has focused on the radical and often dictatorial nature of the change process itself. Receiving less attention but bearing, in our view, at least equal responsibility for reengineering's many dramatic failures is its basic goal: to restructure processes along product flow lines. Yet, as one observes the way processes are organized in most businesses—whether they make products or deliver services—one is struck by the prevalence of the supposedly discredited process stage organization. Are all the smart people who designed and manage these processes hopelessly out of date, or is a process organization sometimes actually a more appropriate choice?

The answer, of course, is that there are compelling reasons for employing a process organization in many situations. Business processes reengineered along product flow lines, like manufacturing processes organized into straight flow cells, work well in certain environments and poorly in others.[27] They generally require different kinds of equipment and skills, as well as an overall increase in equipment capacity (and therefore in investment). They often are more difficult to expand or contract, except in large steps. They tend to constrain the development of markedly different new products and services. Finally, they provide less opportunity for special expertise or exceptionally capable workers. It is ironic that many of the academics who trumpet the virtues of cellular manufacturing, continuous product flows, and companies organized along business rather than functional lines themselves operate out of traditional functional academic organizations—and fiercely resist the use of cross-functional teams in teaching courses or conducting research. We return to these issues in Chapter 10.

1.2.3 The Limits of Emulating "Best Practice"

The ultimate problem that the adherents of lean manufacturing, process reengineering, benchmarking, and other NAOs must confront is that if this new "dominant design" is correct, the strategic role that operations can play is much reduced. In effect, managers are forced to restrict their strategic thinking to deciding which currently fashionable improvement technique to adopt next, and abandon strategic analysis in favor of *benchmarking*—identifying and adopting the "best practices" of other companies. U.S. operations managers are not alone in their surrender to such faddishness. Many Japanese companies similarly fell into the trap of "... following the same strategy. [so] Like passengers on a ferry, they have swamped the vessel by all simultaneously running to the same side of the boat for the best view."[28]

Striving simply to be "lean," or even "world class" is insufficient and, in fact, somewhat simplistic. At best, you end up only as good as (that is, *no better than*) your toughest competitors, and find yourself continually playing catch-up with them. As we argue in the next chapter, long-term success still requires that a company *differentiate* itself from its competitors by offering something unique and valuable to customers—whether this be especially quick service, high reliability, low costs, or innovative products.

As operations managers confronted the difficulties imposed by unstable economic conditions, an increased sense of personal and organizational insecurity, and a recognition that the NAOs for which they had such high expectations had severe limitations, they have also found themselves forced to address a new and peculiar set of operating issues associated with the rapid growth of the New World Economy.

1.3 MANAGING IN THE NEW WORLD ECONOMY

As mentioned in this chapter's introductory section, the end of the twentieth century ushered in what came to be called the *New World Economy,* which combined increasing globalization, advances in information technology, and new forms of corporate organization in ways that redefined the role of operations management. None of these aspects were novel by themselves, of course. Business has been "international" since nations were first created and traded among themselves, and international corporations date from the trading companies of the Middle Ages. Similarly, "modern" information technology has been progressing rapidly since the development of the computer in the mid-twentieth century—in fact, since the telegraph a hundred years earlier. And companies have been experimenting with different forms of organization for hundreds of years. What made the New World Economy different, however, was the way the newest forms of all three intertwined in complex ways to create whole new industries and approaches to business.

1.3.1 Globalization

Three factors made the New Economy's form of globalization different from that which existed before:

1. *The collapse of the Soviet empire in the late 1980s led to a repudiation of state-controlled central planning around the world.* This failure, when contrasted with the success of Japan and other East Asian countries that had adopted various forms of market capitalism, eventually led more than half the world's population to enter the global market economy during the last

fifteen years of the twentieth century. In addition to Russia and Eastern Europe, China, India, and several Latin American countries opened up their borders to foreign commerce.

2. *Advances in information technology and corporate organization made managing foreign operations much easier than ever before.* This particularly applied to global sourcing.
3. *Companies combined the power of IT with an increased willingness to outsource operations to create novel types of partnerships with customers, suppliers, and even competitors.* These networks interacted in synergistic and self-supporting ways, and rapidly became global in scope as managers recognized that countries they earlier had dismissed as "developing" (and, by implication, incapable of participating in high technology operations) were fully capable of mastering the latest advances in information and process technology.

Indeed, many companies found that these developing countries, which previously had tended to focus on making components and relatively low value-added products, were now becoming tough competitors in high-tech products. Ironically, they often found it easier to train workers who had little previous industrial experience in the skills and discipline required by TQM and lean production than it was to persuade their own older, "experienced" workers to adopt these same techniques. Again and again, visitors to factories in China, Mexico, and Southeast Asia expressed astonishment at the speed with which their workers were able to master the most advanced approaches to production management. In the early 1990s, for example, the Cummins Engine Company's factory in San Luis Potosi, Mexico was judged to be the most successful adopter—in a worldwide network of more than fifty plants—of the new production system that the company had encouraged all its plants to utilize. Similarly, one of the top-rated factories in HP-Compaq's worldwide network was in Penang, Malaysia.

1.3.2 Information Technology and Information-Intensive Operations[29]

In addition to the problems they faced in traditional products and services, managers increasingly struggled to introduce and manage new, information-intensive products. As the New World Economy expanded its reach, they discovered that many of the principles, practices, and methodologies that had proven successful in traditional industries no longer seemed effective in this new context. Partly, this was due to the new opportunities and challenges associated with doing business in new environments. More importantly, though, it was due to the very different assumptions and characteristics of "information-intensive" operations. Although some familiar operations management concepts and techniques continued to be applicable to such operations, many were not. In fact, in some important areas those traditional approaches appeared to be almost 180 degrees off course. In the following sections we will sketch out some of the important differences between the old and new economies, and their implications for operations management teaching and research.

The bulk of these differences arise out of fact that many of the basic assumptions that managers and academics tend to make when thinking about *managing operations* are inappropriate for information-intensive operations. Unfortunately, these assumptions are so deeply embedded in traditional thought processes that the people involved in operations seldom are even aware of how fundamentally they influence the way they look at the world (it is said that the last thing a fish discovers is water) and define their domain. By *domain,* we refer to the kinds of problems that interest them, and the tools they feel need to be mastered in order to address those problems. These basic assumptions include:

- *The organizational unit of analysis is an operating unit* (e.g., a factory, a company, or a division/business unit within a company). Most introductory O.M. courses emphasize problems that occur within relatively small organizational units. The rationale is that within such a bounded organization a manager can exercise control—that is, make decisions and directly oversee their implementation. As one result of this instinctive desire to control operations, almost invariably the "default mode" is a decision to do something yourself—within the organizational unit, rather than involve organizations and people outside your control.
- *Operations management is concerned primarily with stable products and processes.* That is, inputs are transformed into products or services following stable, well-specified processes. Most O.M. teaching and research, in fact, focuses on fabrication/assembly processes, which often are separable from (and relatively independent of) products. As a result, different products can be produced using the same process, and a change in the process will not necessarily require changes in the products produced.
- *The major responsibility of operations managers is to control the flow of materials (and/or information) through a sequence of process steps.* Hence, O.M. tends to emphasize the scheduling and monitoring of production batches through a process, as well as materials handling, inventories, expediting, and throughput time. Even when expanding its scope to include service operations and new product development, O.M. academics tend to emphasize those aspects that involve the control of sequences of activities. This is a consequence both of their focus on fab/assembly processes (O.M. academics do relatively little teaching or research about continuous processes), and their inclination, given their mathematical training, to seek out problems that lend themselves to quantitative analysis.
- *A major concern of operations managers is reducing the variable cost of production.* Mass production, hand-in-hand with mass markets, made it possible to reduce the cost of developing and producing a product, as well as the capital invested in its production process (amortized over their respective lifetimes), to a relatively small fraction of a product's total unit cost. For example, depreciation and amortization usually account for less than 5 percent of the full cost per

unit of fab/assembly products. Similarly, O.M. academics have tended to consider the fixed and overhead costs of production as either being small in comparison with the variable costs or outside the operation manager's control.

This assumption about overhead costs is largely a residue from a century ago, when corporate overhead structures tended to be much simpler (consisting primarily of a works manager, a few foremen, and an accountant), and direct wages were considered a variable cost (hence the term *hourly workers*). The focus on variable costs—and particularly on the direct labor component of variable costs (since operations managers have tended to delegate materials purchasing to others)—has been called into question recently by a number of critics. They point out that the overhead/indirect costs of most operations have been steadily rising over the past 100 years, and now often exceed variable labor cost by a factor of three or four.[30]

- Your *competitors are your enemies,* and the key to prevailing against them lies in *differentiation* (e.g., higher performing products). Hence, companies seek to develop products and processes that are both different and superior—in fact, proprietary, if possible.

1.3.3 What's Different in Information-Intensive Operations?

Implications of a Front-Loaded Cost Structure

In the information-intensive industries, almost all these assumptions come into question. To begin, the production and distribution of information is very different from that of physical products. As alluded to in the previous section, operations managers typically have focused their attention on the cost of producing a specified volume of a product or service during a given time period, where the average cost per unit is composed of a relatively small depreciation/amortization cost and a large variable component (particularly if the cost of materials is included). In addition, they typically assume that economies of scale operate to reduce costs only up to some point, after which the diseconomies of scale and complexity drive costs back up.

The cost structure for most information-intensive products, however, is dominated by the up-front costs associated with developing a new product and creating its associated production/delivery system. The marginal cost of producing and delivering an incremental unit of such products, in contrast, is both generally quite small and essentially independent of the distance between producer and consumer. Creating Microsoft's Office 2000 suite of programs, for example, required the efforts of more than a thousand developers working more than two years. Other examples include the development of large financial or other databases, entertainment products, and Internet services: the first unit costs a lot to produce, but each successive unit costs very little.

Some "physical" products, such as I.C.s and pharmaceuticals, exhibit a similar kind of cost structure. A new state-of-the-art I.C. fabrication facility can now cost well over $2 billion—with the result that depreciation and maintenance account for more than 70 percent of the total cost of the resulting chips. Similarly, the cost of developing, and getting FDA approval of, a new drug and its manufacturing process usually takes at least seven years and can exceed $600 million. This topsy-turvy "costly to produce but cheap to reproduce" world has two direct implications for operations management teaching and research.

First, it suggests that *project* management is at least as important as *process* management. For many years, project management has been included among the topics covered in O.M. textbooks and courses, and more recently product development has received vastly increased attention. But the amount of time O.M. academics spend researching and teaching about project management still accounts for a relatively small proportion of their total efforts. In most introductory courses, the topic is represented by only a class or two—often focusing on the theory and use of critical path analysis (see Chapter 8). In the case of information-intensive products, however, managing the development of that "first unit" effectively and quickly is generally far more important to success than is managing the process for providing additional units.

Although one could argue that managing a *series* of projects is a sort of "process," it is a very different kind of process than the ones O.M. has traditionally focused on. The learning curve, if any, for that kind of process is more discontinuous and much less amenable than traditional processes to the principles of continuous improvement and the use of PDCA (plan-do-check-act) cycles in problem identification and resolution. The clear implication is that much more time and attention needs to be devoted to the particular problems of project management. That's where most of the money is spent, and that's where an important source of competitive advantage lies, for reasons we will explore next.

Second, given the huge impact of initial cost, *achieving low cost is less dependent on effective process management, or even continuous improvement, than it is on high cumulative output.* This emphasis on cumulative volume—and therefore rapid ramp-up—is due only partly to the familiar dynamics of learning curves (where marginal costs decrease at a constant rate with each doubling of volume; see Chapter 3), and to the obvious fact that average cost per unit is calculated by dividing total cost (dominated by the first unit's cost) by cumulative volume. Cumulative volume is also important because—unlike physical resources, which are consumed by or deteriorate with usage—many forms of intellectual capital *gain value* as they are used. For example, *knowledge management* systems that are established for the purpose of sharing or creating new information provide better, more complete information as more parties join and use them.

Implications of the "Network Effect"

Closely related to the enhancement of information as more parties share and contribute to it is the so-called *network effect:* the increasing attractiveness to users of certain kinds of networks as they increase in size. The first telephone (or fax machine) had little value, for example, since there was nobody to call. But as more people acquired telephones, the more useful telephones became, and the more people were encouraged to get one. The value of such a network, therefore, increases *faster* than the volume through it, so *network economies* become more important than *scale economies.*

The interaction of the network effect with the importance of amortizing high initial costs over cumulative volume has several additional implications for operations managers. Most important, *speed to market becomes a key driver of low cost.* Although the notion that speed is a major source of competitive differentiation has long roots,[31] speed to market is even more important for an information-intensive company because the likelihood of gaining volume superiority is greatly enhanced if it can be at the forefront of a developing market. Once a network has established a commanding position in a market, customers and suppliers tend to gravitate to it, causing one Internet CEO to state: "time accounting is more important [for us] than cost accounting."[32] Whereas it often is possible for small producers of traditional products or services to flourish by offering versions targeted to the needs of small niche markets (e.g., Porsche and local banks), larger information networks tend to drive out smaller ones. Why would someone want to participate in a rival Internet auction network, for example, if more potential buyers and sellers can be found at eBay? This "winner take all" effect, in fact, was one of the main theoretical justifications for the U.S. government's antitrust suit against Microsoft, specifically its Windows operating system.

A company can attempt to grow too fast, of course, and lose control over its quality, reliability, and service. Also, simply being first does not necessarily lead to competitive success. The market being attacked also must be large and potentially profitable enough to support the network that eventually dominates. PriceLine's attempt to extend the "name your own price" approach that it had pioneered in flight, hotel, and rental car reservations to groceries and other physical products failed because such products could be stored and therefore did not depreciate rapidly in value as the deadline (e.g., the plane taking off with unoccupied seats) approached. This kind of deadline gave PriceLine considerably more bargaining power with United Airlines than it did with Procter & Gamble, say. The resulting profit margins—more in line with traditional grocery stores—were too low for PriceLine to operate profitably in that business.

The new entrant also needs to offer customers a clear value proposition—some competitive advantage over traditional stores and mail-order houses. E-toys, for example, turned out to have little compelling advantages over Toys 'R' Us and other discount toy stores, nor did Furniture.com over traditional furniture stores. In addition, a company must buttress the competitive advantage associated with being early-to-market by finding ways to increase its customers' cost of switching to a competitor. AOL, for example, introduced its instant messaging system, and Drugstore.com automatically checks new drug orders in the context of previous orders and informs customers about possible drug interactions. Amazon, in addition to posting reviews of the products it offers as well as comparisons with competitive products, provides its customers with suggestions as to other products that they might be interested in, based both on their previous purchases and their responses to a questionnaire. First movers must continually support their initial advantage by aggressively building volume. AOL became the biggest Internet provider not by being first (CompuServe was), but by being extraordinarily aggressive after it entered—just as did the Japanese auto companies when they entered the U.S. market, and Microsoft when it successfully supplanted Lotus 1-2-3 with Excel.

Speed versus Quality versus Flexibility in a Fast-Moving World

Over the past two decades operations managers have learned that fast product development, error-free products, and rapid process throughput time can be supportive of low cost. In fact, improving conformance quality (reducing the incidence of defects) is now often regarded as one of the most effective ways for an old economy company to reduce costs and improve throughput time. Quality is just as critical for an information-intensive company because its sales volume—the key to low cost—comes not just from developing and selling products but also from developing trusted relationships with customers that facilitate ongoing repeat purchases. In information-intensive operations, however, *"quality" is defined, and interacts with speed, rather differently than in the case of its old economy counterpart.* Rather than trying to "get it right the first time," as traditional TQM philosophy teaches, the importance of being early to market and the rapidity of changes in markets and information technology argue that a company simply can't afford to wait to introduce a new product until it is polished, efficient, and contains all desired functions and options. Installing a less-than-optimal but improvable system now may be much more important than waiting to introduce a more elegant system several months from now. In this light, then, *quality* means a product that, although possibly incomplete, is robust, easy to use, mostly bug-free, and easy to expand and improve over time.

Once speed and "satisfactory" performance have established an initial advantage, flexibility becomes an information-intensive product's top priority. Since IT enables easy communication with users, firms are induced to provide a high degree of *customization* to meet the specialized needs of individual users in real time. These needs, in turn, are constantly changing as volumes, markets, technologies, and user sophistication evolve, and can shift rather abruptly from ease of use to reliability to response time. Moreover, the pressure to expand one's network encourages rapid introductions of new products and services. Finally, like other industries having front-loaded cost structures (e.g., airlines, integrated circuits, and telecommunications), any slowing of an information-intensive company's growth tends to cause a precipitous drop in earnings—as was demonstrated forcefully during the economic slowdown that began in early 2000. The combination of these three effects implies that companies' internal processes must not only be highly flexible, they are inherently unstable and always in flux.

Partners, Collaborators, and Co-opetitors

Because of the importance of rapid ramp up and high volume, it often makes sense for an information-intensive company to *encourage others to join with it in providing services through a common network.* Once a network is in place for one purpose (think of a telephone system again), it gains value as other products or services (e.g., fax machines and Internet access providers) are added to it. This increased value, in turn, stimulates the growth of the network and the cumulative volume through it. Joining with others to promote and exploit a network may even be advantageous if those same companies are competitors in other products or networks. Apple Computer, for example, benefits from having Microsoft provide software for its network of MacIntosh users, even though Microsoft is providing a Mac-like operating system for the rival personal computer network. Similarly, in order to speed up its own product development, Boeing shares its design tools with customers and components suppliers around the world—even though both purchase from or supply its competitors.

As far as the ultimate customer is concerned, therefore, the output of a network is not a single product, but a *system* of complementary products that together have the potential to make each individual product (and the network as a whole) more valuable. Therefore, the role of operations management is no longer confined to managing the production and delivery of a product or service through a series of steps within a single *enterprise.* Instead, it expands to facilitating and stimulating the production and delivery of compatible, often reinforcing, products through an *extraprise* (sometimes referred to as a virtual organization) of partnerships and alliances with a shifting group of *complementors* and *co-opetitors.*[33] Microsoft, for example, seeks to create an "ecosystem" in which hardware manufacturers and other software companies can develop complementary products that utilize Microsoft systems.[34] In this light, cooperation among information-intensive companies can be as important as competition.

Since attracting customers to use their network is important to all these co-opetitors, *compatibility* is often as important to a company's success as is *differentiation.* Therefore, while each participant might prefer to attempt to achieve a competitive advantage by differentiating its products and services, all are induced to design compatible products by adopting (or jointly designing) common standards, interfaces, and platforms. The key to Bloomberg's success as a provider of financial information, for example, is not due to its access to proprietary information. Essentially, all of the information it provides comes from public sources. The familiarity of its subscribers with Bloomberg's format for displaying that information, and the tools it provides for analyzing it, however, have forced other companies to make their products compatible with Bloomberg's. Relatedly, the increasing popularity of the Linux operating system and the Java programming language versus their Windows counterparts is due largely to the fact that both are nonproprietary and easily available, thereby facilitating the development of compatible products.

Old Economy companies have long recognized the importance of compatibility as well, of course. The reason Matsushita's VHS format for the videocassette recorder prevailed over the Betamax format employed by Sony, despite the fact that Sony was the first to introduce a commercially successful VCR, was because Matsushita was able to induce a group of other companies to use and support the VHS format. Similarly, the success of IBM's design for the personal computer over the (technically superior) Apple and Unix computers was because IBM made its PC design "open" to all, and eventually induced most other computer manufacturers and software manufacturers to standardize around it. More recently, the widespread adoption of CAD (computer-aided design) has been facilitated by the convergence of most equipment and software producers around two *geometry engines* for representing complex shapes. In information-intensive companies, compatibility becomes the norm rather than the exception. The downside of compatibility, of course, is that it reduces switching costs (see Chapter 4), which means that a company loses some of its ability to deter potential competitors.

In addition to "controlling" their internal operations directly, operations managers have to use *indirect* means to "ride herd" on the often ambiguous and shifting relationships among its co-opetitors. The varied activities of the ever-changing membership of a network alliance do not constitute a stable process, and therefore cannot be controlled in the same way one manages an internal operating process. Instead, one must operate through negotiations, inducements, and (sometimes veiled) threats.

In this sense, an information-intensive network often operates somewhat akin to the way medieval Europe did, where individual kingdoms continually strove to prosper at the expense of others, while at the same time enlisting their support (through a series of shifting alliances) in their mutual defense and aggressions. The fact that such fluid structures defy the kind of orderly analysis and measurement that operations managers have traditionally employed does not mean their management is impossible. Indeed, some of those old medieval kings and queens were quite good at it over rather long periods of time! Managers of information-intensive operations, moreover, have a powerful advantage over those "old pros" in that their communications with other network participants are facilitated by the fact that information transmission today is instantaneous, accurate, and almost costless. In addition, because of their relatively recent origin they are not encumbered by the baggage of a long history of competitive rivalry.

The burden of decisions made in the past seems to be particularly difficult for supply chain extranets. The slower-than-expected success of Covisint, the new B2B (business-to-business) network established by General Motors, Ford, and DaimlerChrysler to reduce the costs, delays, and inventories associated with their purchasing of parts and supplies—from both independent parts suppliers and each other—illustrate the kind of difficulties Old Economy companies experience in such networks. Despite the potentially enormous financial benefits of this kind of integrated supply,[35] Covisint's operations have been hindered by the different technologies, standards, and systems in use at the participating companies—as well as, of course, by antitrust considerations and the deep suspicion of each other's motives engendered by their remembrance of previous attacks and counterattacks. As a result, new, independent B2B facilitators, such as Ariba, Commerce One, and Oracle may well prove to be more successful at facilitating and managing such extranets.[36]

To some extent, operations managers have been forced to acquire a few of these indirect management skills during the past two decades. The inadequacy of traditional *command and control* management techniques when confronted with the challenge of determining and directing all the activities required to achieve the defect rates, throughput times, and product development speed required by today's competitive environment has made it necessary for them to enlist the cooperation and creativity of all their employees. Managers quickly found, however, that their traditional ways of managing weren't very effective with skilled people who worked together in semi-independent teams—sometimes composed of representatives from different functional organizations, and therefore not under their direct control. This new kind of control required a whole new set of skills and attitudes.

Fortunately, however, those same skills have a lot in common with those required to manage a network of semi-independent network allies. Not only must managers of operating networks be good negotiators and diplomats, they must know how to win the trust of others, how to build consensus, how to design incentives that encourage various parties to achieve desired results, and how to lead through example. Unfortunately, these skills have largely been mastered through on-the-job training. They seldom were learned in business schools.

Expanding Globally

The quest for ever-greater volume, together with the fact that the cost of communication is both insignificant and essentially unaffected by distance, drives information-intensive networks to expand globally. This facilitates global alliances among suppliers, customers, and co-opetitors, and makes geographical proximity (which underlay the concept of "geopolitics") unnecessary, but complicates their operations management. Hence, operations managers in the New World Economy have to be much more cosmopolitan than most of their Old Economy counterparts. Not only must they be good negotiators, they must negotiate within the United Nations!

1.3.4 Summarizing the Differences: O.M. in the Old and New Economies

As we compare the assumptions underlying Old Economy operations management with those of the new information-intensive economy, a number of obvious mismatches become apparent. These are summarized in Table 1-1.

1.3.5 Redefining the Boundaries of Organizations and Operations Management

Despite the profound nature of these differences in activities and relationships, they still do not capture the full extent of the changes that the New World Economy forces on operations management. Once one begins to think in terms of an interacting extraprise of mutually supportive organizations, as opposed to a traditional corporate enterprise, it becomes easier to consider possible ways for separating out many of the activities currently being carried out within a company and delegating them to external entities. The recent surge in the outsourcing of parts and services that had previously been produced internally is one clear manifestation of this new mode of thinking. It has been encouraged by the availability of fast communications (which has sharply reduced transaction costs) and a newly cultivated sense of mutual dependence.

Initially, such outsourced work tended to be performed by existing suppliers or corporate spin-offs, such as General Motors' and Ford's recent spin-offs of their internal auto components suppliers. Soon these suppliers were being asked to "bundle" their products with those of other companies so as to provide their customers with larger subsystems.[37] Over time, more and more work was transferred to a new breed of *contract manufacturers* that specialized in performing the mundane manufacturing

Table 1-1 Old Economy vs. New Economy Operations

Issue	Old economy	New economy
Unit of analysis	An operating unit	A network of semi-independent players
Goal	Sell products/services	Develop ongoing relationships with customers, suppliers, and complementors
Domain of O.M.	Products and processes	Systems of complementary products, provided by different organizations organized in networks
Dominant O.M. activity	Managing flows through a stable process	Managing the dynamics of highly flexible products through ever-changing processes and networks
O.M. Tools	Flow analysis, scheduling, expediting, and so on	Project management, negotiating, building consensus, designing incentives, and so on
Primary measures of performance	Incremental unit cost and "quality" (i.e., low defects and/or high performance)	First unit cost and "acceptable quality" (i.e., low defects, ease of use, and improvability)
Competitive imperative	Achieve superiority along some valued dimension(s)	Get high volume quickly and induce others to support your product/network
Performance improvement	Continuous improvement, using PDCA cycles and other Kaizen tools	Learning across development projects
Competition	"Prevail" through differentiation	Jointly prosper through collaboration that results in a dominant standard

activities that Old Economy companies no longer saw value in doing. These contract manufacturers proved to be so effective that companies were encouraged to give them more and more business: first individual parts, then whole modules (e.g., computer motherboards, auto brake assemblies, and even complete car cockpits), and finally whole manufacturing facilities. As a result, the contract manufacturing industry grew at a rate of more than 80 percent a year between 1996 and 2000 (the fastest growth rate of any manufacturing industry), often adding capacity by buying the increasingly underutilized factories of their customers. By 2001, most estimates of the global outsourcing market were in excess of $120 billion, and it was projected that 50 percent of all manufacturing would be outsourced by 2010.[38]

The success of this kind of traditional outsourcing encouraged companies to consider subcontracting other major corporate functions: information systems (which today accounts for about 30 percent of total outsourcing), product development and design, engineering services, packaging, testing, and distribution. As a result, what began as a set of traditional purchasing relationships between customers and suppliers has begun to evolve into "a sort of extended enterprise—a set of partnerships between product developers and specialists in components, distribution, retailing, and manufacturing."[39] In short, it has become a New Economy *extraprise.* Whereas fifteen years ago this trend was viewed as creating *hollow corporations,* today it tends to be regarded as promoting speed, flexibility, and more efficient use of resources (See Chapter 4).

The usual reason given for such increases in efficiency is that "unbundling" the various products and businesses that spring up over time, and for various reasons, under a corporate umbrella allows it to focus on its "core competences." This is a somewhat slippery concept, however, and there are other justifications that are more concrete and just as compelling. First, information technology makes it easier for companies to find alternatives to local, or familiar, suppliers. Local networks of suppliers and customers are fast becoming global in scope, and customers can use networks to band together and demand better terms. Second, unbundling a business makes it harder to subsidize relatively poor-performing products, services, or functions with the profits earned in higher performing ones. This, together with pressure from highly informed (and networked) financial markets, induces companies to redirect their scarce resources to the products and activities in which they have a comparative advantage.

Increasingly, in fact, this kind of outsourcing is becoming intertwined with *co-production,* where a company allocates some of its activities to its own customers. In its simplest manifestation, this is observable in self-service operations: requiring customers to perform the final assembly operation (e.g., Ikea's furniture kits), and asking restaurant customers to assemble their own salads from the salad bar. Like outsourcing, getting customers to do more of the total work often represents a *cost-reducing* activity for the supplier—as well as for the customer, to the extent the supplier shares the resulting savings.

In today's interconnected world, however, co-production is expanding to include such *value-enhancing* activities as having customers track the progress of their packages through FedEx's delivery system, searching out their own airline or hotel reservations, or conducting their own banking transactions. At another level of complexity, it includes a customer's product design group interacting electronically with its supplier's engineers to jointly design a product and the molds required to produce it. At still another, it includes *loyalty-enhancing* activities, such as Charles Schwab's ability to keep track of a customer's stock trades, automatically monitor the performance of those stocks, and offer recommendations based on the customer's emerging portfolio and revealed preferences. Similar services are increasingly being provided by the Web sites of major mail-order houses.

The success of reallocating activities that formerly were conducted within the boundaries of a single company has led some companies to explore even more dramatic ways of restructuring their operations. One recent award-winning article has proposed, in fact, that they consider separating out and outsourcing whole *complexes* of activities, such as managing customer relationships, product innovation, and operations—arguing that "although organizationally intertwined, these … are actually very different. They each play a unique role; they each employ different types of people; and they each have different economic, competitive, and even cultural imperatives."[40] The role of operations management in such an organization clearly would be very different than it is in traditional companies.

1.4 THE INFORMATION ECONOMY'S CHALLENGES FOR OPERATIONS MANAGEMENT

A growing number of companies fall squarely in the new information-intensive economy. To them, as we have seen, many of the assumptions, perspectives, and tools of traditional O.M. are largely irrelevant. They must develop their own approaches, based on the realities and assumptions of their world as described above. Their task is made even more complex, moreover, by two other realities of their world. First, information-intensive assets and products require a workforce that is very different than those of Old Economy companies. The term *knowledge workers* is often used to describe this new breed. Although definitions of the term differ, by many estimates knowledge workers today make up about 30 percent of the workforce in the U.S. and, as with other developed countries, constitute its fastest-growing component.[41] These knowledge workers are highly paid, their output is difficult to measure, and they don't like to be told what to do. Moreover, they tend to respond to different kinds of incentives than do their differently skilled predecessors. Making their management even more difficult, their skills (combined with worldwide shortages of such people) make them highly mobile. Managers, therefore, must operate at the interface of competing pressures: their own need for fast growth and cost control, their knowledge workers' demands for autonomy, and the strong likelihood that if they aren't happy they can easily go elsewhere.

To complicate their world even more, many of these companies are growing—or declining—very rapidly. This presents problems, first because it is difficult to decide how and where to expand or contract the capacity of a system when that capacity is both difficult to measure and multidimensional (in the sense that it includes hardware, software, and skill sets both for the transactions themselves and for providing ongoing service to customers). Second, they must strive to retain and motivate employees while operating around the clock (24/7) and managing continual changes in their products and processes—both internal and external.

The challenges facing Old Economy companies, although historically quite different, are increasingly related, because many of them are combining information-intensive activities with their traditional ones. Traditional hardware is being supplemented with software and information services. Traditional communications with suppliers and customers are being augmented with Internet-based interactions. Traditional supply chains, as mentioned earlier, are expanding into larger B2B networks. Traditional arms-length relationships with competitors are evolving into shifting alliances and consortia. Operations managers in such companies, therefore, must continue managing the required changes and improvements in their traditional operations as they learn to master the skills and tools of the new.

Conversely, many information-intensive companies are finding that simply being able to communicate effortlessly with suppliers and customers is an insufficient basis for building a sustainable business. Not only must they *attract* customers, they must *deliver* what these customers want. "Clicks" have to be supported with "bricks," and the cost of providing on-going service to customers can be substantial (this, in fact, has proven to be the Achilles heel of many of the struggling dot-coms). So at the same time their managers are developing the skills and tools required to function effectively in the New World Economy, they also must master the arcane and supposedly obsolete skills of Old Economy operations management.

In other words, the real challenge facing managers today is not just to recognize that the worlds of New and Old Economy operations are very different and require vastly different assumptions and approaches. It is that these worlds are colliding. The task for managers, therefore, is not simply to create new theories, frameworks, and tools for managing New World Economy operations, but also to learn how to grow, manage, and balance them with traditional operations within the same organization. The challenges facing operations managers today, therefore, are greater than ever before. They must seize the emerging, and often fleeting, opportunities to adapt and innovate without losing sight of the fundamental principles of operations management that made the U.S. economy an industrial powerhouse in the first half of the last century—the principles that, in fact, have underpinned the success of every industrial nation.

1.5 AN OUTLINE OF THIS BOOK

This book focuses on those basic principles that create the foundation for an organization's operational success, and describes how its operating and technological resources can be managed *strategically.* Achieving a competitive advantage through superior operations is what we mean by an *operations edge.* The book is written not only for those involved directly in managing operations, but also for those in other functions who must interact with or oversee operations, because turning operations into a source of competitive advantage requires that everybody be involved. We will address ways for resolving strategic operating issues individually (making decisions) as well as collectively (using systems).

Our emphasis throughout is less on specific tools and techniques, which tend to be sensitive to cultural differences, than on an overall framework for thinking about the management of a firm's operations function. Companies too often treat decisions about operations on an ad hoc basis, regarding them as a series of technical problems that can be surmounted one by one without regard for the interactions among them. Such an approach may result in the creation of serviceable buildings, but it will not create an operations organization that can prevail against competitors whose every action fits together, guided by an underlying consistency of purpose.

The book is organized (following this introductory chapter) into three parts. Chapters 2 through 5 address different aspects of an operations organization's structure and strategy. In Chapters 6 through 8 we turn to issues involved in managing operating technologies. Finally, Chapters 9 through 11 deal with various approaches for encouraging and managing operations improvement.

1.5.1 Operations Strategy

The first step for a company that wants to compete through operations is to "get its act together"—getting everybody marching in the same direction, with common goals and priorities, a shared understanding of how it wants to compete in its business(es), and broad agreement about the kinds of things it will say "no" to. Only then will it be able to achieve coherence between the goals, activities, and needs of various functional groups. Focusing specifically on the operations function, such coherence requires that it be designed and managed in such a way that its capabilities and actions are aligned with the needs of its sister functions and organizations. In addition, the various elements of its overall operating system, both structural (buildings, equipment, and contractual obligations) and infrastructural (policies, practices, and systems), have to be compatible and mutually reinforcing. Once it has achieved both internal consistency and strategic coherence, the next step is to go on the attack by selecting and developing exceptional operating capabilities that open up new strategic opportunities for the business. These issues are the subject of **Chapter 2.**

Once a company's strategic mission and technological basis have been established, it must provide its operations organization with the capacity and capabilities necessary to carry out that strategic mission. Capacity issues are the subject of **Chapter 3.** The *capacity* of an organization, of course, is a complex and multidimensional issue. The same equipment and personnel may have very different capacities and capabilities, depending on how they are organized and managed, the kinds of market demands placed on them, and the economic and social environment in which they are located. Although, as discussed earlier, a number of basic industries today are awash in capacity, many companies—even in these same industries—actually find themselves short of capacity in critical areas. This is particularly true for those that are trying to speed up their product development and delivery processes, and/or offer faster response to customer requests.

For example, as we describe in Chapters 7 and 8, many engineering organizations are understaffed given the number of new product and process design projects they have taken on. The result is that project completion times are delayed, priorities are continually reshuffled, and people burn out after hopping from one "urgent" project to another. Similarly, some companies rationalized, downsized, and subcontracted too much, and then found themselves unable to meet an upturn in the demand for their products and services. Just as bad, the complexity caused when too many activities are shoehorned into limited capacity causes confusion and delays. Chapter 3 addresses ways for thinking about such decisions as how much capacity is "enough" in a given situation, and when additions to or contractions of that capacity ought to be made.

The question of how much capacity is required depends crucially, of course, on how much of the work in developing and delivering its products an organization chooses to do internally. One of the fundamental decisions that must be made when developing a competitive strategy—and therefore an operations strategy—is which activities should be carried out within a company and which should be obtained from outside suppliers. And, for those outsourced activities, how should suppliers be selected, and what kind of relationships should be established with them? As world competition emphasizes ever faster, more accurate responses to fast-changing consumer demands, most companies are learning that they cannot provide adequate service all by themselves. Increasingly, they need to coordinate their activities both with their suppliers and with those organizations that operate between them and the ultimate consumers of their products and services. **Chapter 4** addresses these issues, ranging from simple "make versus buy" decisions to crafting and managing strategic relationships with selected suppliers.

Once a business unit has decided what activities it will engage in and has provided itself with adequate aggregate capacity, it next must decide how that capacity should be divided up among a network of separate operating units. This requires decisions regarding how big, how many, where, and which activities and products (or services) should be associated with each unit. These issues are the subject of **Chapter 5,** and motivate a discussion of operations focus and ways for achieving it—both within an operating unit and across the resulting network of such units. Networks can be structured in different ways, and different network structures exhibit different kinds of behavior and require different management skills and approaches. Moreover, once achieved, the focus of an operating unit, or a network of such units, tends to be elusive. Organizations (like thermodynamic systems) tend to become increasingly complex over time, as individual managers attempt to cope with changing requirements and new opportunities. Therefore, after reviewing some of the pitfalls that operating units and networks can experience, we describe mechanisms for preserving and enforcing focus within different kinds of facilities and network organizations.

1.5.2 Operations Technology

Before they can effectively address the challenges of creating strategies for and managing operations in the New World Economy, managers must understand something about information technology (IT) and the increasing impact it is having on operations. We have found that many managers feel insecure when dealing with the dizzying advances in IT, and so tend to delegate key decisions to "experts." Yet such decisions can have a profound strategic impact. So **Chapter 6** begins by providing a brief introduction to some of the basic aspects of modern information technology (and the Internet), and then describes their implications for strategy and management. In particular, it discusses some of the opportunities that advances in IT create for operations management, and how they can be exploited in furthering a company's operations strategy. In the process, it suggests answers to such questions as: Why have so many attempts to implement IT tools and approaches in the past resulted in disappointing performance? What degree of technical knowledge must managers have in order to avoid repeating these mistakes in the future? And what can be learned from the companies that have succeeded in exploiting the power of IT for competitive advantage?

An operations edge is sharper and more defensible if it incorporates one or more process technologies (many of which may be based on, or facilitated by, IT) that are both competitively valuable and difficult for competitors to acquire. Such technologies, either developed internally or acquired from the outside and modified to meet the company's specific needs, create advantage in two ways. First, they can provide superior operating performance on measures that are most important to the company's competitive strategy—cost, speed, dependability, and so on. Second, they can facilitate faster, more efficient, and effective product development. **Chapter 7** focuses on these issues, and describes different approaches that companies follow in developing superior process technologies. It introduces the notions of "learning by doing" and "learning before doing," and describes circumstances under which it might be preferable to develop such technologies centrally or allow different organizational units to create their own.

As described earlier (section 1.3.2), project management is becoming increasingly critical to the success of many companies, particularly those in information-intensive industries whose projects consume the bulk of their financial and intellectual resources. In addition to the development of new products/services and processes, the subject of most treatments of project management, project teams also are involved in making all the different types of decisions covered in Chapters 2 through 10—from formulating an operations strategy, to developing proposals for capacity expansion or contraction, to selecting and/or developing major new pieces of equipment or IT systems, to making facilities decisions and designing networks, to preparing detailed and persuasive capital investment proposals. Even more important than carrying an individual project through to successful completion, however, is the fact that project teams are incubators of management skills. **Chapter 8,** therefore, not only describes different approaches for managing project teams, but also discusses effective ways to structure and manage a *portfolio* of projects over time, so that they build organizational capabilities while continually seeding later projects with the experience and skills developed in previous ones.

1.5.3 Operating Improvement

Major operations decisions, whether involving capacity, alternative processing equipment and information systems, or the adoption of different improvement initiatives, usually require major capital expenditures. Capital, unfortunately, is in limited supply and closely guarded at most companies. Therefore, proposals for investing capital in different types of operations-related projects inevitably find themselves competing both with one another and with those sponsored by other groups within the firm—all of which seek to increase shareholder value. Before addressing specific operations improvement activities, therefore, **Chapter 9** provides a framework to guide the evaluation and advocacy of different types of investment proposals. Operations managers who are not trained in the logic of investment analysis (who, in fact, often chafe at what they consider the narrowness of the financial mind-set) often find themselves at a disadvantage when trying to justify such investments. We describe not only the traditional approaches for evaluating capital investments, but also why a new approach is sometimes needed when making investment decisions that contain a high degree of "option content."

Getting an operations organization aligned with corporate objectives, focused on achieving superior performance in key competitive dimensions, and having properly designed, sized, and equipped can vastly boost its competitive effectiveness. But that competitive advantage will be short-lived unless it is reinforced by a process of ongoing organizational improvement. **Chapter 10** describes different approaches for inducing ongoing improvement in an organization, both within and across operating units. It also provides examples of the competitive power that accrues to companies that do this particularly well—whether it be reflected in quality, productivity, asset management, response times, or product development. Finally, it contrasts the requirements that different improvement strategies place on a company's resources, managers, and organizational structure.

Chapter 11 pulls all these threads together, and discusses the role that senior managers must play in guiding their operations organizations safely through the rugged terrain ahead of them—and, in the process, creating sources of sustainable competitive advantage. They also must address more subtle issues, such as changing the way the operations organization thinks about itself and is regarded by others.

NOTES

1. For a splendid account of Lewis and Clark's journey of exploration, see Ambrose (1996).

2. Jorgenson and Stiroh (2000), and Oliner and Sichel (2000).

3. For an interesting commentary on the logic behind this assertion—as well as its defects, see "What Did We Gain from Zapping the Deficit?" by Bernstein (1998).

4. On the other hand, some economists argued that the U.S. government's estimates of both personal disposable income and savings were too low. The measure of income did not include capital gains on the sale of appreciated assets, for example, and the estimate of personal savings did not take into account peoples' contributions to 401(k) plans or the value of their assets—in particular, the unrealized (and possibly ephemeral) capital appreciation in their houses and stock portfolios.

5. A survey by Goldman Sachs in late 2002 indicated that capacity utilization in U.S. manufacturing was at its lowest level in twenty years; see "Industry Outlook 2003," *BusinessWeek,* January 13, 2003, p. 97. During the previous decade, three of the top five steel companies had gone bankrupt, as had three of the top five airlines.

6. A "bubble" in the sense that it had been largely based on (and, in turn, fostered) inflated real estate, stock prices, and other tangible assets.

7. For an analysis of productivity trends in Germany, Japan, and the United States, as well a discussion of the strengths and weaknesses of various approaches for measuring productivity growth, see Van Ark and Pilat (1993).

8. This dropped roughly in half when its loans to other countries were netted out. On the other hand, it did not include its citizens' postal savings deposits (amounting to more than $10 trillion), of which about $2 trillion had been invested by the Japanese government in public works projects whose financial viability was questionable. If these off-book liabilities and Japan's future pension obligations were taken into account, its true indebtedness could approach 250 percent of GDP!

9. See "Another Return to Recession," *BusinessWeek,* February 17, 2003, p. 26, and "Japan Seethes over Comparisons to Botswana," *The Wall Street Journal,* May 31, 2002.

10. See Berger et al. (2002).

11. One respected economist's jaundiced opinion was that, "… establishing a single currency will have little if any impact on Eurosclerosis: the forces that keep unemployment high and job creation low will be as strong [afterwards] as they are today … having spent years suffering under the disciplines of the Maastricht treaty, Europe will arrive at the promised land and find that it looks an awful lot like the desert." (Krugman, 1998).

12. Germany's DAX stock index (representing thirty of its leading companies) had the worst performance of any stock index in the developed world, and a poll in late 2002 indicated that "7 percent of the companies surveyed, ranging from small businesses to major corporations, have already decided to leave Germany … an additional 32 percent are thinking about it." "Business Heads for Cheaper Shores," *BusinessWeek,* December 30, 2002, p. 58.

13. See "Three Big Auto Makers Scramble to Raise Vehicle Quality," *The Wall Street Journal,* April 1, 2002, p. B4, and "Autos: A New Industry," *BusinessWeek,* July 15, 2002, pp. 98–106.

14. See *Fall 1991 Survey on Current Trends in Implementing Total Quality: Summary of Findings,* Rath & Strong Management Consultants, and "Many Companies Try Management Fads, Only to See Them Flop," *The Wall Street Journal,* July 6, 1993, p. A1.

15. "Don't Get Hammered by Management Fads," *The Wall Street Journal,* May 21, 2001, p. A22.

16. A recent summary of these efforts is provided by G. Easton and S. Jarrell (1998).

17. Carroll, D. (1997).

18. See "Operation That Rated Hospitals Was Success, But the Patient Died," *The Wall Street Journal,* August 23, 1999, p. 1.

19. Similarly, Lawler and Morhman (1985) reported that, "In a number of cases we studied, the CEO of the company had seen a TV program or read a magazine article praising [quality] circles and decided to give them a try."

20. See Klein (1989), Hackman and Wageman (1995), and Schultz et al. (2003).

21. Schneiderman (1998). A study of more than 500 Canadian companies found that a modest application of "Alternative Work Practices" appeared to have a positive effect, but more extensive application led to lower job satisfaction and commitment (Godard, 2001).

22. In the early 1920s Ford's River Rouge plant's inventory turns were reported to be thirty-five to forty per year—comparable to Toyota's plants in the 1980s.

23. "Toyota Emulates Methods of Europe at New Factory," *The Nikkei Weekly,* December 28, 1991.

24. The best known example is *Reengineering The Corporation* by Hammer and Champy, 1993.

25. Ibid.

26. See Hall et al. (1993) and other references in Chapter 10.

27. For a close analogy, see Johnson and Wemmerlov (1996), which concludes that "whether a cellular layout outperforms the functional layout from which it is derived is a complex function of resource interactions, the level of resource utilizations, the degree of resource pool partitioning, and the degree to which factors such as setup time, move time, batch size, etc. can be simultaneously improved as a result of conversion to a cellular layout."

28. Stalk and Webber (1993), p. 98.

29. Much of the material in sections 1.3.2 through 1.3.4, and 1.4 is based on Hayes (2002).

30. Johnson and Kaplan (1987) provide a historical perspective on this issue, while Hayes et al. (1988, chapter 5) and Goldratt (1986) explore its application to operations management.

31. The article "Time—The Next Source of Competitive Advantage" (Stalk, 1988), for example, fostered a series of OM-related works.

32. Jamie Lerner, CEO of Xuma (an Internet facilitator): Plenary Address at the POMS 1999 Annual Meeting, San Antonio.

33. See Brandenburger and Nalebuff (1996).

34. See "On to the Living Room! Can Microsoft Control the Digital Home?" *BusinessWeek,* January 21, 2002, pp. 68–72.

35. *U.S. News & World Reports* estimated that the industry's supply chain contained more than $230 billion worth of auto parts (January 29, 2001; p. 31).

36. According to Day and Fein (2002), of the 1,500 public B2B exchanges in operation in January 2000, less than 200 were in operation in 2003.

37. See "The Allure of 'Bundling,'" *The Wall Street Journal,* October 7, 2003, p. B1.

38. See "When Everything Is Made in China," *BusinessWeek,* June 17, 2002, p. 20.

39. *BusinessWeek,* August 31, 1998, pp. 110–111.

40. Hagel and Singer (1999), use the term *infrastructure business* instead of *operations,* but their description of its characteristics better matches what most people would consider operations to include.

41. See Davenport (2003); Drucker (1994) provides a particularly insightful commentary on the historical context of the shift to knowledge workers, as well as on some of the imperatives involved in managing them.

Chapter 2

Operations Strategy: Origins and New Directions

2.1 INTRODUCTION

Most of the people employed by most organizations—whether private or public, whether engaged in making products or delivering services—are engaged in its operations function, and most of its physical assets reside there. Within *operations* we include all those activities required to create and deliver a product or service, from procurement through conversion to distribution. In today's fierce global competition, there is a growing recognition that the operations function can be a formidable competitive weapon if designed and managed properly.

An *operations strategy* is a set of goals, policies, and self-imposed restrictions that together describe how the organization proposes to direct and develop all the resources invested in operations so as to best fulfill (and possibly redefine) its mission. In the case of a business organization, this mission usually is expressed in terms of survival, profitability, and growth, and is pursued by trying to differentiate itself from its competitors in some desirable way. A company's operations strategy, therefore, has to begin by specifying how it proposes to support that chosen form of competitive differentiation. By helping weld together the massive resources invested in the operations function into a cohesive, purposeful whole, such a strategy can enable operations to become a powerful source of competitive advantage.

Consider, for example, the case of Southwest Airlines,[1] which began operations in Texas in 1971with little more than "a wing and a prayer." SWA grew steadily during the 1970s and, after the deregulation of the airline industry, began expanding outside Texas. By following a clear and consistent low cost/no frills strategy, it grew steadily until in 2003 it was the fourth largest airline in the United States in terms of domestic passengers flown. Moreover, after thirty years of continuous profitability (in several years it was the only airline in the top ten to show a profit), its market capitalization was greater than the total of its six largest competitors.

It wasn't until the 1990s that any of its major competitors attempted to imitate Southwest's strategy, and all attempts so far have failed. Southwest's approaches to customer service, gate operations, and human resource management had made it so efficient, and its reputation and drawing power were so established, that it no longer appeared vulnerable either to competitors' counterattacks or their attempts to imitate its way of doing business. Its eastward expansion in 1997, in fact, occasioned the *Wall Street Journal* to headline an article: "Competitors Quake as Southwest Air Is Set to Invade Northeast." The reason its competitors waited so long to react, and why they were so ineffective when they did so, is largely due to Southwest's superior operating effectiveness.

Most managers have a fairly good idea of what a business strategy consists of, and they are generally familiar with the basic issues and concerns associated with marketing and financial strategies. But the idea that operations can be a competitive weapon, and that an *operations* strategy is more than simply pursuing "improved efficiency" or "doing whatever is required in order to carry out our other strategies" still is somewhat surprising to many managers. In too many firms, operations has tended to play an essentially neutral role, reflecting an assumption that marketing, sales, or R&D could provide a more effective basis for achieving a competitive advantage. Also, the continual pressure in operations for quick decisions tends to stifle strategic thinking and impels managers to adopt stopgap measures that reflect a variety of concepts and techniques. As a result, these measures are likely to lack a clear, common purpose, so their selection and implementation are disjointed and only indirectly linked to broader issues of general management concern.

This chapter takes a contrasting perspective, showing how an operations organization can be configured and managed *strategically* so as to create a competitive advantage. Before describing the development of the concept of *operations strategy* and some of the debates it has triggered over the years, we review the essential nature of *business* strategy: its purpose, its basis in the underlying attitudes and preferences that shape the way a firm manages itself, and how that strategy is translated into the functional strategies required to implement it. Then we describe the somewhat simplistic, but seductive appeal of "one best way" approaches to managing operations, and contrast such approaches with a "contingency theory" of operations strategy based on the notions of *fit* and *focus.* We provide examples of some of the different ways a firm can pursue a competitive advantage, and how, through a coherent series of decisions, an operations organization can go about creating an operations edge that reinforces that advantage.

Then we address how a company might be able to transform a competitive advantage that is easy to imitate, and therefore temporary, into one that is *sustainable* through the development of operating capabilities that are both important to customers and difficult for competitors to copy. This discussion of *capability-building/learning* is continued in Chapter 10. Finally, we describe how several companies have been able to exploit the role that operations can play in mounting attacks on competitors or fending off their assaults. In the **Appendix,** we discuss issues relating to how one might assess the "quality" of a strategy, and also the concept of a "*corporate* operations strategy."

2.2 THE CONCEPT OF STRATEGY

The word *strategy* (derived from the Greek word for generalship) was initially applied only to warfare. When applied to business "wars" it similarly refers to the establishment of objectives, the setting of direction, and the development and implementation of plans, with the goal (in place of military "victory") of achieving ascendancy over one's adversaries.[2] In order to have the desired competitive impact, therefore, a strategy has to operate over an extended time horizon and embrace a broad spectrum of activities, ranging from resource allocation processes to day-to-day operations. It must mold decisions affecting these different sets of activities into a coherent pattern, both over time and across groups that often compete for the same resources. An effective strategy also usually entails concentrating a company's efforts and resources on a limited range of pursuits. Focusing resources on certain pursuits reduces the resources available for others, however, so a coherent strategy usually requires that a company make trade-offs among various "good things."

The word *strategy* is used in so many contexts that it is useful to identify and contrast three different types of management-related strategies. At the highest level, *corporate strategy* encompasses decisions regarding the industries and markets in which it participates (and, by omission, those in which it will *not*), how it structures itself in order to attack those markets, and how it acquires and allocates key corporate resources to various activities and groups. The second level is associated with each of the corporation's strategic business units (SBUs)—usually a subsidiary, division, or product line.[3] Each SBU might have its own business strategy, which specifies (1) the scope of that business and its relationship to the corporation as a whole, and (2) how it proposes to "position" itself within its particular industry so as to achieve and maintain a competitive advantage (see Section 2.6). A given SBU might achieve a defensible competitive advantage in various ways, including such generic ones as low cost/high volume, product innovation and unique features, or customized service in selected niches. To be effective, this advantage must meet important customer needs, take into account competitors' strengths and weaknesses, and be sustainable given the SBU's capabilities.[4]

The third level is composed of the functional strategies that support the type of competitive advantage being pursued. A typical SBU might have four such functional strategies: a marketing/sales strategy, an operations strategy, a financial/control strategy, and a research/development strategy. Decisions in such areas as pricing, promotion, and field service—all subparts of the marketing functional strategy—clearly would be very different if the desired advantage were high volume/low cost rather than, say, unique features/customized service. Similarly, decisions regarding the product technologies to be pursued, whether to be a technological leader or follower, and whether to emphasize developmental engineering or basic research all constitute subparts of the R&D functional strategy. In some SBUs, other functions might be involved, such as physical distribution, field service, and human resource management.

It should be emphasized that a functional strategy is defined by the *pattern of decisions* actually made, not what is said or written in annual reports or planning documents. Some writers distinguish between an *enunciated* (or planned) strategy and an *implemented* strategy. We do not make that distinction because it suggests that developing a strategy and then implementing it are somehow separable. As will become apparent in this and later chapters, we treat the development of an operations strategy as an interactive process involving both planning and execution at various levels and in different areas.

The activities required to implement a strategy take place along both horizontal and vertical dimensions. Vertical activities are those that relate a given function to the business as a whole, or relate a subfunction to the larger function. Such activities follow classic hierarchical organizational relationships. Horizontal activities are those that cut across multiple functions at fairly low levels in the organization, and require more coordination and consistency among functions than do vertical activities. Examples include quality improvement, product development and rollout, and large-scale engineering/IT projects.

2.2.1 Company Values—The Foundation for Strategy

Formulating and implementing an effective strategy takes a long time and requires the support and coordinated efforts of many people throughout an organization. As a result, once in place, a strategy is difficult to change, so it is essential that it be based on a set of values that are widely shared and expected to endure. Such values encourage certain modes of behavior and suggest how the company ought to behave toward its employees, customers, suppliers, and communities. They not only establish the context within which day-to-day operating decisions are made, they help unify the various corporate, business, and functional strategies adopted by different groups within the company and also set limits on the strategic options available to it. Reinforced through conscious and subconscious behavior at all levels, they create a culture that ties people together, guides their efforts, and gives meaning and purpose to their work.

The degree to which an organization is able to achieve consistency among diverse activities tends to be proportional to the coherence of its values and the extent to which they are shared. The implications of this are particularly important for the operations function because that is where the majority of most companies' people work. In a sense, then, the operations organization is a major "keeper" of the company's values. It is not surprising, therefore, to find that the companies that have built the most formidable operations organizations and are most adept at translating operating capabilities into competitive success tend to be those that are characterized by shared and strongly held values. In fact, if managed properly, the operations function not only can contribute substantially to the competitive success of a business, it also can play an important role in helping to support and enhance the values that provide the foundation for its strategies.

2.3 THE OPERATIONS EDGE: CREATING A COMPETITIVE ADVANTAGE THROUGH OPERATIONS

The purpose of an operations strategy is to guide an operations organization in assembling and aligning the resources that will enable it to implement its company's competitive strategy effectively. The problem that most managers face when attempting to develop an effective operations strategy is not that the task is too complex or difficult. Paradoxically, they often appear to believe that it is too *easy*—that they can easily seek out and emulate the best practices of other companies, particularly those deemed world class. The seductive appeal of *ideal* approaches has occasioned a fierce, and sometimes fairly emotional, debate about the relative merits of three quite different philosophies of operations.

2.3.1 The "American System": Mass Production for Mass Markets

Until the early 1980s, most American managers thought about operations in terms of a paradigm whose roots went back well over a hundred years. The *American System of manufacturing,* with its emphasis on mass markets, standard designs, and mass production using interchangeable parts, revolutionized manufacturing in the middle of the nineteenth century. This new philosophy, modified and elaborated by the concept of *scientific management* promulgated by Frederick Taylor and his disciples, was exploited by such great industrialists as Andrew Carnegie, Henry Ford, and Isaac Singer to transform the United States into an industrial powerhouse by the 1920s.

The ideas that the key to low cost was standardization and high volume, that work was done most efficiently when divided up and assigned to specialists, that managers and staff experts should do the thinking for workers (so they could concentrate on "doing"), that every process was characterized by an innate amount of variation (and hence an irreducible rate of defects), and that communication within an organization should be tightly controlled—so as to avoid possible confusion, and should proceed through a hierarchical chain of command—were accepted as dogma. The "best" manufacturing process was assumed to be based on long runs; it utilized equipment that was specialized for each stage of the process and whose capacities were matched as closely as possible; and it used inventories to buffer different stages both from each other and from the erratic behavior of suppliers and customers. Work should be organized and conducted systematically, in a specified sequence and under tight supervision. In the minds of many top managers, such practices—which collectively formed a cohesive operations strategy—defined the "one best way" (to borrow Taylor's phrase) to design *any* manufacturing or service delivery system; it was the ideal toward which all should strive.

In many continuous process industries, such as petrochemicals, food processing, and paper making, this paradigm remained dominant. During the 1980s, however, its shortcomings became increasingly apparent in many assembly and high-tech industries, and other approaches to operations were found to provide convincing advantages. Rather than a single new approach that could be studied and mastered, however, operations managers now faced a confusing cacophony of expert advice—each advocating different routes to improved competitiveness. The mass production paradigm, although inadequate in many environments, at least offered simplicity and clarity; it allowed limited options as regards technology, organization, work scheduling, inventory and quality control, and performance measurement. People might make different choices, but there was widespread agreement about the underlying premises.

The clearest evidence of this consensus is provided by an analysis of the books written about operations management in the twenty years prior to 1980. Not only was the number small compared with the torrent of books on the subject that appeared during the next two decades, their tables of contents were remarkably similar.

2.3.2 The Japanese System: "Lean Production"

In Japan, however, companies rebuilding from the shambles of World War II were beginning to create an entirely different approach to production. Short on capital, blessed with few natural resources, and faced with small, fragmented markets, they were forced to design new practices that reflected both their lack of resources and the chaotic conditions of their economic environment. Over time, the best ones developed an approach to manufacturing that was claimed by some to be uniformly superior to the American System.

This *lean production system* was characterized by an emphasis on reliability, speed, and flexibility rather than volume and cost. People ought to be broadly trained, rather than specialized, and should work in teams to identify and solve operating problems. Staff was "overhead," and overhead was bad. No amount of rejects was acceptable, so one should work tirelessly to eliminate them. Communication should take place informally and horizontally, among line workers rather than via prescribed hierarchical paths through the organization. Equipment should be general purpose and organized in cells that produced a group of similar parts or products, rather than specialized by process stage. Production throughput time was more important than labor or equipment utilization. Inventory, like defects, was waste. Supplier relationships should be long term and cooperative. Product development activities should be carried out concurrently, not sequentially, and by cross-functional teams.

As discussed in Chapter 1, however, despite many examples of lean production's power, the competitive landscape also is littered with companies that have been bitterly disappointed by their experience with these same practices. Such failures could not always be attributed to mere incompetence, making it difficult to argue that this new philosophy of operations embodied the holy grail—the true "one best way" to organize and manage operations—any more than did the American System. The problem is not that lean production contains fundamental flaws; its successes are too numerous and its converts too committed. At issue is whether it is appropriate in *all* situations. More important, in our view, is that adopting lean production or any other combination of Japanese approaches does not enable operations to create an enduring strategic *advantage.* Nor does emulating other "world class" companies. This kind of approach is essentially imitative in nature, whereas a really useful operations strategy should be based on a sense of the kind of competitive *advantage* that is being pursued and articulate how that advantage is to be achieved. How can a firm achieve any sort of advantage if its only goal is to be "as good as" its best competitors?

2.3.3 A Contingency Theory of Operations Strategy: Fit and Focus

The idea that there was "one best way" to manage operations was disputed by a number of critics over the years,[6] but it received its most effective challenge from Wickham Skinner.[7] The kernel of his argument was three-pronged:

1. Different companies/business units have different strengths and weaknesses and so may choose to compete (i.e., differentiate themselves from competitors) in different ways, requiring them to adopt different "yardsticks of success."
2. Similarly, different ways of configuring, equipping, and managing an operations function result in different operating characteristics, making it easier or harder for a company to achieve a given form of differentiation.
3. Therefore, rather than adopting a "one best way," or even an industry-standard approach, the task for an operations organization is to seek congruence ("fit") between its business unit's chosen approach to competition and the way the operation's function is designed, organized, and managed.

Sometime a corporation exhibits a strong preference for a single form of competitive differentiation, usually reflecting its history or unique resources, so all its SBUs tend to adopt similar competitive strategies. More commonly, though, businesses in different markets or industries choose to compete in different ways. This should not create problems unless one makes the mistake of attempting to service the needs of two or more very dissimilar businesses out of the same operations organization (see our later discussion of "focus" and the Appendix).

Each of these three premises is explored and elaborated on in the following paragraphs.

Different Approaches to Competitive Differentiation

The most critical element of an SBU's competitive strategy, in terms of the implications for its operations strategy, concerns how it chooses to differentiate its products and services from those of its major competitors. Given the myriad choices that customers face when making a purchase, how do they decide which product or service to select? Different customers are attracted by different attributes. In order to appeal to those interested primarily in the cost of the product/service, some companies (such as Southwest Airlines) attempt to achieve a competitive advantage by offering the *lowest price.* Price, however, is not the only basis upon which a business can compete (although many economists appear to assume that it is!). Other companies, such as BMW, seek to attract those who want *higher quality*—in terms of performance, appearance, or features—than that available in competing products, even though accompanied by a higher price. The cost of providing higher quality, however defined, must be balanced against the market's willingness to pay for it, of course.

Another competitive dimension through which some firms seek to differentiate themselves is *dependability.* Although their products or services might be priced higher than those of others, and they may not offer the highest performance or the latest technology, they do work as specified, they are delivered on time, and the company stands ready to mobilize its resources to ensure that any failures are corrected quickly. Caterpillar, IBM, and Sysco often are cited as examples of companies whose strategies emphasize such peace of mind.

Still other important sources of competitive advantage are *flexibility,* either in terms of products or order volumes, and *speed/responsiveness.* A firm that competes on the basis of product flexibility, for instance, must be able to offer a wide product range, deliver nonstandard—even customized—products, and/or take the lead in introducing new products. Smaller firms often adopt such a strategy to compete against larger ones. Others emphasize volume flexibility, exploiting an ability to accelerate or decelerate production very quickly and juggle orders so as to provide unusually rapid delivery. Successful companies in highly cyclical industries, like housing or furniture, often make volume flexibility a primary priority.

Within a given industry each company usually selects just one or two of these competitive dimensions to emphasize. It is difficult and, in fact, potentially dangerous for an SBU to attempt to offer superior performance along all of them. If it does, it usually ends up second best on each dimension to some other company that devotes more of its resources to developing a specific competitive advantage. This implies that the SBU must establish clear priorities regarding the way it intends to position itself relative to its competitors.

Some try to match (or stay within some specified range of) competitors along several competitive dimensions, and thereby offer the "best value" or other form of compromise between competing attributes.[8] But when it comes down to the final attempt at persuasion—the moment of decision at the grocery store shelf, say—it hopes the customer's choice will be swayed by its product's (or service's) specific form of superiority. For example, the authors of two best-selling books about management argue that "Most of what we are doing [in business] is a waste of energy…. Companies succeed when they focus on one big purpose above all else … becoming the best in the world at what they do … [and] articulating a solid rationale for making money over the long haul. The rationale, in turn, is generally based on one key, carefully chosen business ratio."[9]

Different Operating Systems Have Different Performance Characteristics

One does not tell an auto designer simply to "design a vehicle." The designer will immediately want to know that vehicle's primary use: for high-speed driving on superhighways, say, or for carrying large loads, for traversing rough terrain, for commuting in urban areas, or for fun and responsiveness. Different uses imply different designs: the classic "road cruiser," van, SUV, pickup truck, subcompact, or sports car. An attempt to "cover all the bases" typically leads to a mongrel design that can't do anything particularly well. So the trade-offs the designer is forced to make must be both internally coherent and consistent with the priorities required by the vehicle's primary use. They also, of course, reflect the technologies and systems available to the designer at the time they are made. The choices and trade-offs available to the designers of the DC-3 airplane, that is, were very different from those available to the designers of the Boeing 737 that replaced it on many of the same routes forty years later. Similarly, FedEx's initial package tracking system could not incorporate the power of the Internet.

Just as the capabilities and limitations of a vehicle reflect the decisions made by its designers, so an operations organization's inherent strengths and weaknesses reflect the influence of the design decisions made by its managers. As a result, that organization is able to do certain things easily and well, and other things only with difficulty—if at all.

An Operations Organization's Priorities Should Reflect Its SBU's Competitive Strategy

An effective operations organization is not necessarily one that promises the maximum efficiency or process perfection, but rather one that meets the needs of its SBU's competitive strategy. Therefore, once the type of competitive differentiation being pursued has been specified, management must ensure that its operations organization is configured and managed in such a way that it can provide that form of differentiation. The clear implication is that there is no one best way for dealing with *any* business problem—whether one is making, delivering, or selling a product or service, designing a management information or quality system, or measuring performance. In each case, one must make choices that reflect one's context, goals, resources, and personnel. Translating a business strategy into an appropriate collection of buildings, equipment, people, and procedures requires time and perseverance to ensure that literally hundreds of decisions, large and small, collectively support and hone the desired operations edge.[10]

2.3.4 Key Decisions Involved in Operations Strategy Implementation

A useful framework for thinking about the diversity of operations design decisions is provided in Table 2-1. The collective impact of these decisions establishes limits on an operations organization's strategic capabilities.

Table 2-1 Operations Strategy Decision Categories

Structural decisions
• Capacity—amount, type, timing • Sourcing and vertical integration—direction, extent, balance • Facilities—size, location, specialization • Information and process technology—degree of automation, interconnectedness, lead versus follow
Infrastructural policies and systems
• Resource allocation and capital budgeting systems • Human resource systems—selection, skills, compensation, employment security • Work planning and control systems—purchasing, aggregate planning, scheduling, control or inventories and/or waiting time backlog • Quality systems—defect prevention, monitoring, intervention, and elimination • Measurement and reward systems—measures, bonuses, promotion policies • Product and process development systems—leader or follower, project team organization • Organization—centralized versus decentralized, which decisions to delegate, role of staff groups

The first four decision categories in Table 2-1 are typically viewed as structural in nature because they represent decisions regarding the organization's physical bricks-and-mortar attributes, such as the amount of production (or service delivery) capacity provided. Moreover, they typically require a substantial capital investment and, once in place, are difficult to alter or reverse. This aspect has led many organizations to rely on their capital budgeting process as the primary mechanism for assessing structural operations decisions.

The other seven decision categories are termed *infrastructural,* in that they describe the systems, policies, and practices that determine how the organization's structural aspects are to be managed. In that sense they are analogous to the software that directs a computer's hardware to carry out tasks in a specific way. Such systems often do not require highly visible capital investments (ERP systems are a notable exception), although developing and implementing them can involve years of effort and they can be just as difficult, time-consuming, and costly to change as structural decisions.

Structural Decisions

Capacity Hardware and software decisions interact in a variety of sometimes quite subtle ways. As one example, the amount of capacity that a given set of floor space and equipment can provide depends on whether it is operated one shift a day, five days a week, or around the clock. It also depends on the process yield/defect level, which is affected by equipment choices, materials sourcing policies, and a number of organizational practices, including how equipment is designed, monitored and maintained, how employee are selected and trained, quality is assured, work is scheduled, and performance is measured and rewarded. For example, the Oshkosh Truck Company was reported to have been able to more than double its production, without any increase in equipment or people, by replacing its three product-specific production lines with one flexible line and making other improvements in scheduling and production methods.[11] Capacity decisions are the subject of Chapter 3.

Sourcing and Vertical Integration Another major structural aspect of an operations organization encompasses decisions regarding how much of the total work required to create and deliver its products/services will be done internally and how much will be purchased from outside organizations. Some companies choose to be vertically integrated—producing most of their own component parts and services, while others prefer to purchase most of their needs so as to limit their capital investment and amount of internal processing. Tied in with this decision are a number of other decisions pertaining to the way the company's outside suppliers are selected and managed. These issues are covered in Chapter 4.

Facilities Besides the amount of raw capacity that is to be provided, one must decide how that total operating capacity is to be broken up into individual operating units. This includes the number and size of these facilities, where they are located (e.g., near major customers? near low cost labor?), and how each is specialized (by product? by process stage? by region?). Such decisions often are less pertinent for services that require a high degree of direct interaction with customers, since that kind of capacity cannot be stored or transported. For example, an unused airplane seat cannot be saved and used on the next flight, or by a concurrent flight to a different destination. But many service companies have certain "backroom" functions that do not require direct customer interaction and so require these kinds of facilities decisions. Such issues are discussed further in Chapter 5.

Information and Process Technology Another class of structural decisions concerns the selection of information and process technologies. At one level, such decisions require choices among different types of equipment (which usually has been designed by someone outside the firm who has in mind a specific proposed use and desired operating characteristics). At another level, it should specify how this equipment is to be located, connected together, and coordinated. For example, the same pieces of equipment can be organized as independent workstations, permitting a variety of process flow paths that result in a wide range of products or services (a so-called *job shop*), or as a connected processing line down which all products flow continuously. Each choice, of course, implies a supporting set of structural and infrastructural decisions.[12] Information technology is the subject of Chapter 6.

Infrastructural Decisions

As shown in Table 2-1, a company's operations infrastructure is composed of its policies and systems governing a number of activities, from capital budgeting and equipment selection to organizational structure. Each of these systems often has repercussions and implications for other infrastructural and structural elements. Capital budgeting and performance measurement systems, in particular, seem to affect everything else. In addition, human resource policies interact with location and process choices, and sourcing policies interact with facility decisions. Organizational design also is highly dependent on vertical integration decisions, as well as on decisions regarding how various facilities are located, specialized, and interconnected. Therefore, although many managers, like most economists, tend to focus primary attention on the more quantifiable issues associated with structural decisions, a company's infrastructure is at least as critical to its success.

The impact of such infrastructural choices is often underestimated. One study of the operating performances of twelve manufacturing plants belonging to three different companies found that *less than half* the performance variation across plants that belonged to the same company—and which used similar equipment and served the same customers—could be explained by such traditional structural variables as plant size and age, capital-to-labor ratios, and union power.[13] The majority of the performance differences could be attributed to differences in policies, procedures, and systems. Other studies have found similar results in contexts outside of manufacturing. For example, in the case of pharmaceutical process development projects, the underlying development processes and problem-solving strategies appeared to account for the bulk of performance differences.[14]

Fit

The choices made for each of these different types of decisions have varying effects on a company's operating costs, quality, dependability, flexibility, speed/responsiveness, and new product capabilities. For example, most companies that continually adjust their production rates so as to chase demand tend to have higher production costs and less consistent quality than those that try to maintain a level rate of production and absorb demand fluctuations through inventories. If it wants to be able to respond quickly to small orders for customized products and rapid changes in customer requirements, it probably should configure itself so that it has excess capacity, its facilities are tightly coordinated (or individual facilities are focused on supplying the needs of specific customers), its processing equipment and people are organized more like those of a job shop than a continuous flow line, and it has cultivated suppliers who are able to react quickly to changing requirements.

If, on the other hand, it wants to be able to offer low cost and the latest technology, it probably should concentrate the production of those items that require large amounts of capital investment and technological expertise into a small number of facilities, possibly located near engineering universities or other technical centers, and seek out suppliers who are able to match its needs. Some researchers have found evidence that the structural and infrastructural decisions made by many companies tend to exhibit consistent patterns that allow them to be placed into one of just a few categories, which can be characterized by such competitive strategies as *caretakers* versus *innovators*.[15]

Just as the trade-offs made by the designers of an engineered product must be consistent with its intended use, so must these structural and infrastructural decisions mesh together to create a desired set of specific capabilities. Operations has to be able to do things that are considered critical to the company's success without wasting resources on lower-priority pursuits; otherwise some of the things that are really important will not get done. Achieving this kind of consistency—or "fit"—between strategy, structure, and infrastructure in an organization, however, is much more difficult and complex than when designing a product. Whereas the decisions and trade-offs involved in product design are usually made within a relatively short period of time by a group of people who work closely together and are often located near one another, structural and infrastructural decisions usually are made at different points in time by different groups of people who often are physically separated and may seldom interact in the normal course of business.

Only infrequently will a company make a basic change in any one of these categories (this being almost the definition of a "structural" decision), but in any year it probably will make at least one major decision that falls into one of them. Hence, the company's competitive priorities and operations strategy need to be clearly communicated to all these groups, and their structural and infrastructural decisions monitored for consistency. Otherwise, unintended drifting may occur.

Focus: Fit in the Small

The notion of *focus* follows naturally, almost inevitably, from the concept of *fit*. Just as a company must choose, train, and manage a sales force differently if its primary task is to sell expensive capital equipment to engineers, as opposed to selling inexpensive disposables to unsophisticated consumers, a single operations organization is unlikely to be equally effective for businesses that compete in markedly different ways. Different operations structures and infrastructures are required for different missions. Therefore, a single facility, even if equipped with the most modern equipment and systems, will tend to experience both irreconcilable conflicts and low overall effectiveness if it attempts to serve multiple markets that demand different competitive strategies. Such a facility, Skinner conjectured, could only become an effective competitor if it were broken up into two or more "focused factories," each of which "is focused to accomplish the particular manufacturing task demanded by [its specific] strategy ..."[16] This emphasis on simplicity, clarity, and low overhead foreshadowed the later concept of lean production.

It is not, of course, *impossible* for the same operations organization to produce and deliver two different kinds of products/services that compete for customers in two very different ways. Indeed, many companies operate this way. However, one cannot expect that organization to perform both tasks *equally well,* or as well as two different organizations could that each focused its attention on the needs of a specific type of product/service, customer, and form of differentiation.

Most managers argue that it is prohibitively expensive to break up a large facility, containing a variety of technologies and producing a number of products/services for different markets, into two or more separate facilities, each devoted to a smaller number of relatively similar products and/or technologies. They argue that not only do multiple facilities usually require duplicate floor space, equipment investment, and overhead structures, they lack scale economies. But many companies have found just the opposite to be true—that focusing their facilities often causes operating costs to *decrease.* If, for example, one's original facility is situated in an expensive (in terms of construction, labor, or transportation costs) location, and a new business that seeks to compete on the basis of low cost can be operated in a less expensive location, then setting up a new facility to service that business may turn out to be cheaper in the long run than continually piling more and more work into the original plant.

Similarly, equipment that is specialized to the needs of a specific kind of product or service is often less expensive (and/or cheaper to build internally) and easier to operate than multipurpose equipment that has a broader range of capabilities and has to be switched frequently from one product to another. Moreover, adding products and services to a facility increases its complexity, which usually necessitates additional overhead to coordinate production schedules, resolve conflicts, expedite orders, and estimate product costs. As a result, companies that break up a big, complex organization into more focused smaller ones often find that their total overhead costs go down.

The advantages of focusing, and thereby reducing the size of, large and complex operating units has come to be recognized in contexts far removed from manufacturing. The airline industry provides a case in point. Faced with declining revenues and growing competition from such "upstarts" as Southwest, many major airlines have begun to recognize the tremendous costs their complexity has burdened them with. At one time, for example, American Airlines had fourteen separate fleets of airplanes, each of which contained subfleets having different seating configurations and equipment that prevented them from being used interchangeably on its worldwide route structure. For example, a 777 used on its Asian routes could not be substituted for a 777 used on its European routes.[17] To complicate operations further, it allowed its customers considerable flexibility to make last-minute changes in itineraries and seating assignments, and provided a variety of "frills" that were valued by (or accessible to) only a portion of its total passengers.

Other nonmanufacturing industries that have begun experimenting with the focus concept include health care and education. Such efforts, however, sometimes engender a storm of controversy. Some believe, for example, that focused "niche" hospitals essentially add to the complexity and cost of traditional hospitals (which offer a broad spectrum of services) by sending them only patients who have relatively complicated medical problems.[18] A similar argument has been made against the concept of *charter schools,* which are claimed to increase the burdens placed on the traditional school system. An example of how this dynamic played out in one company (Wriston Manufacturing) is provided in Chapter 5 (Section 5.5).

A substantial portion of the advantages of focus can often be obtained through less drastic means, however. A company might, for instance, be able to achieve considerable simplification simply by eliminating products or options that are seldom requested by customers, or segmenting its operations and dividing a given facility into separated work areas—sometimes called *plants within a plant.* A *manufacturing cell,* composed of a relatively small group of people who are given responsibility for a related group of products or services, is an extreme example of this approach. Each cell can have most, if not all, of its own equipment, its own workers, its own work-scheduling and performance-measurement systems, and so on. The basic premise behind the concept of *reengineering* is rooted in a similar idea: that major increases in performance can be achieved by co-locating (or tying together electronically) the various groups and functions involved in performing a complete business process. These might include, for example, all the steps from materials procurement through production to physical delivery (see Chapter 10).

Similarly, an airline might separate its total operations into two separate ones: one hub-and-spoke system and one direct route system, such as Southwest's. The former utilizes hubs located in high-traffic airports (so are subject to congestion delays), and is characterized by periodic "waves" of arrivals and departures, during which the airline's ground facilities are either over- or underutilized. Moreover, managing the hub-and-spoke system's complexity requires considerable slack to ensure passengers and baggage can make transfers to their connecting flights, as well as highly sophisticated information and scheduling systems. In contrast, a direct route system restricts the number of destinations (often to secondary, relatively uncongested airports), and reduces scheduling complexity by assigning each plane to a single route that begins and ends at the same city, and which it repeats day after day. Elaborate information and control systems are replaced by an emphasis on teamwork and fast aircraft turnaround times.[19]

As with the case of *fit,* however, the principle of *focus* is easier to explain than it is to implement. Even though a company might agree that it needs to become more focused, the question remains, "How?" It can focus either around product lines, for example, or around process stages/technologies, or geographic areas, or markets/customer groups, but it cannot focus along several dimensions simultaneously. That is, choosing to focus along any one dimension (e.g., product lines) means giving up focus along another. Once this decision has been made, it must decide *how much* focus is desirable. At one extreme, each product, part, or component service could be assigned to a separate organization—usually an infeasible approach. At the other, all operations could be performed at the same location. Companies engaged in delivering services that cannot be stored or transported sometimes drift toward this extreme, and then begin to experience problems as they expand their range of offerings. Returning to our airline example, instead of segmenting its operations into hub-and-spoke and direct route systems, as described above, it might design separate operating systems for "business" and "leisure" travelers. Once the desired focus has been achieved, the company must guard against losing it. Organizations continually are buffeted by new demands and opportunities. Under pressure to react quickly, and swayed more by the obvious short-term benefits of enlarging—and complicating—an existing operations organization than by the longer-term, less tangible benefits of keeping it small, simple, and focused, the natural tendency of managers is to pile more and more products, technologies, and objectives onto an existing facility rather than create a new locus of activities. As a result, business organizations tend to become steadily more complicated over time. To guard against this tendency, some companies have found it useful to set up "charters" for each facility or division. These charters not only specify what the company wants that facility to do, or to become particularly proficient at (designated as *centers of excellence*), but also alert it to the types of activities that it is *prohibited* from undertaking without express permission from higher levels in the company.

2.3.5 Responding to Evolving Strategies, Markets, and Technologies

Since the ongoing task for an operations organization is to structure and manage itself so as to enhance its company's competitive strategy, as its environment and strategy evolve it usually becomes necessary to make changes in a number of the operations decision categories of Table 2-1. Again and again we have found that the root cause of an operations crisis is that a company's operations policies and people—both workers and managers—over time have become incompatible with its facilities, technology, sourcing, and system choices. Even more subtly, even though its structure may be consistent with its infrastructure, the operations organization may no longer be serving the operating priorities demanded by the company's evolving competitive strategy.

During the early part of its life cycle, for example, a product generally is offered in a variety of configurations, most of which sell in relatively low volumes. As the product matures, however, it typically evolves toward a smaller number of higher-volume, more standardized products. This requires compensating adjustments in the way the company organizes its operations, suggesting that both the competitive strategy and the operating systems of a typical company in the industry might be expected to evolve in a relatively predictable manner over time. One can visualize that likely path, as well as other trajectories that a company might follow, with the help of a *product-process matrix,* as depicted in Figure 2-1.[20] This matrix also allows one to identify a number of the opportunities and pitfalls a company might encounter as it attempts to adjust (or, often more damaging, fails to adjust) to predictable market shifts.

Process Structure—Process Life Cycle Stage	**Product Structure—Product Life Cycle Stage** I Low-volume/ low-standardization, one of a kind	II Low-volume, multiple products	III Higher volume, few major products	IV High-volume/ high-standardization, commodity products	**Priorities**	**Key Management Tasks**
I Jumbled flow (job shop)					Flexibility–quality Product customization Performance	Fast reaction Loading plant, estimating capacity Estimating costs and delivery times Breaking bottlenecks Order tracing and expediting
II Disconnected line flow (batch)						Systemizing diverse elements Developing standards and methods, improvement Balancing process stages
III Connected line flow (assembly line)						Managing large, specialized, and complex operations Meeting material requirements Running equipment at peak efficiency
IV Continuous flow					Dependability–cost	Timing expansion and technological change Raising required capital

Priorities	Flexibility–quality			Dependability–cost
Dominant Competitive Mode	Custom design General purpose High margins	Custom design Quality control Service High margins	Standardized design Volume manufacturing Finished goods inventory Distribution Backup suppliers	Vertical integration Long runs Specialized equipment and processes Economies of scale Standardized material

Figure 2-1 The Product-Process Matrix

2.3.6 Strategy as an Art Form

Understanding the basic concepts of strategic fit and focus does not by itself, of course, ensure an effective solution to a specific competitive problem, any more than understanding the basic laws of physics "solves" how to design an automobile. None of the structural and infrastructural decisions described above has a cleanly delineated impact on all the different competitive dimensions, so they can be made in a variety of imaginative ways. While certain choices may have quite clear-cut implications for specific performance measures (e.g., cost *or* flexibility, innovativeness *or* control/reliability), they may have relatively little effect on others, or the trade-offs among them. The adoption of an MRP system, for example, is unlikely to have much impact on the trade-off between innovativeness and defect rates. It is generally possible, therefore, to achieve a given level of performance along any dimension through different combinations of structural and infrastructural decisions. As a result, two different companies that are each trying to achieve a similar set of competitive priorities may make very different design choices as they configure equally effective operations organizations. One, for example, may rely primarily on structural elements (facilities and equipment choices, say), while another may emphasize infrastructural elements (a just-in-time production scheduling system coupled with a TQM program, say). Similarly, German companies might configure themselves very differently from the Japanese companies they compete against head-to-head.

As a result, designing an effective operations strategy is still somewhat of an art form—constrained here and there by technological and organizational possibilities and guided by informed guesses—just as is product design. This ambiguity does not, however, suggest that anything goes. There are basic principles that underlie these kinds of decisions, and provide guidance as to the reasonable alternatives that managers should consider as they attempt to mold their organizations in creative ways.[21]

2.4 CHALLENGES TO THE OPERATIONS STRATEGY FRAMEWORK

Up to this point, our discussion of this contingency theory of operations strategy framework has been dominated by the notion of *strategic fit;* that is, a company's operating system should reflect its competitive position and strategy. *Focus* provides both a means to achieve this fit and a discipline for maintaining it in the face of the continual barrage of potentially distracting opportunities that confront most business organizations. And the *product-process matrix* helps guide the adjustments in strategy and systems that are likely to be required in a changing world. This framework for operations strategy offered very different guidance to operations managers than did the mass production or lean production paradigms, but it contained important gaps. It could not explain, for example, why several competitors' attempts to duplicate the low-cost strategy of Southwest Airlines—to the point of using the same type of airplanes, flying to the same airports, and offering a similar "no-frills" service—ended in failure. Apparently, by copying the strategy and "best practices" of their leading competitor, they had achieved an appropriate fit between their strategy, their structure, and their infrastructure. But good fit alone proved not to be sufficient for success.

The success of Japanese manufacturers also presented problems for contingency theory advocates. Until the 1980s, many western companies wrapped themselves in the straightjacket of industry practice as regards operations, preferring to compete instead through innovative marketing, new products, or financial maneuvers. The notion that operations, if properly configured and managed, could provide a powerful competitive advantage was essentially a theory in search of practitioners. Then Japanese companies in a number of industries began a furious assault on world markets. Their success initially was ascribed to low wages and government assistance or protection. But as westerners studied Japanese management practices, and realized how vulnerable many western industries had become, they began to understand that Japan's success was primarily a triumph of sheer manufacturing prowess.

In 1980, most Japanese companies were producing similar products to those offered by western companies, and were marketing them in similar ways. What made these products attractive was not just their cost (which usually was less than could be justified by lower Japanese wages and interest rates), but also their low incidence of defects, their reliability, and their durability. Yet observers reported that the facilities and equipment of these companies were usually no better than—and often were inferior to—those of their U.S. and European competitors. Moreover, they often produced myriads of products for different markets in large, unfocused factories. Their success, evidently, was not built around notions of fit and focus.

2.4.1 Challenging the Necessity for Trade Offs

The mass production paradigm, on one hand, held that economies of scale and long production runs were the key to low cost, consistent quality, and dependability. The contingency approach to operations strategy, on the other hand, argued that managers had to decide which competitive dimensions were most important, and if conflicts arose among them when designing an operating system they had to make choices based on a careful analysis of the trade-offs involved. This assertion that a given company couldn't "have it all" was one of the most controversial elements of the contingency approach. It was challenged in the 1980s by the advent of *flexible manufacturing systems* (FMS), which appeared to promise both great flexibility (production lots of one) and low (fully automated "lights out") cost.[22] Tradeoff proponents countered, of course, by pointing out that the contingency approach anticipated that trade-offs might change—but not disappear—as new technologies became available.

A second and more serious challenge was presented by the success of elite Japanese companies that appeared to ignore some of the basic tenets of both the mass production and the contingency paradigms. They acted, for example, as though economies of scale and long runs were not important, nor were trade-offs necessary. Indeed, many Japanese factories appeared to surpass their American counterparts on several competitive dimensions—lower cost, higher quality, greater flexibility, and faster product introductions—all at the same time!

> *The lean producer [in contrast to the mass producer] combines the advantages of craft and mass production, while avoiding the high cost of the former and the rigidity of the latter. ... it requires keeping far less than half the needed inventory on site, resulting in fewer defects, and produces a greater and ever-growing variety of products.*[23]

Even Peter Drucker became a convert, asserting that the factory of the future "will be based on the premise that you not only *can* have both [low cost and flexibility] but you *must* have both."[24] Others suggested that a company could improve almost simultaneously along a number of fronts, which appeared to undercut the notion that trade-offs are required. Tradeoff proponents countered that, just as a 737 could fly slower than its maximum speed, many organizations, because of poor management or lack of information, did not fully exploit the potential of their operating structures and infrastructures. An organization that operated within the limits of its capabilities, therefore, might be able to improve its performance along several dimensions until it reached those limits—at which point the trade-offs became operative.[25]

2.4.2 Challenging the Importance of Focus

Similar questions arose regarding whether operating effectiveness really required focus. Although Japanese factories initially appeared to place great emphasis on restricting product variety and encouraging uninterrupted workflows, during the 1980s many of the best ones embraced product proliferation. Sony, for one, introduced more than 150 versions of its basic Walkman (disclaiming the need for market research, it advocated simply introducing a new model and seeing how it sold).[26] The proponents of lean production claimed that it employs "teams of multiskilled workers at all levels ... and ... highly flexible, increasingly automated machines to produce volumes of products in enormous variety."[27]

This appeared to refute the necessity for focus. Among western operations managers, in fact, there was a growing sense that Japanese companies had effectively made both the mass production paradigm and the contingency approach to operations strategy obsolete by demonstrating that their way of configuring operations was uniformly superior. Furthermore, their new rules of the game appeared widely applicable—not only to vehicle and electronics assembly, but also to medical devices and myriad other products and services.

As more companies adopted these approaches, however, they found that success was elusive, and even successful implementations did not necessarily lead to financial rewards. For example, even though the winners of the National Malcolm Baldrige Award (which recognizes U.S. companies that have been unusually successful at improving their quality, productivity, and customer satisfaction) have done well on average, some have experienced notable failures. One of the early winners, for example, entered Chapter 11 bankruptcy soon after receiving the award, and others (including AT&T, HP, IBM, and Westinghouse) soon afterward began experiencing highly visible problems.

Even more disturbing, a number of Japanese companies began to question many of these same approaches. Not only did they find that many of the practices regarded as central to lean production were not equally effective in every situation, they discovered that widespread use of some of them could create problems for society as a whole. For example, the increasing number of small shipments between suppliers, manufacturers, and customers required by JIT scheduling was congesting the country's road system.[28] They expressed similar concerns about the long-term value of product proliferation and ever-faster new product development.[29] In addition to having to commit ever larger amounts of energy and capital to new products, the costs of the resulting product proliferation were found to be heavy. Worse, too rapid a pace of product introduction appeared to confuse both customers and salespeople ("In what ways is this new model different than the previous one?" becomes ever more difficult to answer), and to induce purchase delays because customers anticipate that waiting a little longer might be rewarded with a superior product. According to two experienced observers of Japanese practices:

> *[the] vision of a production lot of one ... has proven ... excessively expensive, even without considering external costs such as traffic congestion...The proliferation of models ... causes overlaps, redundancies, and product cannibalization—even among the best players. ... And, as market niches multiply—but shrink in size individually—the risk of cannibalization increases until a company's product offerings become so closely bunched that the product differences sweated over by hundreds of engineers become trivial in the eyes of consumers.*[30]

As a result, a number of Japanese producers of everything from automobiles to consumer appliances began to stabilize—or even lengthen—their new product introduction cycles.

Still, some of the criticisms of the contingency approach to operations strategy appeared to be valid, which called for a reevaluation of its basic principles. A strategy based solely on such static concepts as fit, trade-offs, and focus seemed lacking in important respects. A more dynamic framework was needed for the rapidly changing global competition.

2.5 DYNAMIC ORGANIZATIONAL CAPABILITIES

A similar concern was troubling theorists in the competitive strategy field in the mid-1980s. Up to then, the dominant paradigm had been based on the idea that a firm could achieve an enduring competitive advantage by entering industries that were structurally attractive and/or by creating an advantageous position for itself within an industry through deliberate action.[31] This framework offered a systematic approach for thinking about the nature of industrial competition, as well as for analyzing specific competitive situations that a company might face. It also provided a set of concepts and tools that were largely complementary to those of the contingency approach to operations strategy. Using the positioning framework, managers could craft a competitive strategy and establish competitive priorities. Then an operations strategy based on fit and focus could translate those competitive priorities into a set of supportive operations decisions and policies.

Despite the insight this "positioning" framework provided scholars and practitioners, it was essentially static in nature. Just as the old Riccardian notion of comparative advantage could not explain the rising power of Japanese industry in world competition, neither could this position-oriented theory of competitive advantage explain (except, sometimes, in retrospect) the success of Southwest Airlines or of individual Japanese companies. Not only were such relatively small and poorly positioned companies able to compete effectively, they sometimes could transform the very nature of competition in their industries.

Throughout the 1980s, different ways were proposed for addressing this apparent paradox. A growing body of opinion felt the solution lay in the fact that many of the most successful companies tended to focus more on building basic internal operating *capabilities* than on achieving specific market positions or financial goals. The word *capabilities* has been used by different authors in a variety of ways, often interchangeably with the words *resources* and *competences.* We prefer capabilities because it denotes a more dynamic connotation; capabilities can be consciously built, whereas the words *resources* and *competences* often have been used to refer to attributes that are more static in nature. Attempts to measure the value of these organization-specific capabilities suggest they account for roughly 10 percent of the U.S. economy's total output—a bit larger than the value of its physical capital.[32]

Such capabilities, developed over time, could either be very general (such as extremely precise process control that permitted very low defect rates, product reliability, and/or miniaturization) or quite specific, such as a highly responsive and efficient distribution system, or developing experience in particular technologies or markets. Then, as new business opportunities arose out of changes in markets, technologies, and the competitive environment, these companies would exploit those opportunities that were particularly susceptible to the specific capabilities they had created. These new initiatives, in turn, provided the opportunity to create new capabilities.[33]

The key assertion of this emerging view (often referred to as the *resource-based view*) of competitive strategy was that companies succeed in the long run not by building and defending competitive fortresses, or by equipping themselves with the latest technologies or facilities, but primarily by being able to *do* certain things better than their competitors. A company's decision to move production to a low wage area, that is, can provide only a temporary advantage, since its competitors can do the same. It can achieve a *long*-term advantage only if it can become exceptionally good at managing such facilities. Similarly, a company might be able to acquire access to a certain technology but not the ability to mass produce products embodying that technology, to sell them effectively, or to improve that technology over time (just as you might be able to buy the latest golf clubs and balls, but still lose matches because you aren't a very good golfer!). Such skills can be developed only with experience, and over time.

Once achieved, however, such organizational capabilities might be able to provide an enduring advantage over competitors—even those that address the same customer needs and configure their operations similarly. The fact that these capabilities are difficult to imitate or transfer is precisely what gives them value. To the extent that they are organizationally specific, the competitive advantage provided by superior internal capabilities is much more sustainable than one achieved through purchase. Improving an organization's competitiveness, therefore, involves more than simply improving its performance along specific competitive dimensions, such as cost, quality, and flexibility. It also incorporates the possibility of developing new capabilities that provide specific operating advantages. Such new capabilities can open up strategic opportunities that may even lead an organization to adjust its competitive strategy.

This more operations-based and dynamic view of competitive strategy has profound implications for operations strategy, as it both elevates the importance of the operations function (where many of a company's most critical capabilities reside) and raises new issues about the nature of its strategic management. The structural and infrastructural decisions listed in Table 2-1 that were considered the means for implementing a chosen competitive strategy now take on a more dynamic role. Rather than simply providing certain capabilities, they also serve to guide and cultivate the development of desirable *new* capabilities.

2.5.1 Path Dependencies: Reexamining Focus and Tradeoffs from a New Perspective

Under the positioning concept of competitive strategy, once a company has configured itself properly to meet the needs of its competitive strategy there is little operations can do to provide additional differentiation. It could, of course, strive for continual improvement, but as soon as its competitors had similarly aligned their operations structures and infrastructures with their competitive strategies and embarked on comparable improvement programs, they would regain parity. Similarly, adopting lean manufacturing leaves little room for differentiation: once all competitors have adopted TQM, JIT, and other components, how can operations further contribute to a competitive advantage?

A concept of operations strategy that emphasizes the importance of capabilities offers a richer, and less imitable set of ways by which an operations organization can differentiate itself. Our earlier discussion of the various structural and infrastructural decisions that made up the contingency approach, for example, did not take into account the fact that a company can proceed along different *paths* to improvement, and each path may both create new capabilities and impair existing ones. As a result, different choices not only affect operations today (*first-order effects*), but also have important, and sometimes predictable, consequences for the kind of operating capabilities one will be able to acquire in the future (*second-order effects*). This richer set of alternatives makes it possible for the operations function to assume a much more proactive role in a company's competitive success, as will be discussed in Chapter 11. For now we will simply reconsider the implications of the capabilities-based approach for both focus and trade-offs.

Facility Focus

In our earlier discussion of focus, the decision whether to focus operating units by product lines or by process stages might be evaluated as follows. If different products are sold in markets that require different competitive priorities (e.g., low cost in one, innovation in another), focusing along product lines would be preferable.

Different facilities could then tailor their equipment, operating policies, and skill sets to the needs of their particular markets. If, in contrast, different product families competed in roughly similar ways (e.g., low cost), but different segments of the production process required very different technologies, operating policies, and capabilities, then a process focus would be preferable.

A focus choice also has dynamic implications, however, in that it shapes the directions a company can take in the future. Since it is usually easier to transfer learning within a facility than across facilities, the choice of focus will influence how different capabilities are developed and diffused throughout an organization. A network of product-focused facilities, like a company organized around strategic business units, runs the risk of fragmenting its core operating skills. Although all facilities may have certain technologies and skills in common, localized learning can lead to isolated pockets of process expertise. As a result, if events force a unit's closure or sale, valuable knowledge can be forever lost to the company.

A process focus creates reciprocal risks. As a facility accumulates specialized expertise, it may lose its understanding of how different process steps fit together. Over time, this may reduce a company's ability to introduce new products or make other changes that require integrated adjustments throughout the process chain. Similarly, if it expects that certain skills (e.g., ultra high-precision machining) will become increasingly important in the future, it might want to begin building such capabilities in existing facilities, whatever their focus.

Trade-offs

One of the most important functions of the earlier fit and focus-dominated approach to operations strategy was to help an organization understand and properly assess the trade-offs among different performance dimensions (e.g., cost versus flexibility) affected by various structural and infrastructural decisions. Such decisions, however, also have important consequences for organizational learning, so an operations strategy also needs to consider the effect that the selection, development, and exploitation of superior capabilities might have on these trade-offs over time. Neither the fit and focus approach to operations strategy nor the lean production paradigm considers the possibility that decisions designed to help the firm compete one way may induce it over time to develop capabilities that encourage it to compete in a different way.

2.5.2 Strategic Choice in Operations

The transition from the relatively static positioning-based approach to strategy to the dynamic capabilities-based approach not only encourages the operations function to consider a much richer set of alternatives and opportunities, it alters in a fundamental way one's whole approach to strategic planning. Rather than formulating a grand plan in a remote executive suite, and then assigning its implementation to various functional groups, strategy formulation and implementation become much more interactive. A company's strategy might not even become evident until, possibly, after its implementation is well along. Instead, people throughout the organization are continually identifying opportunities, developing new knowledge and capabilities, and testing out their ideas. Initiatives are undertaken, changed in mid-course as new information becomes available and better ideas surface, and sometimes abandoned so that energy can be focused on a different approach.

This, however, raises a question as to how *much* strategic freedom an operations organization should be given. Unless it has a clear sense of purpose, it can easily expend its energies on improvement programs that don't have much impact on things that are competitively very important. However, since the value of a given capability depends partly on the future opportunities that present themselves, how should a company—given the difficulty of predicting the future in today's turbulent world—select which capabilities to develop? Can this be done consciously, or is it essentially a crap shoot, where the lucky winners survive (to be offered up as examples by researchers) and the losers disappear—apparently the victims of simple bad management? Can a company exercise real strategic choice as regards capabilities, or is it largely the prisoner of its history, particularly the capabilities it has developed over time—perhaps by accident?

The capabilities-based concept of strategy also suggests that a company's strategy may lock it into certain modes of behavior. That is, a *sequence* of strategic choices may limit its ability to change its strategy in the future, a type of behavior that is called *path dependency.* Infrastructural elements, in particular, have long-lasting effects because they become deeply embedded in peoples' behavior and profoundly affect what they become good at doing. Therefore, when considering whether to change a structural or infrastructural element a company should consider how such a change might affect its ability to alter its competitive priorities as its situation evolves. A network of general-purpose plants, for example, would make it relatively easy for a firm at some point to adopt a competitive strategy based on improved customer service. It would, however, find it difficult to compete if its industry evolved toward standardized products and more commodity-like competition. A company starting with a different plant network and set of capabilities, however, might find it much easier to achieve dramatic cost reductions while working steadily to improve service levels.

2.6 ATTACKING AND DEFENDING THROUGH OPERATIONS[34]

The implication of a capabilities-based approach is that competitive battles are won not in the boardroom but in the laboratories, on factory floors, at service counters, and in computer rooms. The role of the operations function expands from being simply the implementer of strategy to providing the foundation for—indeed, becoming a driver of—successful strategic attacks and defenses. Companies that fail to fully exploit the strategic power of operations will therefore be both hampered in their own attacks and vulnerable to competitors that do. Nowhere is this clearer than in cases where a weaker competitor successfully attacks a large company that has a powerful, well-entrenched competitive position. Although lacking the advantages of size, customer base, and proprietary technology, they are sometimes able to prevail in a surprisingly short period of time. Why were the former leaders so vulnerable?

Why didn't they react more promptly and vigorously to such attacks—even after extended periods of time? And how are some companies, in contrast, able to defend themselves successfully?

Most studies of such implausible competitive victories focus on cases where the key to the attacker's success was the development of a new technology and/or the identification of an emerging market. But there are many other examples where radical new technologies and markets play little role; the attackers exploit technologies that are available to all, and compete for customers who already are being served by established competitors. In such cases, the key to success is often an operations-based advantage. As discussed above, superior operating capabilities embedded in a company's people and operating processes not only buttress a company's chosen competitive position, they also can provide the basis for a sustainable competitive advantage even when it adopts the *same* competitive position as one or more of its competitors.[35] Moreover, this sort of competitive advantage tends to be less visible to competitors than one that is based on staking out a differentiating competitive position. As a result, they are not prompted to respond as quickly. The sustainability of a competitive advantage that is based on superior operating skills is enhanced, therefore, both because it is difficult to duplicate and because competitors may not perceive its potential effectiveness, or even its existence—until too late.

EXAMPLE 2.1 *The Case of Australian Paper Manufacturers*

Consider, for example, the case of Australian Paper Manufacturers (APM).[36] In 1986, APM (a subsidiary of Amcor, Ltd.), which previously had confined itself to producing paperboard for packaging purposes, decided to enter the Australian market for fine paper. In so doing, it entered into direct competition with giant Australian Pulp and Paper Mills (APPM), the papermaking subsidiary of another Australian conglomerate. Up to that point, APPM had been the only domestic producer of fine papers. Not only did it produce 75 percent of the fine papers then consumed in Australia (imports accounted for the rest), but it owned two of the country's three largest paper merchants, which together distributed almost half the country's fine papers. To compound the risk that APM took on when it mounted its attack, up to then it had never before made fine paper, which was technologically more challenging than paperboard.

Yet not only was APM able to elbow its way into the markets for fine papers, over the next seven years it rapidly expanded its beachhead until it accounted for almost half the total market—which itself had grown by 50 percent. Seven years later, APPM's parent company capitulated, selling all its paper manufacturing and distribution operations to Amcor at far below their replacement price. Why didn't APPM—which had the benefit of size, experience, market control, and access to its parent's financial and managerial resources—react sooner and more effectively to APM's challenge? Why didn't it mount an aggressive counterattack while APM was still relatively weak, and its own position still dominant? We suggest possible answers to these questions in section 2.6.1.

EXAMPLE 2.2 *Crown Equipment Corporation*

It is possible to attribute the inadequacy of APPM's response simply to management complacency and myopia, to the distractions created by problems in its parent company's vast array of other businesses, or to a competitive spirit that had been tamed by many years of market dominance. But such reasons would not explain the longer story of the Crown Equipment Corporation,[37] which was a tiny U.S. producer of TV antenna rotators in 1957 when it decided to enter the forklift truck business.

The success of its first forklift—a small, manual device—despite a crowded field of competitors was due to a then-revolutionary idea: that the tough, no-nonsense people who bought and used forklift trucks did not leave their aesthetic sense behind when they came to work, but would be attracted to equipment that was both easy to use and attractive to look at. Emboldened (and perhaps a bit surprised) by its initial success, Crown decided to try that approach again. Working with an outside design firm, they introduced a medium-duty pallet truck that again not only rapidly gained market acceptance but also won an award from the Industrial Design Institute.

This dual success established the strategy that Crown followed for the next thirty years: it would identify a segment of the forklift truck market where the dominant design was stale or inadequate in essential ways. Then, working with professional designers, it would carefully design—from scratch—a more attractive and ergonomically superior truck that it would market at a premium price (about 10 percent above those of competitive products). Competitors at first derisively referred to Crown as "the pretty truck company," and deluded themselves that Crown's success would not be transferable to bigger trucks, where larger competitors controlled the market.

But in the early 1970s, Crown (which by then was selling over 100 different models of trucks in 80 countries) introduced its first rider truck, which had a lift capacity of 4,500 pounds and brought it face to face with a competitor that held a 75 percent market share. Within four years, Crown's revolutionary new design had captured 40 percent of that market, and Crown soon followed that success into still larger products. By 1990, even though it produced only electric trucks, Crown was the third largest forklift truck producer in the U.S., and tenth in the world.

Why didn't Crown Equipment's competitors react to its long series of new products—even though they had monitored its steady growth over at least two decades? Worse, given the market success of its "pretty trucks," why didn't competitors simply copy its strategy of employing outside design firms to help them redesign their own trucks before Crown's new designs made theirs obsolete? Crown's strategic weakness was, after all, its very consistency.

EXAMPLE 2.3 *Wal-Mart*

Similarly, at the time Wal-Mart[38] became a public corporation in 1972, it operated only thirty relatively small discount stores in rural Arkansas, Missouri, and Oklahoma. It had to sell its common stock in order to get enough money to build its first warehouse. Then, following an unwavering strategy it steadily expanded from that base. A little over ten years later, it had about 650 stores and almost $4.7 billion in sales. By the early 1980s (even though most Americans had never seen a Wal-Mart store), one would think that such larger rivals as Sears and Kmart would have become aware of its stunning progress and the potential threat it posed. They either did not perceive that threat or were unable to respond to it, however, so by 1987 Wal-Mart had almost 1,200 stores, over half as many as Kmart. Moreover, the industry's "country bumpkin" had taken the lead in applying computer technology to tracking sales and coordinating the restocking of its stores, as well in implementing a collaborative continuous replenishment system with P&G. Yet rather than prepare for the predictable head-to-head confrontation as Wal-Mart steadily approached the large cities where it was entrenched, Kmart turned its energies to diversification and building a more up-scale image.

By 1993, the battle was essentially over. Wal-Mart's sales of $67 billion were now more than half again as large as Kmart's, and more than 80 percent of Kmart's stores now faced direct competition from Wal-Mart's (while only half of Wal-Mart's stores competed directly with Kmart's). It was then so financially strapped that it could barely cover its annual dividend. Hamstrung in its attempts to renovate its old stores, Kmart declared bankruptcy in early 2002. Why didn't it react sooner? What should it have done while it still had a chance to change the course of events?

EXAMPLE 2.4 ***An Example of a Successful Counterattack***

That such inertia—verging on paralysis—is a *choice,* not an inevitability, is illustrated by the very different competitive response of the American Connector Company.[39] In the early 1990s, ACC learned that DJC, a Japanese competitor that up to then had confined its activities to Japan and nearby countries, was preparing to enter the U.S. market. Moreover, it apparently was planning to base this assault around a new, highly automated U.S. factory modeled after one it had been operating in Japan for more than five years. That Japanese factory had been able to reduce the manufacturing cost of comparable products to almost a third less than ACC's cost, after adjusting for the different costs of inputs in the United States.

ACC reacted immediately, on a number of fronts. It hired a consulting firm to analyze the approaches to manufacturing that had been adopted in DJC's Japanese factory, and began studying whether and how some of these approaches might be implemented in its own plants. It also initiated an integrated set of marketing moves—including closer communication with customers, more emphasis on customized designs, and selective price cuts. As a result, DJC's U.S. factory was still barely profitable over four years after it started up.

2.6.1 *Attacking* through Operations

All these successful attacks—and several others we will discuss below—were based primarily on the kind of operations-based advantages alluded to in earlier sections. Indeed, an operations advantage was the key to the sustainability of the attacker's success. None were built around a new product or service, a unique technology, or a marketing or financial advantage. Nor did the attackers do anything that could not have been copied by any of their competitors, had they reacted in time. Over time, however, the attackers became so effective at implementing their strategies and extending them into new areas that the approaches they employed were no longer easily copied. Analogously, you can buy the same tennis racquet that Pete Sampras uses, wear the same brand of sneakers (although not get paid for doing so!), and adopt a "big serve and volley" strategy. You might even have beaten him when he was eight years old—but not later.

These successful attackers created and exploited their operating advantage in one or both of two ways. First, they adopted an operations strategy that gave them a competitive advantage along dimensions or in locations that, although valued by certain customers, were not being emphasized by competitors; this is what we referred to earlier as a differentiating "competitive position." Often this form of competitive differentiation was tested and perfected in other geographic regions or in different industries. Second, they reinforced this alternative way of appealing to customers with the development of a tightly integrated system of supporting values, facilities, technologies, capabilities, supplier/customer relationships, human resources, and approaches to motivation that could not be easily copied by other organizations.

And the keys to successful counterattacks were symmetric: the incumbents either persuaded customers that their own competitive advantage was more desirable than the attacker's, they exploited the inherent weaknesses in the attacker's specialized operating systems, and/or they emulated its strategy so quickly that the attacker never had enough time to develop vastly superior operating effectiveness. These different responses provide us with an opportunity to revisit the positioning and capabilities-based approaches to strategy.

Positioning: Appealing to a Different Customer Need

As discussed earlier, different customers are attracted by different attributes of a product or service. Companies such as DJC, Southwest Airlines, and Wal-Mart, for example, have attempted to differentiate themselves by offering the *lowest price*. Others, such as Crown Equipment, sought to attract customers who want higher performance, features, or appearance. Still others, such as ACC, sought to differentiate themselves through superior flexibility or innovativeness. A company that decides to pursue a certain form of differentiation cannot, of course, gain any long-term advantage over its competitors if it continues to use the same operations structure and infrastructure as they do. Strategic fit requires that, having decided what kind of superiority it wants to achieve, it must configure and manage its operations organization so as to provide that form of advantage most effectively.

A company that seeks to provide superior product performance or precision, for example, may need to acquire (or build) special production equipment and design and/or make some of its own components to standards that are higher than those available from external suppliers. It may also locate in regions that give it access to higher worker skills, and adopt internal measurement/reward systems that promote continual improvement in product performance. Its operating systems would be far different than those adopted by DJC, ACC's Japanese competitor, which focused on being the lowest-cost producer and therefore favored product designs that sought the lowest possible material and processing costs while just meeting customers' product specifications, as well as proven manufacturing processes rather than newer processes whose reliability was still in question, and a production control system that gave top priority to achieving the highest possible utilization of its equipment and people.

Reviewing in this light the various examples of competitive attacks described above, one sees that some were based on a company's decision to address a critical need (sometimes a latent need) of some group of customers that its competitors had not given high priority to. Such opportunities often arise when customers' needs evolve over time, or when these competitors attempt to address certain customer needs by making operating choices that impair their ability to meet other needs. APM clawed its way into the Australian fine papers market primarily by offering superior quality (its reconditioned paper machine was able to make much smoother paper) and customer responsiveness. It tried to match its competitors' prices but did not try to match their range of products or the variety of sizes and packages they offered. A large segment of the Australian market, it turned out, was more interested in high quality and rapid, dependable delivery than in a broad range of products and package sizes.

This kind of attack mirrors that followed by Japanese auto producers when they first entered the U.S. market. They offered cars that had fewer surface defects, superior economy and reliability, and low maintenance, all at prices comparable with or lower than their larger competitors. U.S. auto producers had long assumed that American customers were more interested in styling, horsepower, and exotic options—an assumption that proved to be outdated during the 1980s.

Crown Equipment's strategy of designing radically new lift trucks was reinforced by its ability to design and manufacture its own components. Its competitors were constrained from being too innovative because they relied on outside suppliers to provide most of the components (often based on standard designs) incorporated in their products. Crown's ability to customize its products to meet the specific needs of individual customers was similarly due to the fact that it had adopted and perfected a production process whereby batches of varying size were assembled using small teams of broadly skilled workers to perform a sequence of tasks in the same workspace. The flexibility of several of its larger competitors, in contrast, was constrained by their use of assembly lines that were set up for long runs and staffed by workers having more limited skills.

These examples provide another explanation why entrenched competitors often respond to attacks so slowly and ineffectively. Once Company A has configured its operating systems with the goal of achieving superiority along certain competitive dimensions, it becomes very difficult to match the performance that a new competitor has been able to achieve along other dimensions through an operating organization that was expressly designed with those other dimensions in mind. Company A can't adapt effectively to a new set of competitive priorities by making a few simple alterations. A number of interacting changes are required, and this takes time—as well as money and a sense of urgency. Faced with the prospect of such wholesale restructuring, it is easy to delude yourself with the notion that the competitive advantages your new competitor is offering will appeal only to a small segment of the market, or are just a "passing fancy" that customers will soon tire of (and, compounding this leap of faith, will then return to valuing the competitive advantages that you have traditionally provided them). Or that the approach being followed by this competitor (while effective at small volumes, in specific industries, and in certain geographic regions) can't be scaled up or transferred to other industries and regions.

Capabilities: Being Better at the Same Game

Although strategists often assume that it is relatively easy to copy another firm's operations equipment and techniques, superior operating *skills* can only be developed with a conscious effort over an extended period of time. Although it is usually relatively easy to duplicate a *mediocre* operation, there are huge—and competitively significant—differences between mediocre and outstanding performers. Catching up quickly to the effectiveness of a first-rate operation is usually very, very difficult. For example, when Kmart finally attempted to react to Wal-Mart's attack by pouring money into new computerized scanner, procurement, and inventory control systems, it found that its employees lacked the skills necessary to use the new systems effectively and that the data being entered into them were full of errors. Instilling the organizational discipline required to ensure the accuracy of data, and providing the training that enabled its people to use its sophisticated systems effectively, had taken Wal-Mart many years. Kmart could find no shortcut.

Again, even though Southwest Airlines initially based its low-cost strategy on a no-frills approach (no meals, reserved seats, or baggage transfers), its use of secondary airports, and its operation of only a single type of aircraft (Boeing 737s), it soon developed organizational capabilities that created further cost advantages. One study, for example, found that its turnaround times were at least a third less than those of its major competitors (even after adjusting for its lack of meals, smaller airplanes, etc.), and its staffing costs were less than half. Just as important was Southwest's loyal customer base, which was willing and able to board and exit its planes just as fast as it would let them! And the quality of its service, as measured by such variables as late arrivals and customer complaints, was 75 percent better than the average of its nine major U.S. competitors.[40] By the time United Airlines and USAir decided to set up subsidiaries utilizing similar strategies and operating structures, they found they simply couldn't match Southwest's fast turnaround times, its aircraft utilization rates, or its friendly, personal service. It is easy to eliminate meals and baggage service, use direct routes to secondary airports, and buy Boeing 737s, but it is hard to "buy" fast turnarounds, on-time arrivals, and cooperative customers. Both United and USAir, approaching bankruptcy in 2001, were forced to abandon their attempts to compete head-to-head with Southwest. Superior capabilities have to be built and nurtured, step-by-step. In thinking about how to develop such operating capabilities, it is useful to break them into three types: *process-based, systems (coordination)-based,* and *organization-based.*

Process-based capabilities are associated with activities that transform material or information, and tend to provide advantages along such standard competitive dimensions as low cost and/or high conformance quality. An example is the manufacturing process developed by IBM and Toshiba for their joint venture's large liquid-crystal computer displays. The ability to ramp up quickly to produce large displays with high yields allowed them to attack existing competitors with larger and brighter products, guarantee availability early in the product life cycle, and defend against competitors' products as each wave of technology matured.

While process-based capabilities are usually associated with manufacturing industries, service companies also use process technologies to achieve operating advantages. McDonald's meticulously researched and documented procedures for producing fast food, for example, have been its primary defense against attackers that were unable to replicate the high level of product and service consistency that McDonald's maintained throughout its network. Similarly, Fidelity Investments invested millions of dollars in developing state-of-the-art image and audio capture technology, so that transactions made by its customers could be rapidly and accurately entered and verified. This accuracy made it possible to provide superior service—for example, to retrieve information instantaneously when responding to customer inquiries or requests.

Systems (coordination)-based operating capabilities underpin such competitive advantages as short lead times, a broad range of products or services, the ability to customize on demand, and fast new-product development. Such capabilities require broad involvement throughout the entire operating system.

For example, the Allegheny Ludlum Steel Corporation[41] became one of the most profitable U.S. producers of specialty steel as a result of a long effort to improve the way it coordinated the complex steps involved in making small batches of customized steel. It also developed a model of the steel-making process that allowed it to recognize and respond to specific processing patterns. Over a period of six years, it was able to substantially reduce the percent of defective steel it produced, double the effective capacity of its melt shop (with the same equipment), and increase its tons per worker by 40 percent. Moreover, it developed an intricate cost accounting system, based on its own carefully documented experience, that allowed it to estimate precisely the cost of any grade, width, and gauge of steel. The system that Allegheny built gave it capabilities that enabled it not only to survive an industry bloodbath (in 1980 it had ten competitors; by 1998 it had three), but also to show a profit every year.

Organization-based operating capabilities are broader still in nature, and underpin the ability to master new technologies, design and introduce new products, and bring new plants on line significantly faster than one's competitors. As they are even more difficult to replicate, such capabilities are among the most powerful in the operating arsenal.

The classic example of such capabilities was provided by the Lincoln Electric Company[42] during World War II. By then it had become the leading—and lowest cost—producer of arc-welding equipment and supplies in the United States. During the war, in a patriotic attempt to increase the output and reduce the costs of such equipment for the war effort, Lincoln voluntarily offered to share its proprietary manufacturing methods and equipment designs with its competitors. As a result, industry production rose to meet demand without any investment in additional capacity. By the end of the war, those competitors had reduced their manufacturing costs to levels that were close to Lincoln's. But soon, using the same organizational capabilities that had given it cost leadership before the war, Lincoln Electric was able to regain and maintain a cost advantage.

As another example, both Boise Cascade and Union Camp began to install new paper plants in the early 1990s. Despite the fact that both plants employed similar off-the-shelf technology, Boise's ability to bring new plants on line quickly allowed it to get up to full capacity in just over a third the time it took Union Camp. Although it operated the largest paper plant in the world (in Franklin, Virginia), Union Camp had less experience bringing new operations on line. The delay at Union Camp's new plant left it at a significant competitive disadvantage when demand for paper products exploded in 1992.

2.6.2 Sustaining an Operations Edge

None of the successful attacks just described was based on programs of indiscriminate continuous improvement; instead, the attackers methodically developed specific operating capabilities and consciously sought out opportunities to exploit them. Some of the attackers clearly intended to stake out a differentiating competitive position. But they also exploited the fact that those being attacked tended to underestimate the power of the attacker's operating superiority. Not all industries, of course, are populated with competitors that are so slow to react. In more dynamic environments, one could argue, any advantage a company might gain from new operating abilities would be quickly eroded away as defenders and new entrants replicated the operational techniques of the attacker. Therefore, that advantage would be expected to be quite transient.

But even in such environments, operations-based advantages turn out to be surprisingly robust for two reasons. First, innovations in operations are inherently difficult to replicate and slow to diffuse. They often demand substantial organizational change and sometimes even a complete realignment of management philosophy and corporate culture. Toyota, for example, was able to offer superior product quality/reliability while maintaining very competitive (and often lower) prices because of its development of a unique production system. Although based on simple principles, this system required such radical changes in worker training and management practice that other auto producers had to spend more than a decade attempting to copy it. Similarly, if the techniques embodied in Total Quality Management (see Chapter 10), which began sweeping through U.S. industry in the early 1980s, were rapidly and easily diffused, the need for TQM consultants would long since have disappeared.

Second, and just as important, building operating capabilities is a dynamic activity. Ongoing invention is at the core of the most effective operations organizations; they do not stand still while their competitors try to catch up. Those that can consistently create new, more effective ways of delivering value to customers stay ahead of the pack. In the cases described earlier, successful operations innovations were both competitively important and *relentless.* As a result, the advantage they gained was powerful and sustainable. Indeed, the ability to develop new and valuable abilities—to push out the frontiers of your operating performance faster than can your competitors—is the most difficult of all to master. By the time U.S. auto producers had brought their defect rates down to levels approaching those of Toyota, Toyota had reduced its rate even further.

Although some individuals learn and adapt easily, organizations rarely do. They must be structured and managed in a way that facilitates learning and change. For example, unlike many companies that had been dismissive of earlier computer technologies (e.g., minicomputers, engineering workstations, and PCs) when they first appeared, and then were astonishingly slow and inept when they attempted to respond, Microsoft was able to react quickly to the threat of the Internet. Partly this is because even during the time it apparently was focused exclusively on its operating system and applications, Microsoft encouraged a few mavericks within the company to develop their Internet expertise. Then, when it belatedly realized the true magnitude of the threat to its desktop market, it allowed their heretical voices to influence the path of the company.

2.6.3 *Defending* through Operations

The foregoing suggests that a company can defend itself against operations-based attacks using one or more of the following three approaches.

1. *It can exploit its own strengths,* pouring resources into improving its competitive advantage and marketing that advantage more aggressively to customers. This may appear at first glance to be more of a marketing-based than an operations-based defense, but in order for that kind of marketing to be successful, it must be built on a foundation of true operating superiority. The danger with this approach is that sometimes companies pursue their chosen competitive advantage(s) beyond the point of diminishing returns—in effect, "overshooting" their customers' real needs.[43]

   For example, one of the ways ACC defended itself against the attack of DJC was to go to its customers and convince them of the value of purchasing customized products instead of the standardized products that DJC was offering. This would have been very difficult, given the huge cost advantage that DJC would have possessed if its new U.S. plant were able to produce products at a cost comparable to that achieved in its Japanese plant. Thus, ACC also embarked on a program to reduce its manufacturing costs. The smaller its cost disadvantage, the easier it would be for its customers to justify buying ACC's higher-performing products.

2. *It can attack its attacker's operations-based weaknesses.* When that attacker configured its own operations so as to offer superior performance along certain dimensions (e.g., low cost, flexibility, or fast response), it had to make hardware and software choices that constrained its performance along other dimensions. These present points of vulnerability. Again using ACC's response as an example, it realized that one of the keys to DJC's low costs was being able to operate its manufacturing facility close to its theoretical capacity (three shifts a day, 330 days a year), and scheduling long runs so as to minimize changeovers. Therefore, ACC set out to prevent DJC from attracting the sales of high-volume products that would allow it to take full advantage of its production process. It did this not only by aggressively selling its ability to design customized products (see above), but also by cutting its prices on the products that were the most attractive ones for DJC to produce.

3. *It can recognize the seriousness of the attack quickly* and emulate its attacker's strategy before the attacker is able to get too far ahead on the learning curve. Microsoft initially was caught flat-footed by Netscape's approach to software development. Employing the same rapid design-build-test cycles that had been used in constructing the Internet itself over the previous thirty years, Netscape worked closely with sophisticated users and exploited their expertise. Microsoft, accustomed to projects that were more

complex, and so required more rigorous pre-launch testing, simply was not organized to operate in this more volatile world. Fortunately, it had built a software development group (a sort of operations organization) that was capable of adapting to such changes. Even more important, it took its fledgling competitor seriously long before it posed an unstoppable threat to its own sales and profitability. It recognized that Netscape's technology could be applied not just to Internet browsers but also to a vast range of other network computer-based products. Not only did it swallow its pride by admitting it had fallen behind, it was clear-headed about the capabilities it didn't have and the amount of time it would take to develop those capabilities internally. Realizing that developing a browser from scratch would take too long, Microsoft based its new browser on software developed by tiny Spyglass Corporation, which it quickly and elegantly incorporated into its new Windows 95 operating system.

While skeptics (and the U.S. Department of Justice) have accused Microsoft of using its sheer size to bully or bundle its way into markets, one has to acknowledge that it also has been surprisingly quick on its feet and willing to abandon practices that it had employed successfully in the past. Recognizing that it had to do more than simply respond to the threat posed by Netscape's *initial* browser, it changed the way it developed new products—emulating Netscape by releasing early versions of its new browser across the Internet (see Chapter 8). This forced it to navigate its way between existing corporate customers, who were accustomed to debugged software that didn't require a lot of technical support, and hordes of Internet-savvy *netniks* who were clamoring for new products.

2.6.4 Lessons in Attacking and Defending through Operations

Companies that base their attacks, or their defenses, on operations capabilities understand that such capabilities rarely can be developed quickly or bought off the shelf. People must be trained and given experience; new equipment and procedures must be developed and honed; and new approaches to management must be tested, shaped, and given time to insinuate themselves into the organization's culture. Sometimes companies are not even aware of the full potential of the capabilities they are developing until a sudden insight or fortuitous incident reveals how they can be exploited.

Indeed, the fact that such capabilities take such a long time to develop, and can come together quite suddenly, gives them much of their competitive power. Entrenched incumbents tend to delay developing similar capabilities because they view them through the distorting prism of their own approach to structuring operations. In other words, if they are used to large-scale facilities, they tend to consider smaller operations as inefficient; if they have invested massively in automation, they dismiss more worker-intensive operations as unreliable and outdated. They also tend to put too much faith in the power of their own size, asset base, and market position, and assume that they can replicate anything a competitor can do, at a reasonable cost and on demand. Case after case, however, shows none of these assumptions to be valid.

Wal-Mart perfected its innovative approaches to retailing for a dozen years in the rural areas of the American south before attacking large urban areas. Southwest Airlines patiently built its skills—and its confidence—for years in Texas and adjoining states before growing like a lily pad to blanket the United States. During decades in which it produced only motorcycles, Honda became a world leader in the design and manufacture of small, highly efficient, gasoline engines before it suddenly transferred those skills into auto production.

Moreover, new operating capabilities often arise in ways and from sources that are difficult to predict. Putting too much reliance on competitive benchmarking, or on monitoring the innovations of one's direct competitors, can easily misdirect a company's attention away from the new operating capabilities that are developing in apparently unrelated arenas. This is particularly true in the case of *capability pairing,* where previously unconnected (and/or insufficiently developed) capabilities are cultivated and combined in a unique way. It is not necessary that any of these capabilities, by itself, be proprietary or even uncommon. They may have been developed for different purposes and different markets, so entrenched competitors are unlikely to perceive in them any danger. But when they are combined and focused on a new market segment or competitive approach, those being attacked often find it difficult to respond. They might be able to develop or acquire either one of those capabilities, but, in the short term, rarely can they master both.

For example, Federal Express rose from obscurity using such a capability pairing strategy: it combined a hub-and-spoke route structure (which its competitors knew about but thought inefficient) with continuous package tracking using state-of-the-art bar code, computer, and transmission technologies. Then, in 1994, while other companies were ignoring the Internet, FedEx became the first major company to conduct business over it. It recognized the importance of *time* when building new operating capabilities, and was determined to keep would-be rivals from coming at it from a blind spot. Although it recognized that the Internet might be a dead end, it was more concerned with developing skills that could give it a new source of competitive advantage. Two years later, FedEx's Web site was averaging nearly 1.4 million hits a month, providing customers with faster and better information while helping FedEx manage its customer service and other resources more effectively.

Similarly, many Japanese companies spent decades improving the precision of their manufacturing processes, reducing defect levels to parts per million, speeding up their process throughput times using just-in-time (JIT) techniques, and instilling a climate of continuous improvement before attacking the U.S. steel, auto, consumer electronics, machine tool, and office equipment markets. Producing the personal camcorder was the culmination of impressive skills in design, automation, mechatronics, and miniaturization that Japanese consumer electronics companies cultivated for over a quarter of a century, first in miniature radios, then in television sets, pocket calculators, and VCRs. When all those highly honed skills came together, the U.S. manufacturers of consumer electronics and photographic equipment found that they were simply incapable of making comparable products.

Effective defenders are quick to recognize such latent threats. They understand that developing new operating capabilities takes time, and are constantly scanning the horizon of their markets and technologies for companies that might combine hitherto unconnected skills and invade their territory. Small companies, particularly those in other countries or different industries, are especially dangerous. Being relatively invisible, the operating capabilities they are developing (and the way these capabilities are being translated into competitive advantage) can escape the detection of companies whose attention and competitive energies are focused primarily on their large, immediate competitors. Many such threats are emerging today from small startups that combine their knowledge of the new information technologies with other operations expertise to attack long-established firms.

As these examples show, strategies that combine new operating capabilities with existing ones in novel ways can be surprisingly powerful. But the most sustainable advantages are those based on an organization's ability to *improve.* A company that has been shielded from tough competition for several years (as was APPM) tends to have a particularly tough time defending itself against sudden attacks. It not only waits too long before taking threats seriously, but when it does respond it finds that it has forgotten how to move—and learn—quickly.

2.7 CONCLUSION

In today's fiercely contested and ever-changing competitive environment, operations strategy requires more than simply choosing which currently fashionable improvement technique to adopt, or trying to copy the "best practices" of other companies. Long-term success requires that a company *differentiate* itself from its competitors by offering something unique and valuable to customers—whether this be *especially* quick service, high reliability, low costs, or innovative products. The companies that are able to develop an operations edge and turn their operations organizations into sources of competitive advantage are those that harness various initiatives and improvement programs in the service of a broader operations strategy that emphasizes the selection and growth of unique operating capabilities.

Rather than confining their improvement efforts to finding and emulating "best" practice, companies should seek out *new* practice, continually asking themselves: "How would a competitor that possessed those new capabilities and understood our own weaknesses go about attacking us?" and "If we were subjected to such an attack, how could we respond?" In addition, they should seek out and study fast-growing competitors to learn about the innovative operating methods they have developed. If you are successful and growing, even though small, you probably are doing something different than the "big guys." A company's size tells little about the quality of its ideas, or its potential to become a competitive juggernaut in the future.

NOTES

1. See the case "Southwest Airlines: 1993 (A)" (HBS Publishing: 9-694-023).
2. See, for example, Andrews (1971), Ghemawat (2002), and Porter (1980).
3. We tend to use the terms *company, firm,* and *SBU* interchangeably throughout this book, implicitly assuming that a company or firm is a corporation that has only one SBU.
4. See Porter (1980).
5. See Abernathy and Corcoran (1983), Chandler (1991), and Hayes et al. (1988), Chapter 2.

6. For example, in a course developed at the Harvard Business School during the late 1940s, Professor John McLean adopted what he called the *industry approach.* By devoting a number of classes to a single industry he was able to demonstrate to his students that companies within the same industry often adopted different competitive strategies, as well as very different policies regarding such important manufacturing issues as the location of facilities, production control methods, make vs. buy, and the administrative structure of plants. The basic notions in that course had a powerful impact on its students—among them a young Wickham Skinner.

7. Skinner (1969), Skinner (1974).

8. Hill (1989), for example, differentiates between competitive dimensions that represent "order qualifiers" (i.e., that induce a potential customer to include the company's products among the set they select from), and "order winners": the dimensions that matter most to them in making a purchase.

9. See Collins and Porras (1994) and Collins (2001).

10. Ward and Duray (2000) report on research that suggests a somewhat different relationship between a firm's competitive strategy and its operations strategy. Rather than being the *context* within which its operations strategy is crafted, they suggest that competitive strategy appears instead to act "as a *mediator* between an organization's environment and its … strategy."

11. See Mulligan and Nanni (2002).

12. Empirical support for the relationship between competitive priorities and process choice is provided by Safizadeh et al. (1996) and Ward et al. (1998).

13. Hayes et al. (1988), Chapter 6.

14. Pisano (1994).

15. See Miller and Roth (1994) and Frohlich and Dixon (2001).

16. Skinner (1974).

17. See "Large Air Carriers Are Beginning to Discover Benefits of Simplicity," *The Wall Street Journal,* August 14, 2002.

18. See, for example, "How to Fix America's Schools," *BusinessWeek,* March 19, 2001, and "Niche Hospitals Draw Criticism From Lawmakers," *The Wall Street Journal,* May 16, 2003, p. B6.

19. See Hansson et al. (2002).

20. Hayes and Wheelwright (1979a and 1979b) provided the initial statement of this concept. More recent attempts to validate the concept by, among others, Safizadeh et al. (1996), and Das and Narasimhan (2001) have provided some empirical support for it.

21. See, for example, "Linking quality management to manufacturing strategy: an empirical investigation of customer focus practices," Sousa (2003).

22. Eventually, as we discuss in Chapter 6, it was found that FMS systems were neither as flexible as expected nor were they cost competitive in many environments.

23. Womack et al. (1990), p. 13.

24. Drucker (1990), p. 98; see also Ferdows and DeMeyer (1990), who suggest that organizations should follow a specific sequence when improving their performance along several dimensions.

25. This argument is elaborated on in Hayes and Pisano (1996) and Schmenner and Swink (1998).

26. See Sanderson and Uzumeri (1991).

27. Womack et al. (1990).

28. See, in particular, Cusumano (1994).

29. See "Japan's Dark Side of Time" (Stalk and Webber, 1993), as well as Crawford (1992), and Meyer and Utterback (1995).

30. Ealey and Mercer (1992).

31. Porter (1980) provides one of the earliest and most cited discussions of this concept.

32. See Atkeson and Kehoe (2001).

33. See, for example, Hayes (1985), Prahalad and Hamel (1990), Teece and Pisano (1994), and Wernerfelt (1984).

34. Much of the material in section 2.6 is drawn from Hayes and Upton (1998).

35. For an opposing view, see "What is Strategy?" by Michael E. Porter (1996), where he argues that "Operational Effectiveness Is Not Strategy."

36. "Australian Paper Manufacturers (A)" (HBS Publishing: 9-691-041).

37. "Crown Equipment Corporation: Design Services Strategy" (HBS Publishing: 9-991-031).

38. "Wal-Mart Stores, Inc." (HBS Publishing: 9-794-024).

39. A disguised name; see "American Connector Company (A)" (HBS Publishing: 9-693-035).

40. Gittell (1995).

41. Now Allegheny-Teledyne, Inc.; see "Allegheny Ludlum Steel Corporation" (HBS Publishing: 9-686-087).

42. See "The Lincoln Electric Company" (HBS Publishing: 9-376-028).

43. Christensen (1997) provides a number of examples.

Appendix

2A.1 EVALUATING AN OPERATIONS STRATEGY

The ultimate test of any strategy is whether it leads to competitive success over the long term. Before that outcome becomes known, however, it is still possible to assess the logical content and structure of a given strategy. Criteria generally fall into two groups, as indicated in Table 2A-1. The first group assesses various types of consistency (both within the operations function and across other functions). The other group assesses the degree to which the strategy enhances the competitive advantage the firm is seeking. The more consistent a set of structural and infrastructural decisions are, and the more they support the firm's desired competitive advantage (business strategy), the more effective the operation strategy is likely to be.

Moreover, it needs to be emphasized again that:

1. An operations strategy is determined by the pattern of the decisions actually made (that is, by what managers *do*), not by what corporate documents say is its strategy.
2. Although individual decisions are usually driven by, and in support of, specific products, markets, or technologies, the primary function of an operations strategy is to guide the business in putting together the set of operating capabilities that will enable it to pursue its chosen competitive strategy over the long term.

Table 2A-1 Criteria for Evaluating an Operations Strategy

Consistency (internal and external)
• Between the operations strategy and the overall business strategy
• Among the decision categories that make up the operations strategy
• Between the operations strategy and other functions' strategies
Contribution (to competitive advantage)
• Making trade-offs explicit, enabling operations to set priorities that enhance the competitive advantage
• Directing attention to opportunities that complement the business strategy
• Promoting clarity regarding the operations strategy throughout the firm
• Providing the operating capabilities that will be required in the future

2A.2 THE CONCEPT OF A *CORPORATE* OPERATIONS STRATEGY

Given the notion that an operations strategy must be tailored to the needs of a specific business, what value is there to carrying our conceptualization one step higher—to the level of a *corporate* operations strategy for a multibusiness firm? Using the preceding definitions of different levels of strategy, and the major decision categories (Table 2-1) that collectively determine an SBU's operations strategy, we shall consider two definitions of a corporate operations strategy and the implications of each.

The first assumes that a corporate operations strategy exists only to the extent that each of its SBUs adopts the same (or very similar) operations strategies. Indeed, most references to a corporate operations strategy seem to imply this definition. However, some reflection suggests that such a definition is not likely to be very useful. Since each SBU has unique aspects, and therefore a unique business strategy, a common operations strategy is unlikely to be appropriate. Even in firms in which several businesses employ similar business strategies (or competitive priorities), usually they are sufficiently different in other respects that they require somewhat different operations strategies.

A second, and somewhat more useful, definition of operations strategy is based on the commonalities among different SBU's structural and infrastructural elements. In Table 2A-2, for example, the operations strategies of three different SBUs (designated A, B, and C) are summarized, as indicated by the symbols (000000, //////, and ++++). Scanning across the various decision categories, it may be possible to identify a few policies regarding certain types of decisions that are common across all (or most) of its businesses. For example, a firm might specify certain size and location characteristics for its individual facilities, or certain personnel policies, independent of the particular business or division involved. Such commonalities are likely the result of a firm's set of common values.

The *corporate* operations strategy under this definition consists of those subparts of each decision category that are governed by common policies across all its SBUs. The choice of which decisions are to be held constant in this manner can vary significantly for different companies. In some, for example, decisions regarding workforce policies may be left entirely to the individual business unit. In others, such as HP-Compaq, a strong corporate culture may dictate that a common set of workforce policies be applied to all business units, whereas work scheduling decisions may be left entirely to individual SBUs.

R&D, particularly that relating to operating processes, is another area where it is often useful to adopt a corporate-wide perspective. A company might decide that it will need a certain technological or operating capability in the future, even though none of its business units has an immediate need for it. Therefore, it might choose to develop that capability at the corporate level, although subsequently it would be transferred to one or more SBUs.

Given the above, it often is useful to consider how the corporate values and preferences that underlie its business strategy also shape its operations strategy. Identifying these preferences can assist a business unit in setting priorities, making

Table 2A-2 The Concept of a Corporate Operations Strategy

Dimensions of a manufacturing strategy	Individual business strategies			Examples of generic (corporate-wide) policies and guidelines
	Business A[a]	Business B[a]	Business C[a]	
Capacity[b]	XXXXXX 000000 000000 000000	XXXXXX ////// ////// //////	XXXXXX ++++++ ++++++ ++++++	A common set of criteria to be used in developing/presenting an investment proposal Policies for the economic or competitive conditions require to plan/start/postpone capacity changes
Facilities[b]	XXXXXX XXXXXX XXXXXX 000000 000000	XXXXXX XXXXXX XXXXXX ////// //////	XXXXXX XXXXXX XXXXXX ++++++ ++++++	Parameters governing the size and location of individual facilities Guidelines for permanent reductions in capacity at mature facilities
Technology[b]	XXXXXX 000000 000000 000000 000000	XXXXXX ////// ////// ////// //////	XXXXXX ++++++ ++++++ ++++++ ++++++	Policies for the organization and layout of production processes Criteria for equipment selection and the levels of automation to be pursued
Vertical integration[b]	XXXXXX 000000 000000	XXXXXX ////// //////	XXXXXX ++++++ ++++++	Policies for make/buy analysis and changes in backward integration Rules for establishing internal transfer prices
Workforce[b]	XXXXXX XXXXXX XXXXXX 000000	XXXXXX XXXXXX XXXXXX //////	XXXXXX XXXXXX XXXXXX ++++++	Establishment of benefit packages and pay scales Policies on unionization, hiring, promotion, and employment stability
Quality[b]	XXXXXX XXXXXX 000000 000000	XXXXXX XXXXXX ////// //////	XXXXXX XXXXXX ++++++ +++++	Standardized reports, reporting relationships, and job definitions Guidelines on performance measures such as the cost of quality, field failures, and expected quality levels
Production planning/Materials control[b]	XXXXXX XXXXXX XXXXXX 000000 000000	XXXXXX XXXXXX XXXXXX ////// //////	XXXXXX XXXXXX XXXXXX ++++++ +++++	Parameters for manufacturing system specifications and hardware approval Rules for measuring and evaluating inventory performance
Organization[b]	XXXXXX 000000 000000	XXXXXX ////// //////	XXXXXX ++++++ ++++++	Definitions of job classifications and direct/indirect staffing levels Policies regarding manufacturing engineering support levels and use of outside services

[a]Each column represents the operations strategy (pattern of manufacturing decisions) that complements a specific business strategy.

[b]Each row represents behavior, practices, and policies in that decision category that are consistent across businesses (indicated by XXXXXX), and those not consistent across all businesses.

trade-offs, and developing more effective functional strategies. Four general types of preferences—dominant orientation, pattern of diversification, attitude toward growth, and choice of competitive priorities—will be described and their implications for operations strategy discussed.

2A.2.1 The Corporation's Dominant Orientation

Some companies, such as Gillette and P&G, have a strong market orientation. They consider their most important expertise to be the ability to understand and respond effectively to the needs of a particular market or consumer group. In exploiting this market knowledge, they may employ a variety of products, materials, and technologies. Other companies, including Corning Glass, Goodyear, DuPont, and Shell Oil, have a material, or product, orientation. They develop multiple uses for their product or material and follow those uses into a variety of markets. Still other companies and businesses are technology oriented (most electronics and chemical companies fall into this class), and tend to follow the lead of their technological expertise into various materials and markets.

2A.2.2 The Pattern of Diversification

A second, and related, preference is the pattern of diversification a company follows. Diversification can be accomplished in several ways: (1) product diversification within a given market; (2) market diversification (geographic or consumer group) with a given product line; (3) process, or vertical, diversification (increasing the span of the process so as to gain more control over vendors or distributors) with a given mix of products and markets; and (4) unrelated (horizontal) diversification, as exemplified by conglomerates. These patterns of diversification are closely interrelated with a company's dominant orientation. They also reflect the company's preference to focus on a relatively narrow set of activities, products, or markets rather than spread itself broadly over many.

Generally speaking, the greater the variety in a company's businesses, the more likely it is that there will be variety in the business strategies pursued and thus in the operations strategies adopted. Unfortunately, the greater the variety of operations strategies, the less likely it is that senior-level corporate managers will be familiar with all the technologies involved or able to fully exploit the potential contribution that operations can make to business success.

2A.2.3 The Attitude toward Growth

The importance of growth is a third factor influencing operations' competitive role. For some companies, growth represents an input to the company's or business unit's planning process; for others it is an output. Every company continually confronts a variety of growth opportunities. Its decision to accept some types and to reject others signals, in a fundamental way, the kind of company it prefers to be. Some companies, for example, in their concentration on a particular market, geographic area, or material, accept the growth permitted by that market or area or material. Other companies, however, are managed so that a certain rate of growth is required if they are to function properly.

The firm's attitude toward growth has a powerful influence on its attitude toward operations as a competitive weapon. On the one hand, in businesses in which high growth is considered essential, operations' primary task is often simply to keep up with that growth. This need tends to take precedence over establishing a competitive advantage on other dimensions of operating effectiveness. Companies or SBUs in which growth is not the primary motivating factor, on the other hand, are more likely to assign a larger and richer strategic role to operations.

Chapter 3

Capacity Strategy

3.1 OVERVIEW

Many managers tend to equate their company's *operations* strategy with its *capacity* strategy. That is, they confine the scope of their strategic thinking about operations to the making of plans for changing its *capacity* (e.g., "We are expanding our Akron plant by 200,000 square feet this year, will consolidate our operations in Europe and reduce their capacity by 20 percent next year, and plan to build a new factory in Singapore, with a capacity of 100,000 units, the year after that"). As pointed out in Chapter 2, however, a comprehensive operations strategy consists of much more than just a sequence of capacity decisions. A coherent capacity strategy does constitute an important element of any operations strategy, however, and often provides a useful starting point when developing one.

There also is a critical difference between a capacity *decision,* which in most organizations is triggered by a request for capital investment, and a capacity *strategy,* which places each such request in the context of a longer-term sequence of decisions. Although much of the literature on capacity planning focuses primarily on how to make specific decisions regarding increases or reductions in capacity, this chapter focuses more on how to sort out and think about several of the issues that affect capacity planning over an extended time period.

As with other major elements of an operations strategy, a capacity strategy must reflect the firm's values, resources, overall approach to competition, and willingness to accept various kinds of risks, as described in Chapter 2. Moreover, it should mesh with and reinforce the firm's other strategies and objectives. Finally, it should embody a mental model of "how the world works" (in a given industry and geographic region)—a series of assumptions and predictions about the long-term behavior of markets, technologies, costs, and competitors' behavior. Such a model would include the following factors:

- Predicted growth and variability of the demand for the firm's products and services
- Costs of building and operating different-sized facilities
- Likely rate and direction of technological evolution
- Expected behavior of competitors (both domestic and foreign)
- Anticipated availability, capabilities, and costs of external suppliers

An operation's capacity often is difficult even to define, much less measure with any accuracy, since it represents a complex interaction of physical space, equipment, operating rates, human resources, system capabilities, company policies, and the rate and dependability of suppliers. As a result, capacity usually can be changed in a variety of ways. For example, the number of passengers that an airplane can carry in one day is a function of the number of hours it is scheduled to operate, the length of a typical flight, the flight delays experienced at the airports it has chosen to serve, and the speed with which it can be "turned around" between flights. Turnaround time, in turn, depends on the number, skill, and motivation of the people assigned to the task, and the extent to which their customers are willing to cooperate with them.

When asked how much capacity they should plan to provide, many managers respond instinctively, "The amount needed to meet expected demand." For reasons we will soon explore, however, a capacity strategy does not consist simply of an estimate of the total demand that is expected to occur at different dates in the future. It requires a careful statement of how much of what kinds of capacity are to be provided over time, given the likely evolution and variability of the firm's activities and operating environment. Although a variety of factors establish limits on an operation's overall capacity, in a given situation one or two key resources are likely to be most critical, so providing those resources will be the most effective means for changing capacity at a particular time. At one point physical space may be most constraining; at others it may be equipment hours or workforce levels; at another, the fluctuation in processing rates or defect levels. Whichever measure is used, we assume in the remainder of this discussion that it is a surrogate for all of the resources required for the business to meet its desired output levels.

This chapter introduces a set of concepts and techniques that are useful both in formulating a capacity strategy and in guiding the individual decisions required to implement one. Section 3.2 examines the various factors that affect capacity and the kinds of problems an operations organization is likely to experience as it approaches its capacity limits. Section 3.3 discusses some of the basic issues that relate capacity to the expected trajectory of demand over time. The concept of a *capacity cushion* is defined, and we suggest some guidelines for thinking about the size of the cushion that might be appropriate in different situations.

Maintaining a capacity cushion at a desired level often is extremely difficult, however, because demand is continually changing and capacity usually is not easy to alter—up or down—in a short period of time. Moreover, for a variety of economic and technical reasons, it often is not possible to increase or reduce capacity in small increments; one must expand or contract in larger chunks—the appropriate size of which will depend on the sizes of existing facilities and their process technologies. While Section 3.3 focuses on the general relationship between demand and capacity, Section 3.4 deals with issues related to the size of these new chunks of capacity. One of the most important of these relationships is that between the cost of a unit of output and the size of the facility in which it is created. The concept of *economies of scale* plays a critical role in the analysis of capacity decisions, as well as in many other types of decisions discussed throughout this book, and so is covered in some detail. We also discuss the equally important concept of *diseconomies of scale.*

Finally, we describe the less familiar topic of *increasing* economies of scale, which is associated primarily with the so-called *network effect* that (as mentioned in Chapter 1) characterizes certain kinds of information intensive operations.

Unlike the more quantitative approaches of earlier sections, Section 3.6 describes different philosophies that can underlie a capacity strategy, and how blind allegiance to any one of them can lead a company into trouble. Section 3.7 concludes with a look at how different capacity decisions are likely to affect the behavior of customers and competitors, and how a business unit's capacity strategy can be integrated with its overall business strategy. Finally, the Appendix to this chapter describes a couple of simple mathematical models that have been proposed for helping one think about alternative capacity expansion strategies. Although the assumptions upon which these calculations are based are perhaps too simple to be applied directly to most real-life decisions, they make it possible for the more mathematically inclined reader to address the important issues in a systematic manner and provide useful insights regarding key relationships.

3.2 HOW CAPACITY AND OPERATIONS MANAGEMENT INTERACT

As noted earlier, although the term *capacity* often is used as though it were precise and easily measurable, identifying an operation's capacity can be highly difficult. Even for a single facility there usually is considerable uncertainty as to how its capacity ought to be measured for planning purposes. For example, an operation's rated capacity is different from both its scheduled capacity and its actual capacity. *Rated* (or "engineering") capacity is based on the maximum speed that equipment and operators can function. Essentially, it represents the theoretical amount of output that could be generated if everything went right and the operation was able to maintain that maximum speed uninterrupted—around the clock, seven days a week. *Scheduled* capacity takes into account the number of hours the facility is scheduled to be in operation during a given period of time (a week, say), as well as the fact that it seldom is able to operate at its maximum speed over a sustained period of time. It represents, for planning purposes, the output that can be expected if it operates at its historical (or standard) rate during that week.

Finally, the operation's *actual* capacity is the consequence of a number of unplanned problems that prevent it from operating as predicted. For example, a *yield problem* (an unexpectedly high percentage of defects) not only reduces the amount of good output, it can consume the productive time of both operators and equipment in reworking defective output. Equipment breakdowns and/or operator problems similarly reduce the amount of time available. Even when equipment and operators are working properly, however, an operation's output can be constrained by unexpected stoppages due to long production changeover times or a lack of jobs to work on because of poor work scheduling, bottlenecks in a prior production stage, or unplanned changes in the work schedule. These are discussed in more detail below.

An operation's actual capacity is affected by at least eight important factors:

1. *Capacity is technologically based.* The process technology used affects an operation's overall capacity and the efficiency with which various resources are consumed.
2. *Capacity depends on the interaction of multiple resource constraints.* Equipment or labor availability, storage space, transport facilities, and so on, can each be a limiting factor or "bottleneck." An operation's capacity, therefore, can fluctuate as one bottleneck is supplanted by another.
3. *Capacity is mix dependent.* Different products/services consume different amounts of various resources, so expressing capacity in terms of aggregate measures, such as sales dollars, can be misleading if there are major changes in the product mix.
4. *Capacity can sometimes be stored.* As a result, it is often difficult to determine how much of a facility's total output is generated by its innate processing capabilities and how much resulted from reducing various in-process inventories. Maintaining excess equipment (to allow regular maintenance) and labor (to fill in for missing employees) represent other "stores" that affect capacity. A measure of capacity that is based on an operation's *maximum* output during a given time period may reflect such cushions and so may not be sustainable over a longer period.
5. *Capacity depends on management policies.* As noted earlier, management policies affect the number of hours worked per week, the amount of final or intermediate products that are stored in inventories, and the capacity cushion that is considered appropriate—all of which directly affect an operation's capacity. Managers also may give more attention to certain types of capacity (such as floor space or machine hours) than to others because they are easier to measure and/or take longer to change. They also can be influenced by accounting rules requiring that labor and materials be expensed during the current time period (which reduces reported profits), but that allow physical plant and equipment to be capitalized and amortized over a longer time interval (increasing reported profits).
6. *Capacity is dynamic.* As a facility gains experience in producing a product or service, and discovers and removes successive bottlenecks, its total capacity tends to expand with time, even without major new investments. This "learning" effect is discussed further in Section 3.4 and Chapter 10.
7. *Capacity is location specific.* Even though a firm's aggregate capacity is the sum of the capacities of each of its facilities, it often is not possible to direct an increase in overall demand to an underutilized facility. As discussed later, transportation costs may make it unprofitable for facilities in some locations to service certain customers or regions, and competitive factors may require proximity to customers. Excess labor, materials, machinery and floor space in the wrong location are not usable capacity.
8. *Capacity is affected by the degree of variability of demand and processing time.* Finally, the capacity of an operation also depends on the variability in the rates at which work arrives and can be processed. This is because a temporary

reduction in the rate jobs arrive, below the rate the operation normally can process them, results in idle time that can never be used again. Similarly, idle time results if an operation completes its work unusually quickly and no other jobs are waiting to be worked on. The capacity represented by an airplane seat whose expected occupant arrived after the flight departed can never be used again; like "darlin' Clementine," it is lost and gone forever.

3.2.1 The Impact of Variability on Capacity

To put this last issue into more quantitative terms, suppose a bank teller's rated capacity for processing bank customers is sixty per hour, but for some reason no customers arrive during a ten-minute interval. As a result, the teller's effective capacity during that hour is at least ten customers less than the usual rate. We say "at least" ten customers because the same phenomenon operates at still smaller time intervals. If the arrival of a new customer takes place several seconds after the teller has finished serving the previous one, those "idle" seconds also are lost forever. The greater the variability in the arrival and/or processing rates, the greater will be the amount of underutilized capacity. The exact amount of this underutilization depends on the arrival and processing rates as well as the specific forms of the probability distributions that govern them. Determining what the actual amount of underutilization is likely to be during any time period is quite complicated in most situations, but we can obtain useful insights by examining a simple case.

Suppose the time between the arrivals of successive customers (work orders) and the time it takes the teller (workstation) to process them are both governed by *exponential* probability distributions. This would occur if customers arrive one at a time and the probability of an arrival during any small time interval (of constant duration) never changed—that is, it doesn't depend on the time of day, on how many customers arrived during the previous few minutes, or on the number of people waiting in line to be served. (For the teller, analogously, it implies that the probability of completing the processing of a given customer during any small period of time stays the same, no matter how many customers are in line or the length of time that customer has already spent being processed.) Under these assumptions, if customers arrive at an average rate of 48 per hour, the probability that one will arrive during any given second during that hour is 1/75 (= 48/60/60) and the average time *between* arrivals will be 1/48th of an hour, or 60/48 = 1.25 minutes.[1] These assumptions might appear to be quite limiting, but they come close enough to describing many actual arrival processes that an analysis of their behavior provides useful insights about the behavior of more complicated situations.[2]

Given the assumptions we made about how customers arrive, it can be shown that if the arrival rate is a (48 per hour in our example) the probability that *no* customers will arrive during some longer period of time (0 to T, say) is equal to e^{-aT} (which is why the probability distribution of interarrival times is called *exponential*). This probability distribution has the characteristic that the *variation* in the arrival rate is proportional to its *average* rate, which allows us to explore the impact that increasing variability has on a system's behavior.

Similarly, if the rate p at which a teller can process customers also obeys those same assumptions, with an average processing time of $1/p$, it can be shown that the percent of time the teller is idle (because there are no customers to serve) during any time period is equal to $(1 - a/p)$. Therefore, if customers arrive at a rate of 48 per hour, and the teller can serve them at a rate of 60 per hour, she will be waiting for somebody to arrive about 20 percent of the time.

Notice that, even though the teller has (60 – 48)/48 = 25 percent *excess* capacity, we might expect to see people waiting in line for service most of the time because some of this capacity has been lost through enforced idle time. In general, for this kind of situation, it can be shown that the average number of customers N in front of the teller (either being served or waiting for service)—which represents the "work-in-process" (WIP) inventory in the system—can be calculated using equation (3-1):

$$N = a/(p - a) \tag{3-1}$$

In our specific example, therefore, even with all that excess capacity there will be, on average, four (= 48/[60 – 48]) customers in the system. And, since the average amount of time a typical customer spends there equals the number of people times the average interarrival time,[3] each of those four people will spend an average of 4/48 = 1/12th hour (that is, 5 minutes) waiting and being served; this represents the "total process throughput time" for an average customer.

Equation (3-1) also implies—and this is the "punch line" for this discussion—that as the rate of arrivals increases and approaches the processing capacity of the teller, both measures of system performance deteriorate rapidly. For example, if the customer arrival rate were to increase from 48 to 54 per hour (that is, by only 12.5 percent), the work-in-process inventory in the system (N) would more than double, from 4 to 9 [=54/(60 – 54)], and the average process throughput time would similarly increase from 5 to more than 11 minutes. And if the arrival rate increased another 5 percent, to 57 per hour (representing 95 percent of the teller's rated capacity), the number of people in the system would skyrocket to 19! The lesson we can draw from this simple example is that, in the face of fluctuating demand, as an operation approaches its capacity limits, congestion and the problems resulting from it can escalate rapidly—as shown in Figure 3-1.

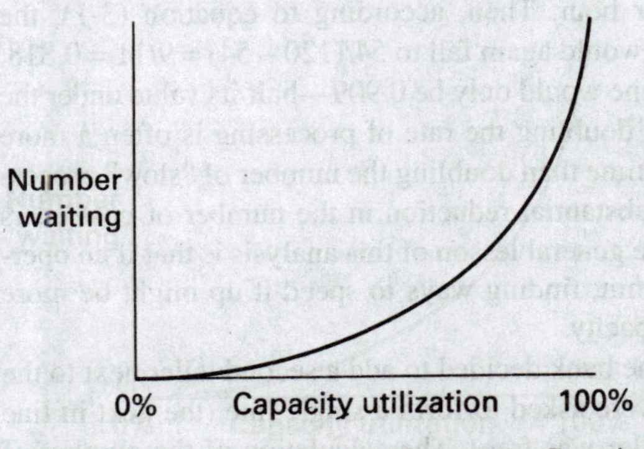

Figure 3-1 General Relationship between Capacity Utilization and Number Waiting

We would not expect to see the same degree of sensitivity of WIP to demand changes in more complex and realistic operating systems, however, because such systems usually comprise a number of workstations, some operating in parallel and others connected in series, often with buffer inventories. These buffers and parallel systems, by ensuring that workstations are less likely to have to wait for work to arrive, effectively eliminate much of the inherent variability in demand that drove the behavior seen in the example above. But our simple single-server example provides suggestive insights about the way congestion in more complex systems builds up as they approach their capacity limits. In the machine tool industry, for example, the time to deliver a new tool rapidly increases as the demand rate approaches industry capacity. Moreover, as companies attempt to reduce inventories by adopting "pull" systems of production scheduling, one might expect them to behave more and more like our simple example.

3.2.2 Alternative Approaches for Expanding Capacity

Let us now extend our example to examine the implications of various ways that the managers of this hypothetical bank might respond to an increase in the customer arrival rate as it approaches 54 per hour (and the number of people in line approaches 9). One way would be to add another teller just like the first one, with his own line. For the moment we will assume that customers, once they have chosen a line, cannot switch to the other line. This might be either because the two lines are separated geographically, or because each teller is specialized to deal with the needs of one of two different types of customers, which are represented equally in the arrivals (in effect, the system would consist of two focused facilities rather than one general facility, the simplest type of the networks discussed in Chapter 5). In either case, the arrival rate at each of the two lines would be cut in half, to 27 per hour. According to equation (3-1), we would expect that the number of customers in each line would fall to 9/11 [= 27/(60 – 27)], or 0.818, so the number in *both* lines would be double that, or 1.636. And the average time a customer would spend in this system would be only 1.818 minutes (= 9/11 × 1/27 × 60 min.).

Now suppose the bank decided instead to provide the single teller with equipment (a new computer system, say) that would double her processing rate (for all customers)—to 120 customers per hour. Then, according to equation (3-1), the number of customers in the system would again fall to 54/(120 – 54) = 9/11 = 0.818, but the average customer waiting time would only be 0.909—half its value under the two-line approach. In other words, doubling the rate of processing is often a more effective way to reduce throughput time than doubling the number of "slow" processors, even though both lead to a substantial reduction in the number of customers and their average waiting time.[4] The general lesson of this analysis is that if an operation is approaching its capacity limit, finding ways to speed it up might be more effective than adding additional capacity.

Now suppose that, as before, the bank decided to add a second teller next to the first one, but this time customers were asked to form a single line (the next in line would be directed to whichever teller was free). The calculation of the number of customers (WIP) in this situation is much more complicated than before, and it is probably easier—as in most other, more complex and realistic cases—to simulate the system's performance characteristics using a computer. It can be shown, however, that there will be an average of 1.13 customers in this two-teller, single line system, and the average time each would spend in the system would be 1.25 minutes. This is somewhat better than the two-teller, two-line system (because it is less likely that a teller/workstation will be idled by a lack of customers), but not as good as for the single very fast teller.

In general, assigning multiple workstations to serve a single long line results in less WIP and shorter throughput times than if each is given its own line. This is why many service organizations (e.g., airline ticket counters and fast food providers) have switched to this type of system, even though it forces all customers to stand in a long—often serpentine—line and continuously shuffle forward. Whether or not customers would prefer to wait in a single long line rather than separate, shorter lines, however, is a complicated issue. Some people object to joining a very long line, no matter how fast it is moving, and may defect. Others like to keep moving, even though in a longer line, and worry about getting trapped in a line with a slow server. And still others seem to enjoy the "game" of jockeying between lines, trying to get through as quickly as possible.

3.2.3 The Consequences of a Capacity Squeeze

When thinking about the consequences of running short of capacity, most managers focus primarily on the resulting loss of potential sales. In later sections of this chapter, particularly when we use simple quantitative models to clarify certain issues, we similarly address the "cost" of lost sales. But as an operation approaches its capacity limit, *stockouts* (incidents where a lack of available goods or processing ability creates the potential for lost sales) are only one—and usually one of the last—of the problems experienced. The symptoms, and costs, of insufficient capacity usually appear long before the first stockout. Assessing the effect of a capacity shortfall only by measuring the incidence of stockouts is somewhat like confining one's analysis of the effect of heart disease to simply estimating the likelihood of a major heart attack.

The first symptom of insufficient capacity is usually an increase in WIP inventory. This is because—as we saw in the simple customer/teller example in the previous section—when the volume of incoming work begins approaching the operation's capacity, the natural variability in arrival and processing rates aggravates the capacity squeeze. Recall that the total number of customers in the system in that example was directly related to the average time a customer (work order) spent in the system: number in system = (total process throughput time) × (arrival rate of new customers).[5] For example, if an average work order spends 4 hours in the system, either waiting or being processed, and new jobs arrive at the rate of 50 per hour (and can be processed at a rate faster than that), at the moment its processing is completed there are, on average, 200 other jobs somewhere in the system behind it.[6] If, for any reason, jobs began to arrive at a rate of 60 per hour, the number of jobs in the system would rise to 240.

Not only does an increase in WIP inventory lead to higher inventory (or customer) management costs, it triggers a number of other problems. *First,* scheduling work becomes much more complex. Some work orders may even get "lost" in the system (temporarily—one hopes!). *Second,* quality problems tend to increase as process throughput times lengthen. To some extent this is due to the increased number of physical movements required in trying to make room for all the partially completed work orders waiting for the next step in their processing, which results in more physical deterioration (e.g., rust, dirt, or scratches). Quality problems also result from delays in recognizing that a problem exists, as often there is no indication that a workstation has begun producing bad parts until a defective part shows up in the next step in its processing. The more WIP inventory, the longer this takes—and the longer until the problem is corrected, the more defectives will be produced. An increase in the rate of defectives produced (and in the time spent correcting them), in turn, reduces the effective capacity of the operating system, aggravating the situation. Moreover, in service environments, where "work orders" are customers waiting in line, as waiting time increases they tend to grow increasingly unhappy, and may defect to competitors.

Third, expediting becomes both more prevalent and more costly. The build-up of WIP inventory and the concurrent increase in processing throughput times may delay the processing of orders from important customers. The pressure those customers apply to speed up the delivery of their orders may induce the operation's managers to pull them out of their natural sequence in the queues waiting to be processed and move them ahead of other customers' work orders. This not only increases the complexity of job tracking, scheduling, and inventory control (all of which cause overhead costs to increase), but it delays the completion of the jobs that were "bumped" behind the favored ones. The customers so bumped, in turn, may become concerned about the impact of those delays on their own operations and request special treatment for their orders as well. Over time more and more work orders require expediting, until eventually the scheduling system breaks down completely: every decision about what to process next has to be made individually.

Not only does expediting lead to additional materials handling, communications, order tracking, and confusion, but if the pressure to expedite a work order becomes so intense that a decision is made to halt the processing of another job so as to begin processing the favored one, the operation will incur the cost of an additional setup and/or changeover. Moreover, to the extent that changeovers consume operator and equipment time, each added one reduces the effective capacity of the operation—further exacerbating the original capacity squeeze.

At some point in this escalating scenario the operation's managers may decide to add additional equipment and/or increase its hours of operation, either through overtime or the hiring of new people—all of which add more costs. Finally, if such actions have the intended effect and capacity is increased to the point where WIP inventory and process throughput times fall back to their normal levels, the need for expediting will decline and quality will improve. The result is a further increase in effective capacity, to the point where the organization may now find itself with *too much!* This may eventually force it to incur the additional costs of *reducing* its workforce. In this context, one can see why the cost of a lost sale, even though highly visible and strategically painful, may not be the biggest cost the operation incurs from a capacity shortfall.

3.3 THE TIMING OF CAPACITY INCREMENTS—THE CAPACITY CUSHION

At its heart, a capacity strategy suggests how the amount and timing of capacity changes should relate to *long-term* changes in demand. Three options, shown in Figure 3-2, illustrate the range of possibilities available when demand is expected to grow steadily.

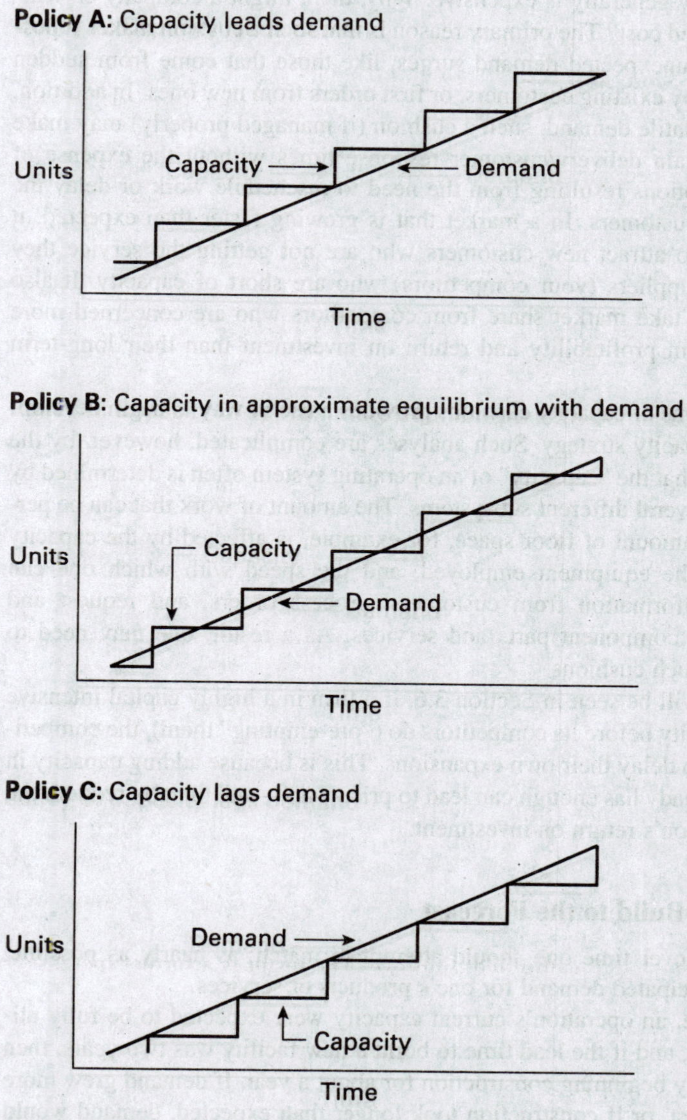

Figure 3-2 Alternative Capacity Expansion Strategies

3.3.1 Policy A: Lead Demand with Capacity

In Policy A, the strategy is to build and maintain extra capacity (analogous to an inventory safety stock) so that the likelihood of running short is less than that of having too much. The greater the capacity provided, the smaller will be the likelihood of running short. The amount of capacity in excess of expected demand is the operation's *capacity cushion.* For example, if the expected monthly demand on a facility is $500,000 worth of goods or services, and it can produce as much as $550,000, it has a 10 percent capacity cushion.[7]

Unused capacity generally is expensive. Why, then, might a company be willing to incur this added cost? The primary reason is that such a cushion makes it possible to respond to unexpected demand surges, like those that come from sudden large orders placed by existing customers, or first orders from new ones. In addition, when faced with volatile demand, such a cushion (if managed properly) may make it possible to maintain delivery/customer response times without the expense of overtime and disruptions resulting from the need to reschedule work or delay the servicing of other customers. In a market that is growing faster than expected, it might enable you to attract new customers who are not getting the service they desire from their suppliers (your competitors) who are short of capacity. It also might allow you to take market share from competitors who are concerned more about their near-term profitability and return on investment than their long-term market position.

Thinking in terms of capacity cushions provides a useful way to begin developing a long-term capacity strategy. Such analyses are complicated, however, by the fact (noted earlier) that the "capacity" of an operating system often is determined by the interaction of several different subsystems. The amount of work that can be performed in a given amount of floor space, for example, is affected by the capacity and flexibility of the equipment employed, and the speed with which one can receive accurate information from customers, process orders, and request and receive supplies of component parts and services. As a result, one may need to determine several such cushions.

Moreover, as will be seen in Section 3.6, if a firm in a highly capital intensive industry adds capacity before its competitors do ("pre-empting" them), the competitors might decide to delay their own expansions. This is because adding capacity in an industry that already has enough can lead to price wars—and thereby reduces the new capacity addition's return on investment.

3.3.2 Policy B: Build to the Forecast

Under this policy, over time one should attempt to match, as nearly as possible, capacity to the anticipated demand for one's products or services.

If, for example, an operation's current capacity were expected to be fully utilized in three years, and if the lead time to build a new facility was two years, then the firm might delay beginning construction for about a year. If demand grew more rapidly than forecast, or if construction took longer than expected, demand would outstrip capacity. As a result, the company would lose potential sales if it did not react by expanding the capacity of existing facilities (through overtime, weekend shifts, etc.), or by subcontracting the deficit to outside companies. On the other hand, if demand fell short of expectations, the company might find itself stretching construction lead times to minimize the excess capacity. However, on average, it would prefer to have "about the right amount" of capacity—the likelihood of having too much being about the same as the likelihood of a shortfall. As we have seen, however, such a policy runs the risk of incurring all the ancillary costs (increased inventories, changeovers, confusion, and overhead) associated with operating close to a capacity limit.

3.3.3 Policy C: Add Capacity Only after Demand Exceeds It

This policy implies that the company's capacity plan will contain a negative cushion, so that the likelihood of running short is greater than the likelihood of having excess capacity.

This is sometimes referred to as a *conservative* capacity strategy, in that it requires less investment than would be required to maintain a positive capacity cushion. It also assures higher average utilization of capacity than do the other two policies, and therefore provides a higher average rate of return on facilities investment. In addition, when new capacity becomes available, it tends to be fully utilized almost immediately. On the other hand, such a policy may also lead to higher average operating costs and a slow deterioration in one's market share over time. For this reason, this policy is not conservative in the sense of being "low risk." It simply substitutes one type of risk (losing potential sales) for another (having underutilized facilities).

We explore the circumstances under which a company might choose each of these contrasting strategies in Section 3.3.5. First, however, we will introduce other factors affecting capacity decisions, including the extent to which economies of scale exist in both constructing facilities and processing jobs.

3.3.4 Alternative Types of Capacity Cushion

Up to now we have used the word *capacity* to refer to *processing* capacity, but if we think of capacity in its most basic sense—as the ability of a business to meet customer demand—one can see that such capacity can be provided in several ways. These vary along a number of important dimensions, including the speed of response, cost, flexibility, and risk of obsolescence.

One obvious way that companies can meet demand that is temporarily greater than their operating rate is by carrying inventories, either of finished goods or of parts and components that can be converted quickly into finished goods. As with the airline seat referred to earlier, most services cannot be inventoried, unfortunately, although some "backroom" services (usually involving the processing of documents or information rather than direct contact with customers) can build WIP inventories. If inventories are possible, they enable the quickest response to a demand surge, but building them for this purpose can be quite risky because it requires that you know exactly which products will be demanded and in what quantities. If your forecasts are wrong, then you not only may not have enough of some products, you also may find yourself with a large inventory of unwanted, and eventually obsolete products.

The more common view of a capacity cushion is that associated with the various resources described earlier: floor space, equipment, and people. This kind of capacity cannot provide the same *speed* of response as can inventories, but it is more *flexible,* in that the specific mix and volumes of products demanded by customers can be produced within the company's normal lead time. Instead of incurring the risk of obsolete inventory, one now incurs the cost of unused capital resources that have a smaller risk of obsolescence.

It is possible, of course, to provide only a partial capacity cushion—of plant and equipment, say, but not of people. Then, if demand increases, overtime will be required and/or additional people hired and trained. This becomes increasingly difficult as the skills required become more and more specialized. For example, one study of the biotech industry at the turn of the century concluded that even if biotech companies were able to obtain sufficient funds for expansion they faced "a looming shortage of the highly trained people needed to design, build, and operate facilities."[8] The tradeoff is between the speed of response and the investment required—just as when deciding whether to hold inventories or provide additional production capacity.[9] Alternatively, one might provide capacity cushions for certain critical products or services and not for others.

If, however, an operation is organized as a collection of work areas, each of which is dedicated to the creation of a small group of products or services, capacity cushions will have to be created for each one. As suggested by our simple bank teller example (Section 3.2.1), the total of these specialized cushions generally will have to be greater than the cushion required for a single facility capable of producing *all* products. On the other hand, both the investment and operating costs of this kind of flexible facility are usually greater than those of several simpler, more specialized facilities.

Similarly, if a product or service is delivered through several regional facilities, each of which supplies a specific geographic region,, more inventory is required to maintain an acceptably low probability of stockout for the system as a whole than would be needed to maintain the same level of service at a single facility that served all regions. In the simplest case, where the probability distributions of demand in each of N different regions are independent of one another and have the same standard deviation σ, it can be shown that the total cushion (i.e., safety stock or excess capacity) required to keep the probability of a stockout throughout the system below some value (95 percent, say) is approximately equal to $\sqrt{N}$ times the cushion required if everything were held in the same location (or produced by the same facility). That is, four storage points need twice the capacity cushion that a single storage point requires to maintain the same probability of a stockout.[10] This phenomenon affects all kinds of inventories—including those consisting of people, computing capacity, fire departments, and urban services. One analysis, for example, estimated that Japan's productive labor supply would be increased by more than 5 percent if there were more mobility of people among firms, since the traditional one-firm-for-life practice in Japan essentially creates a separate inventory of people in each company.[11]

As an example of the various kinds of capacity cushions that might be employed, one consumer appliance company considered a wide range of options. Aware of the uncertainties associated with planning capacity for a product that was still in the early stages of its life cycle, but anticipating substantial demand growth, this firm considered: (1) maintaining its existing production capacity for another six to twelve months (so that its capacity cushion eroded as demand grew), (2) building inventory and working overtime in order to meet unexpected demand surges, (3) adding a second shift at an existing facility, (4) adding floorspace and equipment to that facility, and (5) building a new facility. In deciding among these, management considered (in addition to their respective costs) the likely growth rate of demand, the time required to get capital requests approved by corporate management, and the likely reactions of competitors.

What is best for any organization—where in the series of tradeoffs among speed of response, efficiency, flexibility, and risk it should position itself—depends very much on its specific situation. In a growing market, there usually is relatively little long-term risk associated with having more capacity than is necessary to meet expected demand; almost certainly the company will need that extra capacity relatively soon. If it expects continuing market growth, it simply would be adding capacity a few months before it is absolutely required. Although this might penalize its short-term return on investment, it might enable it to attract new customers from capacity-constrained competitors.

In a stagnant or declining market, however, the penalty associated with excess capacity is much greater. For much of the last third of the twentieth century, for instance, the U.S. steel industry suffered from severe overcapacity. Operating at low utilization rates not only led to high costs per ton, it kept the industry from buying new facilities that embodied more advanced technologies. During this same period, foreign competitors continued to modernize, and thereby steadily improved their costs and quality. This reluctance to invest by the established U.S. giants also encouraged new companies to enter the industry by building new plants incorporating the latest *minimill* technologies. These minimills took an ever-increasing share of the market for steel away from the traditional producers, leaving them with more and more—and increasingly outdated—excess capacity. Three of the five largest traditional producers, including Bethlehem Steel (the second largest), went bankrupt during the 1990s as a result.

3.3.5 Determining the Appropriate Capacity Cushion

From this point on we will confine our analysis to processing capacity alone, although the same general approach would apply to other types of capacity cushions as well. At its most basic level, a decision as to how much capacity cushion to provide (if any) should reflect the relative costs of having more capacity than is needed (the cost of unused plant and equipment and underutilized human resources) versus the costs of not having enough (the cost of overtime, subcontracting, and lost profits). Sometimes referred to as a "newsboy problem," as discussed in the Appendix to this chapter, under very simple assumptions this implies that the size of the capacity cushion should be related to the ratio

$$(C_s - C_x)/C_s \tag{3-2}$$

where: C_s represents the *opportunity loss* per unit from not having enough capacity (s implies short) during a given time period, including lost profit and/or overtime costs, as well as customer displeasure from not receiving proper service

and

C_x represents the annualized cost, during the same time period, of having an unneeded unit of capacity (x implies excess).

In general, if this ratio is greater than 0.5, more capacity than the median forecast of demand should be provided; if it is less than 0.5, a *negative cushion* is called for. Therefore, highly capital intensive industries (C_x large) will tend toward small or even negative capacity cushions (and high average utilization rates), while low capital intensive, high profit margin (C_x small, C_s large) industries will tend toward large capacity cushions and lower utilization rates.

For example, if each added unit of annual operating capacity costs a firm $1 per year in annualized investment and maintenance costs, etc. ($C_x = 1$), and if its lost profit contribution and other costs associated with not being able to satisfy demand out of its own facility, operating at its normal rate, is $3 per unit ($C_s = 3$), then the ratio is (3 – 1)/3 = 0.67. This indicates the need for a positive cushion. More precisely, the total capacity available should be large enough that there is a two-thirds probability of being able to satisfy all demand during the year—or, alternatively, that there is a one-third probability that annual demand would *exceed* the available capacity. If C_s were equal to $2, on the other hand, the ratio would equal 0.5, so capacity should be just large enough that there is a 50 percent likelihood of being able to satisfy demand during the year. That is, the firm should "build to the forecast"—no cushion.

This approach clearly takes a very short-term, simplistic point of view. Building a facility is a long-term proposition, and generally capacity cannot be increased one unit at a time. Nor is it easy to obtain accurate values for the cost parameters required to perform such a calculation. For instance, the *annualized cost of a unit of excess capacity,* C_x, is a convenient fiction: the cost of a unit of capacity usually depends on how many units are added at one time (see Section 3.4) and will change over time as the facility ages, the mix of products and services is altered, and the production technology is modified. Similarly, C_s, the "shortage cost per unit," may include such difficult-to-evaluate components as the future lost profits associated with customers who switch to competitors' products or services because you didn't have enough capacity to meet their needs, and the long-term costs associated with a reputation as an unreliable supplier.

At a basic conceptual level, however, this ratio captures the kind of tradeoff that managers should take into account as they grapple with the question, "How much capacity is enough?" Consider the decision faced by a major pharmaceutical company that was planning to introduce a new drug in 1998, and had to decide in early 1996 how much capacity to provide for its production. At that point in time, when the drug was still undergoing clinical trials, the firm faced a number of uncertainties, including whether the drug would be as efficacious as expected, the size and frequency of an average dosage, whether its use would lead to unanticipated side effects, and how it would compare in these respects with the new competing drugs that were expected to be introduced about the same time by two of its major competitors.

If it achieved expected results along these dimensions, the new drug probably would be able to generate sales of $50 million a month by the end of the first year after its introduction, with a gross margin of $35 million per month. Based on the best information available to it, the company decided that an investment of $240 million in new facilities would provide just enough capacity to meet $50 million worth of demand per month for the new drug during its first year. Given all the uncertainties associated with the new drug, however, management was uncertain as to how much initial production capacity above that average forecast should be provided. The combined interest and maintenance cost each year was expected to come to about 25 percent of the initial investment cost and the expected lifetime of the new facility was twenty-four years.

Although we do not have access to the kind of detailed information needed to calculate the values of C_x and C_s very precisely, the information provided above permits the following very rough estimates for the *first* 1 percent increment in capacity above the average forecast. This was estimated to cost $2.4 million (increasing the total investment to $242.4 million), if one assumed no economies of scale, so:

C_x = $700,000 per year (= $2.4 million/24 + $2.4 million × 25 percent)

C_s = $4.2 million per year (= $35 million × 1 percent × 12)

In other words, if the company found it needed that additional 1 percent capacity during any month (implying sales of at least $50.5 million), the resulting profit would cover the cost of building and maintaining that capacity increment for six months. Looked at another way, the proposed capacity increment would fully recover its costs if only one-sixth of it were needed during the year.

The ratio given by equation (3-2): $(4.2 - 0.7)/4.2 = 0.833$ suggests, in fact, that on the basis of economic considerations alone (and these rough but suggestive calculations), enough production capacity should be provided so that there would be less than a 17 percent probability that demand for the new drug would *exceed* capacity during 1998. (By comparison, one study of biotech drugs that require the cultivation of mammalian cells concluded that "facilities would be profitable if as little as 25 percent of capacity were used."[12]) This would imply a total investment in production capacity for the drug somewhat in excess of $360 million, given the probabilities the company's management ascribed to various possible demand rates. As noted earlier, in this situation, where demand was expected to continue growing after the first year of the new drug's introduction, building a sizable capacity cushion would be much less risky than it would be in a slow growth or cyclical demand environment.

3.4 THE SIZING OF CAPACITY INCREMENTS—SCALE CONSIDERATIONS

Closely tied to the question of how much capacity should be provided to meet forecasted demand are issues relating to the size of the increments of capacity to be added at any point in time. An operating facility's size or, more precisely, its "scale," usually affects the costs of acquiring and operating it. Although it is generally recognized that it seldom costs twice as much to build and operate a facility (or increment of capacity) that is double the size of another, those costs depend on the specific technology and circumstances. This section discusses the underlying causes of scale economies, both positive and negative, and examines their relationship to such concepts as a facility's "optimal" and "minimum economic" scale.

3.4.1 Economies of Scale

A facility's total capital and operating costs generally increase at a slower rate than its capacity or output volume. This concept, called *economies of scale,* often is used—sometimes without careful analysis—as a justification for adding products or services to an existing facility or building a new facility that is bigger than currently needed. Although the concept is based on plentiful evidence of actual cost behavior, so many different phenomena are encompassed by the term that confusion often arises as to what it really means in a specific situation. Moreover, different forms of scale economies (and diseconomies) affect not only capacity decisions, but many of the other types of decisions addressed in this book as well.

Economies of scale can arise for a variety of reasons and derive from many different components of total cost. Therefore, unless the logical connection between the scale economies observed in a given situation and the circumstances and actions that apparently caused them is carefully identified, inaccurate forecasts of future costs can result. The easiest, most logical way to sort out the various causal factors that underlie such economies is according to time period.

Short-Term Economies of Scale

In the very short term, many of the costs of operating a facility are relatively independent of its actual output volume. Hence they are called *period* costs or, unfortunately, *fixed* costs. We say "unfortunately" because the term *fixed costs* often is misconstrued to an even greater extent than is *economies of scale.* All costs are variable over the long run, and are fixed only to the extent that decisions to change them require time to implement. In situations where many of the costs associated with an operation are difficult to change quickly (e.g., the wages of salaried personnel, the costs of depreciation, taxes, and insurance for plant and equipment, interest costs on borrowed capital, and in many settings, even the cost of direct labor), increasing the output will not cause total costs to increase proportionally. In such situations the major increase in total cost will come from the *variable* or *direct* operating costs, such as those associated with operator time, material and energy usage, and wear-dependent equipment costs. Therefore, the cost per unit of output will decrease as total output increases:

$$\frac{\text{fixed costs + variable costs}}{\text{total units produced}} = \frac{\text{fixed costs}}{\text{total units}} + \text{variable cost/unit} \qquad (3\text{-}3)$$

This is sometimes referred to as *spreading the overhead costs* and is characterized as a short-term effect because over time most fixed costs can be changed: salaried personnel can be added or reduced, investment in inventories or equipment can be increased or decreased, and whole areas of a facility can be added or shut down. Also, as facilities reach their capacity limits, new capacity must be added. Since increments usually are added in chunks, the operation can shift rather quickly from operating at full capacity to being underutilized. As a result, this type of scale economy is usually transitory. In order to achieve economies that are more lasting, changes must be made in the way the existing process is *managed.*

Intermediate-Term Economies of Scale

Over a longer time period the firm can exploit increased operating rates to reduce costs in several related ways. In the case of repetitive operations, for example, one can increase the size of the "batches" being processed, thereby reducing the number of changeovers required to satisfy a given volume of sales. The average cost per unit would then be given by:

$$\text{average cost/unit} = \frac{\text{changeover cost}}{\text{total units}} + \text{processing cost/unit} \qquad (3\text{-}4)$$

The extent of the economies achievable through this kind of action depends on how much it costs to make a changeover, which is affected by other factors:

- The actual cost of changing over to a different product (e.g., preparing operators, as well as resetting fixtures, dies, computer programs, and instruction modules, and perhaps adjusting and cleaning internal parts)
- *Run-in* and *run-out* costs (the cost of higher-than-normal errors or defects and reduced labor efficiency at the beginning and end of a new batch)
- The cost of lost output (when people and equipment are operating near full capacity, the time lost during changeovers may result in lost sales or lead to overtime and other costs to compensate for this lost production)

It is also possible to increase batch sizes when demand is stable, of course. Two factors, however, usually make this undesirable. First, increasing the batch size in the absence of a compensating increase in the overall output level will result in higher inventories, requiring additional capital and storage facilities, and increasing the risk of obsolescence. Second, for a given level of total demand, as the batch size increases the time between the production of one batch and the next also increases. If the demand rate fluctuates widely, the firm's finished goods inventory is likely to become unbalanced, which could be costly in terms of increased backorder costs, emergency production runs, and lost sales.

Another way managers can reduce the costs of changeovers when production volume increases is by dedicating resources to specific products, services, or tasks. Creating such dedicated "cells" can facilitate more or less continuous processing, thereby reducing the need for changeovers. Moreover, dedicating equipment and people to the processing of a single product—or group of similar products—makes it possible to tailor skills, tools, and materials handling equipment to the specific requirements of that product group and thus reduce processing throughput times, material waste, maintenance, and so forth. It also may make it possible to use less sophisticated equipment and operators, since the capabilities required to make changeovers, produce a variety of products or services, or introduce a very different product no longer would be required. The effectiveness of such cells, moreover, usually increases as their operators master other skills, including equipment maintenance, quality control, and customer service, allowing them to move from task to task within their cell as bottlenecks or other problems arise.

Relatedly, a final way that scale economies can be exploited in the intermediate term is by using equipment that is specially designed for the needs of a given product or service. When a product's output volume exceeds a certain level it may no longer make sense to utilize general purpose equipment. Higher volume, specialized equipment often leads to lower total costs. To illustrate, Figure 3-3 depicts two alternative approaches to achieving intermediate economies of scale at one chemical plant: using a series of general-purpose processing lines, or using a series of

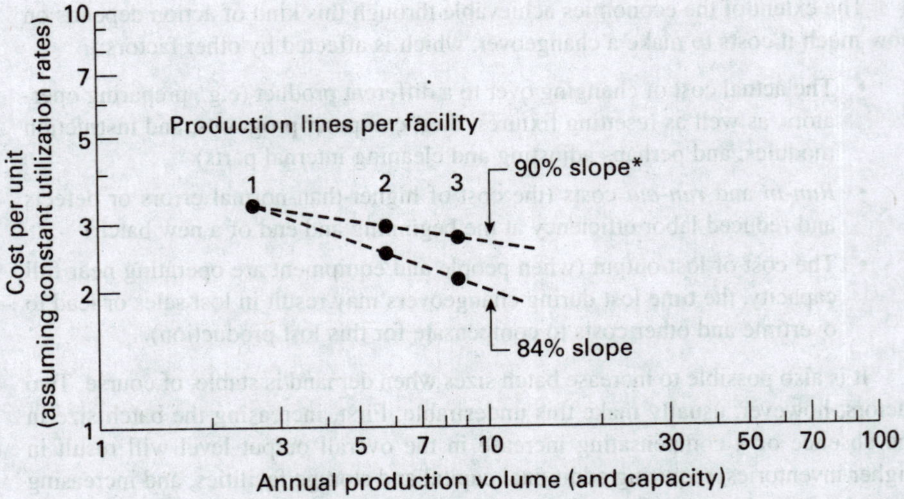

Figure 3-3 Intermedite-Term Scale Economies for a Chemical Plant (Logarithmic Scales)

*The 90 percent slope indicates scale economies from multiple lines of a given size (with no change in product assignments); the 84 percent slope reflects scale economies from more dedicated and specialized multiple lines of that given size.

more specialized lines (the unit costs are hypothetical). It should be noted that the risks associated with dedicated, more specialized (and therefore, usually, less flexible) lines would have to be weighed against their intermediate-term cost advantages.

Long-Term Economies of Scale

When engineers and economists refer to scale economies, they usually mean *long-term* economies. These can be broken into two subcategories: *static* and *dynamic*.

Static economies of scale refers to the economies that arise from using one large facility or piece of equipment rather than a number of smaller ones to create a product or service. This often results in savings because the processing capacity of much equipment is roughly proportional to its interior volume, whereas its cost is more closely related to the equipment's surface area (which is where the materials—cement, metal, and glass—and labor hours are concentrated). Since the volume of a geometric body increases faster than its surface area, both the construction costs and operating costs often follow a curve of the form:

$$C(V) = KV^k \tag{3-5}$$

where $C(V)$ = the cost of an increment of capacity of size V

K = a constant multiplier that depends on various shape parameters

k = a number between 0 and 1 that defines the "degree" of scale economies

Note that no economies of scale exist when $k = 1$; if V doubles, so does $C(V)$. As k gets smaller, the economies of scale become more pronounced. Consider, as an example, the cost of making a steel can. Holding its basic "shape" constant, which implies maintaining the same length-to-diameter ratio, its volume (V units) will increase with the cube of its radius, while its outside surface area will increase only with the square of its radius:

$$C(V) = KV^{2/3} \tag{3-6}$$

This example is not as simplistic as might appear at first glance. Most production units that process liquids (including molten metals) are basically cylinders—large steel cans. Thus, it is not surprising that the cost of chemical reactors, blast furnaces, oil refineries, and ocean freighters all increase roughly according to the two-thirds power of their capacities. For such cost functions, a doubling of capacity causes costs to increase by about 60 percent (since $2^{2/3} = 1.59$).[13]

In practice, k is almost always between 0.6 and 1.0, which has led many industries to adopt a rule of thumb known as *the six-tenths rule* when estimating the costs of different-sized capacity increments. In business situations, of course, this curve seldom is as smooth as equations (3-5) and (3-6) suggest. Only increments of certain sizes may be technologically feasible or available from suppliers. So the actual curve often contains scallops, blank areas, and step changes.

Other factors also underlie construction economies of scale. Some are analogous to the concept of "spreading the fixed costs" that we discussed earlier. For example, certain startup costs often are not directly proportional to the size of the facility: one must employ the services of architects, engineers, and lawyers no matter what size unit is being considered, and their fees are sometimes surprisingly independent of the unit's size. Similarly, the cost of environmental impact statements, negotiations with zoning boards, and governmental agencies tends to increase less rapidly than unit size. The cost per unit of operating such a facility, moreover, can be affected by technological opportunities. More sophisticated measuring instruments, equipment, and controls all become economical at higher volumes. They often make it possible to reduce labor costs, increase output yield, and improve product quality.

Indeed, sometimes building a larger facility allows one to adopt an entirely different processing technology—one that might not function effectively or be economic at low volumes. These technology-related savings, due to using a single large facility rather than several smaller ones, complement those that are a function of simple geometry. Both types are generally classified as *static economies* in that they are embodied in the equipment itself rather than in the skills gained in using the equipment to make/deliver products or services.

"Size" Is Not the Same as "Scale"

There is a critical—and often misunderstood—difference between a facility's *size* and its *scale*. The first refers simply to its physical size or output volume. Scale, however, implies repetitiveness—that multiple units of the *same* type are being processed. Only scale allows a company to fully reap the various advantages described above. For example, if it decides to produce a number of dissimilar products or services in a single large facility (rather than separating their production into smaller, more specialized facilities), the hoped-for "spreading of overhead" described in equation (3-3) is unlikely to occur. This is because the processing of multiple dissimilar products usually causes overhead costs to *increase*—due to scheduling complexity, training, expediting, process control, etc. Similarly, the cost savings associated with larger batch sizes, as depicted in equation (3-4), are achieved only when one produces larger batches of the *same* thing.

Finally, high-volume, more automated equipment that provides a cost advantage through investment economies of scale, as depicted by equation (3-5), often is more costly to change over from one product to another than is smaller, manually operated equipment. As a result, if it is called upon to switch frequently from one product to another, whatever cost savings were achieved through its initial purchase or construction will be dissipated quickly by operating inefficiencies. (An example of such behavior is provided by the experience of a plant in Holland, described in Chapter 5, section 5.2.5.) This confusion between size and scale is the reason many companies have been unable to obtain the cost savings they anticipated when they "rationalized" operations by combining two or more facilities into one.

"Dynamic" Economies of Scale

The term *dynamic* economies of scale refers to the improvement in the total operating cost per unit that results from the skills, systems, and experience that accumulates over time. It recognizes that equipment manufacturers (who, in effect, transmit processing technology between firms) do not completely determine the processing cost of the companies that buy their equipment. Dynamic economies arise from "learning by doing" (discussed further in Chapter 7), as well as from equipment geometry and technology. Therefore, rather than being a function simply of the scale of a facility (or the size of the chunk of capacity being added to it), it is a function of the experience gained through the *accumulated* output of that facility. Such economies represent the combined impact of many, often quite small, changes in equipment, labor capabilities, management methods, product changes, and so forth, as well as from formal R&D programs. A number of studies have documented the powerful impact that such ongoing process improvement can have on process performance over time.[14] We expand on these issues in Chapter 10.

Both static and dynamic economies of scale are illustrated in Figure 3-4, which depicts the marginal costs of production for two competitors. Each is investing in a new facility (making precision components, say, for the same market), but one is just entering the business. For different capital investment levels it may acquire any one of four technologies; their marginal cost relationships are specified by curves C_1 through C_4. The second competitor is an existing producer that will apply its acquired experience, operator capabilities, management skills, and process understanding to the new equipment that replaces its old equipment. If both firms make investments at scale "4," resulting in the same investment level and technology, the experienced firm realizes a marginal cost specified by the lower dotted curve, C_4'.

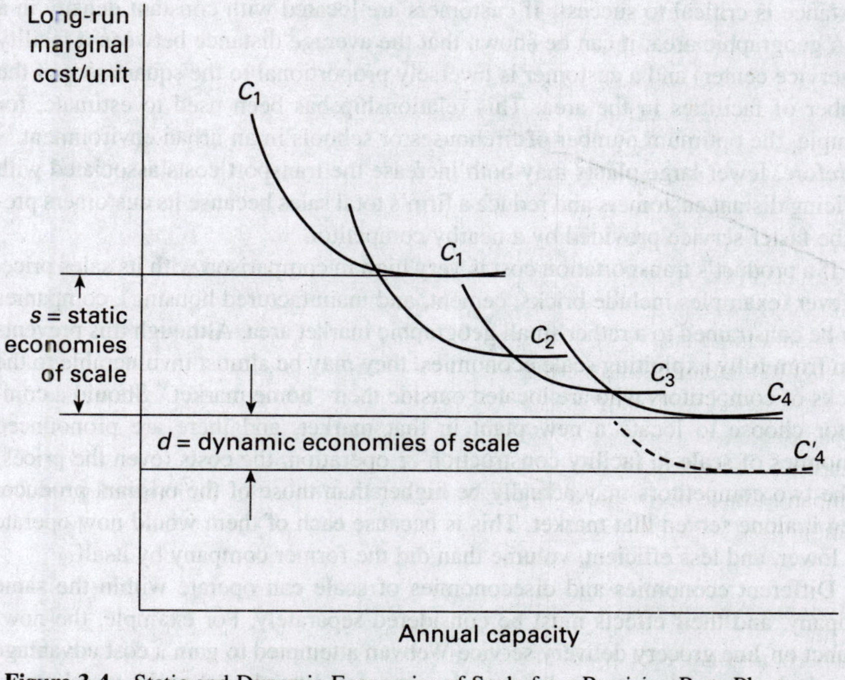

Figure 3-4 Static and Dynamic Economies of Scale for a Precision Parts Plant

Thus, the new firm will realize *static* scale economies of *s* dollars per unit by purchasing the largest facility rather than the smallest one, whereas the established firm will be able to realize an additional *d* dollars per unit as a result of the *dynamic* economies that accrue from its greater experience and accumulated knowledge.

3.4.2 Diseconomies of Scale

As Maynard Keynes observed (and, undoubtedly, many others before him): "There is no such thing as a free lunch." So it is with economies of scale. Increasing the scale of production can enable a firm to reduce certain costs, but it can also cause other costs to increase. These diseconomies of scale fall into four main categories.

Diseconomies of Distribution

Generally, the bigger a processing facility, the larger the geographic area it has to service. Moreover, if the density of its customers decreases rapidly as their distance from the facility increases (as it would if the facility were located in an urban area, say), the distribution costs required to supply an expanding region will probably increase much faster than the sales volume. Even in cases where the company does not incur the transportation costs directly, it may have to pay "freight equalization" or customer transport charges to prevent competitors nearer the customer from gaining a cost advantage.

The same type of distribution diseconomies may affect the *demand* for a firm's products in situations where the response time to customer requests for service or assistance is critical to success. If customers are located with constant density in a given geographic area, it can be shown that the average distance between a facility (or service center) and a customer is inversely proportional to the square root of the number of facilities in the area. This relationship has been used to estimate, for example, the optimum number of firehouses or schools in an urban environment.[15] Therefore, fewer large plants may both increase the transport costs associated with servicing distant customers and reduce a firm's total sales because its customers prefer the faster service provided by a nearby competitor.

If a product's transportation cost is very high in comparison with its sales price, however (examples include bricks, cement, and manufactured housing), companies may be constrained to a rather small geographic market area. Although this prevents them from fully exploiting scale economies, they may be almost invulnerable to the attacks of competitors who are located outside their "home market." Should a competitor choose to locate a new plant in that market, and there are pronounced economies of scale in facility construction or operation, the costs (even the prices) of the two competitors may actually be higher than those of the original producer when it alone served that market. This is because each of them would now operate at a lower, and less efficient, volume than did the former company by itself.

Different economies and diseconomies of scale can operate within the same company, and their effects must be considered separately. For example, the now-defunct on-line grocery delivery service Webvan attempted to gain a cost advantage through the use of twenty-six large-scale, automated "pick and pack" warehouses, costing $30 million each. Unfortunately, Webvan never attained its expected sales volume, so its warehousing economies of scale were dominated by the costs of delivering orders to customer. These costs escalated rapidly as Webvan's customers expanded beyond densely populated urban areas into the suburbs.

Diseconomies of Bureaucratization

As the scale of a facility increases, generally so does the workforce required to operate it. The larger the workforce, the more supervisors, coordinators, and managers are required. Since managers usually feel that the number of people reporting to them (often referred to as their *span of control*) ought to be less than some maximum number (generally ten to twenty), organizations tend to grow like pyramids: as the base of the pyramid (representing the number of operators) grows, so does the number of layers of management—each of which usually requires its own retinue of secretaries and assistants. Whereas a 200-person workforce would normally have at most three organizational levels above the operating level (supervisors, department heads, and the facility manager), a 2,000-person workforce typically has four or five levels. As the number of layers in the management hierarchy grows, communication and coordination become more difficult, so additional support personnel are required.

The results are predictable: management costs increase; the organization's response time (to both external forces and internal crises) deteriorates; and people on the plant floor—the base upon which the pyramid rests—lose their sense of identity and personal loyalty, both to each other and to the firm as a whole. It becomes increasingly likely that the information filtering up or down through the organization gets lost or distorted. Worse, first-level supervisors (on whom the operators depend for direction and support) tend to lose some of their credibility and authority if they are constrained by incorrect or incomplete information.

Another danger arises when the number of people working in a facility becomes large relative to the population in its immediate region. As a community becomes more and more dependent on a single facility or company, it tends to become more concerned about that facility's activities. Often this growing sense of dependence can lead to attempts to become more involved in decisions involving the facility. Eventually this process can lead to open hostility.

The end result is that large facilities tend to attract successful unionization efforts (which has the effect of adding another bureaucracy to the organization), as well as increased public scrutiny. There is some evidence that the frequency of labor disputes also goes up.[16] As a result, many companies "cap" the number of people that can be employed at each of their facilities—limiting it, say, to 3 to 4 percent of the working population within a twenty-mile commuting distance.[17]

Diseconomies of Confusion

Although related to the problems of bureaucratization, the diseconomies that fall into this category arise from a different phenomenon: the tendency for a facility, as it grows in size, to be assigned more and more products, processes, and specializations. As mentioned in our earlier discussion of the difference between size and scale, combining dissimilar activities does not reduce complexity; it merely locates them under the same roof. Unless this complexity is managed carefully, the firm can begin to work at cross-purposes, and even dissolve into chaos.

Our observations suggest that the number of people whose role is primarily one of *coordination* across functional or departmental boundaries tends to increase more than proportionally with the number of separately managed units (departments, functions, process stages, etc.) in a facility. This phenomenon is analogous to one often observed in large networks (railroads, truck lines, computer networks, etc.), where the "supervisory costs" (those associated with supervising the operations of each unit) increase in rough proportion to the number of units, but the "coordination costs" (associated with coordinating the operations of different units) increase with the number of *linkages* between units. In general, the number of links between N nodes in a network is equal to $N(N-1)/2$ so, for example, a network with four units (shipping terminals, product lines, process stages, etc.) has six links among them. If another unit is added to the network, the number of links goes up to ten. In other words, its supervisory costs will increase by 25 percent, but its coordinating costs will increase by 67 percent. Going to six units increases the number of links to fifteen. These and related issues are discussed further in Chapter 5, where we address the topic of facilities focus.

Diseconomies of Vulnerability

The larger a facility, and the more responsibilities a company places on it, the more dependent it becomes on its successful operation. Should it experience a natural disaster (fire, flood, earthquake, etc.) or a human one (strike, accident, mismanagement), the company's performance as a whole may be seriously impaired. To reduce their vulnerability to the kind of risks that are associated with putting "too many eggs in one basket," companies often prefer to divide the production of certain critical products, components, or services among two or more separate locations.

In summary, diseconomies of scale are just as real and important as economies of scale, even though they seldom receive equal attention by economists. The management literature, on the other hand, increasingly recognizes that small companies and plants often outperform their larger competitors. Even today, however, too many companies seem to regard diseconomies of scale as the result of a set of factors that "good" managers should somehow be able to overcome.

3.4.3 Increasing Economies of Scale

Managers and economists tend to focus primarily on the kinds of clearly observable scale economies and diseconomies described above. They can see the advantages to making more of something, and the disadvantages of being too big. The advent of information intensive networks, however, has focused increasing attention on a phenomenon that until recently was of little practical interest: the possibility of *increasing* economies of scale. As pointed out in Chapter 1, the value of certain kinds of networks can increase faster than the number of users, because each new user adds potential value to all the existing users. The more companies join a business-to-business (B2B) network, for example, the more opportunities each will have to locate new/better customers and sources of supply. The result is that large networks can become so valuable they discourage the formation of competing networks, resulting in a "winner take all" monopoly. The dominance of Microsoft's Windows operating system, which has induced applications programmers, computer manufacturers, and Internet providers to configure their products and services around it (implicitly "joining" its network of Windows-users), was one of the reasons the United States and other countries instituted antitrust suits against the company.

3.4.4 Optimal Economic Size

The previous discussion of the economies and diseconomies of scale leads naturally to the notion of an *optimal* facility size. The basic concept is straightforward: as the size of a facility increases it can exploit more and more scale economies but it also becomes increasingly subject to diseconomies. That is, the marginal cost curve goes down over some range, then begins to increase. Management's task, therefore, is to select the size that allows it to create and deliver its products and services at the lowest cost, or with the highest total profit (which sometimes leads to a different answer), and at the same time is compatible with the company's values and attitudes regarding competitive priorities, desirable working environments, and risks of various types.

Consider the following highly stylized but illustrative example. Suppose a company's *total* cost of production follows a "six-tenths" rule, as depicted in equation (3-6): $C_P(V) = KV^{2/3}$, and the cost of shipping its (single) product is proportional to the distance in miles: $C_T(m) = k\,m$, where both K and k are constants. The *average* cost of producing V units, therefore, is $C_P(V)/V = KV^{-1/3}$. If one assumes that the demand for the company's product has uniform density d in a circular area around the plant, then V units will service an area of radius $R(V)$ miles, satisfying $V = [\pi R^2(V)]\, d$. The *average* distance involved in transporting products within an area of this radius can be shown to be ⅔ R(V), so the average cost of producing *and* transporting V units is equal to $K\,V^{-1/3} + \frac{2}{3}\,k(V/d\,\pi)^{1/2}$. The V value that minimizes this total cost function can then be found either by graphing it or by differentiating it with respect to V and solving for the value at which the derivative equals zero.

Determining the best size for a facility in practice involves rough approximations, and is usually based more on "gut feeling" than on factual data. It is difficult both because it is hard to distinguish the impact of "bad management" from "wrong size," and because it depends on a number of situational factors, such as the facility's age and its general environment—labor, government, market, competition, and technology—all of which change over time. Over the past several decades, technologies have been developed in a number of industries that permit efficient operation at much smaller volumes than was true in the past. Steel minimills and in-store photographic film developing units are but two common examples of this trend.

In spite of these measurement difficulties, as well as the large number of studies showing little evidence that facility size has much effect on performance,[18] management behavior in a number of industries appears to reflect a belief that there is an optimal economic size for a facility. Most are stated in terms of ceilings on the maximum sales revenue to be generated, the number of workers employed, or the floor space to be provided. One study,[19] for example, found that employment ceilings ranged from about three hundred for firms in highly competitive, labor-intensive industries like apparel, shoes, and metalworking, to six thousand in capital- or technology-intensive industries like transportation equipment and electronics. A few industries, such as aerospace, appeared to have no ceilings at all. Also, as an industry matured its firms tended to use smaller facilities than when it was growing rapidly; some even dismantled facilities they felt excessively large. The reasons managers gave for preferring smaller facilities included the following:

- The confusion, complexity, and difficulty of maintaining control over larger facilities
- A management philosophy as regards employee motivation and incentives, including the maximum number of management layers desired
- The desire to avoid unionization
- A concern about becoming too dominant in the local community

All of these reasons relate directly to factors identified previously and reflect management's need to balance the economies and diseconomies of scale.

The concept of a *minimum* economic size follows naturally from the previous discussion: it is the smallest facility that is competitively and operationally viable. Clearly, that minimum size depends on an industry's technology, the market served, the nature of competition, and several other factors. Schematically, it can be depicted as in Figure 3-5.

In Figure 3-5, strong economies of scale (indicated by the curvature of the total cost curve) occur up to point A. Therefore, the average cost per unit decreases rapidly

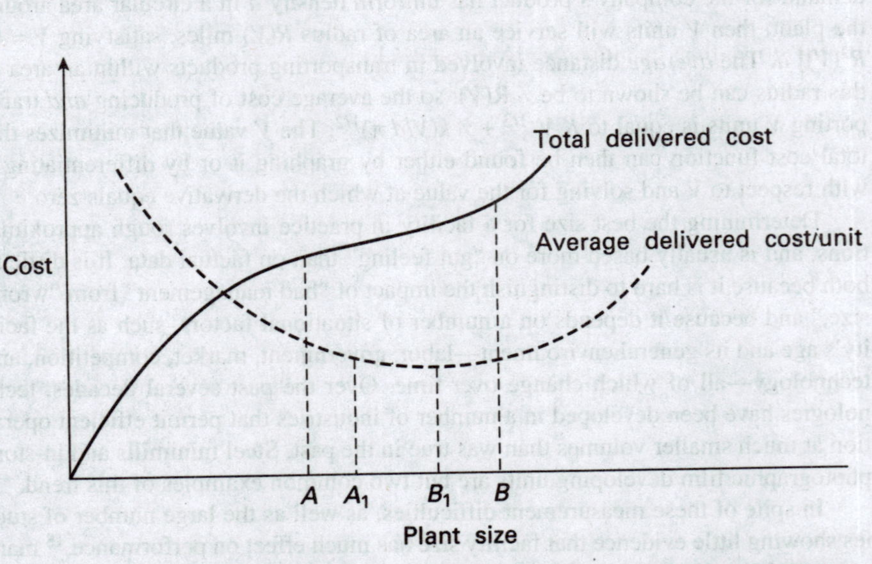

Figure 3-5 Conceptual Presentation of Total Delivered Cost and Average Cost/Unit

up to that point. Between points A and B the total cost curve flattens out, indicating that the increase in the total delivered cost is approximately proportional to the increase in plant size over that range. The average cost per unit, therefore, varies only slightly between A and B. Beyond point B the average cost curve increases, indicating that diseconomies of scale outweigh economies of scale.

Building a facility bigger than size A leads to some improvement in cost, but not a compelling one; any size in the range from A to B is likely to be cost-competitive (or "economic"). Looking only at this cost curve, Facility A can be considered the *minimum economic size.* It may, however, not be the minimum *feasible* size, as only facilities larger than size A_1 may be viable for technological or organizational reasons. For example, equipment may come only in certain sizes, or the cost of certain overhead functions necessitates processing volumes above a certain level. So, while point A_1 might be the minimum *feasible* economic size in this industry, a facility of size B_1 would be the *optimal* economic size.

It should be reemphasized that the minimum economic size is a somewhat elusive concept, because there are no clear breaks in the curve depicted in Figure 3-5. Nor, as discussed in Chapter 2, do all firms compete solely on the basis of delivered cost. Hence, the size of the minimum economic facility is a matter of judgment that depends very much on the individual company and its competitive strategy, just as does the "optimal" size. Studies of plant sizes in the same industry, for example,[20] have shown that the median-sized plant varies widely among different countries and often is substantially smaller than the theoretical minimum economic plant. These studies also suggest that the average facility size tends to increase as the size of the total market in a given country increases, whereas the kinds of technological and economic considerations that tend to permeate discussion of economies of scale are largely independent of market size. These results do not imply that business managers are not "rational" as much as they suggest that when making decisions they take more factors into consideration, and have more ways of influencing a facility's operating costs, than economists give them credit for.

3.5 DEVELOPING A CAPACITY STRATEGY

If strong construction scale economies exist, it probably does not make sense for a company to try to match the growth in demand for its product with a series of small capacity additions. Capacity should be added in larger chunks, which raises the questions: "How big should these chunks be?" and "When should they be added?" In practice, of course, these questions are complicated by a number of related issues having to do with whether the capacity increment is being added to an existing facility or in a separate location, and organizational complications associated with putting it in place and managing it effectively. The sizes of the increments may also be restricted to the capacities of the equipment available from suppliers, or by financial constraints.

To address these questions we return to the three types of strategies depicted in Figure 3-2. In our earlier discussion of capacity cushions we assumed it was possible to keep such a cushion within acceptable limits through careful choice of capacity increments. If scale economies make it advisable to add capacity in rather large chunks (compared with existing capacity), however, it may not be possible to fine-tune a capacity cushion as suggested by the simple ratio of equation (3-2).

Under such circumstances, a sequence like that depicted in Figure 3-6 provides a more appropriate framework for thinking about this problem. If we assume that demand is growing at a rate of G units per year, and that the company is adding capacity in chunks of V units every T years, the company's capacity cushion will be very large immediately after a new increment has been added (at time t_1, for example), so it would be almost impossible for the company to run short during this period. However, the probability of running short approaches 100 percent as time t_2 approaches. The question is: How much of an expected deficit (D) should the company *plan for* toward the end of this period—just before a new increment is added?

The basic tradeoffs that must be made involve, first, the reduction in the cost per unit that comes from adding a larger chunk of capacity; second, the cost of operating an underutilized facility until demand grows to the point when this additional capacity is needed; and third, the costs associated with being short of capacity during the final portion of the firm's capacity replenishment cycle. Therefore, while a firm that overbuilds will be paying both capital (interest) charges for some amount of unused capacity and the costs of maintaining it so that it can be used when it is needed, it might end up with a more cost-effective facility and reduced shortage costs.

Two other factors must also be considered. First, during periods of sustained economic growth many companies run out of capacity and place orders for new equipment at about the same time, causing equipment costs to rise rapidly. Second, building capacity before it is needed increases the risk of technological obsolescence. In many industries, major technological advances have occurred with shocking suddenness. Although this is particularly true of industries that depend heavily on computer or information technology, no industry is immune to such disruption. The technology of plate glass production, for example, was completely overturned in the late 1950s when the float glass process was introduced by Pilkington Glass, Ltd., a relatively small English firm. Similarly, the steel industry was destabilized in

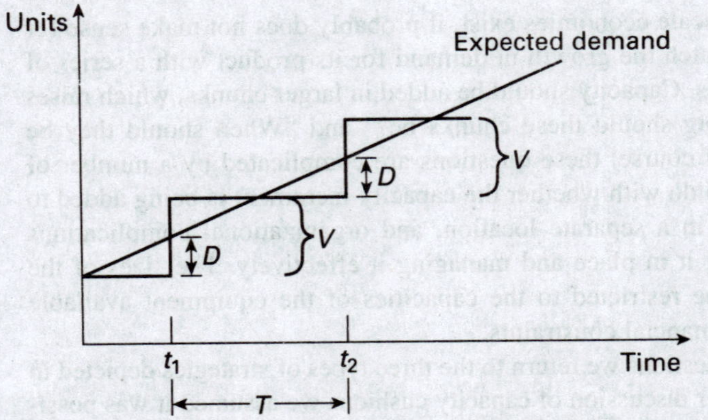

Figure 3-6 Capacity Expansion Strategy over Two Cycles

the late 1980s when relatively small minimills developed the ability to produce cold rolled sheet steel. And the publishing industry, whose technology had been relatively stable for more than 200 years (since Gutenberg, according to some), experienced a series of profound technological changes after 1960 that made desktop publishing possible—and obsoleted much of the industry's traditional equipment and skills.

Assuming that such adjustments can be made properly, and that future costs and demand growth are roughly predictable, one can estimate the net cash flows that will result over time from adding capacity increments of a given size in such a way that the firm keeps roughly abreast of a specified pattern of growth in demand. Then some approach, such as discounted present value (to be discussed in Chapter 9), can be used to aggregate these net cash flows. This provides a means for evaluating the financial impact of any given sequence of capacity increments and demand growth rates. If rather restrictive assumptions are made about the demand pattern and costs, the discounted present value of certain simple capacity strategies can be obtained directly through mathematical manipulation, as described in the Appendix to this chapter.

Given the complexities and uncertainties associated with estimating costs and demand growth, it usually is unrealistic to try to develop a capacity expansion plan by attempting to minimize a single summary measure as described above. Such an analysis is of questionable value unless it takes place within a conceptual framework that guides one in the right direction when assessing alternatives. The next section seeks to provide that kind of general guidance.

3.6 FOUR PHILOSOPHIES OF CAPACITY EXPANSION

The foregoing discussion has sought to separate the capacity expansion decision into its two basic components: (1) the general relationship between capacity and demand, and (2) the amount of the capacity increase that is appropriate at a given time. It also provides some insight into the circumstances that might lead companies to make different choices in different situations. In doing this we employed some simple models to evaluate the impact of different capacity strategies. Those models, unfortunately, require a somewhat unrealistic ability to forecast the evolution of costs and demand, and usually hold all but a few factors constant so as to simplify the analysis. Since most managers are not blessed with such prescience, they generally find it useful to supplement this kind of formal analysis with more intuitive approaches for making capacity decisions. In practice, companies tend to adopt one of the following four different philosophies with respect to capacity expansion:

1. *Don't add capacity until the need for it develops* (Policy A in Figure 3-2). Usually, the need for additional capacity is greatest during periods of rapid demand growth, such as at the peak of a business cycle. Firms that adopt this approach, therefore, often find themselves motivated to expand their capacity at about the same time as their competitors do. These simultaneous expansion decisions not only can drive up construction costs for everybody, they also lead to sudden large increases in industry capacity,

which—because of the delays between the time that orders for new capacity are placed and when it becomes available—often occur at about the time the industry growth rate slackens. Bloated capacity, coupled with slowing growth, then increases the competitive pressure on everyone in the industry. To avoid such boom and bust cycles, some companies prefer an alternative approach.

2. *Try to outguess the market by following a countercyclical strategy.* This approach suggests that the firm should add capacity at a *low* point in the business cycle, when it (as well as its competitors) still has excess capacity. This course of action can result in reduced construction costs for the maverick firm, but it is obviously riskier. The manager who recommends building a plant at such a time is in a very vulnerable position. She becomes, in effect, a "soothsayer"—and subject to all the slings and arrows of that profession. Therefore, some companies adopt a third approach, which represents a modified version of the second:

3. *Build for the long haul* (usually Policy B or C in Figure 3-2). This is analogous, in a sense, to "dollar averaging" in the stock market. It is based on the idea that only a genius or a fool tries to outguess the market on a continual basis, and that it takes only one mistake to have your classification downgraded. Instead, if a company's managers believe in the need for maintaining or increasing its market position in the industry over the long haul, they should simply decide how much capacity will be needed at some comfortably distant point in the future and base their decisions regarding the size and time-spacing of capacity additions around this goal.

Strategies 2 and 3 both launch a firm along a capacity expansion path that may be out of step with the moves of competitors. This can be risky, particularly if the firm is relatively small and a few giants dominate the industry. If the firm "guesses right" by building capacity at the right time, and the industry leaders guess wrong, then the small firm may reap substantial rewards (temporarily, at least). But if it guesses wrong and the leaders guess right, the firm's competitive position—even its survival—may be jeopardized. Depending on how averse they are to such risks, some managers adopt a fourth expansion strategy:

4. *Follow the leader(s).* This strategy is: "Build when they build." If they are right, you benefit too. If they (and you) are wrong together, then neither you nor they will gain any competitive advantage. If the leaders do exercise some control over industry prices, they may respond to their misfortune by raising prices when industry capacity is tight, or by not dropping them when excess industry capacity is available. In either case, your firm will be able to hide under their price umbrella.[21]

Believing that the only thing worse than making a bad strategic decision is to be the only one in their industry to make that decision, many companies follow this strategy. The behavior of airline companies around the world in the mid-1990s provides a telling example: the major airlines were buying new planes, so everybody else did, too. Unfortunately, just as the new planes became available, the recession of the early 2000s and the events of September 11, 2001 resulted in sharply reduced air travel. This led to hundreds of perfectly usable airplanes being mothballed, eventually over 10 percent of the total—mute testimony that following the leaders is not always a winning strategy. Companies that built automobiles, I.C.s, and commercial office or hotel space experienced similar problems during the same period.

The popularity of the "follow-the-leader" approach can create a different kind of problem, moreover, in that its apparent predictability may lead some companies to attempt to "game" the system by trying to outguess the market (a version of strategy 2). Consider the dilemma faced by a major biotech company, which we will call "Biopharm." It was running out of manufacturing capacity for its products in late 2003, at a time when the biotech industry as a whole was experiencing a capacity shortfall. Although in the past Biopharm had not been reluctant to make use of contract manufacturers to supplement its own facilities, its suppliers were reaching the limits of their capacity as well and might not be able to provide the amount of additional capacity Biopharm required *when* it needed it. Therefore, it began making plans to invest several hundred million dollars in building its own new facilities.

Its decision was complicated, however, by a report prepared by a well-known investment bank that indicated that many other biotech firms were also planning to expand capacity for the same reason.[22] If all these companies went ahead with their plans, within the next two or three years (the time frame in which Biopharm expected to outstrip its existing capacity) the industry was projected to have considerable *excess* capacity. This caused Biopharm to reconsider its planned expansion. Could it depend on the rest of the industry to go ahead with their proposed expansions? If so, it probably could avoid making a huge investment in new capacity. But what if several of these other companies—all of whom received the same report—decided similarly to cancel their expansion plans? Instead of simplifying the expansion decision making, therefore, the follow-the-leader approach was forcing Biopharm into an even more complex analysis based on game theory.

In short, pursuing any one of these "philosophies" of expansion over an extended period of time can get a company into trouble. Each expansion situation should be evaluated in light of the company's evolving circumstances, competitive situation, and business strategy as described in the next section.

3.7 INTEGRATING A FIRM'S CAPACITY STRATEGY WITH ITS BUSINESS STRATEGY

Most of our discussion of capacity strategy thus far has made two implicit but critical assumptions: (1) a capacity strategy deals with expansion, and (2) expansion occurs as a *reaction* to increased demand. Although such assumptions provide a useful starting point for capacity analysis, they encourage a mechanistic analysis that is too narrow to deal adequately with the full range of considerations that managers need to take into account. Now we turn to a discussion of how capacity expansion can be used *proactively:* to influence—not simply react to—the demand for a firm's products and thereby support its business strategy.

For example, as suggested in Section 3.3, a capacity increase may both stimulate demand growth (since "supply creates its own demand") and make competitors more hesitant to add capacity themselves. This is because a company that adds new capacity also adds to the total capacity in the industry. As we saw in Section 3.4.1, moreover, if construction costs are subject to strong economies of scale each capacity increment is likely to be fairly large. Smaller competitors may become uneasy about adding to their own capacity after such a large increment has come on-stream, fearing that too much capacity will lead to a price war and other forms of cutthroat competition. Therefore, by continually investing in new capacity and reducing costs a financially strong company may be able to "preempt" its competitors from adding capacity as fast as it does. Not only can it thereby satisfy its own capacity needs, it also may force its competitors to alter their plans.

Wal-Mart, for example, essentially backed into this strategy early in its history. Its large established competitors had already established strong positions in the major U.S. cities, but had largely avoided the smaller southern cities, so Wal-Mart chose to locate stores in relatively small towns in the southeast. Not only did it face little competition from other large discounters in these areas, but also its low prices attracted customers from the whole geographic region around its stores. By the time its large competitors finally began to realize the sales potential in these regions, they found that Wal-Mart had "locked them out": there was profitable opportunity for only one large discount store in a given area—and Wal-Mart was already there.

Over time, as less aggressive competitors' share of industry capacity shrinks and the average age of their facilities rises above those of their more aggressive competitors, they may be driven slowly out of the market, leaving their former customers to the victors—as was the case with Kmart (see Chapter 2) and the large integrated U.S. steel companies. Although the firms that refused to invest may feel that their reluctance to add new capacity was logical (and probably can justify it with analyses showing that such capacity additions would not have met some desired return on investment), a series of such apparently logical steps can lead to disaster. In retrospect, one sees that adding capacity employing up-to-date technology may be justified even when a company already has excess capacity. In a sense, such an investment represents the "ante" that allows a company to stay in the game. We will return to this issue in Chapter 9, when we discuss the "option value" of a facilities investment.

The strategy that is best for a given company depends on a variety of factors, including its size, its tolerance for risk, its industry's competitive structure, and its ability to differentiate itself in that industry (or, alternatively, to influence the behavior of competitors).[23] Managers can delude themselves into thinking that their competitors will respond "rationally" to a preemptive capacity addition. Instead, those competitors may decide to add capacity as well and hope that some other firm—an even "greater fool"—will reduce its capacity or even exit the industry.

As a result of such behavior, a number of industries have found themselves so overbuilt that literally years were required before their members could regain some semblance of profitability. As described in Chapter 1, the long economic boom in Asia seems to have fostered that kind of behavior. It led, first, to massive over investment in several major industries, such as automobiles and semiconductors and, second, to a financial collapse in the late 1990s when the bank loans that enabled those investments could not be repaid.

Fearing that kind of outcome, a company that operates under a severe cost disadvantage, or pursues a different approach to gaining a competitive advantage, may even attempt to insulate itself from the other companies in its industry by adding capacity that is specialized to its own peculiar needs, and build for the long haul. As one example of this kind of strategy, Trus Joist Corporation, a manufacturer of roof and floor support systems for the construction market, has sought to differentiate itself on the basis of high quality and fast delivery of customized products, rather than low cost. It therefore has followed a policy of maintaining production capacity 20 percent in excess of projected peak seasonal demand.[24] This strategy has enabled it to guarantee delivery within three weeks of order receipt—even in peak periods when its competitors' delivery times usually lengthened. To make such a capacity cushion economically feasible, Trus Joist pursued complementary moves in product design, facilities development, and production technology. Rather than taking conventional industry plant size economics as given, or simply following industry practice, it simply did whatever was required to implement its chosen strategy.

The *location* of new capacity also can help support a firm's strategic objectives. For example, building a new factory in a geographical area where you have not previously had any production capability not only improves your ability to service the existing demand for your products in that area, it also brings you closer to existing and potential customers. Your workers and managers become neighbors of these customers, and your proximity encourages relationships that may prove stronger than those established by more distant competitors. In effect, you become an "insider" in that community and thereby reap all the advantages of that position.

NOTES

1. In general, if the probability that a customer arrives during any very short period of time Δt is equal to $(a \times \Delta t)$, then the average time *between* arrivals is $1/a$.

2. For additional information about this specific situation, as well as about more complicated "waiting line," or "queuing," models; see chapter 20 in Wagner (1975).

3. In the case of exponential interarrival and service times, the average time that someone would spend in a stable system (that is, the average number of people in the system stays the same over time) from the time she arrives until she leaves is equal to: $T = 1/(p - a)$. This is because (see footnote 5) the average number of people in a line is equal to the average rate at which they arrive (and, equivalently, depart) times the average amount of time each spends in line: $N = a \times T$, implying that $T = N/a$. In our example, $T = a/(p - a) \times 1/a = 1/(p - a)$.

4. This is because each of the tellers is idle 55 percent (= 1 − 27/60) of the time, which reduces their effective capacity. Even though the faster teller has the same percentage of idle time (= 1 − 54/120), her customers spend less time being processed, and this faster processing time translates into less total waiting time. In fact, if customers arrive at a rate of 54 per hour it is easy to show that a single fast server is better than two normal (that is, 60 customer-per-hour) servers as long as her processing rate is greater than 87 customers per hour.

5. This rather commonsensical relationship between processing throughput time T, WIP, and arrival time a: WIP = $a \times T$ (or, equivalently, T = WIP/a) often is referred to as "Little's Law" after the man who first proved that this was true in general, not just for arrival and processing times governed by the exponential distribution.

6. Recall our example in the previous section, where the probability of a new customer arriving during any second was 1/75; if the average customer spends 5 minutes (= 300 seconds) in the system, one would expect that there would be four customers (= 300 × 1/75), on average, in the system at any time.

7. A 10 percent capacity cushion can be turned around and viewed as a "90 percent capacity utilization," or, more accurately, a capacity utilization of 1/(1.0 + 0.1) = 0.91.

8. Lohmeyer et al (2002).

9. A third step, and one that implies a still slower response time but potentially less committed investment and the attendant risk of losses through product or process obsolescence, would be a capacity cushion in the form of cash or a loan agreement that is specifically earmarked for plant and equipment expansion. If this cash/loan is kept separate, and the procedures for authorizing its use are set up in advance, when demand grows to the point where additional capacity is called for, it will not be necessary to go through the full capital appropriations process in order to authorize construction. Holding capacity in this form slows the response time considerably, to a matter of months or years instead of weeks, but it can speed up the expansion process.

10. This approximation becomes exact if each item's demand is governed by independent Normal probability distributions, or as N becomes very large.

11. See Ono and Rebick (2003).

12. Lohmeyer et al., 2002.

13. In keeping with the terminology used later in discussing "dynamic" economies of scale, or learning curves (see below, as well as Chapter 10), it is sometimes convenient to measure scale economies in terms of the percentage of cost reduction associated with each *doubling* of capacity. In cases where doubling a facility's capacity causes its cost to go up by 60 percent this corresponds to a scale ratio of 1.6/2 = 0.8; that is, each doubling of capacity is accompanied by a reduction in unit cost to 80 percent of its previous value.

14. For example, Stobaugh and Townsend (1975) estimated the contribution of static and dynamic scale economies, among other factors, for 82 petrochemical products over a five-year planning horizon. Their analysis suggested that the impact of dynamic economies exceeded that of static economies by a two-to-one factor. The reductions attributed to greater product standardization alone roughly equaled those from static scale economies. Similarly, other classic studies of the semiconductor (Tilton, 1971) and rayon (Jarmin, 1994) industries found that the most successful competitive strategies were those based on dynamic rather than static scale economies.

15. Kolesar and Blum (1973) demonstrate that the average distance = k (area served/number of plants)$^{1/2}$.

16 For example, Prais (1973) reported that less than 10 percent of the plants employing fewer than 400 workers in the U.K. experienced strikes during 1971–1973, while more than 50 percent of the plants employing more than 5,000 workers experienced strikes during that same period.

17. See, for example, Schmenner (1982), pp. 10–11.

18. For example, Hayes et al. (1988, chapter 6) analyzed the "total factor productivity" of a number of plants being operated by the same company, making similar products for similar customers, and found that plant size had essentially no impact on performance. Looking at organizations in general, Gooding and Wagner (1985) reviewed thirty-one published field studies of the size-performance relationship and reported there was no significant positive relationship between organizational size and efficiency.

19. Schmenner (1982).

20. See, for example, Scherer et al. (1975) and Weiss (1975).

21. Note that both strategies 1 and 4 can cause several companies in an industry to expand capacity at about the same time. A cynical outsider (an antitrust regulator, say) might claim that this is evidence of collusion. It is usually nothing of the sort—any more than a long line waiting to buy tickets for a hit show represents collusion. But how can one prove that one isn't colluding? Usually only with lots of lawyers, time, and money!

22. See "Q-Series: The State of Biomanufacturing," UBS Investment Research, June 20, 2003, which estimated that worldwide capacity for biotherapeutics was about 2,242 kg. in 2003 (slightly less than the total demand anticipated in 2004), but was expected to rise to almost 8000 kg. by 2006.

23. See, for example, Lieberman (1987).

24. See "Trus Joist Corporation" (Harvard Case Services 9-675-207).

Appendix

3A.1 JUSTIFYING THE SIMPLE FORMULA (3-2) FOR ESTIMATING THE AMOUNT OF CAPACITY CUSHION WARRANTED BY A GIVEN COST STRUCTURE AND DEMAND DISTRIBUTION

A number of different kinds of models have been proposed for determining the "optimal" (implying some measure of lowest cost) capacity expansion strategy. We used one of the simplest—the familiar "newsboy" model—in section 3.3.5 to analyze the decision faced by a pharmaceutical company that had to decide how big a facility to build for the production of a new drug. The name *newsboy* derives from the stylized decision faced by a boy who buys a certain number of newspapers at a wholesale price each day with the hope of selling them on the street for a higher price. Knowing that a paper left over at the end of the day is valueless, the newsboy must balance the cost of buying too many papers, and having to throw some away, against the potential lost revenue from not having enough to meet that day's demand. The newsboy's decision is myopic in that he only has to make a decision for the current day; whatever decision he makes will not affect the next day's decision. Moreover, the cost of buying papers (e.g., adding new capacity) is proportional to the amount added—that is, no economies of scale.

If, after deciding to buy n papers, the newsboy begins to consider whether he should buy "one more," he must estimate whether the expected revenue he might gain from selling that paper (which is equivalent, in this case, to C_s in Section 3.3.5) is greater than the cost of buying it (C_x). The probability of selling that paper is the probability that the demand for papers that day is greater than n. Therefore, he should buy that extra paper as long as:

$$C_s \Pr(\text{demand} > n) > C_x \text{ or, equivalently, } \Pr(\text{demand} > n) > C_x / C_s.$$

Alternatively, if he prefers to think in terms of the probability of *not* selling that additional paper, he should keep buying additional papers until Pr(demand < n + 1) = 1 – Pr(demand > n) = $1 - C_x / C_s = (C_s - C_x)/C_s$, which is equation (3-2).

3A.2 MODELS FOR EVALUATING SIMPLE CAPACITY EXPANSION STRATEGIES

A number of somewhat more complicated models have been proposed that incorporate different, more realistic assumptions. Some, for example, include economies of scale and allow one to consider a series of capacity additions (possibly of different sizes) over time. Others make different assumptions as to the nature of the demand-generating process, and whether stockouts result in lost sales or just deferred ones.

In order to make their analyses simple enough to allow closed form solutions, however, attempts to make a model more "realistic" by adding complexity to certain aspects usually forces one to simplify other aspects.[1]

In this Appendix we first consider two of the simplest models,[2] which allow one to evaluate a variety of alternative strategies but limit the ways demand can change over time and ignore any uncertainty about the future.

3A.2A THE DISCOUNTED PRESENT VALUE OF SIMPLE CAPACITY STRATEGIES IN A GROWING MARKET, ASSUMING NO SHORTFALLS IN CAPACITY ARE PERMITTED

If we assume that demand is growing by G units each year, it can be shown that the TDC, or total discounted cost[3] of adding capacity increments of size V at each point in time where demand equals existing capacity (Policy A in Figure 3-2), and assuming these increments cost the same each time, is proportional to:

$$TDC\ (V,G,i) = \frac{C(V)}{(1 - e^{-iV/G})} \qquad \text{(3A-1)}$$

where: $C(V)$ = the cost of a chunk of capacity of size V

i = the annual cost of a dollar's worth of excess capacity (including the cost of interest, maintenance, insurance and obsolescence, but deducting the rate of inflation)

Under the assumption of linear demand growth, the time T between successive additions of capacity will always be the same: $T = V/G$.

On the other hand, if demand is predicted to grow at a constant *percentage* rate, g, each year (rather than a constant amount, as before), and we continue to add capacity at constant time intervals,[4] the size of successive capacity increments will have to increase steadily as the unit growth per year increases. If the cost of any increment is $C(V)$, the discounted cost of adding a capacity increment every T years can be shown to be proportional to:

$$TDC\ (V,g,i,d_o) = \frac{C[V(T)]}{(1 - e^{-(i-kg)T})} \qquad \text{(3A-1)}$$

where: T = is the time between capacity additions

g = is the *percentage* growth in demand each year

i = is the net annual cost of underutilized facilities (as in equation 3A-1),

d_o = is the demand at time period t_o, so that $D(t_o + T) = d_o e^{gT}$

$V(T)$ = is the increase in demand that occurs between time t_o and time $(t_o + T)$, when the first increment is needed.

Since $D(t_o + T) = d_o e^{gT}$, for any value of T after t_o,

$$V(T) = V(t + T) - V(t) = d_o e^{g(t+T)} - d_o e^{gt} = d_o e^{gt}(e^{gT} - 1) \qquad \text{(3A-3)}$$

In general, one could substitute possible values of V into either of these equations and determine the value that minimizes the long-run discounted cost of this kind of capacity strategy. Note that in both cases we have assumed that capacity can be added as soon as it runs out, implying that one can forecast demand exactly over the lead time required to add new capacity (we will relax this assumption, allowing demand to outstrip capacity, in section 3A.2b). If, for example, the construction cost has the form $C(V) = KV^k$, the optimal capacity increment can be calculated directly by solving for T in the following equations:

(a) arithmetic demand growth:[5]

$$(e^{iT} - 1) = iT/k, \text{ or}$$

(b) geometric demand growth:

$$[e^{(i-kg)T} - 1] = (i - kg)\,(1 - e^{-gT})/kg$$

and then using the resulting value to solve for V, using either $V = GT$ (if growth is linear), or $V = d_o e^{gT}$ (if growth is exponential).

A Numerical Example

Assume the following:

i = 15 percent

G = 3,000 units per year

$C(V) = 0.0335\ V^{0.7}$

The calculations of *TDC* for various values of V when demand is growing by a constant amount G each year, in millions of dollars (e.g., a plant having an annual capacity of 12,000 tons costs \$24 million), are as follows:

V	$C(V)$ (in mill.)	$1 - e^{-iV/G}$	$TDC(V,G,i)$ (in mill.)
10,000	\$21.14	0.39347	\$53.72
12,000	24.01	0.45119	53.23
14,000	26.75	0.50342	53.14
16,000	29.37	0.55067	53.34
18,000	31.90	0.59343	53.75

The optimal value of V therefore appears to be about 13,500 tons, or roughly 4.5 year's worth of demand growth. Note, however, that the curve depicting the total discounted cost is quite flat between 12,000 and 16,000 tons, so any value in that range would probably be acceptable, given the roughness of the assumptions made.

3A.2B A MINIMUM COST CAPACITY STRATEGY WHEN SHORTFALLS ARE PERMITTED

Assuming that the company never runs short of capacity in a growing environment is generally unrealistic. This section of the Appendix, therefore, focuses on the analysis of capacity strategies in cases where capacity is permitted to lag behind demand.

It can be shown that if a positive penalty cost (C_p) is attached to every unit that is demanded but cannot be supplied, if demand is growing at a constant amount G per year, and if the cost of an increment of capacity V is given by $C(V) = KV^k$, then the optimal amount of S, the expected shortfall right before a new increment of capacity is slated to become available, is proportional to the ratio (i/C_p): the time value of money tied up in unused facilities divided by the penalty cost per unit.[6] Unfortunately, the impact of the value of C_p on both S and the size of the increment V that should be added is extremely complicated. About the best that can be said is that both V and S increase as the penalty cost decreases; in fact, if C_p is very large, it will not be advisable *ever* to run short of capacity. Therefore, $S = 0$ and the problem reduces to one we discussed earlier (see Figure 3-2, Policy A).

The reason that V increases as C_p gets smaller becomes clear when one remembers that S, the amount of the shortage right before a new capacity increment becomes available, also increases as C_p gets smaller (because the ratio i/C_p gets larger). Therefore, when a new capacity increment is added, it quickly becomes fully utilized because of the pent-up (or redirected) demand represented by S. Since each new increment is soon operating at capacity, there is less cost attached to building a larger increment and reaping the benefits of construction and operating economies of scale. If there is no penalty for not meeting demand (that is, it can be deferred indefinitely without cost), the company will *never* build any capacity and the shortage S will increase indefinitely as demand increases. An example can help illustrate these points.

Using the same assumptions as in the example in the first section of this Appendix: annual growth in demand G = 3,000 tons, the annual cost of underutilized facilities i = 15 percent, an economies of scale exponent of $k = 0.7$, and a plant of size 12,000 tons costing $24 million, then the following values can be shown to be approximately optimal:

Penalty cost per ton short (C_p)	Optimal increment of capacity (V)	Expected shortage (S) just before next increment arrives
$10,000	13,500	0
200	16,000	2,900
100	19,500	6,700
50	30,000	18,000
25	83,000	73,400

As in our previous example, rather large changes in these optimal values have relatively little impact on the total discounted cost function—doubling (or halving) the *V* values given above, for example, causes total discounted costs to increase by less than 8 percent.

Again, the nature of the assumptions involved should be stressed—particularly that demand is growing at a constant, known amount each year, and that the penalty cost is a constant value per unit short, no matter how large the amount of undercapacity or how long it has existed. As emphasized earlier, however, one seldom can compress all the implications of not being able to meet demand into a simple "penalty cost per unit." Customers may decide to take their business elsewhere, to "more reliable suppliers" or "suppliers who are willing to grow with us"; new competitors may be encouraged to enter the business; and existing competitors may mistake your "rationality" for weakness and be emboldened to attack your markets. Therefore, while suggestive, this analytical formulation of the problem and the insights one can gain from it are probably too simplified to be applied directly to an actual capacity decision. This approach, however, does allow one to better understand and approximate the various tradeoffs that must be taken into account when making such decisions, and to examine their interaction in a systematic way.

Other capacity planning models have been proposed that assume demand follows a Brownian motion process (i.e., a Markovian random walk), as is often used to model fluctuations in the prices of equities and other financial securities over time. Under very simple assumptions regarding the cost of capacity additions and the nature of the capacity expansion process, one is able to obtain closed form (albeit, rather complex) solutions.[7]

Finally, one study compared three of the capacity expansion models described in this chapter—the simple "newsboy" model, the model analyzed in section 3A.2A, and a formulation incorporating Brownian motion with drift—with actual capacity behavior in the petrochemical industry. Interestingly enough, this comparison suggested that the simple newsboy model appeared to provide the best overall fit with that industry's experience![8]

NOTES

1. Two comprehensive surveys of a number of such models are provided by Freidenfeld (1981) and Luss (1982).

2. First discussed in Manne (1967).

3. A brief discussion of the rationale for using the discounted present value as a summary measure for a series of cash flows stretching into the future is provided in Chapter 9. This Appendix is intended for readers who have some technical training in that and other quantitative techniques. Further information about the calculations on this and the next several pages is contained in Manne (1967). See, in particular, Chapters 2, 9, and 10.

4. Surprisingly, Smith (1980) has shown that for several different cost functions and demand patterns, adding capacity at equal time intervals is the *optimal* strategy.

5. This is obtained by expressing Equation A3-II.1 in terms of $T = V/G$, differentiating with respect to T, and solving for the value of T at which the derivative is equal to zero.

6. For details, see Manne (1967), Chapter 10.

7. See, for example, Luss (1982), and Dixit and Pindyck (1994), particularly Chapter 11, part 2.

8. Lieberman (1989).

Chapter 4

Determining Organizational Boundaries: Vertical Integration and Outsourcing

4.1 INTRODUCTION

One of the most fundamental strategic decisions every company faces is which activities should be conducted in-house and which should be "outsourced" from various partners and suppliers. Such span of ownership, or vertical integration, decisions ultimately define the very essence of the firm's business model and determine whom it considers its customers, suppliers, competitors, and partners. Moreover, these decisions can have a profound impact on competitive performance.

Unfortunately, managers attempting to develop vertical integration strategies must negotiate their way through advice that seems to change with the times. In the mid-1980s, *BusinessWeek* warned of the dire consequences that would result from extensive outsourcing and even coined the pejorative term *hollow corporation* to describe companies that possessed no manufacturing capabilities of their own. But in a more recent article the same magazine trumpeted the virtues of outsourcing and argued, "The effect on innovation could be huge. Spinning off manufacturing and other non-core functions allows industrial titans to focus new investment where it gets the most bang: on research and marketing."[1]

The relevant issue, as framed in this book, is not whether vertical integration is a good strategy *in general,* or whether outsourcing is better, but *under what conditions* should an organization vertically integrate, and under what conditions should it outsource? In this chapter, we introduce a framework to help one identify the circumstances under which different decisions about outsourcing and vertical integration can create—or undermine—a strategic advantage.

4.2 TRENDS AND EVIDENCE

Historically, many U.S. industries were characterized by a high degree of vertical integration. A pillar of Henry Ford's original system was integration from the production of wood and steel through final auto assembly. IBM was vertically integrated for much of its history, designing and producing its own components and writing its own software. Over the past decade, however, there has been a clear trend toward outsourcing and vertical disintegration. Ford and General Motors have both spun-off major chunks of their parts divisions. Whereas electronics companies once designed and manufactured most of their components and systems in-house, contract manufacturers now account for more than $100 billion in revenues and have been growing at a rate roughly three times that of the overall electronics market. Whereas pharmaceutical companies historically conducted most of their R&D in their own labs, a growing share of their R&D budgets is now spent on alliances with new biotechnology firms, and clinical trials are routinely sub-contracted to specialists such as Quintiles or Covance. A web of alliances characterizes the business models of the vast majority of companies competing in the telecommunications space.

Some observers regard these trends as clear indications of the superiority of extensive outsourcing, and of focusing on a narrow set of "core competences." Vertical integration is deemed to be too costly, inflexible, and distracting for companies competing in fast-paced environments. In particular, manufacturing is often cited as a *nonstrategic* activity that can and should be outsourced. Increasingly, moreover, companies are outsourcing services and high-tech activities such as R&D, product design, accounting, software, and information systems management. One study by Forrester Research in 2003 predicted that U.S. companies would move more than three million of such jobs (representing over $130 billion in wages) out of the country over the next fifteen years.[2]

Recent research and case studies also have tended to focus on the benefits of outsourcing. For example, a study of product development in the automobile industry[3] found that a portion of Japanese automobile companies' advantages in engineering productivity could be traced to their more effective use of suppliers in the product development cycle. Japanese automobile manufacturers have tended, on average, to be less vertically integrated than their American and European competitors. Moreover, they typically encourage their suppliers to take on greater responsibilities for the design and development of components and subsystems. In their attempts to become more cost competitive and flexible, U.S. automobile companies have followed these foreign competitors' lead by outsourcing a far greater percentage of their component design and manufacturing needs. Dell Computer, the most consistently profitable personal computer maker over the past ten years, neither designs nor manufacturers any of the internal components that go into its machines, focusing strictly on basic design, configuration, assembly, and distribution. Yet, it has crafted an enormously well coordinated set of linkages with its suppliers that provide it unmatched flexibility in that industry.

The chief advantage of outsourcing lies in the economies of specialization (or "focus"), as discussed in Chapter 2. By focusing its resources and attention on a narrow set of activities or competences, an organization should be able to perform them better than an organization that spreads itself more broadly. In addition, outsourcing enables a company to take advantage of suppliers' lower factor costs (particularly wages), and thereby harness the power of market forces to drive down costs and/or improve quality. Or, it might simply exploit a supplier's willingness to accept a lower rate of profitability and/or return on assets than its own shareholders demand.

However, as with most strategic decisions, the issue is more complex than it first appears. There are also costs and risks associated with outsourcing, and many counter-examples to the outsourcing success stories. Drawing general conclusions about the relative success or failure of vertical integration, based on what is working or not working in a particular industry at a particular time, is dangerous. There are many examples of industries where the relative merits of vertical integration versus outsourcing have changed over time. The disk drive industry provides a good example. Until the late 1970s, vertically integrated firms dominated that industry. Nonintegrated disk drive firms then gained the upper hand from the late 1970s through the early 1990s. Today, vertically integrated disk drive manufacturers appear to be gaining competitive advantage once again.[4] Similarly, in the early 1980s, IBM was widely praised for outsourcing both the microprocessor (to Intel), and the operating system (to Microsoft) of its then-fledgling Personal Computer. By the early 1990s, the strategic wisdom of that choice began to look quite suspect.[5]

In the 1980s, a new breed of semiconductor companies, such as Weitek and LSI Logic, which specialized in chip design and contracted out all manufacturing, were widely touted to provide models of the "new" I.C. industry. This view changed in the early 1990s, however, when manufacturing capacity in the industry became tight and the fabless firms found themselves unable to line up contractors to meet their delivery commitments. Fabless design firms also discovered that some of their customers were deciding that it was just as easy for them to perform their own design in-house and secure their own manufacturing contractors. In contrast, Intel (clearly among the most successful I.C. manufacturing companies over the past fifteen years) has long pursued a strategy of vertical integration. It carries out all major operating functions—R&D, manufacturing, and marketing—in-house, and is vertically integrated into chipsets and subassemblies. Similarly, during the early years of the twenty-first century, Samsung emerged as a market leader in several high technology markets, including digital cell phones, LCD displays, DRAMs, and large-screen TVs, while following a vertical integration strategy. Its CEO, in fact, asserted, "If we get out of manufacturing, we will lose."[6] On the other hand, Taiwan Semiconductor Manufacturing Company (TSMC), which specializes in contract manufacturing, is one of the fastest growing semiconductor companies in the world.

It also should be recognized that vertical dis-integration by one set of firms may, on the flip side, lead to *increasing* vertical integration by those firms' suppliers. For instance, Solectron, the largest contract manufacturer of electronic products, initially confined itself solely to production. As electronics companies changed their strategies to focus on final systems design and assembly, Solectron saw an opportunity to vertically backward into the design of components and subassemblies. Recently, it has chosen to integrate further into procurement and logistics. In the drug industry, contract research organizations (CROs) initially only conducted clinical trials under contract to drug companies. Increasingly, however, CROs are vertically integrating into other aspects of the drug development process, including process development, manufacturing, and even earlier stage pre-clinical development. Even the Internet world is not as "virtual" as it seems. Amazon, for instance, has built up a vast infrastructure of warehouses and logistical operations to support its online retail operations.

The complexities of a vertical integration strategy can be seen in the January 2000 merger of America On-Line (AOL), the largest Internet subscriber service, and Time Warner, an owner of cable services and major news publications. At the time, Steve Case, founder and chairman of AOL proclaimed that such a merger would provide AOL with access to the cable network it needed to offer high speed broadband Internet services and a vast array of content (e.g., CNN online). Other media companies had followed a similar strategy of acquiring "content" providers. It is important to note, however, that vertical integration through merger is just one possible way for a company like AOL to access broadband cable infrastructure and content. A plausible alternative might have been to form some type of long-term contractual alliance with Time Warner that fell short of outright acquisition. Licensing content and contracting for access to a cable infrastructure was another alternative. Each approach, of course, involves its own set of challenges and risks. As AOL-Time Warner and other media companies have learned, acquisition is only the first step toward integration; getting all the various units to work together can be a more serious challenge. Alliances and licensing, however, also involve potential risks. For all the challenges of getting newly acquired units to cooperate, it may be even more difficult to achieve cooperation across independently owned companies.

These examples suggest that one-best-way prescriptions about vertical integration are misleading. There are situations where vertical integration is more appropriate than outsourcing, and conversely where outsourcing is more appropriate. In the next section, we lay out a framework to help managers develop appropriate strategies around vertical integration.

4.3 FRAMING VERTICAL INTEGRATION AND SOURCING DECISIONS

Traditionally, vertical integration decisions have been framed in terms of "make" versus "buy." Although the methods in practice varied, the basic idea was to take each component part or service and conduct a thorough analysis of the costs and risks of making versus buying it. One of the chief problems with traditional make-versus-buy analyses was their failure to take into account some of the critical strategic issues that could not be measured purely in terms of production and delivery costs.

One approach, known as value-chain analysis,[7] takes a more activity-based approach. The value chain framework divides a firm into the set of major activities (e.g., inbound logistics, operations, outbound logistics/distribution, sales and marketing, procurement, technology development, and administrative infrastructure) that it uses in creating value. Under a value chain lens, vertical integration decisions are not viewed in terms of which *parts or services* to make or buy, but rather, in terms of the underlying *set of activities* to undertake internally. For instance, under traditional make-buy analyses, an automobile manufacturer might weigh the total costs of producing brakes internally versus the price and related logistical costs of purchasing them externally. With a value chain analysis, all of the distinct activities (design, machining, assembly, logistics) required for brakes are first identified and the costs associated with each are assessed. The purpose of value chain analysis is to get a picture of the total system costs, and the implications that "make" decisions have on those costs. At first glance, this does not appear to be very different from traditional make versus buy. However, value chain analysis takes into account that the same set of activities (e.g., design) might support multiple products, and outsourcing one product can have cost implications for others that share resources. Value chain analysis also allows one to consider the cost impact of linkages across products (scope economies), as well as across activities in the value chain when making vertical integration decisions.

Value chain analysis is limited, however, by the fact that it is concerned almost exclusively with the configuration of activities that minimizes *cost,* given a firm's overall competitive strategy. Only issues associated with economies of scale and scope are taken into consideration, so value chain analysis provides little guidance about *where* specific activities ought to take place (i.e., inside or outside the firm). Value chain analysis also is limited in that vertical integration decisions are essentially decisions about *ownership,* but activities are not "owned" in any meaningful sense. What is owned are the underlying assets, resources, and capabilities that make those activities possible.

This suggests that the most appropriate units of analysis for vertical integration and outsourcing decisions are resources and capabilities. Moreover, it implies that a decision to outsource an activity is also a decision to enable a supplier or partner to invest in and own a certain set of underlying assets, such as intellectual property, physical plant and equipment, and relationships with other suppliers. Conversely, a decision to integrate vertically is a decision to invest in and own those assets oneself. An asset-based approach to vertical integration is particularly relevant today, given the increasingly important role of intellectual property, know-how, information, reputation, and other intangible assets in achieving competitive advantage.

In the next section we lay out a framework for vertical integration that focuses on the choices between the assets and capabilities a company should own and those that it can access through relationships with partners, customers, and suppliers.

4.3.1 What Are the Choices?

As stated above, vertical integration and outsourcing essentially offer different approaches for gaining access to an asset of some type. Vertical integration involves ownership of the assets, whereas outsourcing involves some type of contractual relationship with another entity (a supplier, customer, or partner) that owns the asset. In reality, there is a continuum of governance structures and contractual arrangements into which firms can enter to gain access to assets,[8] as depicted in Figure 4-1.

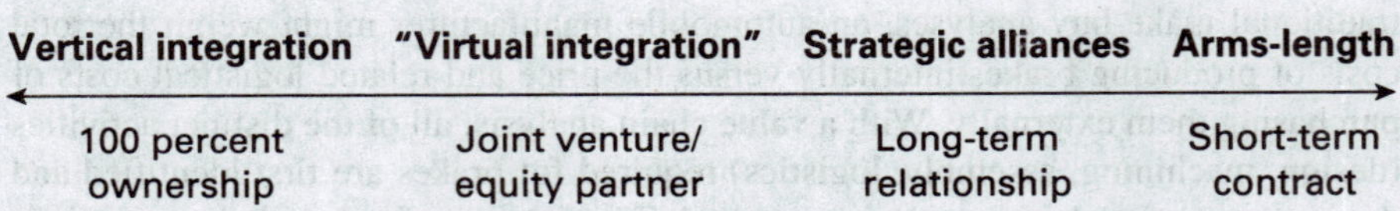

Figure 4-1 Continuum of Governance Structures

Obviously, the labels in Figure 4-1 do not convey the true complexity and nuances of arrangements seen in practice. There are, for instance, an enormous number of variants of "long-term" relationships, as well as of "joint ventures." The purpose of the diagram is to illustrate that when making vertical integration choices, companies are choosing along a continuum with some types of relationships being "closer" to full vertical integration and others being "closer" to a pure arms-length exchange.

How do relationships differ along this continuum? Posed another way, what difference does it make if a company owns an asset, jointly owns it with another party, or does not own it at all but instead contracts with someone who does? One way to think about these choices is to consider differences in how they govern decisions, information flows, and activities between the two parties. Full ownership of a set of assets (as in vertical integration) clearly provides some degrees of freedom in terms of control. Ownership entitles the company to establish operating strategies and policies, hire and fire employees, settle internal disputes, write contracts with other entities, and make detailed operating decisions about how those assets are used (do we ship order A or B today?) without seeking the permission of an outside party. This does not mean the company can do whatever it wants. Its management is still constrained by legal and regulatory boundaries, as well as by market forces and the realities of organizational inertia. However, with ownership comes a certain degree of discretion,[9] including the right to cede operational decisions to another party. Ownership also has legal implications of terms of the organization's ability to lay claim to certain physical and intangible properties, such as trademarks, patents, and copyrights.

At the other extreme are arms-length or "spot-market" transactions. These do not involve any type of vertical ownership of assets. In a spot-market, two parties having no common ownership contract with one another to buy/sell a product or service at an agreed upon price and time. The ultimate mechanism of control in an arms-length relationship, aside from legal action to enforce the contract, is that failing to perform as expected may result in losing future business.

Many types of relationships lie somewhere in between pure spot-market exchanges and complete ownership. The term *virtual* integration is sometimes used to connote a relationship that involves a very high degree of coordination and cooperation between two independent firms. Several studies of the automobile industry, for example, have found that Japanese companies have tended to engage in longer-term, more cooperative "partnerships" with selected groups of suppliers. Other examples can be found in the organization of supply chains in the retail sector, such as Wal-Mart's close links with its suppliers. In general, these partnerships include extensive sharing of information, cooperative design efforts, and implicit (if not explicit) promises that the relationship will be enduring. Supply partners sometimes even "control" operations within the other's organization. For example, as described in Chapter 5, Procter & Gamble controls the inventories of its products in Wal-Mart stores.

At first glance, virtual integration appears to encompass the best of both worlds. It provides a higher degree of coordination and information exchange than arms-length contractual relationships while avoiding some of the organizational costs (including bureaucracy, overhead costs, and loss of incentives) characteristic of many captive supply situations. It is not surprising that virtual integration has been trumpeted by some academics and practitioners as *the* best way to organize both supply chains and product development.

The fact that virtual integration encompasses many of the best features of both "markets" and "vertical integration" does not, however, mean that it is universally superior to those alternative arrangements. While it may contain the "best of both worlds," there is no reason to believe that it can avoid the worst of both as well. For instance, committing to a long-term partnership with a supplier will almost certainly reduce a company's flexibility to change suppliers quickly if the supplier does not perform as expected or technological changes render the supplier's capabilities obsolete. One study,[10] for example, has found that long-term supplier commitments have made Japanese disk-drive manufacturers slower than their U.S. counterparts in adopting new component technologies.

Likewise, while partnership-type relationships enable a greater degree of close coordination than can be provided through arms-length relationships, they may not provide the degree of integration found within well-functioning organizations. Consider the "Power PC" alliance between Motorola, IBM, and Apple Computer. When first announced in 1991, the alliance set out to challenge the dominance of Intel and Microsoft in personal computing by developing a high-performing PC microprocessor, a new operating system, and a host of complimentary chips and software applications. Virtually all of the collaborative projects failed amidst conflicts among the three partners and the difficulties of coordinating the development of a complex system across three very different organizations. In June 1998, IBM and Motorola announced the dissolution of the alliance.

The point of this example is not that alliances are bad; rather, like vertical integration, arms-length agreements, and other governance structures, such alliances are appropriate under some conditions, but not all. Different choices along the vertical integration arms-length relationship continuum are warranted under different circumstances.

One of the challenges of assessing vertical integration strategies is that they are rarely "all or nothing" decisions. At any point in time, a company may be vertically integrated into certain assets, manage others through joint ventures and alliances, and utilize arms-length market exchanges for others. Take as an example Dell Computer, which does not perform any electronic component manufacturing. Its personal computers contain microprocessors, memory chips, graphics cards, disk drives, and other components designed and manufactured by outside suppliers. Like other PC manufacturers, it licenses the Windows operating system from Microsoft. However, Dell has vertically integrated into a set of assets that support its "make to order" operating strategy. For instance, Dell has created a set of proprietary logistical processes that range from the design of its Web page through its information systems infrastructure (a process that has proven difficult for others to imitate). Importantly, it also owns the data about what people are buying and in which combinations. It also has vertically integrated into final assembly facilities that have been designed to efficiently produce in lot sizes of one. Finally, while it outsources components, Dell utilizes longer-term relationships with its suppliers and links them into its information system to support quick response.

Thus, it is not meaningful to say that Dell is "not vertically integrated." Instead, the apparent power of Dell's operating strategy is that it is vertically integrated into a set of proprietary assets that give it a competitive advantage over other PC manufacturers that have vertically integrated into a different set of assets. As a result, it has been able to reduce its total inventory to less than four days of sales (compared with the average high-tech company's fifty days), and actually receives payment from a sale to a customer before its suppliers require payment for supporting that sale![11]

Careful examination reveals that most companies' vertical integration strategies operate at a fine level of granularity. Consider the following examples:

- Sun Microsystems designs the "SPARC" chips used in its high performance workstations, but subcontracts the fabrication of those chips to specialized chip makers (while maintaining ownership of the intellectual property).
- A pharmaceutical company may purchase information on genetic targets from a genomics company, contract with a specialist in combinatorial chemistry for rapid synthesis and screening of candidate compounds, and even utilize a contract research organization to conduct clinical trials, but retain ownership of the intellectual property (patents, experimental data, trademarks, etc.) of the drug that eventually comes to market.
- Internet companies that provide search capabilities, like Yahoo!, may utilize (under license) proprietary search algorithms and software developed by third parties. A Yahoo! user may access content created and owned by media companies like Time Warner, but delivered through a server infrastructure owned and operated by a company like Akamai.
- It is common in franchise businesses (e.g., McDonald's) for the franchiser to maintain ownership of the brand name, the process technology, and even the land used by the franchises. Franchisees are "independent" businesses, but they do not own many of the key assets used in their operations.

4.4 FACTORS INFLUENCING VERTICAL INTEGRATION DECISIONS

Deciding among vertical integration, *virtual integration,* or a more arms-length relationship, requires consideration of three sets of factors: (1) capabilities/resources; (2) coordination requirements; and (3) strategic control and risks. All three are examined next.

4.4.1 Capabilities/Resources

One of the first issues a company must face in developing a vertical integration strategy is a need to assess its resource constraints and the limits of its organizational and operating capabilities. In some cases vertical integration is not feasible because the company simply lacks the financial resources to acquire or build the required assets. This is an extremely common situation for start-up companies. In the biotechnology industry, the enormous costs of building a clinical development infrastructure has led many companies to rely on contract research organizations or partnerships with established pharmaceutical companies for drug development. However, such constraints are not limited to start-ups. Consider one of the largest manufacturers in the world: Boeing. Because the development of a new generation aircraft costs upwards of $10 billion, even a company as large as Boeing must rely on an extensive array of subcontractors to develop and manufacture major portions of the aircraft. Boeing focuses most of its resources on the aircraft's design, the manufacture of its avionics, and its final assembly.

Capability limits also play an important role. No company can do all things well. Intel is clearly a very technically skilled organization with vast financial resources, but it has chosen to let other organizations develop the equipment it uses in manufacturing semiconductors. Indeed, Intel even makes substantial investments in applied research focused on advancing the technology of photolithography, but it does this by funding research carried out by universities and outside partners. One of the reasons for such a strategy is that the design of semiconductor devices requires a very different set of technical skills than does equipment design. In wireless communications, developing mobile phones that can access the Internet has become a major area of activity. A company like Motorola is adept at developing such devices, but it lacks capabilities to develop the tailored Web browsers and Internet user interfaces needed to make such a product useful. Given the readily available software development skills and installed user base of companies like Yahoo!, Netscape, or Microsoft, a partnership with one of them would be a more feasible strategy. In arenas such as the Internet or pharmaceuticals, technological advance is so rapid and so dispersed among organizations that it is simply infeasible for any one enterprise—no matter how large or skilled—to be the world's expert at everything. Companies like Microsoft, Intel, and Sun have entered into literally hundreds of licensing and co-development agreements with niche players and start-ups that are developing new information technologies.

The *time* required to build or acquire a certain set of capabilities can also impose a "hard" constraint on a company's vertical integration strategy. In the short-term, a company might simply be unable to vertically integrate regardless of its strategic desirability. In rapidly evolving environments, the time required to build or even acquire certain capabilities may be prohibitive. In those cases, the company needs to craft alternative arrangements, such as virtual integration.

Just because a company *can* do something, however, does not mean that it *should.* Investing in building one new set of capabilities detracts resources and management attention from other potentially high-value possibilities. And conversely, just because a company lacks the capabilities in the short term to vertically integrate does not mean that over the long run it should not be building those capabilities.

To get a sense of direction about where vertical integration might be most valuable, one needs to consider the other two sets of factors: coordination, and strategic control and risks.

4.4.2 Coordination Requirements

Historically, the arguments for vertical integration were rooted in the need to carefully coordinate activities and assets. Henry Ford created a fully integrated supply chain in 1920s because his production system required a high degree of design and scheduling coordination between raw material processes, component fabrication, and final assembly. The need for coordination in and of itself, however, does not automatically warrant common ownership of assets. Financial markets, like the New York Stock Exchange or the NASDAQ, provide a tremendous amount of coordination between buyers and sellers who operate at arms length.

Vertical integration, longer-term partnerships and alliances, and arms-length relationships all can achieve various degrees of coordination. Each, however, is more effective at addressing different types of coordination problems and challenges. In designing a vertical integration strategy the objective is to choose the governance structure that best addresses the *specific types* of coordination that need to be provided.

Coordination requires information exchange. The Internet has clearly been a powerful force in enabling organizations that are geographically dispersed to quickly and efficiently exchange certain types of information that are vital for coordinating their operations. This has had two effects. In some cases, it has enabled companies to forge tighter operational links with their suppliers and customers. Dell Computer, as discussed earlier, has utilized the Internet very effectively to achieve a high degree of coordination throughout its supply chain without extensive vertical ownership. In this case, the Internet has facilitated "virtual integration." In others, as described in Chapter 1, third-party intermediaries have attempted (with mixed results) to use the Internet to spawn spot-markets.

In the Internet age, the term *information* tends to convey an image of the kind of data that can be stored, processed, and communicated electronically. Information comes in different shapes and forms, however, with important implications for supply-chain strategy. An important distinction must be made between information that can be codified and interpreted in a standard way, and information that is tacit and requires specific experience or capabilities to interpret.[12]

Many types of coordination problems in operational settings require information that can, in fact, be fairly well codified and interpreted in a relatively unambiguous way. Examples would be information on costs, prices, quantities and dates of specific models shipped and delivered, inventory levels, defect rates, and production schedules. Many elements of the design of certain products (such as layout, part specifications, materials, interfaces between components, etc.) can be codified in blueprints and CAD models. Similarly, *standardized module interfaces* can codify much of what designers of different parts of a system need to know about each others' designs in order to coordinate their tasks. One of the advantages of codified information is that it can be shared relatively quickly and efficiently. New information technologies are making it even quicker and more efficient to share codified information across large numbers of people and organizations spread over wide distances. When different companies can quickly and easily share requisite information (via documents or electronically formatted data), vertical integration is not necessary to achieve coordination.

In retail supply chains, for example, better coordination between different parts of the supply chain—from producer through retailer—can significantly reduce the costs of stock-outs and excess inventories,[13] as will be discussed in Chapter 5. Adjusting production to reflect what is actually selling at the store level requires that information about retail sales and inventory levels be rapidly shared throughout the supply chain. Because the relevant information can be codified and captured, processed, and transmitted electronically, better coordination in retail supply chains does not require vertical integration. It can be achieved across separate companies using appropriate information technologies (e.g., point of sale terminals) and contractual agreements delineating operating policies that must be followed. It is no coincidence that the trend toward outsourcing has accelerated in recent years as the Internet and other technologies that facilitate information exchange became available. The new technologies have improved the coordination efficiency of outsourcing.

Similarly, if part designs and specifications can be codified precisely and conveyed in standard ways, coordination between R&D and manufacturing may not require vertical integration.[14] It is not that coordination between R&D and manufacturing isn't necessary, rather, that such coordination can be achieved through the exchange of well documented and standardized information between the organizations. This may help to explain why the contract manufacturing of printed circuit boards in the electronics industry has become such a big business. Printed circuit boards designs, while very complex, can be fully specified in writing and transmitted electronically to suppliers. Modular product designs, in which the interfaces between different components or subsystems are well-specified and standardized, are also likely to enable sufficient coordination without vertical integration.[15] In analyzing the disk drive industry, nonintegrated firms appear to have gained competitive advantage during the period when disk drive designs became modular. Standard interfaces embodied all of the information required by designers of different subsystems (heads, disks, controllers, etc.) to coordinate their work. Since there was no need for extensive communication between designers of different parts of the system, there was no advantage to being vertically integrated.[16]

There are many types of situations, however, where the information required for close coordination is not easy to capture in codified format, or to interpret properly, because it is idiosyncratic and "tacit." A good example would be the interface between R&D and manufacturing in biotechnology. Genetically engineered processes are enormously complex. Moreover, they are relatively new and many scientists in the field describe them as "more art than science."[17] Many of the nuances of these processes are not well understood, even by the most highly skilled R&D and manufacturing personnel in the industry. As a result, it is extremely difficult to describe the process in its entirety via documentation. Processes developed at laboratory scale often do not work as expected (if at all!) when transferred to a full-scale production facility.

Uncovering the reasons for these problems typically requires extensive experimentation and iteration of the process. In addition, there are subtle but important interactions between the product and the process technology. Minor alterations in the process can have a significant impact on the quality and character of the product being made. As a result, process development requires extensive coordination and communication between process R&D and manufacturing. Successfully transferring the process from the lab to the plant requires R&D personnel to go to the plant, often for an extended period of time, to set up the process and supervise initial test batches. Process problems encountered at large scale may require changes to the process (e.g., reaction temperatures), the production environment (e.g., a new piece of equipment), or both.

Can one carry out such an endeavor via a partnership with an outside contractor? The answer is certainly yes. Indeed, in the biotechnology industry there are firms that specialize in producing products for others. However, when process development and manufacturing are organizationally separated the costs and time required to develop, transfer, and scale-up a new production process, are likely going to be higher than when an organization completely controls both activities.[18] This is because manufacturing processes and techniques within the industry to date have been fairly idiosyncratic. Different firms have evolved different approaches based on their prior experiences. As a result, when biotechnology firms engage manufacturing subcontractors, both organizations must come up to speed on the details and nuances of each other's technology. This is quite a different situation than printed circuit board production, where design information can be rapidly transferred to subcontractors, and the details of the production process are not critical to the design of the board.

Difficulty in exchanging information may also be due to the fact that certain kinds of information require interpretation. Consider a statement by an automobile executive that the company's next new model should be "exciting." What this means in practice, and how it will manifest itself in a design, probably will be very different depending on whether the company is Volvo or Porsche. The experience of the designers within each of those companies enables them to interpret such information within specific frames of references about past projects. A joint team—of designers from both Porsche and Volvo, say—might have more difficulty coordinating their efforts than would a team *within* either one because of the lack of shared experiences. And, it would almost certainly be highly ineffective to attempt to coordinate the efforts of such a joint team using arms-length directions.

Where the critical information about design requirements or production tends to be tacit and idiosyncratic, advanced information technologies do little to solve coordination problems. When information is tacit, coordination generally requires extensive face-to-face communication on an ongoing basis. It may also be facilitated by prior experience in working together and a common base of understanding (e.g., "we learned from our last project that certain kinds of design do not work well with that supplier's manufacturing capabilities"). Although this kind of information can be communicated across firm boundaries, it does raise the investment required in a supplier relationship. As a result, under these circumstances companies tend to develop relationships with other organizations that lean more toward the vertically integrated end of the spectrum.

All these factors explain why many companies that sought to reduce costs by outsourcing IT functions or software development to low-wage countries have not received the benefits they expected. First, the productivity of their foreign suppliers' people is generally substantially less than that of U.S. workers, and this productivity gap is increased by the aforementioned problems of communication. Monitoring and managing the supplier's activities, moreover, often involves considerable travel back and forth, and sometimes extended stays in both directions. On top of these ongoing costs, there are considerable up-front expenditures associated with selecting the vendor and managing the transition of the work to be done, which sometimes requires that foreign personnel come to the United States to be trained (during which time they must be paid U.S. wages and expenses). Finally, there are hidden costs associated with the fact that foreign workers are generally less willing to point out potential problems in a job specification or offer suggestions for improving it. The accumulation of all these factors often results in a company saving less than 25 percent from outsourcing, even though its foreign supplier's wage rate is one-forth or one-fifth of that in the United States.[19]

In contrast, by integrating vertically a company can create specialized organizational processes (e.g., a project management system) and structures (e.g., a project team organization) that facilitate coordination and information exchange. In addition, vertical integration can facilitate the kind of learning that occurs through repeated interactions between particular groups or functions (e.g., design and manufacturing, manufacturing and marketing, component design and system design) or functions.[20] Such learning will be most valuable when the critical knowledge lies at the interfaces of functions and technologies.

4.4.3 Strategic Control and Risks

The third facet of vertical integration strategy concerns the implications of outsourcing for strategic control and risks. Creating a highly efficient supply chain does not guarantee that your company will extract any additional profits from it. A good example would be the supply chain characterizing most of the personal computer industry. It could be argued that IBM, by adopting a modular design approach and by outsourcing key components of its first personal computer (PC), helped to create a highly efficient supply chain for the PC industry. Outsourcing major subassemblies, such as printed circuit boards and even final assembly, has often been an efficiency-enhancing strategy. On the other hand, the eventual result of IBM's decision was that companies selling PCs today capture only a small share of the added value of the entire PC supply chain. In contrast, two "component" suppliers—Intel and Microsoft—appear to have captured the lion's share of total supply chain profits. One of the implications of the term *strategic* control is that supply chains need to be designed not just to create value, but to *capture* that value as well.

Vertical integration also is warranted when one seeks to avoid two types of strategic risks: the risk of "lock-in" associated with a high costs of switching partners,[21] and risks related to the leakage of intellectual property. Switching costs are created when either one or both parties must make investments that are valuable only in the context of a specific relationship. Economists sometimes refer to these as *relationship-specific* or *transaction-specific* investments.[22] Because relationship-specific investments, by definition, have much less value when used outside the context of a specific relationship, they create a major cost of switching for either the supplier, the buyer, or both, and thus provide a rationale for longer-term, more integrated sourcing strategies. Various examples of relationship-specific investments are described below.[23]

Lock-In from Specialized Contracts and Partnerships

One of the chief benefits often cited for not being vertically integrated is the ability to switch suppliers or partners. The ability to switch partners creates flexibility to respond to changing technologies and also can act as a credible inducement for improved supplier performance. However, switching is a two-edged sword. If you are free to find another supplier or customer, your partner presumably has the same luxury. In some cases, the cost consequences of switching partners are minimal. For instance, if your organization uses a commodity product, it may not matter precisely who your supplier is on any given day, as long as the product meets some agreed-upon quality specifications, price, and delivery requirements. A supplier that fails to perform can quickly be replaced, and the impact on the operation is likely to be negligible. There's no need, for example, for a bread manufacturer to redesign its ovens to accommodate a new supplier's wheat flour. Likewise, because the supplier does not have to tailor its wheat flour to the needs of any specific customer, the cost of changing customers is also relatively low.

If switching costs are inherently low, as in the case of a commodity product or service, outsourcing enables a company to take full advantage of the benefits of the market-based arrangements discussed above. Indeed, companies that face low switching costs may prefer to use very short-term contracts with suppliers or make spot-market purchases. These mechanisms provide the most flexibility, with little risk other than the financial risks associated with broad-based changes in market prices. Indeed, these are exactly the kind of circumstances where Internet-based exchange markets are likely to work best.

Many companies enter into long-term contracts to hedge against the risks of rising prices, but it should be recognized that such long-term contracts carry their own risks. Hedging, after all, cuts both ways. If the market price of the good or service in question falls, a long-term supply contract leaves the buyer saddled with comparatively higher costs. For many types of commodity products, such hedging can generally be achieved more efficiently via separate contracts bought and sold in the relevant future market.

Certain Internet services also create the potential for lock-in. For instance, once Internet users establish e-mail accounts and have e-mail addresses, they prefer not to change e-mail providers. The same would be true of services such as online bill paying. It certainly is not impossible to change e-mail providers or online bill paying services, but many users prefer to avoid the set-up costs and the "hassle" of doing so. As a result, such services have the potential to *capture* customers and their Internet traffic, and traffic is a valuable commodity on the Internet. There are two ways whereby a portal might provide such access to e-mail. One is to create its own e-mail service; the other is to give users access to the e-mail service of a third party. The second option is clearly much riskier, because that third party then gains partial control over the portal's traffic. If users' loyalty is attached to the provider of their e-mail rather than to their portal, the portal will become dependent on the e-mail provider. It should be no surprise, then, that both Yahoo! and AOL offer their own e-mail services, rather than making third-party services available to their users.

One might argue that such risks can be mitigated by long-term contracts. Such contracts do offer more protection than short-term contracts, but they may not offer fail-safe protection. Given the considerable uncertainties and complexities associated with most business activities, it is virtually impossible for any long-term contract to specify all the possible contingencies that might arise. In addition, there are some behaviors that are impossible to specify and enforce in a contractual relationship (e.g., a promise to use "best efforts" to accomplish a certain task). Most long-term agreements, by necessity, leave significant room for renegotiation and adaptation as circumstances and technologies change. Of course, entering into such a renegotiation when facing the high cost of switching partners is not an attractive bargaining position to be in.[24]

Even where two companies have a history of good working relationships and have established a high level of trust, unforeseen circumstances can create vulnerabilities. A good example of this happened to Crown Equipment Corporation, described in Chapter 2. For thirty years the company contracted all of its industrial design requirements to a single industrial design firm, Richardson-Smith (RS). The relationship between these two companies was both deep and successful. Not only did a senior executive at Crown and a cofounder of RS develop a very close professional and personal relationship over this time period, but also the Crown engineers and the RS designers worked extremely well together. One Crown engineer commented that the designers from RS were viewed and treated no differently than "internal" members of project teams. This changed, however, when RS decided to sell out to a much larger, European-based design firm that had a different approach to doing business. Ultimately, Crown decided to create an in-house design department to provide the "Crown-specific" design capabilities the new design firm was no longer willing to satisfy.

Although we do not want to downplay the role of trust and mutual cooperation (these are critical!), companies need to recognize the cruel reality that a majority of partnerships end in "divorce." Even where trust and a spirit of cooperation exist, the story of Crown demonstrates that unforeseen events like a change in ownership or shifts in personnel can have a significant impact on a relationship. As companies grapple with new strategic conditions, their interests and those of their "partners" may diverge. McDonald's franchising strategy proved to be absolutely critical during the company's rapid growth phase, but its franchisees also have limited the company's flexibility to alter its strategy in the slower growth, more competitive environment in which it now finds itself.

Lock-In from Specialized Assets

There are other situations where the nature of investments in technology, plant and equipment, or intangible assets causes the cost of switching partners to be so high that a company is effectively locked in to a particular partner over some time period.

Historically, many of these cases of "lock-in" have occurred when companies made investments in physical assets that were geographically colocated, as when a supplier built its plant across the street from a major customer. Good managers recognize the risks of making such specialized investments without strong contractual safeguards, such as "take or pay" contracts and buy-out provisions.

High switching costs and lock-in also can occur when the only assets at stake are intangible. Consider Internet portals such as Yahoo! or AOL—locations on the Internet that serve as entry points for large amounts of traffic. A portal is more valuable to users of the Internet when it has access to a rich array of ancillary services and content (e.g., shopping, news, travel agencies, e-mail, on-line banking) and can direct users to the information they seek. Of course, the value of that portal to the *providers* of ancillary services is directly proportional to both the traffic it garners and its ability to steer users to specific services. A portal thus serves as a middleman between the millions of Internet users on the one hand and the thousands of providers of ancillary services on the other.

In order to join a portal's group of providers of ancillary services and content, an on-line retailer might agree to pay a small percentage of the customer's total purchase to the portal that originated that customer. Relationships between portals and content/ancillary service providers, however, are potentially subject to switching costs. For example, by having access to a large number of providers of content and ancillary service, a portal both makes itself a more attractive site to visit for Internet users and increases its value to providers of content and services. The problem for content and service providers is that as a portal garners a greater and greater share of Internet traffic, the bargaining power between the portal and the content/service providers begins to shift. When a portal is small, it needs to attract content and service providers. However, once it has established a reputation as a site with plenty of good content, and has created a highly loyal user base, its providers of content and services become vulnerable to losing access to the portal. This puts the portal in a position where it can extract higher prices from those providers.

In the next two sections we explore in greater detail the impact that both physical and intangible assets may have on lock-in.

Physical Assets

In some contexts, a company is required to customize a physical asset to the needs of a specific customer, or accommodate the inputs of a particular supplier. Perhaps the best example of this occurs with the tools, dies, molds, and fixtures used in the production of physical components. For instance, the dies used to stamp the fenders of 1999 Ford Explorers have essentially no value unless they are used to produce fenders for a 1999 Ford Explorer. A supplier cannot redeploy that asset to produce, say, a fender for a Ford Escort or a Toyota Corolla, or any other vehicle. Specialized physical investments are sometimes also needed in chain retail stores or restaurants that seek to provide the same unique physical environment or layout (Benihana Restaurants and McDonald's are good examples). Investments in specialized physical assets create the same kind of risks discussed above for location-specific investments. Once made, such investments leave a company with a severely weakened bargaining position in future negotiations, since the assets cannot be easily switched to alternative uses. Long-term agreements can help mitigate these risks. Another common strategy that is short of vertical integration is *quasi-integration,* whereby one partner will own the specialized physical assets required by the other. In the automobile industry, for example, it is common for OEMs to buy the specialized tools and fixtures used by their component suppliers. This transfers risk from the supplier to the OEM. In some franchise arrangements, the franchiser retains ownership of the property and physical infrastructure, while all other assets of the franchise are owned by the franchisee.

For certain types of assets, value is almost strictly a function of *location.* Consider the coaxial cable commonly used for cable television. A 100-foot strand of coaxial cable has virtually no value by itself. However, when that piece of cable is located between a cable modem in a home and a broadband communications infrastructure, that same asset now becomes worth a monthly revenue of $50 to $100. A company that has invested in such location-specific assets is in a position to extract significant value from those that require access to them. This might help explain why Internet service providers such as AOL were willing to pay significant premiums to acquire cable operators. Conceivably, they could have negotiated long-term contracts with cable operators to "lease" access to their cable infrastructures, but such arrangements would have been very risky for them over the long term. The cable operator is the owner of the scarce, difficult-to-imitate asset (the physical cable running to the home), and would be in a position to extract significant concessions from the service provider.

Intangible Assets

The most valuable specialized assets in a buyer-supplier relationship are often intangible. These include both reputation and intellectual property, such as technology and *know-how.* For instance, if a supplier is responsible for developing critical technologies used by a specific customer, it can gain specialized expertise about that customer's unique needs. This customer-specific knowledge is only valuable to the supplier if it continues to have a relationship with that customer. Likewise, the buyer might find it costly to switch to alternative suppliers that have general expertise, but lack the detailed, specialized knowledge of its unique needs.

For example, Japanese automobile producers have relied relatively heavily on their suppliers to develop and design component and subsystems. These suppliers were required to develop "Honda-specific" and "Toyota-specific" design expertise. This may help explain why Japanese automobile companies have traditionally relied on longer-term relationships with their suppliers, rather than the short-term, arms-length contracting approach traditionally used by U.S. auto companies. Relying on suppliers to develop customer-specific expertise poses risks to both suppliers and customers, however. Without some sort of guarantee that the relationship would be long-term, a supplier probably would be hesitant to invest significantly in "Honda-specific" expertise. Similarly, an OEM like Honda would be hesitant to trust its supplier to develop unique capabilities to which it would need access in the future. Interestingly, as U.S. automobile companies began to emulate their Japanese competitors' strategy of outsourcing more design work to suppliers, they also have had to move away from their traditional contracting approach in favor of longer-term partnership-type agreements. There is evidence, however, that this change has proven difficult to implement. During the late 1980s, General Motors asked its suppliers to invest heavily in R&D for new GM products, which required relatively substantial GM-specific investments. When Ignacio Lopez became head of worldwide procurement for GM in 1992, however, he adopted a "get tough" approach with suppliers, leading to the termination of many supplier agreements. If buyers cannot make credible long-term commitments to suppliers, vertical integration may be the only way to foster investments in specialized design capabilities.

Buyers also can be vulnerable if they come to rely on suppliers for specialized technology or expertise. The chief reason PC manufacturers have not, in general, been highly profitable is that they are essentially locked-in to Intel and Microsoft. Both companies have developed specialized capabilities and intellectual property that have made it extremely difficult for other suppliers to enter the market. Given the need to maintain compatibility with the prevailing technology standard, PC manufacturers have had little choice but to buy their microprocessors from Intel and their operating systems from Microsoft. The PC industry is a good example of a situation where lock-in occurred over time as a prevailing standard emerged. When IBM's PC division first decided to buy microprocessors from Intel and to license its operating system from Microsoft, it had the upper hand in the bargaining. It could have chosen other operating systems (e.g., the 8-bit CP/M or even a proprietary system) and microprocessor designs (such as Motorola's architecture). By choosing Intel's design and Microsoft's operating system, however, IBM made them the industry standard. As more software and peripherals were developed for the Intel-Microsoft standard, it became increasingly difficult for PC manufacturers, including IBM, to seek alternative sources of supply for microprocessors and operating systems.

The presence of specialized learning curves (the result of the dynamic economies of scale described in Chapter 3 and further discussed in Chapter 10) also can create lock-in. Consider a company that wants to outsource the production of a certain part. If it has several possible suppliers, it should be able to strike a fairly attractive deal, so outsourcing ought to be quite attractive. However, the decision is more complicated if the manufacturing process is complex and subject to a significant learning curve. As the chosen supplier gains experience and comes down the learning curve, the company's flexibility to switch suppliers drops significantly. Although other suppliers might continue to be interested in becoming a supplier, they will be increasingly less attractive options in the future because they would have to start at the top of the learning curve. As shown in Figure 4-2, after producing n units the experienced supplier has a cost advantage of $(C_0 - C_n)$ over the alternative supplier. In extreme cases, alternative suppliers may drop out of the market completely and thus be unavailable at a later date. Although an initial contract may have spelled out a way to share the gains from learning-curve cost reductions, when it comes time to renegotiate the contract the experienced supplier will be in a strong bargaining position, as the buyer's next best alternative is to purchase from an inexperienced, higher cost supplier. Only by vertically integrating into the production of

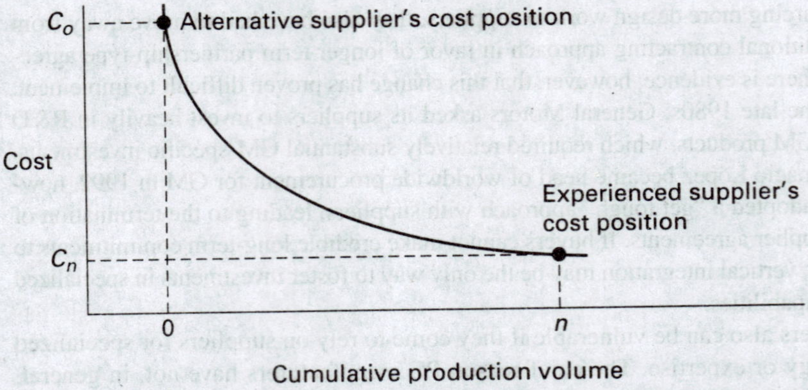

Figure 4-2 The Cost Advantage of Accumulated Experience

the component would the company be able to capture 100 percent of the learning curve related cost savings.

Corporate reputation and brand image can also be critical specialized assets, as well as a source of tension between suppliers and buyers. Consider a fast-food restaurant chain such as McDonald's. The reputation of its brand is a critical specialized asset of the McDonald's Corporation. Wherever people see a McDonald's restaurant, they have certain expectations about the quality of its food and service, so when McDonald's sets up a new franchise, it effectively licenses the franchise operator's use of this critical asset. A franchisee that, for short-term gain, cuts corners on food quality, service, or restaurant cleanliness potentially destroys the long-term value of the McDonald's brand name. This is one reason why companies that license the use of their name to others, or set up franchises, do not rely strictly on arms-length contracts. McDonald's' franchise agreements, for example, specify in detail the quality standards that franchise operators must meet and the operating procedures they must follow. McDonald's further assures quality by carefully controlling the raw materials and ingredients used by its franchises. It also has the right to inspect franchise operators to ensure that they are meeting the terms of the agreement. Thus, although the franchise operators are "independent," they contractually give up some of their operating independence to McDonald's Corporation. Through such agreements a company is able to achieve some of the control aspects of vertical integration while keeping some of the incentive properties of market-based approaches.

4.4.4 Protecting Intellectual Property

We have stressed throughout this book that intangible assets—in particular, capabilities and intellectual capital—are perhaps *the* most important operating assets in companies today. Possession of proprietary technology and methods, data about customers, collective organizational knowledge about how to operate facilities at high efficiency, and other forms of intellectual capital can make a dramatic difference in a company's performance over time. Almost all companies recognize the value of their intellectual capital and seek to protect it vigorously from unintended leakage.

Vertical integration and outsourcing strategies play an important role in a company's overall approach to protecting intellectual capital. Outsourcing and other kinds of collaborative arrangements between companies often involve exchanges or transfers of intellectual property. In such exchanges, contractual stipulations are generally made about how such property can be used. If the intellectual property in question can be readily identified and protected contractually, collaborative arrangements and outsourcing present no particular risks of leakage. For instance, Microsoft sells its Windows operating system to PC manufacturers without fear that competitors will reverse engineer their system and begin selling their own versions of Windows. Microsoft has created strong intellectual property protection around Windows through both formal legal mechanisms (e.g., copyrights) and by not revealing the source code that underlies the system. With such well-delineated boundaries around its intellectual property, Microsoft is able to collaborate with a host of other companies, including PC manufacturers, software vendors, and component suppliers (like Intel), without losing control of its technology. Vertical integration into computer hardware—the strategy pursued by Apple—is simply not needed to extract the full value of its technology.

In contrast, where intellectual property is less protected legally or inherently easier to copy, then organizations must be careful when entering into collaborative relationships that require such knowledge to be revealed. For example, through operating experience a company may learn many valuable "tricks" about how to optimize a given process. This kind of production process knowledge can be quite valuable, but is often difficult to patent. As a result, companies often prefer to rely on laws relating to "Trade Secrets" to protect such knowledge. Collaboration or outsourcing that exposes such knowledge to outside parties creates risks. Trade-secret law does protect leakage, but generally is not as strong as patent protection. Moreover, if the knowledge concerns an operating process, subsequent "infringement" might be quite difficult to detect because the process is hidden behind corporate walls; in contrast, infringements of product technology are exposed in the marketplace.

In particular, it might be very difficult in practice to prevent intellectual property from diffusing if an outsourcing partner also has relationships with an organization's competitors. Although a contract may stipulate very specific fields of use, and prohibit the application of the technology to the partner's other projects, unintentional spillovers may be difficult to prevent, even when supposed "Chinese Walls" are in place. Consider a situation where the same production facility produces both your product and a competitor's product, or where an R&D team carries out projects for both your firm and one of your competitors. If intellectual property is not well protected by legal mechanisms, and is inherently easy to imitate, vertical integration can be a useful way to inhibit unintended leakage.

Another issue concerns the degree to which parties can identify and delineate boundaries around "who owns what" ahead of time. In the biotechnology field, for example, Amgen and Johnson & Johnson collaborated on the development of a drug called Erythropoetin, and divided the rights to its commercialization according to its therapeutic uses. They wound up in a legal dispute over whether use of the product for "*pre*-dialysis" patients should be considered part of the "dialysis" market (which was allocated to Amgen) or to the "all other markets" category (which was allocated to J & J).

Technological change also can blur clear boundaries between agreed upon fields of use. For instance, Intel and AMD signed an agreement in 1976 giving AMD perpetual rights to all of Intel's micro-code for use in "microcomputers." In 1987, Intel terminated the agreement arguing that a *microcomputer* was different from a *microprocessor,* so AMD had no right to Intel's microprocessor code. The result was an eight-year legal battle, costing hundreds of millions of dollars, that eventually ended in a compromise settlement.

4.5 SUMMARY

This chapter has attempted to provide a framework that will help managers make appropriate choices about organizational boundaries and the structure of supplier relationships. This framework is summarized in Figure 4-3. For illustrative purposes, we list only the polar extremes—recognizing, of course, that the distinctions indicated are a matter of degree rather than kind.

This framework provides a richer and more useful way to think about vertical integration than the simplistic exhortation to "focus on core competencies." We do not wish to undercut the value of the notions of core competencies and organizational focus, which were emphasized in earlier chapters. The challenge, as we stated there, is to choose the appropriate *level* of focus. Under certain conditions, as described in this chapter, an extremely narrow vertical focus may not always be the most strategically advantageous operating posture. Problems associated with coordination, strategic control, and intellectual property can dissipate the benefits of "sticking to your knitting."

A company, moreover, needs to distinguish between what its core competencies *are* today and what they *should be* in the future if it is to succeed in the long-run. This framework provides a useful way to think about the kinds of capabilities that it may find it valuable to have in-house, and depicts the set of conditions under which an organization with a narrow vertical focus may need to build new internal capabilities in specific technologies, activities, or regions.

Intel is an excellent example of a company that recognized this distinction in the mid-1980s.[25] During the early 1980s, Intel found itself being squeezed out of the market for memory chips (a device it had invented) by such Japanese competitors as Hitachi, Fujitsu, and NEC, which had nurtured stronger capabilities to develop and rapidly scale-up complex semiconductor manufacturing processes. It was clear by 1985 that Intel's "knitting" lay in its ability to design complex I.C.s, not in manufacturing or developing processes for more standardized chips. As a result, faced with growing financial losses, Intel was forced to exit the memory chip market. As Intel shifted its focus to the microprocessor market (again, a device that it had invented), it retained a powerful lesson learned from the memory market: it was essential to develop strong capabilities in process development and manufacturing.

A "stick to your knitting" strategy would have suggested that Intel focus on the design of microprocessors and use outside partners to manufacture them. Given the close connection between semiconductor product development and process development, however, relying on outside parties for manufacturing would likely have created significant costs in terms of longer development lead times. Over several years during the mid- and late-1980s, Intel invested heavily in building world-class capabilities in process development and manufacturing. These capabilities are one of the chief reasons it has been able to maintain approximately 90 percent of the personal computer microprocessor market, despite the ability of competitors like AMD and Cyrix to "clone" Intel designs relatively quickly. Expanding its capabilities beyond its original core capability of product design has been a critical ingredient in Intel's sustained success.

The idea of core competence must be balanced against the problems of coordination, strategic control, and intellectual property protection that we have discussed in this chapter. A careful analysis of these factors is needed to determine areas where an organization may need to build new operating capabilities, as described in

	← Vertical integration	Arms-length relationships →
Coordination	"Messy" interfaces; adjacent tasks involve a high degree of mutual adaptation, exchange of "tacit" knowledge, and learning-by-doing. Requisite information is highly idiosyncratic.	Standardized interfaces between adjacent tasks; requisite information is highly codified and standardized (prices, quantities, delivery schedules, etc.)
Strategic control	Very high: significant investments in highly durable relationship-specific assets needed for optimal execution of tasks. Investments cannot be recovered if relationship terminates. • Co-location of specialized facilities • Investments in brand equity • Large proprietary learning curves • Long-term investments in idiosyncratic R&D programs	Very low: assets applicable to businesses with a large number of other potential customers or suppliers
Intellectual property	Unclear or weak intellectual property protection Easy-to-imitate technology "Messy" interfaces between different technological components	Strong intellectual property protection Difficult-to-imitate technology "Clean" boundaries between different technological components

Figure 4-3 A Framework for Organizational Boundaries

Chapter 2, not simply apply existing capabilities most effectively. Ultimately, an organization's vertical integration strategy is an integral part of its longer-term "capability-creation" strategy.

NOTES

1. "Souping Up The Supply Chain," *BusinessWeek* (August 31, 1998): 110–112.
2. See "Outsourcing Abroad Draws Debate at Home," *The Wall Street Journal,* July 14, 2003, p. A2.
3. Clark and Fujimoto (1990).
4. Christensen (1998).
5. Chesbrough and Teece (1996).
6. "The Samsung Way," *BusinessWeek* (June 16, 2003): 56–64.
7. See Porter (1985).
8. In the economics literature, this range is often referred to as the "markets" versus "hierarchies" continuum; see Williamson (1975, 1985).
9. Grossman and Hart (1986) use the term "residual rights of control" to formally characterize this discretion. In their model of organizational boundaries, vertical integration is determined by which parties have residual rights of control.
10. Chesbrough (1998).
11. See "Does Dell Stack Up?" *CFO-IT Magazine* (Fall 2003): 39–43.
12. The distinction between "codified" and "tacit" knowledge is discussed in Chapter 10, and its implications for vertical integration are explored in Teece (1976, 1982).
13. Fisher et al. (1994).
14. Teece (1986).
15. See Teece (1986) and Chesbrough and Teece (1996).
16. Christensen et al. (1998).
17. See Pisano (1996) for a more detailed discussion of biotechnology processes.
18. Ibid.
19. See "The Hidden Costs of Offshore Outsourcing," *CIO Magazine* (September 1, 2003): 60–66.
20. See Chapter 8 for additional discussion of this issue. Pisano (1996) provides evidence of learning across projects and the importance of repeated interactions.
21. See Williamson (1975), Monteverde and Teece (1982), and Ghemawat (1991) for fuller discussions of lock-in and the impact of switching costs on vertical integration decisions.
22. Joskow (1987), Williamson (1975).
23. These categories are from Williamson (1975).
24. Williamson (1975), Teece and Monteverde (1982a, b), Joskow (1987), Pisano (1989, 1990).
25. Information from this section drawn from "Intel-PED (A)," (Harvard Business School case #693-056), and "Intel Corporation: 1968–1997, (Harvard Business School case #797-137).

Chapter 5

Designing and Managing Operating Networks

5.1 INTRODUCTION

Most companies either belong to a multi-unit network as a supplier or/and customer, or operate one of their own (manufacturing plants, warehouses, retail stores, service centers, etc). Although the traditional multiplant manufacturing network is the kind that comes most readily to mind, networks can be even more important in the operations of service companies. Some of the most important strategic decisions a retail company makes, for example, concern the size, scope, number, and location of its stores. New technologies, moreover, are encouraging the expansion of many networks. This is clearly evident in the banking sector, where automated teller machines (ATMs) now are not only considered part of a retail bank's network, they can be even more critical to its competitive success than its network of traditional branches.

The configuration of an operating network has major implications for its cost structure, asset utilization, delivery lead times, stability, responsiveness, flexibility, customer service, and its company's financial performance. Like all other aspects of a company's operations, however, there is no "one best way" to organize and manage a network. Different network structures have different strengths and weaknesses, and a given network cannot do everything equally well. Designing an operations network, therefore, is like designing any operating system, in that choices must be made regarding its (1) *structure* (the number, location, scope, and specialization of the units belonging to the network); (2) *infrastructure* (degree of centralization, policies, incentives, measures and controls, etc.); and (3) *ownership and governance* (who owns which facilities/units). Chapter 4 addressed ownership and governance issues, and this chapter will focus on the first two.

Networks are ubiquitous in today's world. In addition to the familiar facility and communication networks, there are an increasing number of nontraditional kinds, including collaborations to facilitate purchasing, ownership, product design, marketing, and servicing. Companies are driven to join networks, despite their natural fear of losing some control over their operations, because they recognize that a group of firms, if connected appropriately, are often able to accomplish tasks that are beyond the capabilities of any single participant. Surprisingly, as various kinds of networks are examined from different perspectives, it increasingly appears that they all share certain characteristics and principles. According to one knowledgeable observer, "… no matter what organizational level we look at, the same robust and universal laws that govern nature's webs seem to greet us."[1] One of these principles is that the sensitivity of a network to external shocks depends largely on the way it is structured. In particular, networks that have multiple "hubs" (components that have unusually numerous and rich connections to other components) appear to be more stable than those whose components are roughly equal in power and influence.[2]

5.2 THE RATIONALE FOR MULTIFACILITY NETWORKS

Before launching into issues relating to the design and operation of a multiunit operation, it is useful to ask: Why might a company not want to do everything (all operations for all customers) under one roof? Indeed, much of our coverage of capacity decisions in Chapter 3 made the implicit assumption that an operation's capacity was (or could be considered to be) centralized in one location. In some contexts the answer is relatively obvious: There are limits to how far a customer will travel to a retail outlet, for example, so total revenue growth beyond a certain limit requires expanding the number of branches. Similarly, if after-sales service is critical, companies generally find it advisable to provide a large geographically dispersed network of local service centers, even if the original product was manufactured centrally. In other contexts, however, the rationale might be less obvious and involve a strategic choice. For example, most manufacturing companies start out with a single plant to supply their chosen market. At some point, however, the capacity of the original plant is reached or new products are introduced and the company faces perhaps its first major strategic operating decision: Should it expand capacity at the original site or add another facility?

There are a number of benefits for keeping operations centralized, which argue for expanding the original facility. First, up to a certain point, it may be possible to "spread the overhead" (take advantage of the underutilized fixed costs already in place) and exploit economies of scale, as described in Chapter 3. Second, keeping production "under one roof" enables a company to make use of the unique capabilities and skills developed there, and avoids the challenge of transferring technology and operating know-how to new sites. Third, centralization avoids the logistical complexity associated with coordinating production and information flows across sites.

As a given facility is assigned responsibility for more and more activities and as it expands its geographic coverage, however, its management becomes more and more difficult. Moreover, the problems associated with providing it with the necessary materials and skills, as well as of transporting products to, and/or servicing, remote customers, become increasingly complex and costly. As discussed in Chapter 3, beyond some volume level (its *minimum efficient scale*) the marginal costs of production may start to increase. Moreover, the *size* of a facility (that is, its total capacity or output) is not the same as its *scale*. Scale involves the repetitive performance of *similar* activities, so tends to decrease as the number of products and processes assigned to a facility—which usually requires an expansion in its size—increases. As described in Chapters 2 and 3, each new product or process tends to bring with it additional costs (often hidden, but nonetheless real) associated with managing the added operational complexity.

To reduce this complexity, Skinner[3] argued that a given facility ought to limit the scope of its operations in some way so as to facilitate the ability of its managers to concentrate all their attention on a narrow set of operating goals, problems and processes. This allows them to focus on attempting to achieve *exceptional* performance within a limited range of activities rather than merely adequate performance across a wider range. In Section 5.3, we discuss how to think about some of the different ways a facility can be focused.

This conjecture has been tested in a variety of contexts with sometimes ambiguous results, possibly because (as described below) it is possible to focus a given operation in different ways, and measuring any given form of focus can be tricky. As a result, while some studies have not produced evidence that focus improves performance, others have demonstrated substantial improvements and suggested that the result depends on the specific kind of focus applied.[4] In addition to a number of anecdotal reports of the successful application of focus at individual companies,[5] at least two consulting firms have reported major improvements due to focus in broad studies of several hundred factories around the world.[6]

Dividing up all the tasks involved in a total operation into more easily managed packets and assigning them to separate operating units usually results in the creation of a multifacility operating network. Such a network not only enables a company to expand its geographic reach, it allows it to take advantage of multiple markets, labor pools, skills, and cost structures. For instance, New York-based banks with large credit card businesses seldom locate their customer service call centers in New York. Instead, they typically place such centers in smaller towns in rural areas—and sometimes even in other low-cost English-speaking locales, such as India and the Philippines. Multiunit operations also can help a company cut overall costs by reducing its logistic and transportation costs. If such costs constitute a significant fraction of total costs (as for bulky products), a company is motivated to build plants closer to the geographic markets it serves. Alternatively, it can locate warehouses geographically so as to optimize logistic costs and response times.

However, as a company adds facilities in pursuit of such benefits, it also finds itself facing significant new management challenges and issues. Creating a network does not necessarily *reduce* the problems of managing a large, complex organization. It simply *replaces* one set of problems with another that may be easier to deal with—or may lead to disaster. Despite the "network effect" described in Chapter 1, which holds that the value of an information-based network increases roughly with the square of the number of participating units, *operating* networks (like other operating systems, as we saw in Chapter 3, Section 3.4.2) also experience *dis*economies as their size increases. As a network expands, for example, not only do the units composing it lose some of their sense of community and commitment, but also it becomes increasingly difficult for a central group to monitor and control their activities. Many networks attempt to deal with these problems through a version of the focus concept: they divide their facilities into a small number of semi-separable "clusters" (often around geographical lines), each under its own management but with a common hub.

A network's overall effectiveness therefore requires not only that each individual facility within it be managed effectively, but also that they all be buttressed with effective overall network policies and strategies. Unless a company deals with these issues proactively the advantages of multi-facility operations can be quickly dissipated in a tangle of complexity and confusion.

5.3 DESIGNING THE MULTIFACILITY NETWORK: *STRUCTURE*

In Chapter 2, we described how the structure and infrastructure of an operations organization tends to affect its performance along different competitive dimensions. In this section we similarly discuss various alternatives for structuring an operations *network,* and suggest how different forms of network structure are likely to influence its behavior, management, and performance. In the next section we will provide a similar discussion of the way different infrastructural decisions affect network behavior and management.

When an operations organization decides to divide up its activities and assign different sets of activities to separate operating units—thereby creating an operations network—it faces three key structural decisions: *how many* different facilities should be utilized (and, relatedly, how big should each be), where should they be *located,* and how should each be *specialized?*

5.3.1 Number and Size

Managing a single very large and complex facility may be more difficult than managing a smaller, simpler one, but the coordination and control of a large number of separate facilities can be even more difficult—and such problems tend to increase with their number. A network composed of a few large facilities, for example, may be easier to coordinate and better able to exploit economies of scale than one composed of a larger number of smaller facilities. However, small, focused facilities also have important advantages. Being easier to manage (and therefore easier to staff with effective managers), they tend to be more flexible and responsive to changing market demands and quicker to adapt to new technologies and approaches. As discussed in Chapter 2, moreover, the advantages of focus—including simple, lean overhead structures, easy communication, and rapid learning that comes from performing a reduced number of tasks repetitively—can often lead to better quality and lower overall costs.

5.3.2 Location

Once an organization decides to create a new facility, it must decide where that facility should be located. Near major markets or customers? Near sources of raw materials? Close to low cost labor, or to pools of special skills? Each approach has advantages in different situations—and disadvantages in others. For example, a producer of high tech electronic equipment may decide to locate the design of its products near a technology center, but perform their final assembly in a low cost area such as China. This may reduce its direct labor costs, but cause overhead costs to increase—both at the corporate level, which has to coordinate the necessary production schedules and shipments, and in the assembly plant itself because of problems associated with locating and importing the necessary components, a lack of reliable transportation, and/or a requirement that ownership (and often management) be shared with a domestic company. It also requires more investment in logistics inventories, lengthens the total production throughput time, and complicates the process of incorporating design changes in the product. Finally, finding good local managers is often difficult, and bringing in expatriate managers is usually very expensive. On the other hand, while most of these problems would be considerably reduced if the company located the assembly facility near a center of technology such as Silicon Valley, the high labor rates there might undermine its products' competitiveness.

5.3.3 Specialization

This brings us back to the notion of operations "focus"—simplifying the management and increasing the effectiveness of a large, complex operation by breaking it up into subsets, each comprising a relatively narrow range of activities, and dedicating a separate facility to each subset. An operations organization can do this in a number of different ways, however. One common way is by *product line:* each facility is assigned to produce a restricted set of similar products (similar in the sense that they require compatible process technologies and management systems). Specializing in this way requires some system for satisfying the needs of a customer that requests a number of products or services that are produced by different facilities. Later we will characterize this as a form of *horizontal* network structure, in that different facilities are capable of supplying customers directly and do not require large amounts of inputs from their "sister" facilities in order to perform their tasks. As an example, the Medical Products Company[7] produced a wide range of hypodermic syringes for the European market in several different facilities. Small syringes used for insulin injection were produced at a plant in Ireland, while larger syringes were produced at other plants in Spain and Ireland, and less expensive "two-piece" syringes were produced at a different Spanish plant as well as one in Germany. Syringes were sent to customers either directly from the plants, or indirectly via a European warehouse.

A common variant of a product-specialized structure is to further organize facilities around *production volumes.* Facilities that produce large volumes of relatively standardized products usually require different equipment and management systems than those that produce a large number of different products in small volumes. Rather than combine the production of both low and high volume products in the same facility, therefore, many companies prefer to assign them to separate facilities. For example, the Wriston Manufacturing Corporation,[8] which produced trucks and other large scale transportation equipment, assigned one plant to produce the initial runs of all new products, as well as the low-volume replacement parts of aging product lines. Once the sales volume for a product exceeded a certain level, its production was shifted to another facility that was specifically designed for medium-volume manufacturing. Then, if its sales volume increased to the point where mass production equipment and techniques were appropriate, it was shifted either to a general-purpose high-volume plant or to a new plant built specifically for its needs. The advantages of this approach should be obvious. In a later section we will describe some of its disadvantages.

A third, very popular way to specialize facilities is by *process stage:* an operating process that consists of a series of very different processing technologies is divided up so that different facilities are each responsible for one process stage (or a small number of them). This creates a "vertical" network structure, in that creating the final product or service requires the passage of materials and information through a chain of such specialized facilities. An organization that produces electronic products using proprietary integrated circuits, for example, might have one facility that builds individual "I.C. chips" on silicon wafers, another that breaks the wafers apart into individual chips and "packages" them with electrical leads and protective coatings, and still others that incorporate the chips into modules (such as motherboards) or complete products. Our earlier example of a hypothetical "Chinese" assembly plant was a simpler example of this.

One advantage of this approach is that each different process stage can be separately managed by people particularly skilled in its specific technology(s). Another advantage is that grouping all the production for a given stage into a few facilities—rather than trying to perform all process stages in each of a larger number of product-focused facilities—makes it possible to take advantage of economies of scale. Finally, since different process technologies involve different cost structures and require different inputs and skills, different process stages can be located in the geographic regions that are most supportive of their requirements and characteristics. Our producer of electronic equipment, for example, might locate its I.C. fabrication in regions where there is a high concentration of engineers and its packaging and assembly operations (which require relatively large amounts of semi-skilled labor) in locations where labor costs are low.

The major disadvantages of organizing by process stage are just as obvious. First, scheduling production through a chain of specialized facilities can be quite complex, as is managing the network so as to ensure that schedules are adhered to, and to take appropriate action when they are not. Second, a series of transfers between different facilities takes time and can incur high transport costs as well as a large investment in in-transit inventories. Third, satisfying an ultimate customer requires that all the facilities involved in producing the products required by that customer perform their assigned activities properly and on time—since a breakdown at any stage will disrupt deliveries of all the products that depend upon that stage. Therefore, such networks often require some sort of back-up capability—either duplicate facilities, "flexible" facilities that are designed so that they can switch rapidly from one set of products to another, or outside suppliers that can provide products on short notice.

Another common approach to specializing facilities is by *geographic region:* one group of facilities is devoted to supplying Region A (e.g., Asia), while another supplies the needs of Region B, and so on. This allows the company as a whole to better serve the specialized needs of local customers. On the other hand, for the reasons described in Chapter 3 (section 3.3.1), regional specialization often requires a higher investment in facilities and inventory buffers.

5.3.4 Mixed Networks

In practice, most operations organizations do not adopt a single approach to facilities specialization. For various reasons—some planned and others almost accidental—some facilities may be specialized by product family, others by process stage (thereby creating a "two-dimensional" network), and still others by geographic region. For example, Wal-Mart has many suppliers, distribution facilities, and retail stores in different countries. Therefore, it must simultaneously manage the horizontal relationships across its stores within each geographic region and the vertical relationships between those stores and its worldwide network of suppliers and distributors. Similarly, the manufacturing organization of the pharmaceutical company Merck in mid-1997 comprised nine large "chemical" plants that produced basic chemical intermediates and/or transformed them into more complex drugs, and twenty "pharmaceutical" plants that took these bulk pharmaceuticals and packaged them into various dose sizes, with appropriate labels and instructions. Most of the chemical plants were in the United States, while the packaging plants were located close to major markets.

In the next section, we will discuss in more detail some of the disadvantages of mixing facility specializations, which can have profound implications for organization performance and morale. As an example, one often hears managers complain about what we have come to call, generically, their "European plant" problem. Their U.S. plants, they claim, are relatively efficient and reliable, but their "European plant" (wherever it might be in the world) is a constant source of problems. Its productivity is low; its inventories are high; it cannot maintain consistent quality, and its delivery times are excessive. Upon investigation, it usually is found that their U.S. facility network has a relatively clear structure, either along product or process lines. It also is serving a relatively homogenous market that employs the same language and currency. The "European plant," on the other hand, typically is trying to provide a much wider range of products to meet the specialized needs of several different countries, all speaking different languages. In addition, it usually is producing some of those products' parts and components that are difficult to obtain locally and expensive to import from the company's specialized component plants in the United States. Accommodating and managing this level of complexity tends to be much more difficult than for the more focused U.S. plants, and as a result the performance of the "European plant" suffers by comparison.

Each form of facility specialization, of course, requires a matching set of specialized capabilities. As a result, many companies have found it difficult to transfer managers or other highly skilled people between facilities that are specialized in different ways. One of the problems experienced by the Wriston company, for example, was attracting good managers to its small volume/new products facility. Managers trained in its higher-volume facilities, with their simpler product lines, long runs, and greater use of automated processing equipment, were loath to move to a facility that was required to produce hundreds of low-volume "cats and dogs" products on antiquated general-purpose equipment. Worse, if a new product became successful, its production soon was moved to one of the higher volume plants; only the unsuccessful ones stayed put. As we shall see, this approach to pursuing product success eventually led to the plant's failure.

"Orchestrated" Networks

Before turning to a discussion of the reasons for choosing one form of multifacility network over another, we should emphasize that these different kinds of networks are not the only ones that operations managers need to know about. Increasingly, as discussed in Chapters 1 and 4, one sees companies that have redefined—usually by narrowing—the boundaries of their activities and transferred the unwanted activities to other companies. Most do this in a passive way, simply seeking out a supplier and establishing a traditional buyer-seller relationship. Some companies, however, take a more active role in establishing and managing the new collaborative network that results, seeking to become its major hub.

For example, Wal-Mart expanded its role well beyond the usual kind of supplier network that competitors like Sears and Kmart had developed. Instead, early on (starting with P&G, the provider of some of its largest-selling products), it sought to establish very closely coupled relationships with its suppliers through the introduction of "Retail Link," an IT system that provided them with up-to-the-minute information about sales of individual items at its stores. These suppliers, as a result, took on some of the responsibility for initiating production and deliveries. Another example of a supplier taking on a more proactive role is provided by the Taiwan Semiconductor Manufacturing Company, an I.C. "foundry" that fabricates customized chips for other companies. TSMC has expanded its influence over its network of customers and equipment providers by providing designers with a set of sophisticated software tools that allow them to create designs without having to worry about the manufacturing problems associated with different design choices. These tools include a *component library,* developed by TSMC, that enables them to create almost any I.C. design by selecting among and assembling a set of standard I.C. components.[9]

Nike, the world's largest provider of sporting footwear and apparel, now relies extensively on suppliers for the bulk of its production and logistics. It organizes the supply chain, for each product, from materials sourcing to assembly to delivery. It provides general guidance to individual firms—most of them in Asia, thousands of miles away from its major markets, and coordinates the interfaces between them, but otherwise does not attempt to manage their activities. Li & Fung, a trading company based in Hong Kong, goes a step even further. It produces no products of its own, and to supply the clothes and accessories ordered by its customers, largely located in the United States and Europe, it "orchestrates" the operations of a network of more than six thousand focused providers in forty countries. For a given order it selects and organizes specialists in product development, raw material production, manufacturing, and delivery—all of which might be in different countries. Then it rides herd on the process as it unfolds, stepping in to solve problems and occasionally bringing in new suppliers to provide assistance. Similarly, Menichetti, a supplier of fashionable apparel products to U.S. and European markets, operates as the orchestrator (or, as Massimo Menichetti called himself, the "Impannetore") of a large network of small Italian producers.[10] These orchestrators' only product, in a sense, is their process.

Microsoft's network is of an even different kind, in that it is composed primarily of independent collaborators rather than suppliers. Microsoft understands that in order to make its software products more attractive to potential customers, it needs to enhance them with a wide array of complementary software and hardware. It obviously cannot provide all these enhancements itself, so it has cultivated a network of collaborating firms to work with it in providing them. It encourages and orchestrates their activities through a variety of initiatives, from providing early information about new software packages that it is developing, to training seminars, to the creation of application interfaces that allow them to link their products seamlessly with Microsoft's.[11]

5.3.5 Selecting between Horizontal and Vertical Network Structures

As one reviews the preceding discussion of the various ways a network of facilities can be structured, it becomes clear that decisions regarding how to focus an individual facility involve a number of options and tradeoffs. Moreover, a collection of such decisions can create, implicitly or explicitly, a focus for a whole network. For example, specializing facilities by product family (or by product volume or geographic region within a product family) creates a product-focused, or *horizontal,* network structure in which sister facilities are relatively independent of one another. Conversely, specializing by process stage creates a process-focused, or *vertical,* network because each facility is dependent on others for key inputs and its "customers" often are sister facilities. As we shall see, horizontal and vertical networks behave in very different ways, and require very different management infrastructures and styles. A process-organized facility generally tends to have an engineering mind-set, whereas a product-organized facility tends to have a marketing mind-set and a location-organized facility a regional mind-set.

Too often companies make decisions to focus along one dimension or another in an ad hoc manner, without thinking about their long-term consequences. There are some general guidelines that should affect such decisions, however, and they reflect the relationship between the characteristics of different types of networks and the organization's competitive strategy, as described in Chapter 2. One is that a network should be structured in such a way that the facilities within it all have compatible strategic priorities. This suggests that if most of a company's process technologies are characterized by large economies of scale, and if low cost has a higher priority in its competitive strategy than does fast delivery or flexible responsiveness to customer requests, then different process stages probably ought to be separated out into dedicated facilities. The same is true if a given process technology is so complex and fast changing that it requires the total attention of a substantial number of very highly skilled technologists (who might be less effective in, or attracted to, a facility that was primarily focused on end products).

In contrast, if process technologies are not too complex or their output can be purchased from external sources, and the company's competitive strategy requires close interaction with a fast moving market, a network of smaller facilities located close to major markets (i.e., a horizontal product and/or regionally-focused network) is likely to be more appropriate. A product focus also facilitates the alignment of priorities within a product development team, and between such teams and their marketing and operations functional groups. On the one hand, restricting each facility to the production of a portion of the total number of products reduces the complexity of production scheduling. On the other hand, it also can lead to the duplication of facility overhead, make it harder to shift capacity across facilities, and impede attempts to transfer and retain learning across facilities.[12]

Unfortunately, there isn't always a clear match between competitive priorities and different network structures. Moreover, different forms of network organization can either facilitate or undermine the desired *focus* of individual facilities. One company, for example, was considering whether to move from a region-organized network to a product line-organized network. Analyzing the implications the two approaches had for the way individual plants might be focused, as shown in Table 5-1 below, suggests that its existing regional organization had led to a wide range of processes and activities within each plant, and that a product line organization would better promote facilities focus.

In a sense, the structure of a network determines its "grain," establishing what is relatively easy to do within it and what is relatively hard to do. The dirty truth of the matter is that, as when establishing any set of priorities, one cannot have things both ways. Focusing one way precludes you from focusing another way, so tradeoffs must be made. If one attempts to focus different facilities in different ways, one is likely to end up with an unmanageable hodge-podge. We will expand upon the

Table 5-1 Assessing the Differences between Alternative Ways of Focusing a Plant Network

Type of focus	By region		By product line	
Key decisions	United States	Europe	High end	Low end
capacity utilization	75–100 percent	75–100 percent	75 percent	100 percent
lay-out	batch & in-line	batch & in-line	batch	in-line
facility size	varies	varies	0.5 mil/yr	2.0 mil/yr
sourcing	varies	varies	partners	arm-length
process technology	automation	automation	manual	automation
workforce	hi & lo skills	hi & lo skills	high skill	low skill
quality	varies	varies	performance	low defects
prod'n run length	varies	varies	short	long
performance metrics	varies	varies	delivery	cost

reasons for this in the next section, where we discuss the infrastructural issues associated with different types of networks.

An example that illustrates all these considerations is provided by the European Division of Alden Products, Inc.,[13] a U.S.-based producer of premium household products. Until the mid-1960s, it supplied the needs of its major European countries through a number of relatively small and independent local plants. Then, faced with rapid growth in many of these markets and the increasing difficulty of staffing, managing, and coordinating this multiplant network, it decided to consolidate all production for continental Europe into one large modern plant in Holland. All the production processes for all its products were located in this Uniplant. Over the next twenty years, the size of that plant was increased several times, and in 1989 it faced the need for another expansion. By this time, however, the Uniplant was experiencing severe problems. Its direct labor productivity had stagnated; its overhead costs were soaring; and its delivery times were increasing even as its inventories rose. Worse, increasing complaints about its lack of responsiveness and generally poor service were being received from Alden's country managers, who were being forced to purchase products from the Uniplant for their customers. Its long success had fostered impending failure.

Six alternatives for expanding manufacturing capacity were proposed. The first was simply to enlarge the existing Uniplant, as had been done several times before. The second was to separate the plant's two major product lines (liquid and aerosol products) into two independent facilities next to each other in Holland. The third was to create a sister to the Uniplant in southern Europe—where the demand for its products was growing faster. The Uniplant would continue to supply all the products sold in northern Europe, while the new plant would supply all the products needed in the south. A variation of this approach, Alternative 4, was to specialize the two plants by production volume: the Uniplant would continue to produce the higher volume products for all of Europe, while the new plant would specialize in producing the lower volume products. Alternative 5 was to continue centralizing all purchasing of chemicals, and the processes that converted them into bulk liquid products, at the Uniplant, together with all aerosol products. The bulk liquid products would be shipped to smaller bottling plants located close to major markets. The final alternative was to outsource the bottling of most products to local *contract fillers*—independent companies that specialized in performing the bottling operation. In short, Alden Products had to decide whether to expand in place, outsource much of its production, or to create a product line-focused network, a process stage-focused network, or a geographic-focused network.

Even though Alden Products' competitive strategy placed much higher emphasis on having a broad product line, introducing lots of innovative new products, and responding rapidly to the changing needs of important markets than it did on low cost operations, the Uniplant had been designed and managed so as to efficiently produce long runs of a relatively small number of products. In short, the Uniplant's problems were caused largely by the fact that its structure and infrastructure were at odds with its company's competitive strategy.

Which of the alternative ways for reconfiguring its European operations would be more consistent with the priorities implied by that strategy? The first two alternatives (either a larger or a sister Uniplant) would essentially create duplicates of the current plant—and likely either duplicate or exacerbate its problems as well—without dealing with the basic incompatibility of company strategy and plant structure. Alternatives 3, 4, 5, and 6 each attempted to deal with that incompatibility in a different way. Choosing among them would require a careful analysis of the production, logistics, and overhead costs associated with each, as well as of the different types of infrastructures that would be required for each type of network—the topic of the next section.

Given the differences in the processes appropriate for producing high-volume versus low-volume products and Alden's need to respond quickly to changing market demands, however, our earlier discussion of the need to fit a network's structure to its company's technology and competitive strategy suggests that a combination of Alternatives 3 and 4—adding a new facility in southern Europe that could efficiently produce low-volume products—was likely to have been a good choice. Instead, the company decided to continue with its previous expansion policy and increased the capacity of the Uniplant once again. A few years later, after two more such expansions, the performance of the Uniplant had deteriorated to the point where Alden's European organization was in crisis. Under pressure to resolve the crisis quickly, Alden was forced to adopt a version of Alternative 6: retaining the production of only the highest volume products (as well as a few proprietary new products) at the Uniplant, and outsourcing the bulk of its lower volume products to local contract fillers.

5.4 MANAGING THE NETWORK: *INFRASTRUCTURE*

Deciding on the structure of an operating network—as discussed in the previous section—is a critical first step in developing a purposeful multiunit operating strategy. Indeed, companies often respond to crises or major operating problems in a network by changing its structure. For example, they often embark on "rationalization" programs involving some combination of facility closings and the realignment of products, processes, volumes, and/or geographical responsibilities among the remaining ones. Such rationalizations can yield large benefits and better link the company's operations to its overall strategy, but they usually are not sufficient by themselves. Unless the network's software—the policies, procedures, and systems that we have called its *infrastructure*—are also aligned with the needs of the company's competitive strategy, restructuring by itself will not solve its problems.

Analogously, redesigning a computer system's hardware generally requires a corresponding redesign of at least some of its software. Few people would consider buying a brand new personal computer containing the latest and fastest microprocessor, most advanced BUS architectures, and most sophisticated graphics capabilities if it utilized the same software that had been created for less-powerful machines. The new computer might operate without errors, but its overall performance would likely be unsatisfactory. Yet, this is what many companies essentially do in the wake of plant "rationalization" programs: they redesign their operating networks, create new missions for their plants, and even invest in new technologies, but leave in place many of the old policies, procedures, and systems.

The hospital industry provides an example of the limitations of attempting to address a broad strategic problem through structural solutions alone. In the 1990s, faced with declining reimbursement rates from managed care organizations and government insurance programs (such as Medicare), as well as intensifying competition from less expensive community hospitals, many major teaching hospitals embarked on strategies to create "integrated delivery networks" or IDNs. The concept behind IDNs was that a single umbrella organization could provide a complete continuum of services, from primary health care (e.g., routine physicals and diagnostics) to the most complex and specialized procedures (such as heart surgery and organ transplants). IDNs also could exploit the advantages of focus, by having different organizations in the network specialize in different types of care. For instance, community-based doctors would provide primary care while suburban hospitals in the network could specialize in secondary care and routine medical services (such as diagnostic services, routine surgery, and follow-up care). The urban academic hospitals could then focus on providing more complex services and procedures to the sickest patients, a mission much more in line with their research orientation.

Advocates of the IDN concept argued that it would greatly reduce the cost of care by simplifying the costly and cumbersome hand-overs from one provider to another, by enabling better alignment of incentives, and by facilitating the diffusion of best-practice approaches to health care. At the same time, providers would enjoy all the benefits of focus since no one organization would be asked to do it all. In the pursuit of this strategy, many academic medical centers merged with cross-town rivals and embarked on a spree of acquisitions of suburban hospitals, diagnostics centers, and primary care physician practices.

Unfortunately, not only have IDNs not proven to be the promised panacea, they have experienced several high profile failures. In San Francisco, the merger of two prestigious academic medical centers—at Stanford University and the University of California at San Francisco—was eventually disbanded after experiencing significant financial difficulties. Similarly, Boston's Care Group—a product of a merger of the Beth Israel and Deaconess hospitals (both affiliated with the Harvard Medical School), and the acquisition of several community hospitals—experienced major financial problems and was forced to contemplate closing or divesting several of its hospitals.

With the benefit of hindsight, the failure of the IDNs could be seen to be due largely to infrastructural problems. The benefits of integration were never fully realized because hospital managers and physicians were either unwilling or unable to implement the required changes in processes, procedures, and systems needed to create a truly "seamless" system. Thus, some hospitals in the same network continued to use different and incompatible information systems, which prevented the sharing of critical patient information as they moved from one provider to the next. In some cases it has proven virtually impossible to get physicians from different hospitals in the same network to agree upon common standards or protocols. Although such networks were supposed to create a spirit of cooperation among one-time-competitors, long-standing rivalries have proven devilishly difficult to cool, particularly when hard decisions need to be made about cutting staff, eliminating redundant facilities, and reallocating investments. In other cases, genuine desires to coordinate care across providers have been foiled by incompatibilities in different computer systems used for billing and patient care. In the next section we examine some of the critical aspects of a network's operating policies and procedures that influence its operating effectiveness.

5.5 MANAGING DIFFERENT NETWORK STRUCTURES

The challenges of managing a network differ depending on its basic architecture, in particular the differences between the horizontal and vertical structures described earlier. Managing a *horizontal network* typically requires decisions regarding the degree of autonomy that individual facilities should be given, and which practices should be standardized across the network. In contrast, the key challenges in managing a *vertical* network—a chain of operations that include a sequence of formal or informal buyer-supplier relationships—revolve around how to coordinate the flows of goods and materials along the chain in order to meet delivery promises, minimize the costs of either under- or over-stocking, and facilitate the development and introduction of new products.

These alternative network structures have important implications for the activities and responsibilities of a company's central operations organization. This group's task is both to oversee the network's operations and to instill and maintain its sense of priorities and mission, even where individual units have quite different sets of responsibilities. It can accomplish this both directly, by establishing and monitoring the structural decisions and policies described in Chapter 2 (such as capacity planning, process technology, logistics, and human resource policies), and indirectly through the recruitment and development of facility managers, and the way it measures and evaluates their performance. Depending on the type of network, however, there are a variety of ways for carrying out these responsibilities, as described next.

5.5.1 Horizontal Networks

Horizontal networks tend to be better suited for less complex and less capital-intensive technologies, whose scale economies are not great enough to require large facilities, and where flexibility and product innovation are more important than careful planning and tight control. Authority in such a network tends to be decentralized, which promotes flexibility and responsiveness. Their facilities often have profit responsibility (particularly if the network is organized geographically), and operate almost like semi-independent small businesses.

In such a decentralized organization, facility managers must be broadly skilled and somewhat entrepreneurial. Their focus on specific products promotes identification with the needs of those products' customers, so these managers often become responsible for the whole gamut of activities associated with developing, introducing, producing, and delivering products, and responding to customer problems and new needs as they arise. This means the corporate operations staff has to put considerable emphasis on recruiting and developing managers who are capable of taking on such a broad range of responsibilities, as well as on monitoring, evaluating, and rewarding their performance. Although removed from day-to-day facility operations, the central staff also seeks to maintain control and direction by developing, communicating, and coordinating common policies, standards, and procedures.

A horizontal network also differs from a vertical network in its approach to managing the development and introduction of new process technology. Although individual facilities in a vertical network are focused on specific process technologies, and so tend to be staffed with experts in that technology, each of the facilities in a product-focused horizontal network usually contain several different process technologies, and as a result facilities are likely to find it difficult to keep up to date technologically. The selection and development of new process technologies therefore become, essentially by default, a corporate responsibility—usually assigned to a central process technology group.

5.5.2 Vertical Networks

Vertical networks are more appropriate for complex, divisible, and capital-intensive processes. Since each facility is only one of several that add value to the final product, and its customers are often sister facilities, it tends to have little identification with either the final product or its end users. Nor does it typically have control over the prices at which its outputs are transferred to other facilities, so tends to be treated as a cost center.

A process-focused vertical network can facilitate low-cost production if there are substantial economies of scale and/or advantages stemming from the use of a superior process technology. These cost advantages may be offset, however, by the large central overhead and logistics costs required to manage such a network effectively. Issues relating to capacity (and the balance of capacities in different facilities), logistics, and technological change are critical, and absorb much of the central staff's attention, as does the coordination of various facilities' responses to changes in sales volumes and product mixes. It is difficult for such a network, with its chain of individual processes, to make major changes in the rate of output because of the pipeline momentum in the system. It also experiences difficulties and delays when trying to introduce new products, since authority is not assigned along product lines.

These contrasts in the issues that horizontal and vertical networks must deal with imply very different allocations of responsibilities between a company's central operations group and its individual facilities, as well as the policies and practices affecting measurement and control, skill requirements, and managers' career paths. In a horizontal network, the central staff tends to confine itself to collecting and disseminating information, coordinating decisions across functional groups (principally between marketing and operations), assisting in manager training and development, and providing consulting services. In contrast, the central staff of a vertical network must take a much more active role in making the system "work," since addressing the needs of its ultimate customers requires not only that each link in the facility chain complete its assigned responsibilities satisfactorily but that goods and information move from one to the other in a timely and cost-effective manner. These contrasting management structures, in turn, require very different management skills and attitudes in their respective facilities, which has important implications for the kind of people recruited into those positions and how they are developed and motivated.

5.5.3 Centralization versus Decentralization

Once a company begins to separate the production of a given product or service into more than one site, it faces a fundamental decision about the degree of autonomy to give each site in setting its own policies and procedures. Consider a multinational corporation that has assembly operations located in facilities around the world. To what extent should each facility be allowed to make its own decisions with respect to the selection of process technologies, quality standards and procedures, human resource policies (pay, promotion, training, etc.), and production planning and inventory control methods? One approach might be to let facility managers choose what they think best for their own operation. At the other extreme, a company (like McDonald's) might centralize all critical operating decisions and essentially mandate standardized policies and procedures for all its facilities. In reality, most companies operate somewhere in between the two extremes, but finding the appropriate middle ground is often a source of intense disagreement between facility managers (who tend to prefer to set their own course) and corporate directors of operations who usually prefer a more centralized approach.

Centralized Networks

The choice between highly autonomous and highly centralized approaches involves complex trade-offs. The benefits of a highly centralized approach include, first, that the standardization of critical operating decisions may improve communication and coordination across the network. For instance, if every plant that assembled similar products were allowed complete freedom in planning its production of various products, without considering the production and inventory decisions of other assembly plants, it is likely that the total network would either greatly under-produce or over-produce certain items. If stockouts were costly, each plant might choose to produce somewhat more than the forecasted demand (as described in Chapter 3). If all plants, as a result, accumulated substantial "buffer" inventories, the total inventory costs across the entire network would be higher than desirable. Centralizing production decisions can avoid such local optimization, and lead to better inventory management across the network. Standardizing information systems, databases, part numbers, and other protocols also can help facilitate the exchange of necessary information.

The benefits of such standardization sound obvious, but in our research and case writing we have come across countless examples where facilities are not able to share basic production planning or inventory information because of incompatible information systems—as was the case for many of the failed IDNs described in Section 5.5. In the late 1990s, for example, the food products giant Nestlé S.A. discovered that it was utilizing nine different general ledgers, multiple purchasing systems, and twenty-eight points of customer entry throughout its far-flung plant network. "We had no clue how much volume we were doing with a particular vendor because every factory set up their own vendor [system] and purchased on their own," stated the Nestlé V.P. responsible for Corporate Information Systems.[14] This complexity and incompatibility were the principle drivers behind Nestlé's decision (and those of many other companies around the world) to adopt an enterprise resource planning system.

Second, centralization has benefits where customers value uniformity in a product or service experience regardless of its location. Thus, as described in Chapter 4, a McDonald's franchise has virtually no discretion over how its facilities look or are laid out. Moreover, every franchise must follow detailed operating procedures that cover all aspects of operations, including precise cooking times, temperature settings, and portions for all food items. McDonald's does this because its core strategy is to provide customers with a highly uniform product and experience, regardless of whether a McDonald's is in Athens, Georgia or Athens, Greece.

Although it operates at the other end of the technology spectrum, Intel seeks similar process standardization. Under its "Copy Exact" strategy, every Intel plant producing the same product must utilize the same process technologies, equipment, and procedures that were developed or chosen during the process-development phase.[15] Once the process technology is tested and validated in one of the company's Technical Development Fabs (essentially full-scale pilot plants), the process is "frozen" and replicated throughout the network. This facilitates the ramp-up of new products and enables Intel to assure its customers that their microprocessors have the same specifications and quality standards no matter where they were produced. We return to this example in our discussion of process development in Chapter 7.

In some industries such as automobile, electronics, and aerospace, large OEM customers often will insist that all supplier plants follow a common set of policies and procedures. Many companies now demand that their suppliers become ISO certified. A supplier to such a customer therefore would have to require that all its plants implement the same ISO program. In regulated industries, such as pharmaceuticals, common standards are enforced by regulatory agencies.

A third reason companies centralize certain operating policies and procedures is to ensure that all their facilities adopt common ethical standards and business practices. This issue is particularly salient for companies that have operations in countries with very different labor laws, environmental standards, and cultural norms. Increasingly, multinational corporations are establishing common global policies for such issues as worker safety, employment practices, and environmental impact.

Finally, companies may standardize policies and procedures across facility networks in an attempt to ensure that "best practices" are communicated and adopted widely. As described in Chapter 2, Section 2.3.4, in multiplant networks it is not at all unusual to find large variations in performance across plants making the same product and using essentially the same process technologies. Studies have shown that these variations are largely the result of sometimes rather subtle differences in such operating practices as maintenance, material handling, employee training, and so on. Adopting known best practices, then, can help improve performance across the entire network.

One might wonder why it would ever be necessary to *mandate* standardization. Why wouldn't facility managers be willing—even anxious—to adopt best practices from another facility if this would lead to a performance improvement in their own facilities? Yet, even when confronted with comparative data that show the clear superiority of another approach, managers of lagging facilities often will resist the idea of adopting that superior practice, arguing that their particular facility has *special* requirements or constraints that make adoption impractical ("it won't work here"). Occasionally, such a stance is well-founded. More often, however, the resistance of a facility's managers reflects a defensive attitude and a concern that adoption of another facility's practices is an admission of their own shortcomings. To overcome these largely psychological barriers to adoption, some companies force the adoption of perceived best practices. This issue is picked up again in Chapter 10, where we discuss in greater depth the issue of transferring best practice from one facility to another.

Decentralized Networks

The arguments for decentralizing decision making and allowing a higher degree of plant autonomy can be equally compelling. First, if facilities are focused by market segment or geographic regions, more autonomy enables greater responsiveness to the needs of those different customer bases. For example, in the early 1990s John Crane Ltd. produced high precision seals used in chemical processing and paper making at two factories in the United Kingdom.[16] One site was responsible for producing standard seals, while the other focused on specialized (custom-designed) seals and spare parts. The custom/spare parts business required very fast turnaround. Thus, the policies in that plant had to support a make-to-order strategy. In the standard product line, however, lower cost was a much higher priority for customers. Therefore, that plant adopted policies oriented around long-production runs (to amortize set-up costs) and high machine utilization. Given the differences in the two markets, it would have been counter-productive to insist that both plants follow the same policies and procedures.

Second, giving different facilities some discretion over policies and procedures enables them to adapt more easily and effectively to local operating conditions and constraints. A facility operating in a high wage welfare state, such as in Western Europe, would want to adopt different technologies and human resource strategies than a sister facility operating in a low-wage developing country. Similarly, plants in locations with poor transportation infrastructures probably would find it necessary to hold more inventory than would those located at major transportation and shipping hubs.

Finally, permitting some autonomy facilitates experimentation in practices, policies, and processes, and such experimentation can lead to superior performance. If facilities are forced to follow centrally dictated standard procedures, there is a clear risk of stifling innovation and learning, as will be discussed in Chapter 7.[17]

In summary, the choice between a centralized/standardized approach and a more decentralized approach involves tricky trade-offs. The advantages and disadvantages of each approach are summarized in Table 5-2. Since there are very few (if

Table 5-2 Situations Where Centralization or Decentralization Is More Appropriate

Centralized/standardized when different facilities:	Decentralized/autonomous when facilities:
1. Produce similar products	**1.** Produce different products
2. Serve similar customers who value uniformity	**2.** Serve customers with different needs
3. Operate in environments with similar constraints and/or resources	**3.** Operate in very different local environments

any) completely centralized or completely decentralized networks, in most cases the choice between approaches is made at the level of individual policies and procedures. Thus, for instance, a given company might give its facilities wide discretion over specific production planning and inventory control policies, but insist that they use the same information system to implement those policies.

5.5.4 Implementing and Maintaining Focus

Despite the intuitive appeal of the concept of focus, and considerable evidence of its value, most managers are reluctant (and find it difficult) to implement and/or maintain focus in their own organizations. There are at least six reasons for this reluctance, most of which are the result of the difficult trade-offs that have to be made:

1. It is costly and expensive to split up an existing facility, and managers worry about losing the supposed benefits of a large (albeit unfocused) facility.
2. There are different ways to achieve "focus," which leads to internal disagreement about how best it might be achieved in a specific situation—and some studies have indicated that this choice can be critical to success (see footnote 4).
3. Managers are reluctant to lose the expertise of certain people who are likely to leave if a facility is focused in a way that reduces the value of their specialized knowledge. For example, a facility that is focused along product lines is likely to have less appeal to specialists in, or experienced managers of, a specific process technology.
4. Focus might lead to a reduction in the efficiency of the capital invested in equipment and facilities (as discussed earlier, if they are subject to economies of scale, two small facilities or machines will probably cost more to acquire than one bigger unit—although this additional investment might be reduced by making use of less costly equipment and facilities that are limited in the range of activities they can undertake).
5. Managers are unwilling to lose the capacity cushion that an unfocused (that is, a "general purpose") facility provides; for example, the usable capacity of a network of focused facilities will decrease if one of them experiences operating problems or the product mix shifts so that it has to operate well

above or below capacity (this is analogous to the problem of specialized waiting lines that was described in Chapter 3, and also reflects a "don't put all your eggs in one basket" mentality).

6. Above all, it is difficult to measure (using the usual accounting metrics) the financial benefits of focus in a given situation, whereas it generally is relatively easy to measure its costs; this is particularly true when the intent of focus is to improve some nonfinancial aspect of operations, such as delivery speed or reliability.

Another difficulty is even more subtle. That is the common practice of attempting to solve operating problems through structural solutions alone. As we have already illustrated, simply changing the structure of a network without making reinforcing changes in its infrastructure is unlikely to unlock the full potential of focused facilities. An incompatibility between structure and infrastructure, such as when a process-focused network is reconfigured to be a product-focused network without changing the management policies and styles of the facility or corporate manager, is more likely to lead to confusion and frustration. As a result, over time, focus disappears.

Plant Charters

Even without such incompatibility, focus is constantly under attack. A facility's manager is continually subjected, usually under some pressure, to requests to take on new assignments because of unexpected developments. The pressure from superiors is reinforced by the manager's desire to be a "good citizen," a sense of obligation to one's fellow managers, and wanting to show that one is a "can-do" person. It is hard to say no to such requests, even when they violate the nature of the focus of one's operating unit.

To make it easier for their facility managers to say "no" when it is appropriate, some companies have created mission statements, or *charters* for each of their focused facilities. Such a charter needs to be unambiguous and fairly brief so that it can be easily understood, communicated, and remembered. It should both state what the facility is expected to do and be good at, as well as (perhaps more important) what it should *not* do unless given specific authorization from a higher level of management. Above all, it should clearly indicate how a given facility is supposed to be *different* from other facilities in the network. Too many operating units have mission statements that have the universality of the Boy Scout oath, promising everything (e.g., "We will provide low cost and high quality, as well as fast, flexible response, while delighting our customers and valuing our employees") but delivering little.

5.6 THE DYNAMICS OF HORIZONTAL NETWORKS

Horizontal networks are continually being forced to adjust to changing product volumes and mixes by juggling products and/or components and customers. They also are subject to patterns of behavior that can lead either to exceptional success or total failure.

For example, one of the most striking and insidious dynamics one sees in horizontal networks is the way power shifts over time among facilities, and between facilities and their corporate office. Even in a well designed and managed network (irrespective of which type it is), unfortunately, growth in scale or scope tends to muddy the clear divisions of responsibilities among corporate and facility management. Whichever group feels it is not receiving the desired support from the other seeks to take on more of the other's responsibilities. For example, as a company's sales and product offerings increase, the resulting increase in complexity often causes the central organization to begin to lose control over the activities of its facility network. When this is recognized—usually in conjunction with some sort of crisis—the natural inclination is to centralize control and strengthen the central organization. Over time a series of such decisions inevitably reduces the authority of facility managers. As they lose power, the best route to advancement in the organization comes to be seen to be an assignment to the central group, so the best young managers gravitate there. Once there, these ambitious, energetic managers tend to take over tasks that they feel they can do better than others, so the strong get stronger and the weak get weaker. Eventually the organization finds that its strategies and investments—carefully crafted by its central group—are proving ineffective because they are not being implemented effectively at the facility level.

However, delegating too much responsibility to a product-oriented manager in a horizontal network may also lead to problems. For example, when faced with a need to expand capacity, such managers are likely to opt to *expand in place,* continually adding to their existing facility, or building nearby satellite facilities. This appears to offer the easiest, fastest, and (in the short term) least costly way to meet the market's demands. Over time, however, as we saw in the case of Alden Products' Uniplant, a series of such decisions can lead to the creation of a huge, complex facility that has lost the flexibility and responsiveness that a product-focused organization needs to have.

Another example of the strong getting stronger is when certain facilities come to be regarded as particularly effective, causing investment and management talent to be shifted to them. Often these resources are provided—either directly or indirectly—by the less effective facilities, which further undermines their effectiveness. The problems experienced by the Wriston Manufacturing Company (introduced in Section 5.3) provide a clear example of this dynamic. Although its horizontal network of assembly plants was structured very rationally, with each plant specifically equipped and managed so as to be able to efficiently produce product families having a restricted range of production volumes, over time the network experienced increasing difficulties.

At first it appeared that only one plant was having problems. This plant, in Detroit, had been assigned the role of producing all the division's low-volume (and newest) products. Over time, however, its costs steadily escalated and its profitability declined, while its physical plant deteriorated. During a market downturn in 1992, the Detroit plant began losing money. Much of its equipment was obsolete (its average age was over thirty-three years), the plant's layout was fragmented and inefficient, its unionized workforce was aging and increasingly hostile, and its plant manager (who was experiencing health problems) appeared unable to turn the situation around. As a result, the division manager was contemplating closing the plant anu transferring its products to two of his other plants

How had this situation developed in a network whose structure apparently was so logical? Its problems were all due to its infrastructure. First, all plants were profit centers, and expected to exceed a corporate mandated minimum return on assets (ROA) each year. Second, plant managers were not given control over the prices for their products. These were set by division management, based on customer considerations and estimates of each product's "full cost." These cost estimates, in turn, included allocations for both plant overhead and corporate overhead, based on each plant's production volume, and the same product costing system was used in each plant. Third, plants essentially competed with each other for investment funds: those with the highest ROA received the most new investment. As a result of its deteriorating profitability, therefore, the amount reinvested in the Detroit plant had been less than its annual depreciation for several years. This lack of investment, and the resulting deterioration of its facilities, led to recurring rumors that the plant was going to be shut down, which caused increasing morale problems with the unionized workforce. Fourth, because of its increasing problems the Detroit plant was not an attractive assignment for promising new managers. They preferred assignments at one of the newer, better performing plants, so the Detroit plant's managers tended to be older, more "traditional," and—over time—worn down.

The problem was that these infrastructural decisions were the same for each plant, even though different plants—by design—had very different missions and production problems. A plant producing mostly low-volume products on manually operated equipment, for example, would naturally experience higher set-up and inventory costs than a plant that produced mostly high-volume products on automated equipment. Using the same cost accounting system for each plant, therefore, automatically penalized the Detroit plant—which could not recoup its higher costs by increasing its prices. The practice of rewarding plants that generated high profitability with higher investment had the effect, over time, of starving the Detroit plant of new investment and sent it into a downward spiral, making it an increasingly unpleasant place to work. Only managers who didn't have attractive employment options outside the company (generally those who were less capable and dynamic) could be persuaded to take on assignments there.

5.7 THE DYNAMICS OF VERTICAL NETWORKS

As described above, better communication, access to global markets, and financial pressures all have encouraged many companies to rely more on a distributed network of other companies, rather than solely on their own, in-house operations. This has led to an increasing number of supply chains that not only are long (in that they involve several operating units), but are shared among different firms, none of which necessarily owns the whole chain. These networks are *vertical* in the sense that products might flow all the way from raw material producers to component manufacturers to assemblers to distributors, and so on. For example, Intel and Maxtor make disk drives that are assembled by Hewlett-Packard/Compaq into computers. These computers are subsequently shipped to Ingram Micro (one of the two large computer distributors in the United States). From there, the products make their way to value-added resellers (VARs), which then deliver/install them at customer sites. This approach allows each party in the chain to focus on its strengths and avoid those activities in which it has no comparative advantage. At the same time, however, such vertical networks are prone to a range of coordination problems (beyond the difficulties of merely performing all the transactions), as described below.

5.7.1 Vertical Supply Chain Dynamics: The Bullwhip Effect

One of the most intriguing and frustrating aspects of the management of vertical supply chains is known as the *bullwhip effect.* The nature and impact of this effect has been demonstrated to thousands of managers and business school students by a simulation known as "The Beer Game."[18] In this game there are four players, each representing a different role in a simple supply chain: the Factory, the Distributor, the Warehouse and the Retailer. As depicted in Figure 5-1, each player holds inventory, receives orders from its downstream customer, and places orders with its supplier (the factory creates a production order). Only the retailer sees the actual consumer demand. Over the course of thirty-five weeks or so, each player places weekly orders based on information about its own inventory, backlog, and demand history. They are not permitted to communicate with upstream or downstream players except through the orders they place. There are costs associated with both stockouts and holding inventory, and the objective is to minimize total costs.

One aspect of the game that makes it rather complex is that there are both ordering lags (two weeks) and shipping lags (two weeks), in keeping with those one might see in an actual supply chain. Simulations of the operation of this vertical chain, whether conducted by inexperienced college students or seasoned executives, reveals a behavior that is both consistent and startling. Even though final demand begins at four units per week, then rises to eight units per week and remains constant thereafter, the supply chain convulses as a result of the information and shipment lags, as well as the "rational" behavior of its participants. Figure 5-2 depicts some typical performance patterns (based on actual experience) that have been observed with this game.

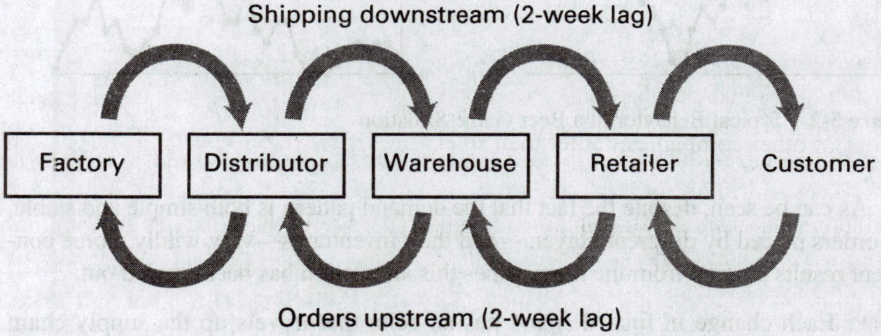

Figure 5-1 The Beer Game

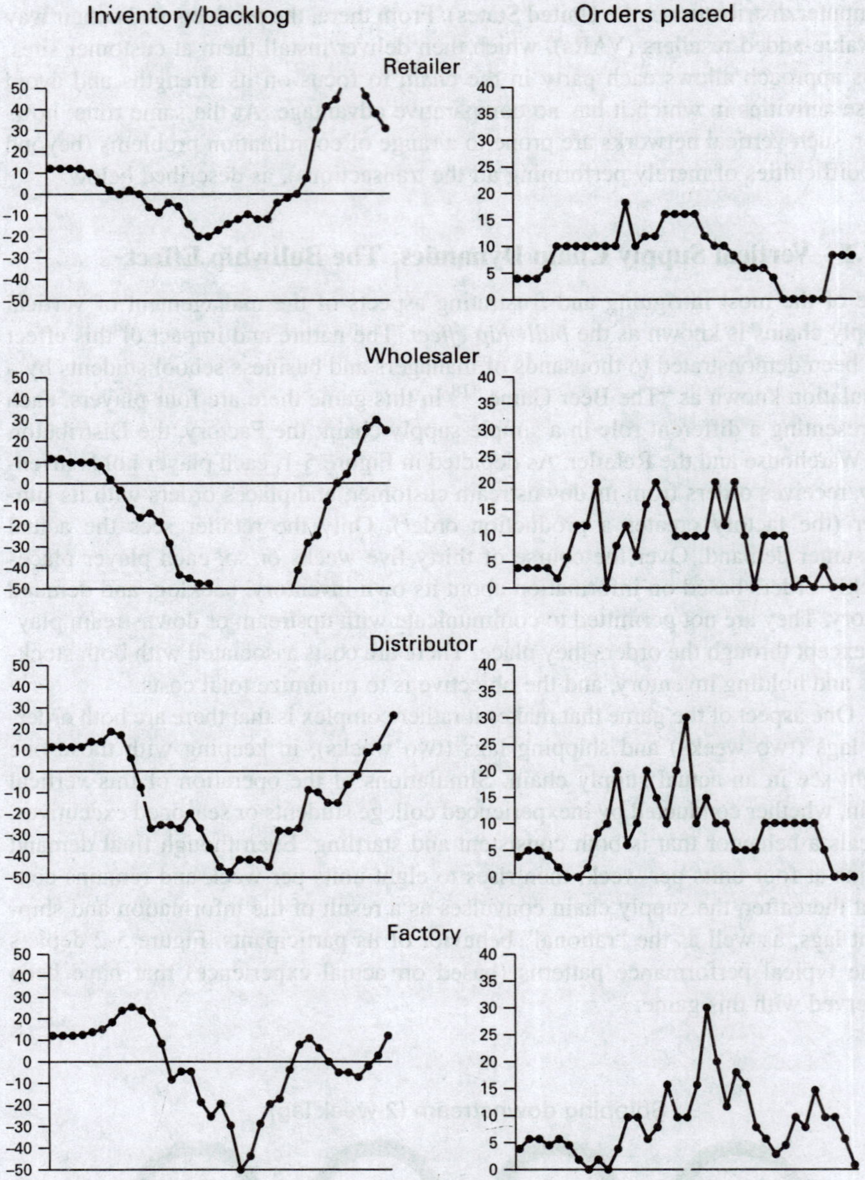

Figure 5-2 Typical Behavior in a Beer Game Situation

As can be seen, despite the fact that the demand pattern is both simple and stable, the orders placed by different players—and their inventories—vary wildly. Some consistent results emerge from the many times this simulation has been carried out:

- Each change in final demand has an echo that travels up the supply chain (towards the factory), with a consistent lag.

- Fluctuations get larger as one moves back up the channel.
- Factories can be starved for orders for many weeks, even though final demand stays the same or even increases! They also can maintain heavy backlogs during the weeks just before or just after plant shut downs.

This behavior, generally known as the bullwhip effect, triggers enlightening post-simulation discussions with participants. Why do they behave the way they do? Since players cannot communicate directly with their partners in the channel, it is easy to point the finger of blame on the idiotic decisions made by someone else further up or down the channel! "Why did my customer order so much, and then stop ordering just as I ramped up production?" "What happened to all those orders I asked for but never got; why wasn't my supplier delivering?"

The answer lies in the fact that each player has to act independently, only able to communicate with other players in the channel through their orders and deliveries. If a player in the channel overreacts to the orders received (and decides to build a safety stock, for example), everyone else is compelled to react. However, the lags are such that it might be several weeks before supply finally reaches the source of demand, and by then the demand might have disappeared or have been fulfilled by inventory elsewhere in the channel.

Very, very few simulations result in a steady, controlled flow of material from the factory to the customer. Almost all result in the kind of instability shown in Figure 5-2. Few people understand how powerful the effect is until they participate in the simulation and experience it for themselves.[19] Would it be better, one can ask, if the smartest person in the channel were allowed to make *all* the decisions, being supplied with complete information about the amount of inventory at each stage and actual customer demand? Yes, undoubtedly respond the players. But what if the *least* sophisticated person controlled the channel? Yes—begrudgingly—the players say: Even that would be better than allowing each to act independently.

It is important to point out that ownership of the total supply chain by a single company will not necessarily solve the problem. As described in Section 5.5, many facilities and operating groups act independently, with their own incentives and objectives, in spite of being part of a larger organization. The effect is most destructive when the different operations in a company's vertical network are encouraged to act autonomously—as in the beer game.

In the real world, of course, there are telephones, fax-machine and all manner of potentially powerful electronic links to make communication easier, and relieve a major cause of the bullwhip effect. However, the real world also contains multiple products (often of sufficient variety to preclude a discussion of each SKU), variable pricing, promotions, bulk discounts, the effects of perceived shortages (causing buyers to order more than they need), and a host of incentives that conspire to make the effect worse.

This effect is an enormous source of cost for real supply chains: the U.S. textile industry, for example, is estimated to incur costs in excess of $100 billion per year for unneeded inventory, returns of unsold goods, and poor service.[20] U.S. retail value-chain sales in1997, for example, were approximately $2.6 trillion. To support these sales, retailers held $300 billion in inventories, while merchant wholesalers held $250 billion to supply the retailers. The combined inventories held by the multiple tiers of manufacturers were valued at $450 billion, so the total inventory in the value chain was estimated at $1 trillion.[21] Much of this inventory (probably 25 percent to 50 percent) results directly from the bullwhip effect.

It has been argued that the aggregation of the resulting instabilities of many such supply chains has fuelled the waves of boom and recession that have been a constant feature of the capitalist world since the eighteenth century.

5.7.2 Dealing with the Coordination Problem

The bullwhip effect can be alleviated through a variety of ways:

1. *Reduce the number of stages in the supply chain.* This can be done, for example, by eliminating regional warehouses and/or delivering directly from the factory to the retailer, which is the approach that Wal-Mart has taken, or bypassing retail stores and selling directly to consumers, the approach taken by Dell Computer. The ability to remove intermediate stages (called *dis-intermediation*) has been one of the major drivers of Web-based, direct-to-consumer (D2C) businesses.
2. *Communicate consumer demand directly up the supply chain.* Retailers can make consumer demand data directly available to upstream stages, so they can base their production/ordering decision making on a richer understanding of likely future demand than is provided by orders from their immediate customers.
3. *Reduce ordering and shipping delays.* Companies can use electronic links to reduce the cost of placing orders, allowing more frequent orders for smaller amounts. The higher transportation costs resulting from smaller orders can be countered by combining orders for an assortments of products into one truckload, or hiring external logistics companies to handle shipping. Also, companies can reduce long lead times by working to improve internal operating effectiveness (see Chapter 10).
4. *Reduce demand destabilizing practices.* Promotions, special sales, and price discounts artificially stimulate demand, and tend to "borrow" it from following periods. Reducing such practices provides a clearer picture of real consumer demand and removes the incentives for consumers to stockpile.
5. *Counter customer "gaming" during shortages.* When a product is in short supply, suppliers can allocate it to customers on the basis of their previous sales records, rather than on their current orders; this discourages them from overordering. They can also eliminate generous return policies, so customers are less likely to cancel orders.

Which of these possible corrective actions is more effective in improving supply chain performance seems to depend on the particular context. A series of recent experiments,[22] however, provides some partial insights and tantalizing conjectures. A modified, Web-based version of the beer game simulation was used to investigate various ways for "beating the bullwhip" with the help of information technology.

Each experimental condition corresponded to a different type of 'real world' IT effort, and was conducted with hundreds of supply-chain simulation runs.

One experiment compared the effect of *sharing actual demand* data among all supply chain participants with that of *reducing the time lag* between one player's actions and another player's awareness of it. This experiment indicated that, compared with demand sharing, a shorter response lag led to superior customer satisfaction and lower cost. On the other hand, demand sharing did a better job of reducing the magnitude of the bullwhip fluctuations.

A second experiment concentrated on two different kinds of time lag: shortening the time to deliver an order after receiving it and shortening the time between orders (implying more frequent orders). This revealed that *shortening delivery times* was about as effective as *shortening order interarrival times* in lowering total supply-chain cost, but that shorter delivery lags also improved customer satisfaction, while shorter order lags did not.

The goal of this work was to understand which initiatives, alone and in combination, had the greatest effect on each of three different performance outcomes. Its results again strongly support our theme throughout this book—that there is no "one best way" to deploy IT in the circumstances modeled by this game, since various performance measures were differentially affected by the various approaches.

5.7.3 An Example: Managing the Bullwhip

Barilla SpA, an Italian manufacturer of pasta products, provides an excellent example of how one company attempted to solve the problems the bullwhip effect created for its manufacturing and distribution operations—and the difficulties it encountered in the process.[23] In spite of a fairly constant (and high!) consumption of pasta in Italy, Barilla experienced wild swings in demand at its main distribution center (DC) in Pedrigiano. This distribution center delivered to its customers' distribution centers, which then supplied retailers. In some weeks the demand for pasta on the Pedrigiano DC might rise as high as 80,000 kg, then fall to only 4,000 kg the next week. With an average demand of 30,000 kg, the DC experienced a weekly standard deviation of 22,700 kg! Keeping enough inventory to ensure that it could satisfy customer orders under such circumstances had become extraordinarily expensive, and Barilla suffered from both high inventories *and* poor order fill rates. With retailers cutting back on their own inventories, the demand for good service from Barilla was increasing. Its managers recognized that something needed to be done.

In attempting to deal with this problem, Barilla introduced a program called just-in-time distribution (JITD). Brando Vitali, director of logistics at Barilla explained the concept:

> *… rather than send product to the distributors according to their internal planning processes, we should look at all of the distributors' data and send only what is needed at the stores—no more, no less. … In my opinion, we could improve operations for ourselves* ***and*** *our customers if we were responsible for creating the delivery schedules. … We could try to reduce our own distribution costs, inventory levels and ultimately, our manufacturing costs if we didn't have to respond to the volatile demand patterns of the distributor.*

We have always had the mentality that orders were an unchangeable input into our process, and therefore that one of the most important capabilities we needed to achieve was flexibility to respond to those inputs. But in reality, demand from the end-consumer is the input.

How would this work? Every day, each distributor would provide us data on what Barilla products it had shipped out of its warehouse to retailers during the previous day, as well as the current stock level for each Barilla SKU. Then we could look at all of the data and make replenishment decisions based on our own forecasts ... we would just be responding to sell-through information one step behind the retailer. Ideally, we would use actual retail sell-through data, but that's hard to come by […] given that most grocers in Italy aren't equipped yet with the necessary bar-code scanners and computer linkages.

Vitali's vision thus adopted two of the approaches suggested in the previous section for ameliorating the bullwhip effect: Reduce the autonomy of one of the stages in the channel by allowing one player to make fast decisions for the good of the whole channel, using information that is closer to the real demand signal.

While the vision was sound, Barilla's "solution" created new, largely unforeseen problems. The *implementation* of the plan—where the rubber met the road—was much more challenging than expected. First was the problem faced by Barilla's downstream distributors. What would their managers' jobs be, if not to manage stocks at their warehouses? Why should they hand over information to Barilla solely for the sake of Barilla's convenience? Many were unconvinced of the advantages they would gain from Vitali's plan. One distributor offered to *sell* Barilla the information it wanted, but would not relinquish decision rights over what got ordered, and when. This was far from what Barilla wanted.

Ultimately, Barilla recognized that it needed to create a *demonstration project* to convince its downstream partners that the JITD program would both work and be better for them. To do so, it tested JITD on two of its own distribution depots, in Florence and Milan. The results were surprisingly good. Fill rates rose from 98.8 percent to 99.8 percent, even as inventory levels fell from ten days to four days. Eventually, Barilla was able to sell the idea to Cortese, a long-time distributor of Barilla products, with remarkable results. Stockouts at Cortese fell from about 6 percent to practically zero, and inventories were halved. Even with this powerful evidence, broader implementation of JITD was a long, slow haul. It had taken five years since the inception of the idea just to get to this first customer approval.

Not only did Barilla face resistance from its external partners, but also there was considerable internal resistance to the plan. What, for example, would now be the job of its salespeople in a world where the amount sold was determined by its logistics staff? What new role would they have? Their bonuses depended on how much they sold—but JITD gave them little influence over sales.

5.7.4 Some Concluding Thoughts on Supply Chain Management

Although the advantages of reducing the bullwhip effect in a supply chain—by tying the various participants closer together—are obvious in theory, hundreds of companies have experienced difficulties similar to those faced by Barilla. Knowing the pain that will be involved, few companies feel they have the ability, resources, and credibility to drive the changes required. The supply chains that lead the way are generally those where one of the participants is exceptionally powerful. Which one this is depends very much on where it is and who is involved. In the case of Barilla, for example, in Italy it was by far the most powerful player; the retail grocery chains were much weaker by comparison. When Barilla entered the U.S. market, on the other hand, it had no such power. In the U.S. market, the giant retailers tend to have greater power than most of their suppliers. As a result, Wal-Mart (the largest company in the world in terms of sales) was able over time to build its supply chain and weld it into a tightly linked system, sometimes in partnership with its largest suppliers. P&G, one of these partners, in turn exerts its power in the supply chains it dominates to allow its salespeople to restock retailers' shelves directly—without going through the usual ordering/delivery process.

In spite of the clear systemic advantages of schemes like Barilla's, the problems of implementing such strategies rarely lie with technology. Rather, they are founded in people and power. Individuals feel threatened and potentially usurped by the mechanistic models of *vendor-managed inventory.* Corporations rightfully have concerns about handing over information and decision rights concerning their inventory levels. If the resulting gains are systemic then, quite reasonably, the various companies in the chain ought to work out equitable ways to share the spoils. In spite of new technologies, the mountains that supply-chain managers need to cross before reaching the promised land present a difficult and arduous journey, one that is likely to grind slowly on for many years to come. Technology may facilitate solutions, but it is custom, practice, trust, and culture—the infrastructure of supply chains—that ultimately determine the ability to overcome the inherent challenges of coordinating vertical networks.

NOTES

1. Barabasi (2002).
2. See Tu (2000) and Iansiti and Levien (2003).
3. Skinner (1974).
4. Mukherjee et al. (2000), for example, argue that the "focus" achieved by reducing product variety in a given facility does not by itself necessarily lead to improved performance, as this depends critically on how "different" the various products really are in terms of their manufacture. What they find to be critical, by examining sixteen different production lines, is whether a line is asked to carry out tasks that are outside its normal capabilities.
5. See, for example, Ruwe and Skinner (1987) and the case "Copeland Corporation" (HBS case #9-686-088).
6. Reported in Harmon (1992) and Rommel et al. (1995).
7. A disguised name; see the case "Medical Products Company" (HBS case #9-694-065).
8. A disguised name: see the case "Wriston Manufacturing Corporation" (HBS case #9-698-049).
9. See Iansiti (2002).
10. See Brown et al. (2002), "Li & Fung (Trading), Ltd." (HBS case number 9-396-075), and "Massimo Menichetti (B)" (HBS case number 9-686-135).

11. Cusumano and Gawer (2002) provides more information about this and other types of collaborator networks.

12. See Hayes and Schmenner (1978).

13 A disguised name; see the case "Alden Products, Inc.—European Manufacturing" (HBS case 9-697-099).

14. See "Nestlé's ERP Odyssey," *CIO Magazine* (May 15, 2002): 62–70.

15. See "Intel—PED (A)" (HBS case 9-693-056).

16. See "John Crane UK Ltd." (HBS case 9-691-021).

17. This issue is rather complex because, as noted above, standardization is often advocated as a means for diffusing best practices.

18. Developed by Jay Forrester and Jon Sterman at MIT.

19. One of the worst-performing players we have observed, in fact, was an executive who recently had managed a Beer Game exercise for his own company!

20. Based on U.S. Commerce Department sales and inventory reports.

21. See the Web site: www.cpfr.org/InventoryTraditional.html.

22. Conducted by Professor Andrew McAfee at the Harvard Business School.

23. See "Barilla SpA (A)-(D)" (HBS case numbers 9-694-046, and 9-965-064, 065, and 066).

Chapter 6

Information Technology and Operations

6.1 INTRODUCTION

Information technology (IT) has become an increasingly critical part of an operations manager's job. Indeed, many operations managers are now charged with managing not only the physical aspects of operations, but also the technologies required to deal with the ever-growing torrent of information needed for those operations. In this chapter, we will begin by understanding how the role of IT in operations has changed over time, and look at two important technologies having a broad impact on many companies: enterprise resource planning (ERP) and the Internet. We will then look at systems integration (both within and outside the company), and explore the critical and increasing role that IT-based standards play in allowing companies to fit their IT systems to their changing operating imperatives. We then present two potential long-term hazards faced by operations managers as they deploy new IT systems, and examine alternative strategies for building an IT capability in light of those hazards. Finally, we emphasize that IT shares a fundamental principle with operations in general: While many technologies may be widely available to all, it is the *way* those technologies are combined and exploited that provides them with the potential to deliver a powerful, and ongoing, competitive advantage. We will revisit and expand upon some of these same issues in Chapter 7, where we discuss different approaches to developing *operating* process technologies.

6.2 THE EXPANDING ROLE OF IT

6.2.1 IT in Operations

In the 1960s, the IT presence in companies was characterized by mainframe computers, hard-wired terminals, card readers, and customized programs. Such programs often focused on running the payrolls and customer billings of mid- to large-size companies, and thus it was natural for IT to report to the chief financial officer.[1] With the 1970s came the ability to share the resources of a mainframe or minicomputer with "virtual operating systems" that allowed a distributed group of users to interact with the mainframe as if it were dedicated to each of them alone.

This fostered a much more eclectic use of IT, and exposed many more people to its capabilities.

In particular, it allowed the deployment of programs like MAPICS, one of the best-known packages for running Material Requirements Planning (MRP), a system used to plan and manage manufacturing operations. MRP relied on a database containing, for each product, a current inventory level, a demand forecast, a bill of materials (BOM) that specified the type and number of components needed for each product, and an estimate of its manufacturing/purchasing lead time. Given these four pieces of information, the MRP system worked back from specific delivery dates and determined which, how many, and when components should be made or ordered. MRP, of course, has become much more sophisticated over the years, but the fundamental principles remain the same: to allow manufacturers to decide how much of what to make/order, and when to do so. The advent of software such as MRP brought the realization that IT had become an important tool for supporting operations. Operations managers were compelled (sometimes reluctantly!) to take advantage of these new control technologies, which appeared to have the potential to simplify a shop's information flows and assure timely and accurate delivery of products.

The 1980s brought an explosive increase in the computing power available on microprocessors, fueling the advent of the microcomputer. This, along with spreadsheet and word-processing capabilities, allowed managers to have (physically, rather than virtually, as before) their own personal machine, sometimes possessing the ability to network with the rest of their organization, to share files,

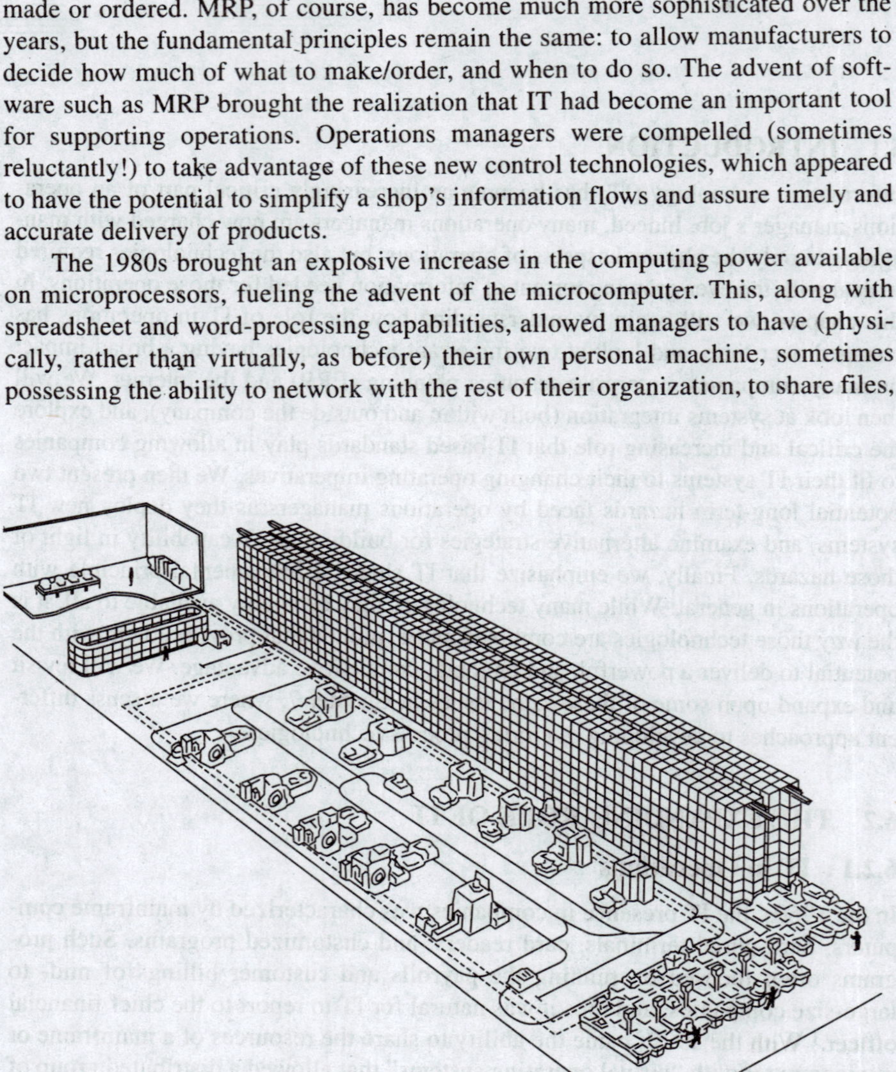

Figure 6-1 A Flexible Manufacturing System

and to run shared programs. At the same time, advances in robotics, sensors and material-handling technologies (such as Automated Guided Vehicles, or AGVs) allowed the development of the first *flexible manufacturing systems* (FMS), an example of which is depicted in Figure 6-1.

The goal of many FMS vendors was to progress, ultimately, to a "lights out" factory, in which robots, machines, and computers would carry out all information flows, machining, and materials handling. The term *lights out* conveyed the idea that operations managers would be able to close the doors, turn the lights out, and simply let the computers and machinery do their work. Indeed, at least one such factory was built by Yamazaki-Mazak machine tools in Japan, which ran its third shift with no lights. Although it was used as a production facility for its machine tools, it also fulfilled an important marketing role: to show the potential of Mazak's technology.

While many FMSs were installed, the promise of the lights-out factory faded as companies' product ranges exploded, stretching the automated machinery beyond what it could do without manual intervention. In addition, the applicability of the technology was primarily limited to small-batch machined goods, which meant that the vast majority of manufacturing industries were beyond its reach. Most manufacturers realized that their operating systems would require people to make them work, at least for the foreseeable future.

Meanwhile, a series of impressive IT developments began to make it possible to link the activities of *design* and manufacturing. Computer-aided design (CAD) systems, which initially were simple two-dimensional drafting tools, developed the capability to depict three-dimensional solid models. This permitted a range of additional tools to emerge, such as finite-element programs (to predict stress and distortion) and routines that detected interference in 3-D space.

One of the most significant consequences of the development of 3-D modeling was the advent of computer-aided manufacturing (CAM), which used the three-dimensional representation of an object to design the process for manufacturing it. These *part-programs* defined paths, cutters, speeds, and feeds, and could be downloaded to specified machine tools to make the component.

John Crane (UK) Ltd. used these technologies to develop a powerful competitive advantage in the market for specialized engineering seals in the early 1990s.[2] For many years Crane had been a pioneer in the design and manufacture of mechanical seals. It invented, for example, the "gas-seal," which uses a gaseous barrier to keep two fluids from mixing through the bearing of a rotating shaft. Gradually, many of Crane's seals became commoditized, and cheap "knock-off" products manufactured in the Far East became available throughout the world. Crane struggled as it progressively shifted its business away from commodity seals to more specialized seals. In this arena, seals often were custom made, or older-model seals that were no longer made were reproduced. A number of other companies already were operating in the specialized seal market, however, and Crane had to find a compelling way to differentiate itself if it were to achieve success.

Seals generally represent only a small part of the cost of a piece of capital equipment (such as a paper plant), but their failure can bring the whole plant to a stop. Quick response was usually the primary customer need in this situation, so delivery lead-time (rather than price) became the principle operating challenge in

Crane's new world. As it restructured its physical manufacturing operations to adapt to its changing priorities, Crane turned to information technology to help it forge a new competitive advantage. It built its own CAD-CAM system to take engineers' designs and automatically generate part-programs for making the parts. Its competitors, however, were using off-the-shelf CAD-CAM systems that, while they worked, were not tuned precisely to the world of mechanical seals. These systems often demanded time-consuming manual intervention to rewrite the part-programs.

The system built by Crane, by contrast, not only produced customized parts the first time, but it also could be improved over time. Operators would make suggestions when they saw the machine tool using suboptimal processes, and production engineers would then adjust the software to take advantage of their experience. Over time, Crane built a system that was unmatched anywhere in the world. In concert with its new, just-in-time physical operations it gained and maintained a major presence in the specialized seal business, providing a compelling example of the use of IT to build powerful *new* operating capabilities, rather than simply to "support" manufacturing.

6.2.2 Expansion of IT to Business and Network Operations

The Crane example addresses the *manufacturing process* level. In recent years, however, IT-related operating processes have grown to encompass many of a firm's activities at the coordinative or *business process* level. Reflecting its growing importance during the 1980s, many companies began to recognize IT's potential to create a broader source of competitive advantage. In 1986, William Gruber coined the term *chief information officer,*[3] or CIO, to reflect the need for this emerging resource to be managed more effectively. Unlike traditional DP (data-processing) managers, who were responsible for simply controlling and maintaining the various IT systems around a company, the more senior role of the CIO was to guide the exploitation of the new opportunities that were emerging as a result of IT-based capabilities, as well as to manage the increasingly cross-functional span of those technologies.

One of the consequences of the expanding applications and role of IT was the tangle of tools that grew up in many firms: MRP systems often had trouble speaking to financial systems; sales management systems generally could not communicate with compensation systems, and so on. In addition, IT began to reach *outside* the firm's operations, giving companies the ability to communicate with each other to coordinate deliveries and place orders. In response to these trends, two new sets of technologies emerged to create critical new areas of opportunity—and challenge—for operations managers: enterprise resource planning systems (ERP) and the Internet.

6.2.3 Enterprise Resource Planning

ERP is an enterprise-wide information system that aims to integrate most of a company's IT-based business processes. These large systems, costing from $5 million to $250 million to implement, enjoyed dramatic growth in the 1990s.[4] The growth of sales of the principle ERP vendors is depicted in Figure 6-2. By 2002, in spite of a somewhat slower growth rate due to the "tech meltdown," the annual revenue of the largest vendor, SAP, had grown to more than $7.5 billion.

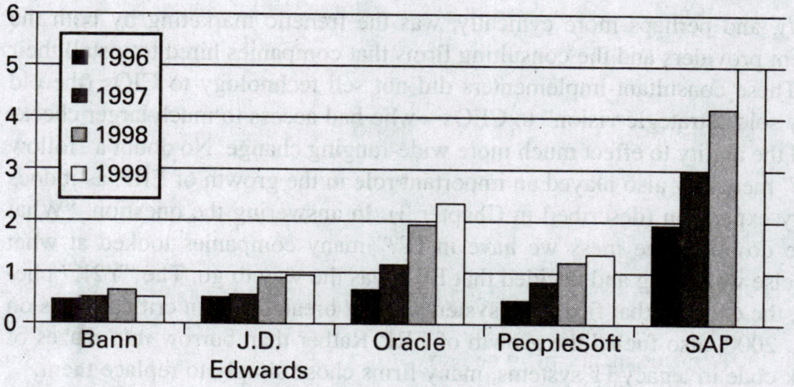

Figure 6-2 Revenues of Top ERP Vendors, 1996–1999

ERP's success resulted from the confluence of a number of factors. *First,* as described above, many companies (and particularly their CEOs) had become frustrated that different parts of their organizations used idiosyncratic, often local, information systems. These alien systems caused data to be presented in inconsistent ways, making comparisons and aggregations very difficult. In some cases, accessing information from elsewhere in the organization had become impossible from a technical point of view, as the systems often could not talk to one another at all. This unfortunate state of affairs commonly emerged when firms made a series of acquisitions of companies having incompatible information systems, or unthinkingly gave their internal groups local control over information technology without requiring common standards for data representation and interchange between sites. Most companies did not anticipate that it would soon be possible for information systems to be networked across even the most remote sites. These factors were compounded in governmental organizations, where the differing emphases of various political parties and philosophies, combined with the rapid, election-induced turnover of personnel (as well as the complacency associated with civil service regulations), and the lack of competitive pressure, has fostered IT anarchy. When the U.S. government decided to establish its Office of Homeland Security in 2002, for example, it discovered that its border security agencies alone employed eleven different databases—none of them compatible with the others!

Second was the growing influence of the *process-view* of organizations, which suggested that firms be reengineered around the family of processes (e.g., order fulfillment, billing, and payment processing) necessary to run the business, rather than around the various departments and functional groups that might be involved in those processes (see Chapter 10). ERP provided an opportunity to change the way a company worked, first forcing those processes to be specified exactly and then cementing them into its *modus operandi* through software. Since the software didn't allow people to do things the old way, the "reengineered" way became the only way that people could work.

Finally, and perhaps more cynically, was the frenetic marketing by both the ERP system providers and the consulting firms that companies hired to install their systems. These consultant-implementers did not sell technology to CIOs (the old way), they sold "strategic vision" to CEOs—who had access to much larger checkbooks and the ability to effect much more wide-ranging change. No doubt a "follow the leader" mentality also played an important role in the growth of ERP, as it does in capacity expansion (described in Chapter 3). In answering the question, "What should we do about the mess we have in IT?" many companies looked at what everyone else was doing and decided that ERP was the way to go. The "Y2K" phenomenon, the concern that firms' IT systems might break down in critical ways on January 1, 2000, also fueled the growth of ERP. Rather than burrow into mazes of patchwork code in legacy IT systems, many firms chose simply to replace them.[5]

Unfortunately, many of these new "organ implants" failed. One study found that 50 percent of such major IT initiatives were abandoned, and another 40 percent were delivered late and/or over budget.[6] Other studies have estimated a 70 percent failure rate in process-enabling IT initiatives,[7] and a staggering 84 percent failure rate in customer relations management (CRM) initiatives.[8]

This does not imply that ERP and other major IT systems have not brought tremendous benefits to many firms. Rather, it says that they have not been the right solution for *all* firms in *every* situation—as might be predicted from our discussion of the concept of fit earlier in this book. We will discuss both the potential and the pitfalls of ERP, and different approaches for implementing it and other major new IT initiatives, later in this chapter.

6.2.4 The Impact of the Internet

The growth of the Internet in the 1990s was fueled primarily by the World Wide Web (WWW). In late 1990, Tim Berners-Lee invented the technology behind the WWW at CERN in Switzerland. The idea behind the Web was to merge computer networking and hypertext into a powerful and easy-to-use global information system. Hypertext is text with links to other information, on the model of references in a scientific paper or cross-references in a dictionary. With electronic documents, these cross-references can be accessed with a mouse-click, and thanks to the WWW, they can be anywhere in the world.

The Internet had been growing steadily since the late 1960s, and by the 1990s it had become the worldwide 'plumbing' for e-mail and file transfers. The WWW provided a clear 'window' into that vast network, so that normal humans as well as computer nerds could now use it. The implications of the WWW for operations managers have been immense. First, it allowed the installation of *intranets* (private, company-only webs) that used the same technology as the rest of the WWW, and provided the ability to share documents and information within a company in a standard and readable form. Second, these intranets were often extended to become *extranets,* which allowed selected outside organizations to have access to some of the data available inside the firm.

These Internet-enabled networks made it possible for companies to begin to share information with partners, customers and suppliers in a seamless way.

Although EDI (electronic data interchange) had stumbled along for many years using dedicated links and proprietary protocols, this new *lingua franca* made it possible for companies to share information with even the most remote suppliers and customers. Among the thousands of possible examples, *BusinessWeek* reported on fifty of the most innovative projects using the Web that various organizations had under way in late 2003; these ranged from collaborations with suppliers to customer service to operational streamlining.[9] Web-based networks also facilitated outsourcing of an increasing number of IT activities, and created the foundation for *utility computing*—where companies could access the computing power residing in other companies' computer networks whenever their own ran short of capacity. All this was made possible largely by an acceptance of global, open standards.[10] We will talk more about the importance of such standards later in this chapter.

6.3 THE CHALLENGES OF INTEGRATION, STANDARDS, AND FIT

6.3.1 Making IT Decisions that "Fit"

IT today has become all-pervasive. Its tentacles now stretch to embrace not only the whole firm, but the firm's suppliers, partners, and customers as well. IT's role for many years was simply to *support* operations; today it is at the *heart of* operations. When combined with superior physical processes, it can be forged into a powerful weapon—providing firms with new abilities to compete through operations. It has grown to be an essential part of the operations manager's job, either alone or in combination with the other systems overseen by the CIO. Indeed, IT has come to dominate the capital spent on fixed investment by firms, and has continued to displace traditional investments through booms and busts since the 1970s (see Figure 6-3).

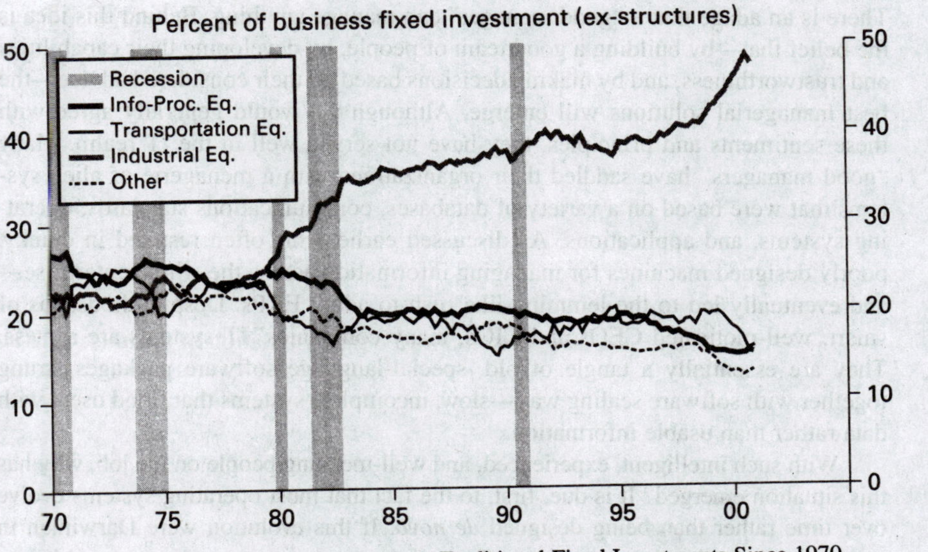

Figure 6-3 Percent Expenditure on IT vs. Traditional Fixed Investments Since 1970

For IT professionals of the 1960s the concepts of *fit* and *focus,* as described in Chapter 2, would have had little meaning: there generally was only one basic way to run payroll! Today, however, the situation is very different. The choices are vast, whether concerning the technology to be used, who builds the software, how much information to share, or what standards are to be used in the company.

Like any other engineered system, a given IT system is good at doing certain things but not so good at others. This requires choices, and the concepts of fit and focus play key roles in making such choices. Which IT choices will fit with the firm's long-term competitive objectives? Which will allow it to focus its operations' efforts on building the capabilities that will deliver those objectives?

Many firms, however, do not find themselves in a position to make IT decisions that "fit." They are saddled with multiple operating systems and a cacophony of communications standards, resulting in excessive, ongoing expense that delivers little apparent value. A chaotic information system is much like a chaotic factory operation, in that it cannot be managed so as to provide desired competitive priorities until it is brought under control through the adoption of common operating principles and standard practices. These *principles,* in turn, provide the stable foundation upon which managers can grow and mold IT to their best advantage. One of the most important of these basic principles relates to the custodianship of technical standards, which has a major impact on the ability of an IT system to integrate groups both inside and outside the firm, and maintain that integration over time. To see how managers can make the most of that potential to facilitate communication and coordination across the firm, we first must understand how companies get themselves in trouble. Then we can explore how standardization, paradoxically, *increases* a company's ability to change and improve an IT system over time.

6.3.2 How Did We Get into This Mess?

There is an adage that a "good manager" can manage anything. Behind this idea is the belief that—by building a good team of people, by developing their capabilities and trustworthiness, and by making decisions based on their considered advice—the best managerial solutions will emerge. Although we would generally agree with these sentiments and principles, they have not served well in the IT realm. Many "good managers" have saddled their organizations with a menagerie of alien systems that were based on a variety of databases, communications standards, operating systems, and applications. As discussed earlier, this often resulted in clunky, poorly designed machines for managing information across the whole enterprise—and eventually led to the lemming-like rush to adopt ERPs. Despite thousands of smart, well-motivated CEOs and CIOs, many companies' IT systems are a mess. They are essentially a tangle of old, special-language software packages strung together with software sealing wax—slow, incomplete systems that flood users with data rather than usable information.

With such intelligent, experienced, and well-meaning people on the job, why has this situation emerged? It is due, first, to the fact that most operating systems evolve over time rather than being designed *de novo.* If this evolution were Darwinian in nature, one would expect corporate information systems to grow stronger and leaner with each generation, with weaknesses being bred out and strengths being reinforced. This is not what we see. Although managers are often eager to introduce new systems, they tend to be loath to eliminate the old systems the new ones are supposed to replace. They either fear that they may somehow lose critical information or access in the process, or feel the need to provide a backup for units that are unprepared to make the switchover. Second, it results from an over-reliance on the idea that local needs demand local solutions. Local managers (those who manage departments, plants, joint-ventures, geographic regions, divisions, etc.) often will cling tenaciously to this idea, for the reasons discussed in Chapter 5. Given that IT is so important to their operations, they want to retain control over their own destiny by selecting information technology that is "just right" for their needs. We return to this theme in our discussion of process development in Chapter 7.

Unfettered by clearly illuminated principles, trade-offs, or constraints from their leaders, local or departmental managers usually will do the "right thing"—from their own point of view. They will build the locally optimal solution, and pay far less attention to the overall requirements of the firm as a whole. This is the "Let a Hundred Flowers Bloom" approach to IT. In theory, this encourages innovation and local experimentation so that good solutions will ultimately emerge. In practice, it resulted in the chaos described above and caused thousands of firms to turn to ERP for their salvation. An ERP system forces managers to adopt a whole-enterprise perspective by restricting their ability to make local experiments and improvements—unless, of course, the hundred flowers include competing ERP systems as well!

Celanese, a $4.5 billion global chemicals manufacturer, provides an extreme example of what can go wrong with this approach. In 2001, it finally faced up to the fact that its policy of giving its five business units almost complete autonomy had led them over time to adopt fourteen different major IT systems, including thirteen separate SAP systems, in three different versions across five different data centers. For many years, Celanese had operated as a holding company, and tried to arrive at decisions affecting the whole corporation on a consensus basis. The fierce independence of its subsidiaries, however, tended to undermine consensus, so hard decisions affecting IT had been avoided for many years. In order to reduce the cost and complexity of its multiple systems, Celanese ordered its CIO to replace all fourteen IT systems with a single one (called "OneSAP") over a two-year period. One of the managers involved in this Herculean effort commented, "we're trying to become one company … [which requires having] to make people feel pain to an almost near-death experience. That's the only way to get to the ultimate goal." Celanese hoped, as a result of this rationalization, to realize operating savings of 30 to 50 percent.[11]

This vignette illustrates vividly that one of top management's primary purposes should be to ensure that the IT decisions made by managers throughout an organization fit together in a coherent way. This usually will mean some sacrifice on the part of local managers. Although their choices might be optimal from a local point-of-view, the corporate leader's job is to point out the sacrifices that need to be made for the good of the whole, and to help guide ongoing decisions with a vision and set of principles for the whole organization.

Unfortunately, in the case of IT many of the trade-offs necessary to sustain an integrated information system over time are tediously technical. When faced with making and enforcing such trade-offs—concerning database standards, communications standards, and so on—senior managers will often, through lack of knowledge, back off and defer to their regional and functional managers. These managers, in turn, usually turn for help to their local IT experts and consultants. They usually will ask, "Will our systems be compatible?" but as we describe later, this is an imprecise question. *All* systems are ultimately compatible, given an infinite amount of software engineers, time, and money.

No company, unfortunately, has infinite resources. For example, Kellogg, the giant breakfast cereal producer, teamed with Oracle, the second-largest software company in the world, in an ambitious attempt to create a massive software package dubbed CPG (for consumer packaged goods). CPG proposed to integrate four complex systems from four different vendors—Oracle's ERP system, an asset management system provided by Indus, a supply-chain management system provided by Manugistics, and an order management system provided by IMI—into a seamless whole. Oracle pledged to take full responsibility for the integration and support of CPG. After three years of trying, however, the software was still not working as promised because of the difficulties of integrating the four alien systems and companies, each of which had its own view on how data should be represented and communicated. Tri Valley Growers, a farm co-op in San Ramon, California, went bankrupt after spending millions in the attempt to implement the same system, and according to one industry observer, "No one ever got [all the pieces of] CPG up and running."[12]

At the very least, senior managers' technical knowledge must embrace standards and principles that allow evolution, innovation, and experimentation to take place, and that their evolving systems are able to integrate with, be maintained by, and be consistent with the enterprise as a whole. In order to show why such understanding is becoming increasingly important, and why asking whether two systems are "compatible" is the wrong question, we will use communication standards as an example. This will demand some tolerance for dry detail on the part of the reader, but will ultimately, we trust, enable senior operations managers to ask more informed questions about their evolving information technology and better understand some of the important trends in IT.

6.3.3 Selecting Standards

The trouble with standards is—there are so many to choose from.
—Anonymous

To understand the idea of a communications standard, it is important to recognize that such standards exist at many levels. For example, as shown in Figure 6-4, the Internet relies on low-level protocols such as *ethernet* to carry digital bits from one place to another. This standard addresses such prosaic issues as 'what voltage should represent a 1?" The next level (in this example, TCP/IP—the protocol of the Internet) relies on the lower standards to get its work done. This standard addresses questions like, "How do I make sure packets of bits get to the right place, and in the

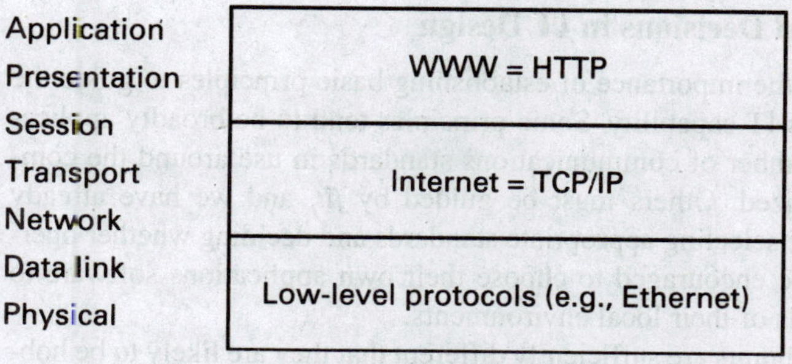

Figure 6-4 Internet Open Protocol Stack

right order?" The next level (in this example, HTTP), tells the receiving computer how to display the data by, for example, having a protocol to distinguish text from graphics. This protocol relies on all the levels of protocol beneath it. In the case of most Internet protocols, the protocol stack is *vertically modular.* This means that we can run TCP/IP over a variety of low-level protocols. We can use the ethernet or a modem; TCP/IP would even work over a semaphore link—which would demand even more patience than the average modem!

Why is such technical detail important in operations? It reveals that computers communicate at many different levels, and an agreement must be reached about the appropriate protocols at each of these levels. Systems may be compatible at one level of the stack, but not at another. Also, the 1990s saw a rapidly converging consensus about the standards that should be applied at various levels, making it much easier to connect computers that would hitherto have been described as *incompatible.* Moreover, many of these standards were *open* standards, meaning that no license fees are necessary to use them, so even small companies can afford to be members of a rapidly growing community of computers that can communicate easily with one another. Finally, the growth of the open protocol stack has come from the bottom up. It began with physical layers (such as ethernet), which gave rise to TCP/IP (the basis for the Internet), which over the last few years gave rise to the World Wide Web.

Even higher-level standards (such as those for specific business processes) are continuing to emerge. (Appendix 6.A describes the enormous potential that such standards provide for integrating *across* firms.) By buttressing existing standards with promising emerging ones, companies can create systems that permit ever-more-sophisticated integration—not only across the various systems in current use, but also incorporating as-yet-unanticipated future systems. Moreover, as emphasized earlier, not only must a company adopt standardized technical and business interfaces, it must choose whether to centralize control of information technology or delegate that control to local managers. These choices, however, should reflect an attempt to create an IT infrastructure that supports a firm's strategic objectives, not a mind-set that sees a monolithic, centralized design as a technical necessity because the firm has failed to develop adequate IT capabilities.

6.3.4 Principles and Decisions in IT Design

Earlier we emphasized the importance of establishing basic principles to guide the development of a firm's IT capability. Some principles tend to be broadly applicable, such as that the number of communications standards in use around the company should be minimized. Others must be guided by *fit,* and we have already introduced two of these: selecting appropriate standards and deciding whether operating subunits should be encouraged to choose their own applications software to reflect the specific needs of their local environments.

Sometimes such subunits are sufficiently different that they are likely to be hobbled by a "one-size-fits-all" solution. However, a company with very similar business units might do well to run the gauntlet of local objections and encourage use of a single system. This almost always will reduce costs, and given some soak time, may actually end up being favored by local managers. Decisions regarding where local control of IT should end and central coordination begin should be shaped by the firm's overall strategy, rather than based on a "best practice" approach. As described in Chapter 2, this means such decisions should be guided by how a particular business chooses to compete in its particular competitive environment.

Whatever decision is made, senior managers need to keep some key points in mind. First, although its importance is often underestimated, keeping informed about, and taking advantage of, standards has become one of their most critical responsibilities. Second, steering one's organization through the blizzard of technologies that emerge over time requires some detailed knowledge. Without such knowledge, operations managers tend to avoid making the key decisions required to maintain the coherence of their IT infrastructure over time. As a result, they lose the power to affect choices that could enable or constrain different operations strategies in the future.

Later in the chapter, we will expand further on the strategic choices and principles that are necessary in developing a company's IT base. First, however, we want to alert the reader to some of the potential strategic hazards encountered in deploying IT, which emphasize the need for carefully selecting the appropriate principles for guiding development.

6.4 STRATEGIC HAZARDS

Two common strategic hazards, with echoes in other chapters of this book, have become particularly salient in the IT arena: hazards to distinctiveness and hazards to strategic flexibility.

6.4.1 Hazards to Distinctiveness: The Rebirth of the "One Best Way"

Many companies install packaged corporate software (such as ERP) as a way of importing "best practices" from others (insofar as those practices are embodied in the software vendors' products), and applying them across their whole enterprise. This approach might work well in companies that fall far short of superior practice. In others, however, it might cement them into a set of "best" practices that, while effective in certain other industries, are hopelessly inadequate for the particular business at hand. For example, in the electronics distribution industry, salespeople have a base price from which they set custom prices for every customer. Rapid response is critical for such people. To set the price, they need to know how much inventory is on hand and the company's sales history with that particular customer, as well as a range of other data such as the prevailing market scarcity of the product.

In order to access these data, one well-known ERP system (at least in its plain vanilla form) requires salespeople to bring up multiple "screens" on their computers. This causes them to become frustrated and less effective, so the new system becomes a barrier to effectiveness rather than an aid. A better solution—for this kind of business, at least—would be to have all these data available on one well laid-out screen. This is a comparatively minor example, but thousands of such issues can arise when using a "one size fits all" program.

Of course, software packages can be modified to accommodate such local needs, but each such change can be expensive and time-consuming, adding up to a very expensive and lengthy implementation project. Software that forces a company to adopt *best practice* is similar in philosophy to the *one best way* approach to operations (as exemplified by "lean manufacturing;" see Chapter 2). By restricting its ability to create distinctiveness, there is a real danger that *best* practice—imported through IT and available to all—eventually becomes *standard* practice in an industry. IT thereby becomes just an expensive competitive leveler, from which no one gains any advantage. We return to this issue in Section 6.6.

We advocate a very different approach, one that demands a contingent view of operations: different companies may choose different ways of doing things, not only because they have different strengths and weaknesses, different business environments, and different competitive strategies, but also because this is the only way their operations organization can participate in creating a distinctive competitive advantage. Such an advantage can sometimes be achieved using packaged software, as the ability to customize it increases. If not managed carefully, however, IT's potential to be restrict operational flexibility has ramifications that may encumber a company for years, as described below.

6.4.2 Hazards to Strategic Flexibility: IT as "Liquid Concrete"

One of the misleading aspects of the word *software* is that "soft" is its first half. This suggests something that is easily malleable, whose shape can be altered at will. The reality for operations IT, of course, is very different—as it is with other elements of the operations infrastructure. As one manager observed: "I can easily change a piece of structural steel: get a guy with a flame-cutter, and it's done. Software is a nightmare to change: whenever we change it, it messes something else up."

Such experiences are typical. Software has become so complex and interdependent that it is difficult for engineers to make small changes without causing much broader ramifications. Although vertical and horizontal modularity certainly help, there are some systems that are so difficult to change that the systems themselves ultimately come to *define* the firm's operations. The only way to break out of this "soft" straightjacket is through a *strategic leap,* as described in Chapter 10: replacing the whole system, or at least, substantial parts of it. Hence the popularity of ERP systems and process reengineering.

This, however, runs counter to what many operations managers have learned through hard experience. The last half of the twentieth century saw a shift in the role of operations managers from merely being users and custodians of capital equipment to emphasizing ongoing improvement and local innovation. As pointed out in Chapter 2, managers are realizing that the key to creating competitive advantage through operations lies in developing distinctive capabilities rather than solely in buying the latest equipment and technology. Dogged, incremental improvement and an increasing reliance on one's internal capacity to create and improve new process technology have characterized the approaches used for developing such capabilities. Many leading companies have provided examples of the benefits of this approach:

1. It makes ongoing improvement a part of everyone's job—not just that of a select few.
2. The deep knowledge that is developed allows the operation to adapt to new requirements, remain flexible as business requirements change, and develop new capabilities through experimentation and invention.

Many companies' approaches to selecting and implementing information systems, however, reflect a movement in the opposite direction. Enterprise resource planning systems, as the name suggests, pervade the whole company and shape the way the business works at many levels. More and more firms are installing ERP, and the application of ever-more-powerful IT systems in operations is increasingly characterized by very large implementation projects. Because these systems are so complex and monolithic, they often make it forbiddingly expensive and difficult to conduct local experimentation (which might improve performance or adapt better to changing requirements). In short, the information systems adopted by many companies have come to mirror many of the features traditionally associated with large, sophisticated, capital-intensive production equipment.

Moreover, they tend to lock a company into using a single software vendor, which both restricts its ability to take advantage of the advances made by alternative vendors and creates major problems if its own vendor experiences internal problems or goes out of business. The attempt by Oracle to acquire PeopleSoft in 2003, for example, was regarded with horror by many of those who had adopted PeopleSoft's ERP software. As one affected CIO phrased it, switching ERP vendors "is the equivalent of performing a brain transplant. It's expensive, and it might kill us."[13]

Operations managers already have had experience with this type of information system. MRP provides a compelling example in the manufacturing realm. Although many of the original MRP systems initially provided enormous benefits, most were found to be stubbornly difficult to adapt over time. For example, one of the key data elements in an MRP database is the lead time for a given component to be made on the shop floor. This is entered either when the system is installed or when the component is introduced to the product line. Over time, one would expect that this lead time would be reduced. As the process stabilizes, operators gain skill, and set-ups become easier, the time required to make a batch of the item might fall to half or a third of what it was originally. In theory, the data should be changed to reflect this new capability. In practice, it rarely is, and the planning system progressively bases its directives on more and more inaccurate information.

There are a number of consequences of this. One of the most common is that planners begin to second-guess the information in their IT system. One of the authors has worked in an environment in which the "real" system for determining what should be made, and when, was run on the back of cigarette packets. Nobody trusted the IT system, and since nobody trusted or used the system as much as they should have, data were not entered into it. Which meant that people trusted the system even less ..., and so on. Of course, a critic might rightly point out that such behavior reflects a lack of discipline in the operation, poor training of employees, or a lack of leadership on the part of the managers. It nevertheless also reflects the danger that the fit between an IT system and the way the operation it seeks to support actually works may deteriorate.

Unfortunately, any system installation reflects the world as it is at a given point in time. Without determined action, it will ensure that it stays that way. This trend toward monolithic systems is puzzling, given the growing importance of information systems during a period of increasing pressure on operations to be *agile.* Today's demands for increased long-term flexibility, broader product ranges, and rapid response all require information systems that are adaptable and have the capacity to be molded to the distinctive and changing needs of the business. Indeed, the need to be in control of one's technological evolution has caused a number of firms to reach out to the explosively growing arena of open-source technologies to provide solutions to their corporate computing needs (see Appendix 6.B).

6.5 IMPLEMENTING IT SYSTEMS: TWO APPROACHES

Give this background, we can now address another principle for guiding the design and management of a firm's information systems. This concerns where the firm should position itself between two archetypes, at the opposite ends of a spectrum of choice, for implementing IT projects.

The first archetypal model of how an organization might approach the design and expansion of its IT base, which we term *installation-based,* is characterized by progressive waves of large software systems. These are put out to tender or are bought "off-the-shelf" from outside suppliers and consultants. They gradually become obsolete as time goes by. IT projects within this model are large, long, and complex, and only begin to deliver value when fully installed. Much of the involvement of the ultimate users of the system takes place at the very beginning of the project (to determine requirements), and toward the end, after most of the technical work has been done (to provide training and help confer "ownership" of the system). The major challenges with this approach are: (1) specifying precisely in advance all the requirements of the system, (2) managing the vendor or the IT group to avoid cost and delivery overruns, and (3) finding ways to insure against premature obsolescence, given the possibility that circumstances may have changed by the time the system is fully installed. The goal of this model is not necessarily to build a system that can be improved after implementation, but to ensure that the new system performs *as originally promised.*

The second model (*path-based*) views IT development as a "path," in which multiple technical phases (such as networking, software and processing devices) overlap, evolve, and are mutually dependent. In these circumstances, a company's systems are continually being renewed at different levels, and the prime concern is integrating them and ensuring their compatibility with existing modules. Projects are small and fast and intended to start paying off quickly, delivering value and allowing local experimentation all along the way. It is analogous to the incremental improvement approach to operations in general that is discussed in Chapter 10 (particularly Sections 10.6 and 10.7). Users are intimately involved throughout the process, and this approach requires less long-range planning and large project management but more ongoing direction-setting and internal technical expertise. The differences between the two models are summarized in Table 6-1.

The path-based approach to the development of operations information systems promises many of the same advantages associated with incremental ongoing improvement. There is an important additional consideration, however: information systems are highly interdependent. Although it is frequently possible to adjust a lathe or milling machine in isolation, any change in an information system is likely to cause failure in other systems that rely on the data it produces. Similarly, a change in a networking protocol will only be useful if the other devices on the

Table 6-1 Installation-Based and Path-Based Models for IT Development

	Installation-based	Path-based
Role of IT	Supportive/peripheral to operations	Integral part of operations
Project size and number	Large, few, infrequent	Small, many, frequent
Development approach	Buy, configure, then install	Prototype and evolve
Delivery of value	When project is complete	Ongoing
Source of technology/software	Heavy use of proprietary interconnection code, proprietary standards	Use of common standards
Primary functional concerns	Control, efficiency, accommodating all requirements at once	Integration, interconnection, flexibility, progressive delivery of requirements
Locus of technical control	Vendor/IT group	Internal operation itself
Experimentation	Limited	Frequent opportunities
Primary managerial effort	Installation, project and vendor management	Ongoing management of interconnection standards

network are able to translate that protocol. With information systems, in other words, local changes are more likely to have global consequences. For this reason, enterprise information systems require the specification of an encompassing architecture that defines how all the components of a system will function and fit together as a coherent whole.[14] The *installation-based* approach to information systems management satisfies these architectural needs through a monolithic design: the system is designed at a single point in time, so that all its components fit well, and function together.

A path-based approach to information systems, by contrast, does not demand that all components be specified (or even anticipated) in advance. It regards preexisting *legacy systems* as a fact of life, and accepts at the outset that new modules and new technologies will be added, and that the total system will evolve progressively as time goes on. Rather than specifying precisely *which* components will form part of the whole, a path-based system simply specifies the principles that guide *how* they will be added or altered. As such, the architectural metaphor is closer to that of a town or city rather than a building.[15] For information systems, these include how various subsystems should *communicate,* rather than how they should *operate* internally. In other words, it demands *horizontal* modularity.

In this sense it exhibits a close parallel to the kind of modularity found in physical products. For example, a camera manufacturer may produce a variety of lenses for its range of cameras. Multiple lenses can be used on an individual camera, and the same lens can be used with multiple cameras. The guiding principle (except when there is a major design change) is that the *interface* must stay the same, regardless of how an individual camera or lens works internally. Indeed, the lens or camera can be made and sold by other manufacturers provided they conform to the interface specifications.[16]

This principle is one of the foundations of object-oriented programming, yet its advantages are similar at the enterprise-computing level. It results in modular systems, in which the different modules may be provided by various vendors as long as they contain the required interfaces. This allows local change and adaptation with less complex or severe global consequences. It also makes it possible for operations and department managers to select and adapt subsystems that are appropriate to the task at hand (provided they conform to the specified interconnection standards), rather than be constrained to use the subsystem dictated by the single vendor of a total system.

However, the theme of this book is that no approach is best for every situation, and the preceding paragraphs do not do justice to those companies for whom monolithic solutions have proven highly effective. Reports of the demise of ERP systems and their providers in the late 1990s were greatly exaggerated! Figure 6-5 depicts the spectrum of choice for implementing information technology, and discuss the circumstances under which one might tend to lean one way or the other.

The spectrum in Figure 6-5 (API means *application program interfaces,* discussed below) suggests the extent to which software assembly and development is either customized or standardized. The different ends of this spectrum roughly mirror the two archetypal development approaches just discussed, and any choice along this spectrum demands supporting decisions that are consistent with that choice.

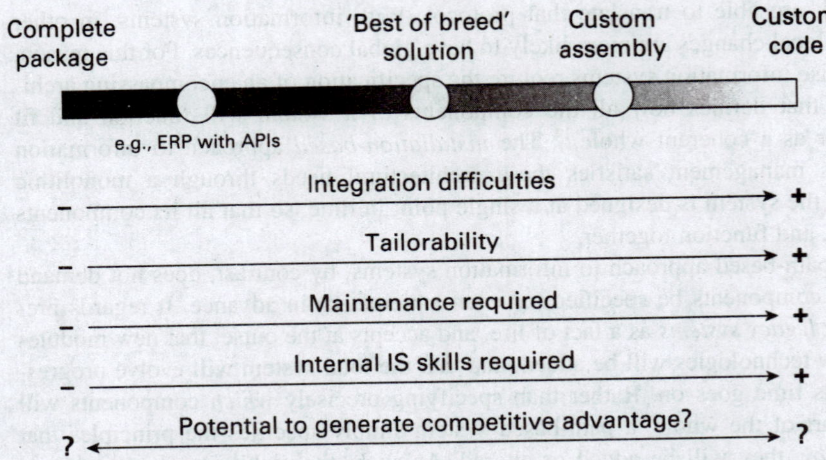

Figure 6-5 Spectrum of IT Options

Either extreme of the spectrum is generally untenable. The extreme left-hand side depicts a situation in which the firm buys all of its software in one, complete, off-the-shelf, unmodified package. This is rarely likely to be useful, because every firm's business processes contain certain idiosyncrasies. The other end of the spectrum represents completely custom code, developed in house. This also is not a useful position: it mirrors the situation common in the early days of computing when applications software was carved out of a block of solid Cobol and customized precisely to a firm's requirements. Those old software packages were outrageously expensive, and typically were the brainchildren of a few engineers who inevitably would then move on, leaving the system unmaintainable.

The central region of the spectrum is where the real choices lie. For example, it is possible to customize ERP systems to individual firms' requirements with the use of application programming interfaces (APIs). These allow programmers some limited access to the system, so that they can write or plug-in certain functionality themselves. These might include, for example, an existing materials-handling system or a more appropriate human resource management (HRM) system. The underlying ERP system retains ultimate control, but is tailored more precisely to the firm's specific requirements than are permitted by the standard "switches" in the basic system package. The development approach is still primarily installation-based, though a small sprinkling of path-based principles might still be useful for some occasional ongoing modifications. For what competitive situation might this solution be most appropriate?

We can imagine a company that has grown by acquisition over many years. As with the case of Celanese, discussed earlier, each acquisition brought with it its own flavor of IT, with intensely loyal devotees in each subsidiary. To simplify the assimilation of each acquisition, corporate IT built bridges to those information systems, allowing them to interact with the rest of the organization in a basic (often batch-based) way. Even though the company's basic priorities and approaches to operations have not changed over the years, the costs of its archaic and fractionated business processes continue to rise because of their inability to serve the business as a whole. In response, the company engages a consulting firm to evaluate its processes, redesign them, and install an ERP system (appropriately flavored) to bring the company up to date. It focuses on best practice to make sure that the new and expensive investment in information technology delivers capabilities in line with those of its major competitors.

For such a firm this solution might make sense. It has fallen so far behind that a monolithic system is the only way it can get to where it needs to be within a survivable time period. With one large project it is able to solve some of its most difficult enterprise-wide computing problems. In addition, a company with outdated business practices and mediocre internal IT development groups can gain access to a set of practices and software far superior to those it currently has in place.

In the middle of the spectrum is the *best-of-breed* approach. This approach is characterized by selecting standard, large modules (such as a financial system or an HR system), buying them from best-of-breed vendors, and then assembling them together to build a whole that is much more tailored and distinctive. Its downside is the project's requirement for local expertise and its technical uncertainty. It might founder because of unanticipated compatibility problems, or the whole might end up being worse than off-the-shelf solutions. This is the problem with reinventing the wheel: it only makes sense if you can really build a wheel that works better, and fits your cart better, than any other wheel! At the same time, there is the potential to provide capabilities that both differentiate the operation from its competitors and provide superior value to its customers.

A number of firms in similar industries have made different choices within this part of the spectrum. Compaq, for example, prior to its merger with HP, went ahead with a comparatively plain-vanilla ERP implementation. Dell, after abandoning a proposed ERP system, eventually chose a best-of-breed approach that reflected its unique way of competing through operations. It also gave it more ability to renew its IT resources on an ongoing basis.

Further to the right on the spectrum is "Internet-land." Firms using this approach do not cement together five to ten large building blocks to build the information systems. Rather, they weave together hundreds of tiny threads of software, often available free over the Internet. Such a firm (often small) might rely on Linux servers, running MySQL as a database, coupled with large numbers of server-based applets (small pieces of code). Information technology designed and built in this way is very, very risky without the appropriate expertise, and may deliver *less* ability to continuously improve. However, if you are in the business of inventing a new business, one that changes every day and must be highly flexible, then this is the way to go. The techniques developed by companies such as Yahoo!, Google, RedHat, and Amazon.com provide outstanding ability to change and improve as time goes on. These companies have adopted a path-based approach to IT development: their systems are continually improving and developing. Although they might not all be successful, this approach has begun to infiltrate a number of very established companies. These include some major banks that use it in building ever-improving Web sites, and manufacturing companies that are able to provide more and more information about in-progress orders to their customers.

Operations managers must make a choice about which approach is most appropriate for their company, given its resources, strategic position, and competitive strategy. As with any other aspect of operations, *fit* should be the over-riding concern rather than "best" (or, worse, most-fashionable) practice.

With any choice, however, an important question often goes unasked. Preoccupied with the question: "Will the system do what we want?", they fail to address the question: "How will we improve it afterwards?" This oversight saddles the firm with a system that, sooner or later, will fall behind its competitors. Just as important, it will fail to foster the development of new capabilities. Many firms opt for the safe approach of a consultant-based information system because their lack of knowledge (and resulting lack of confidence) induces uncertainty. A better approach for such a company would be to redirect its resources to developing the knowledge and skills required to build an innovative system that provides new and distinctive capabilities.

6.6 MAKING IT "MATTER"

Mastering the power of IT today is clearly a critical part of an operations manager's responsibilities. Although some of its aspects and considerations are peculiar to IT, the operations strategy framework introduced in Chapter 2 is still applicable when IT is introduced as part of the operating system.

It needs to be emphasized again, however, that simply being at the "leading edge" in adopting the latest, most powerful IT systems does not inevitably lead to any lasting competitive advantage, any more than does buying the most modern equipment or licensing the latest product technology. Consider the dilemma experienced by three companies that dominated the manufacture of customized building products in Spain (they faced minimal competition from imports). All were able to deliver their products, on average, in about two months. Each then installed a similar large ERP system, spending many hundreds of millions of pesetas in the process. Amazingly, each project was completed on time and succeeded in reducing its company's delivery lead times to three weeks. At the end of a year following these implementations, no one had gained any additional market share or profit. Where was the benefit from all this money, time, and effort? This is clearly an example of the "competitive leveling" hazard described earlier in this chapter.

This phenomenon, observed in industry after industry, has led some to question whether IT, because it is so widely available, really "matters"—that is, how can it ever provide any competitive advantage?[17] The same argument, however, could be applied to money and employees. Both are available to all. What makes them sources of competitive advantage is *how they are managed.* Recall from Chapter 2 that Southwest Airlines used the same planes that any of its competitors could have bought, flew into airports that were available to all, and followed a "no frills" strategy that was relatively easy to copy. But it was consistently profitable, while those that tried to imitate its operations were not.

When IT is incorporated as an integral part of an operation's infrastructure, moreover, it adds to the ability of that organization to provide a source of competitive advantage. The basic principle of competing through operations is that competitive advantage comes through the development and application of operating capabilities that both provide value to customers and are difficult to replicate. Coupling the innovative capabilities available through IT with those associated with physical operations, as did John Crane, has the potential to deliver enormous value to customers, whether through decreased lead times, greater ability to customize products, lower prices, or better quality.

Although it is possible for competitors to *imitate* a company's IT systems, we have repeatedly emphasized how difficult it is to extract the full potential from any set of IT resources. This opens up ample opportunity to create competitive advantage—as well as comparable "opportunities" to fall behind the pack. Operations is hard. Operations—integrated with IT—is even harder. Companies like Dell and Federal Express have recognized this; their superior skill in managing IT has heightened their operations-based competitive advantage. Others, such as Fox-Meyer Drug (which was put out of business as a direct result of a failing IT installation), have been crushed by their inability to keep up in the new arms race. For those companies that can seize and master the great challenges involved, the combination of rapidly evolving IT and superior operations will provide powerful new capabilities, and hence windows of advantage, for years to come.

NOTES

1. Indeed, many firms still run legacy organizations in which IT reports—bizarrely—to the CFO, whose skills may lie squarely in accounting and finance, but who generally have little or no education in IT.

2. See "John Crane UK Ltd.: The CAD-CAM Link" (HBS case number 9-691-021).

3. Gruber (1986).

4. http://www.geneseo.edu/~mpp2/erppaper.htm.

5. An interesting conundrum emerges here. There was, ultimately, no significant impact from the predicted Y2K problem, despite small armies of people holed up in the hills with supplies of canned food. On the one hand, this appeared to justify Y2K-related investment, since it appeared to have fended off the problem. On the other hand, the problem might have been considerably over-estimated in first place, obviating the many millions spent on IT and consultants to ensure post-millennial survival.

6. McDonagh (2001).

7. Davenport (1995).

8. Ware (2003). See also McAfee (2003b).

9. Green (2003).

10. An open standard is (roughly) one that is not proprietary, or under that control of a particular company or person. It is available for use by all, for free.

11. See Berinato (2003), which concludes that "'OneSAP' has the power to transform the company. Or, if it fails, debilitate it."

12. Koch (2001).

13. James Prevo, CIO of Green Mountain Coffee Roasters, as quoted in Verity (2003).

14. See Henderson and Clark (1990).

15. For an elegant example of architectural principles at this level, see Alexander, Ishikawa and Silverstein (1977).

16. Assuming of course, that the permission of the owner of the intellectual property pertaining to the interface is obtained.

17. This is the basic argument in "IT doesn't matter;" Carr (2003), which pointed out that "studies of corporate IT spending consistently show that greater expenditures rarely translate into superior financial results. In fact, the opposite is usually true."

Appendix

6A.1 STANDARDS AND INTEGRATION OUTSIDE THE FIRM

As described in this chapter, the IT standards used in a company can have a major impact on its ability to maintain the integration of its systems over time. But what about the operations outside its internal control? Within a company, it is comparatively straightforward to ensure that the standards selected are adopted throughout. Outside its four walls, the problem is much harder. Ideally, there would be an open standard defining how firms communicate with one another. Everyone would employ this standard, and thus (as with a telephone system) would be able to speak with anyone else. Will we continue to see growth of *open* standards upward in the fashion described earlier in this chapter? For example, could there be a common language for computers to communicate the placement of an order, or a late shipment notification, so that even firms that have never done business together before can seamlessly begin to do so?

The answer, so far at least, is "no"—at least not between firms in different industries. Industries are idiosyncratic and have such varied requirements that up to now attempts to create widely accepted business-to-business standards have been fragmented and unsuccessful. Moreover, computer-to-computer links require many more levels of agreement than do human-computer interactions. The latter only need agreement at the lowest level because people can decipher and interpret documents even when they do not have the same format, while computers are "like Old Testament Gods: all rules and no mercy."[1] However, within industries there are now a number of successful examples of firms banding together and agreeing on such high-level standards. One example from the computer industry may help to show how these intercompany standards are emerging.

An Example of the Application of New Communication Standards

The RosettaNet is a consortium of more than 400 of the world's leading IT, electronic components (EC) and integrated circuit (IC) companies, all working to create, implement and promote open e-business process standards. Figure 6A-1 depicts the various original groups of partners in the consortium. Putting this consortium together required dozens of high-level meetings to discuss the details of how these companies' computers will communicate regarding such business processes as purchasing, returns, rebates, delivery acknowledgments, and so on. New computer languages, such as XML (eXtended Markup Language) promise to greatly facilitate the implementation of such communication.

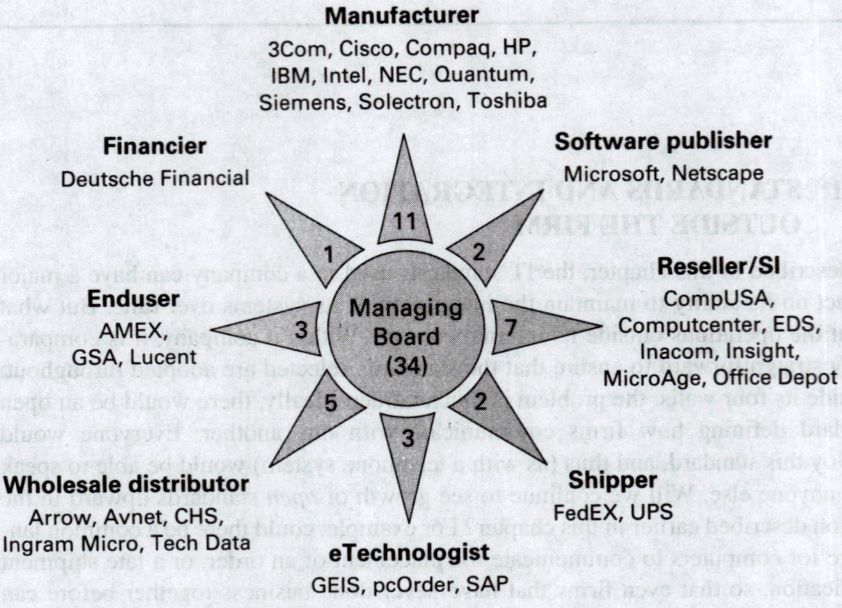

Figure 6A-1 Original RosettaNet Partners

Lauded as a more flexible and cost-effective successor to EDI (Electronic Data Interchange), XML has the potential to allow trading partners to exchange and utilize much more extensive and intricate data than ever before. However, as with many new computer languages, XML is still in flux as regards such basics as terminology, formats, and interfaces, and it is unclear whether most companies really need (or want!) to use its full information-sharing potential. Moreover, XML is only a language to implement a higher-level language. It is a language for saying things—it does not necessarily know what to say. The "what to say" is the part where agreement is needed. What, for example, should our computer say to yours to let you know that we're out of stock, and how should it say it?

Since computers are less flexible in their interpretation of language than people, these specifications must be tightly defined. In spite of the difficulties of getting a large group of companies to agree on how this should be done, the potential gains have made the proposition worthwhile.

RosettaNet is now used for a myriad of transactions between its partners. By establishing a common language, and standard processes for the electronic sharing of business information, RosettaNet has opened the lines of communication and delivered new opportunities for everyone involved. The businesses that provide the tools and services that help implement RosettaNet processes gain exposure and business relationships, while the companies that adopt its standards engage in dynamic, flexible trading-partner relationships that can reduce costs and raise productivity. End users enjoy speed and uniformity in purchasing practices.[2]

The RosettaNet standards and software are well ahead of the field, but other industries are likely to develop similar solutions over time. The logic of developing business-to-business standards that enable firms to build rich, process-based connections, rather than just exchanging bits and bytes, is compelling. For most industries, this is a matter of *when* rather than *if.* For operations managers, this calls for vigilance about the standards that are emerging in their industry. Some industries, for example, have attempted to build these standards through industry associations, which often takes too long to have any impact. Others have enlisted the most powerful firms in an industry to set standards. Covisint[3] for example, is an independent company with joint ownership by Ford, DaimlerChrysler, General Motors, Renault/Nissan, Commerce One, and Oracle. As well as building the infrastructure necessary for process-based transactions, this group might eventually *define* business-to-business standards for the thousands of companies involved in the automobile industry. A lower-tier company unprepared or unwilling to adopt these standards, may quickly find itself unable to compete.

Although the promise of such industry hubs is enticing, Covisint itself (along with many similar hubs) has faced numerous implementation challenges. When first announced in February 2000, Covisint's founding partners expected it to be operational within thirty days and predicted that it would eventually handle U.S.$750 billion in annual purchasing. Its launch, however, was delayed by technological difficulties, regulatory reviews, and administrative squabbles, and it now appears that it will be several years before Covisint comes close to its original goals.[4] This demonstrates the tremendous difficulties—as pointed out in Chapter 1—of overhauling the business practices of a network of companies, steeped in years of tradition.[5] Although the technological issues associated with hubs are being overcome quickly, hubs must also overcome a myriad cultural barriers—a far more daunting task.

Perhaps the real promise of common standards that enable IT-based business-to-business communication lies with smaller groups of companies that have less ambitious goals. New sets of tools are emerging to facilitate the development of intercompany connectivity (as well as intracompany integration). In the Open Software community there is increasing agreement on high-level connectivity.[6] Proprietary software toolboxes, such as Sun's J2EE framework and Microsoft's Visual Studio and .NET initiative, promise to make the business of wiring companies and organization together easier than it ever has been.

For managers more generally, it will become increasingly important to be aware of the emerging high-level standards in one's industry. Suppliers that cannot communicate using the standards that become agreed upon may find themselves "out of the club" and unable to do business in the way their partners demand. The solution is to keep informed about the standards in each of the industries in which a company operates, and to build information technology that can easily be connected to other firms using those standards.

6A.2 OPEN SOURCE SOFTWARE

Because of the cost, inflexibility, and strategic hazards of packaged, proprietary software, a number of firms (such as the Burlington Coat Factory and IBM) have turned to the open-source community to provide the software for certain subsystems. Open-source software—such as *MySQL* (a database program), the Linux operating system, and the Apache Web server—is developed by thousands of programmers around the world who build the software as a hobby in their "spare time." Their goal is to write elegant code that works and solves a particular problem. What's more, they make the software and the source code available over the Internet for free. This "bizarre" phenomenon[7] has made the Apache Web server the most common server on the Internet, as well as the most reliable.

The reliability results from the fact that there are now many thousands of eyes looking at and improving the source code, rather than the finite development resources available to a proprietary software firm. To ensure that this distributed development work is integrated and focused, each open source project usually has a project manager (who often is the instigator of the project) and/or a Web page (such as www.sourceforge.net) that facilitates communication among the programmers who have volunteered to work on the project. Programmers are guided by the principle that in getting their particular job done they must not "break" anything else in the overall system.

For companies, open-source software has the advantage that its users can alter and adapt the code themselves as time goes by and their needs change. It also is usually well documented, because the whole development approach demands that other people can easily understand how the code works. Sony Electronics, Sallie Mae, and DaimlerChrysler, among many others, all have taken advantage of Linux-based systems in their day-to-day operations.

NOTES

1. McAfee (2003a) provides this quote, which is attributed to Joseph Campbell.
2. www.rosettanet.org.
3. www.covisint.com.
4. www.ecommercetimes.com.
5. See also McAfee (2003a).
6. Low-level connectivity is the ability to exchange "bits and bytes." High-level connectivity is the ability to connect computers at much more abstract and meaningful levels—to allow, for example one company's systems to place an order with another company's. See, for example, www.osf.org/bus_area/interoperability/.
7. See Raymond (1999) for further insight.

Chapter 7

Creating an Edge through New Process Development

7.1 INTRODUCTION

The competitive power of new *product* development is increasingly recognized by academics and practitioners alike. Over the past two decades, dozens of articles and books have been written about how to make product development cycles both faster and more effective.[1] MBA and executive-level courses on new product development are proliferating throughout the country. Major consulting firms, including McKinsey, Booz-Allen, and Bain, have made improving product development a staple of their client services, while dozens of "boutique" consulting firms now make it their principle specialty. Across a wide range of industries, it would be hard to find senior managers who are not actively trying to improve their company's product development performance. Efforts to improve product development now receive the kind of resources and attention that productivity and quality improvement received during the 1980s.

The development of new operating *process* technologies, however, has engendered far less excitement among academics and practitioners, let alone the public at large. This is perhaps not surprising because we, as consumers, often come into direct contact with innovative new products in our daily lives but rarely glimpse the operating processes hidden behind facility walls. But the reasons run deeper. During the 1990s, as discussed in Chapter 4, there was a growing perception by many companies that operations no longer constituted a strategic—or core—competence, at least for those that competed in technologically dynamic contexts. Process superiority, in fact, has come to be viewed as of strategic importance only in those "mature" industries where U.S., European, and today even many Japanese companies find themselves at a comparative disadvantage relative to rivals from newly industrialized countries. Indeed, U.S. companies may have focused increasing attention on new product development *because* they saw it as a way to compete against offshore rivals that possessed stronger operating competencies.

The perception that superior process capabilities are less critical to competitive success than product development ignores the fact that many new products and services are completely dependent on the development and execution of complex, novel, and often enormously costly processes. The latest generation of computer memory chips, for example, requires production facilities (*fabs*) costing more than $2 billion but having useful economic lives of just a few years. Moreover, the true value of these processes lies not just in their physical aspects (e.g., buildings, tooling, machinery, and computers), but also in the intellectual capital embedded within them. It comprises knowledge about such difficult to observe and imitate process details as tool designs, reaction conditions, assembly sequences, and quality assurance methods that reside in the heads of the scientists and engineers who created those processes.

The importance of process innovation is not limited to manufacturing industries. Its role may be even greater in service settings where customers interact directly with the operating environment, since new services often require new operating capabilities. For instance, online trading is clearly a breakthrough service in the financial services industry and, judging from its growing volume, has been a very successful "product" innovation. Yet online trading would not be possible without significant investments in information technology and the development of new processes for executing trades.

Although many companies continue to regard operations as a bottleneck in, rather than a facilitator of, product development, most now recognize that their operations organizations ought not to be passive bystanders in the development process. They discarded the old approach where R&D "threw designs over the wall" into operations long ago, and adopted various approaches for ensuring that the designs of new products and services were compatible with existing operating capabilities so that their operations organizations were not caught off guard. Despite these improvements, their operations organizations still play an essentially passive role in the development process: they are considered to have "done their job" as long as they do not complicate and impede the new product development project too badly. We assert that operations needs to play a much more *proactive* role in the product development process, and that process development can be a competitive weapon for enhancing an organization's overall innovative capabilities.

This chapter discusses how effective process development can play a powerful role in creating a competitive edge by facilitating both new product development and overall operating effectiveness. We also describe the managerial actions and organizational behavior patterns that help build such process development capabilities over time.

7.2 HOW PROCESS DEVELOPMENT AND OPERATIONS INTERACT TO FACILITATE NEW PRODUCT DEVELOPMENT

Operational excellence often is viewed as critical only in industries, such as steel and commodity chemicals, where low cost is the primary driver of competition. While it is true that operations plays an important role in those contexts, it also has strategic leverage in a much broader range of industries, including those where cost is not the highest competitive priority.

7.2.1 The Product Life Cycle Concept Revisited

The idea that superior operating processes become important only as industries mature became prevalent in the 1970s, with the development of the product life cycle model of innovation.[2] This model (see Figure 7-1) posited that during the early phases of a product's life, when its basic concepts were still being formed, the rate of product innovation would exceed that of process innovation. Once producers and consumers had gained sufficient experience with alternative versions of the product, a "dominant design" would emerge (such as the internal combustion, gasoline powered, steel body automobile), and opportunities for radical product innovation would begin to recede. At this point, competition would shift to reducing the cost of that dominant design, and firms would focus increasingly on process innovation. Thus, according to the product life cycle model, process innovation becomes important only later in the life of an industry.

The product life cycle model provides a plausible logic that helps explain the patterns of innovation observed in many industries.[3] It also draws attention to the critical competitive impact of the emergence of a dominant design, and provides insight into why established firms in mature industries tend to experience difficulties adapting to radical product or process innovations.[4] Yet the assumptions of the model are not always applicable. First, it focuses on cost reduction as the primary goal of process innovation. This implies that firms have an incentive to develop new processes only in the intermediate phases of an industry's life, after opportunities for new product innovation have been depleted and production volumes are sufficiently high to justify specialized equipment. Such potential competitive advantages as time to market and rapid production ramp-up are ignored.

Second, lurking beneath the model is an assumption that the organizational competencies required for product innovation are fundamentally different from—and

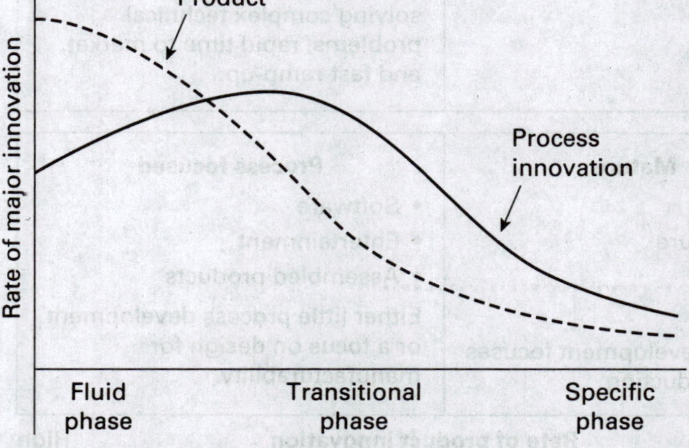

Figure 7-1 The Product Life Cycle Model

potentially in conflict with—the capabilities required for process innovation. Indeed, investments in specialized process technologies are often viewed as a potential hindrance to further product innovation, by causing firms to hesitate introducing new products that would make their existing process technologies obsolete. This would suggest that such investments should be deferred as long as possible. Yet there are many organizations where strong product and process R&D capabilities not only coexist peacefully, but actually complement one another. In the biotechnology, semiconductor, advanced materials, health care, and many service industries, new products cannot be commercialized without breakthroughs in process technology. Intel Corporation, as an example, is able to continually introduce ever higher-performing microprocessors because it also has built strong capabilities to develop and scale-up the complex manufacturing processes required to produce these sophisticated devices.

7.2.2 Mapping the Context

The matrix in Figure 7-2 depicts the respective roles of operations and process development in different types of industries. The two left-hand quadrants represent

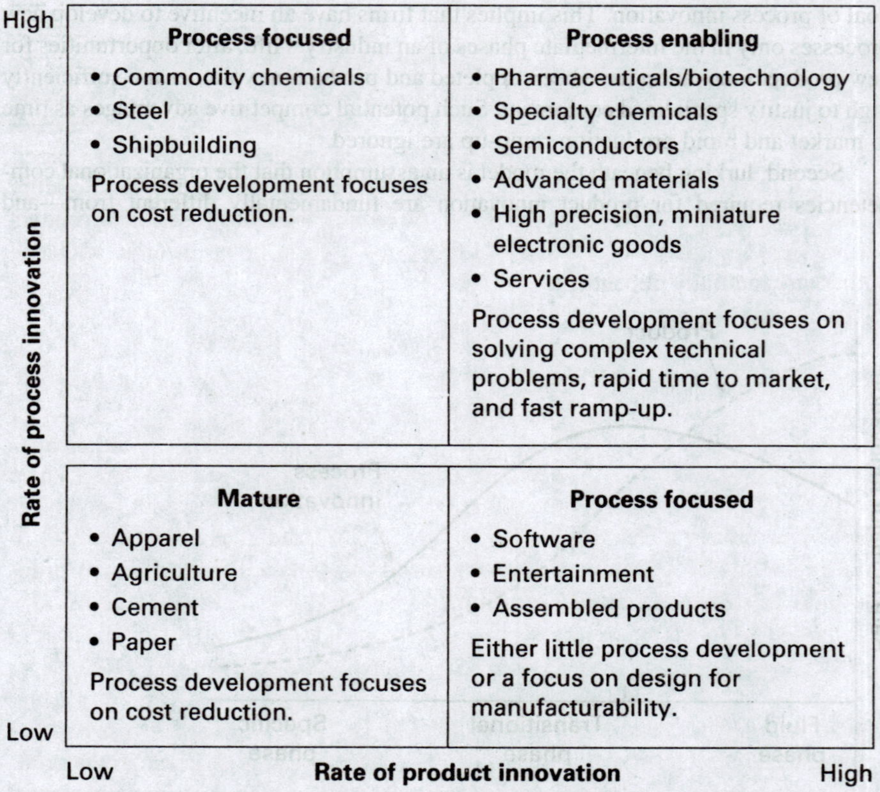

Figure 7-2 The Relationship between Product and Process Innovation

two aspects of the mature phase of the Product Life Cycle model, where product innovation decreases. Both encompass industries whose products have become relatively standardized, so product innovation is sluggish. However, process innovation continues actively in the upper left-hand quadrant ("process focused"), containing such industries as commodity chemicals and steel, while both product and process innovations have slowed to a crawl in the lower-left quadrant (e.g., agriculture and cement). In both quadrants, the number one priority of operations is improving productivity through better capacity utilization, incremental improvement, and the adoption of new, more efficient process technologies.

The lower right-hand quadrant ("product focused"), by contrast, represents the emerging/fluid phase of the product life cycle model: industries where product innovation is rampant, but process technologies are relatively stable. In this quadrant, which includes many assembled goods, the critical challenge facing operations is to ensure that the designs of products or services are compatible with existing process and operational capabilities. The principles and methods of Design for Manufacturability (discussed later) are well suited for these situations.[5]

The product life cycle model, however, ignores the upper right-hand quadrant ("process enabling," or product-process co-specificity), which encompasses such industries as pharmaceuticals, semiconductors, specialty chemicals, advanced materials, and most services. In these industries, not only do both product and process technologies evolve rapidly, they must be carefully synchronized. Even in some assembled products, the connection between product and process might be tighter than assumed by the product life cycle model. For example, producing miniaturized product designs for medical devices, instruments, and consumer electronics often requires the development of processes having extremely high precision.[6] It is in this quadrant that the capability for fast, efficient, and high-quality process development has a direct effect on the commercial success of new product introductions. Product and process capabilities, far from being at odds with one another, are mutually dependent.

7.3 LEVERAGING PROCESS DEVELOPMENT CAPABILITIES FOR COMPETITIVE ADVANTAGE

Although superior process development and operational capabilities can reduce operating costs (certainly one important dimension of competition), the real power of these capabilities often lies in how they help companies achieve faster time to market, smoother production ramp-up, enhanced customer acceptance of new products, and/or a stronger proprietary position.

7.3.1 Accelerated Time to Market

Perhaps no issue has drawn more attention in both the academic literature and the popular business press in recent years than the strategic value of getting new products to market faster.[7] The benefits of reducing product development lead times, particularly in information-intensive industries (see Chapter 1, Section 1.3), are well known. In some contexts, even short delays in product introduction can be deadly if first movers are able to gain a stranglehold on the market. In an attempt to shorten lead times, many companies have adopted approaches that employ simultaneous engineering and overlapping product and process design cycles. There is compelling evidence that, if managed properly, simultaneous product and process design facilitates significantly shorter development lead times than does a purely sequential approach.[8] Less attention, however, generally is given to reducing the time required for *process* development, despite the fact that compressing process development times may translate directly into shorter overall product development lead times. Process development can be a bottleneck for product launch, particularly where process technologies are relatively complex and need to be customized to the design of a specific product. In these contexts, further shortening the product development lead time hinges directly on an ability to speed up process development.

Moreover, companies usually find that in order for process design to be successfully carried out in parallel with product design, a far more flexible process development capability is required than was necessary under the traditional sequential approach. When product and process design are done sequentially, process developers begin their task with relatively complete knowledge of product specifications. Although they face intense time pressures, they also have the luxury of working around a relatively fixed set of product specifications. Under simultaneous engineering, on the other hand, process developers must be able to respond quickly to an almost continuous flow of information about evolving product specifications.[9]

In addition to its direct effect on accelerating a product's time to market, process development skills may influence the total product development lead time in more subtle ways. For example, in contexts such as pharmaceuticals, semiconductors, and automobiles, some process development must take place before functional prototypes or representative product samples can be fabricated. Slow process development at this stage can delay and prolong prototyping lead times, which, in turn, delays the entire project. Similarly, a process that is incapable of producing sufficient quantities of test materials can severely restrict a company's ability to conduct needed tests. Even worse, where problems in process technology result in prototypes that are of low or variable quality, test results may be inaccurate or unreliable. This is an especially important issue in situations where relatively large volumes of test batches must be manufactured to allow for thorough product evaluation by potential future customers, users, or regulatory agencies (as is the case for pharmaceuticals and some specialty chemicals).

Another strategic advantage of being able to develop processes rapidly is that it allows a company to wait longer before initiating process development, without delaying the launch of a new product. As a result, fast process development can make it less imperative for an organization to adopt simultaneous engineering. In environments where commercial success is far from guaranteed and complete technical failure is a serious possibility, the ability to carry out development sequentially, without extending the new product introduction date, can reduce the financial risks associated with its development. Pharmaceutical companies know this well: only a tiny fraction of new molecular entities discovered in their R&D labs ever reach the market. If they can delay process development and engineering until late in the development cycle, such firms can reduce the risk of investing resources in a project that may be terminated, or of making commitments to process technologies that may be made obsolete by unanticipated product design changes. But in order to be able to afford to wait, the company must have fast cycle process development capabilities.

7.3.2 Rapid Ramp-Up

When a new product is first manufactured it may take weeks or even months before productivity, capacity, quality, yields, and other performance measures reach their projected long-term levels. This period is generally known as *ramp-up,* and it occurs for two reasons. First, as operators become familiar with a process, they move down a learning curve—becoming more effective at carrying out necessary operating tasks. Second, it is during this initial period of production that many process problems are identified and fixed. In the automobile industry, for example, it often takes six months or more before a factory is able to produce a new model at full-scale production volumes. In semiconductors, initial manufacturing yields for new devices may be less than 5 percent, but could climb over 80 percent within several months.[10] Ramp-up also is important in service settings. Many new Internet retailers learned this lesson painfully during the holiday season of 1999, when their logistical systems proved incapable of handling surging demand and their customer support systems couldn't deal with the resulting customer complaints.

Effective and thorough process development before commercial launch can contribute significantly to a smooth, rapid ramp-up for three reasons. First, the faster a firm can expand production without adding more capital, the faster it can generate sales revenues and recoup development investments. This clearly has implications for the numerator of the new product's return on net assets (RONA). Quick ramp-up can also enhance RONA by reducing the size of the denominator. Typically, the capital expenditure required to produce a new product is determined by both the product's estimated demand and the productivity of its production process (that is, its output per unit of capital). For any given level of demand, higher productivity implies a lower capital investment. All else being equal, a firm with the capability to increase yields or productivity quickly will tend to invest less capital in operations than will a firm whose ramp-up is more gradual.

Beyond these financial reasons, however, rapid ramp-up can play a critical strategic role. The faster and more effectively a firm can ramp-up production, the faster it can penetrate the market, gain broad acceptance of its product, and begin to accumulate high-volume production experience that may lead to lower future production costs. There are many examples where companies have been first to market with innovative product designs, but problems during ramp-up led to poor quality and severe product shortages, creating a window of opportunity for competitors. In contrast, Plus Development Corporation was able to capture and hold 65 percent of the market for "plug-in" hard disk drives, despite the entry of dozens of competitors, because it and its manufacturing joint venture partner focused on designing their product and process for quick ramp-up and trouble-free production.[11] Plus was able to reach factory yields of over 99 percent within three months of starting commercial production (compared to an industry norm of about six months) and achieve much higher levels of dependability than its competitors. Fast ramp-up not only allowed Plus to penetrate the market more deeply than its competitors, but it also proved critical in building the company's reputation for reliable delivery and reliable products. In most markets, customers have long memories, so difficult ramp-ups that lead to poor-quality products or unreliable service can have devastating and lasting impacts on a company's reputation.

7.3.3 Enhanced Customer Acceptance

Most consumers, unless they are operations management aficionados, are not concerned with the details of the production process used to make a product. Prospective car buyers, for example, generally want to learn about the engine, the size of the trunk, and how well the car rides. Although they might be interested in knowing the location of production, they probably do not care at all about the nature of the production control system (JIT versus MRP), whether the company uses empowered cross-functional teams, or which software was used in the factory's programmable logic controllers. Yet the features of the product they do care about (e.g., size, weight, reliability, and environmental impact) are directly affected, in many contexts, by the specifics of its production process. The Kodak FunSaver, a single-use disposable camera, provides one example. To appeal to environmentally conscious consumers, Kodak integrated recycling directly into the FunSaver's main production process.

In some cases, a strong process development capability will allow an organization to fundamentally alter its basic product concept. In 1988, Johnson & Johnson's Vistakon division introduced the first disposable contact lens—the Acuvue.[12] While the concept of a "disposable" lens was novel, its design was not. The Acuvue was fabricated from the same basic type of polymer used for other soft lenses and, although the lens was thinner (to permit greater oxygen permeability), its basic dimensions were similar to those of existing lenses. What was novel was its manufacturing process. To make disposability possible, over a five-year period Vistakon participated in the development of a process (described in more detail in Chapter 11) that reduced manufacturing costs by an order of magnitude and dramatically tightened tolerances. Thus, the lenses could be profitably sold at a price that permitted weekly disposal, and their consistency was so good that users did not perceive differences in fit or corrective power from one week to the next. Rapid production ramp-up allowed Vistakon to market Acuvue nationally within just a few months. Although major competitors soon introduced their own disposable lenses, it took them from six months to a year to ramp up production and begin national marketing, and Vistakon was able to maintain its lead in the disposable market. Within three years of its introduction, the Acuvue lens achieved worldwide sales of more than $225 million (compared to Vistakon's total sales of $20 million prior to the Acuvue), captured approximately 25 percent of the U.S. market for contact lenses, and catapulted Vistakon into a leading position in that industry.

7.3.4 Stronger Proprietary Position

Great new products represent a two-edged sword. On the one hand, they attract buyers willing to pay premium prices, generate profits, and make a company the envy of its competitors. On the other, the better and more successful the product, the more competitors will strive to imitate it—and such imitators can be swift and ruthless. EMI, for example, invented the diagnostic imaging technology known as CAT scanning but was knocked out of the market within years by established imaging companies. Bowmar may have invented the calculator, but it was Texas Instruments, Hewlett Packard, and (later) Sharp that came to dominate the business. Product patents tend not to play a significant role in protecting intellectual property except in a few industries, such as chemicals and pharmaceuticals. Even where patents do provide protection, long lead times between the discovery of the patentable technology and its commercialization may mean that patent protection expires relatively soon into (or even before the start of) the commercial life of the product.

Innovative process technologies can provide a way for organizations to extend the proprietary position of a product. Would-be imitators may be able to reverse engineer a product, but can still be blocked from entry if they cannot determine how to manufacture the product at competitive cost and quality levels. For these reasons, product designs that are inherently difficult to manufacture can create opportunities to use proprietary processes as a barrier to imitation. The Gillette Sensor razor provides an excellent example. The three-bladed Sensor has proven to be one of the most successful products in Gillette's history and a major driver of its earnings growth in recent years. Yet despite licensing its *product* patents, no generic versions of the Sensor have reached the market. The complex manufacturing process (which was not shared with others) has proven a major barrier to entry.[13]

7.4 ACHIEVING SPEED, EFFICIENCY, AND QUALITY IN THE DEVELOPMENT OF NEW PROCESSES

In the previous section we identified some of the ways process innovation can be used as a proactive, competitive weapon in the race to develop new products or services. In this section, we consider ways for turning this potential into reality.

Before delving into the decisions that effect process development performance, it is useful to frame the essential challenge facing an organization that needs to develop a new process technology and then transfer it into an operating setting. At a highly simplistic level, a process technology is akin to a "recipe." It encompasses input specifications, the sequence of tasks that must be performed, the equipment that must be utilized, the parameters at which equipment must be operated, the expected intermediate outputs, means for controlling the process, and ways of checking the quality throughout. As anyone who has tried out a new recipe for the first time can attest, however, the jump from having the recipe to creating gourmet fare can be quite challenging. One reason is that the recipe, no matter how well written and how detailed, generally cannot capture all the subtle—but possibly critical—nuances of the process. A second reason relates to changes in scale. The recipe designed to prepare four servings may need to be tweaked in order to serve a dinner party of twelve.

Finally, the recipe that Chef Emeril uses to create a mouth-watering soufflé can lead to a pile of mush in the hands of a less-skilled chef.

Although highly simplified, the cooking recipe analogy captures two critical challenges of process development and transfer. The first is that transferring a technology from the lab to the operating floor is complex because the "devil is in the details." Most companies now recognize that simply transferring documents seldom works, because not all the relevant details can be codified and clearly communicated in writing (this is what we referred to in Chapter 4, Section 4.4.2, as *tacit knowledge*). As a result, most companies in both manufacturing and service settings routinely deploy "technology transfer teams" to ensure that face-to-face communication supplements the process documentation.

The second issue, and one that even more organizations tend to struggle with, is that the right "recipe" is contingent on operating conditions and scale. Almost every organization can recount horror stories of processes that worked wonderfully in the lab and in small-scale pilot runs, but simply did not work when attempted at full scale under real operating conditions. In these cases, R&D generally blames operations for not implementing the process as designed, and operations blames R&D for not communicating the process adequately. Management blames the technology transfer process but, in fact, the problem often lies not with the *transfer* of the process but with the fact that the process was not actually designed to run at full scale, under normal operating conditions, using typical operators. A better technology transfer process does not solve this problem. Instead, it simply ensures that the *wrong* process is more smoothly handed over to operations.

The critical challenge of process development, then, is to develop and transfer to operations, in a timely and efficient manner, a process that not only can produce the desired product but also achieves desired performance (in terms of costs, quality, flexibility, reliability, responsiveness, etc.) when utilized under "real" operating conditions. The challenge becomes even more complex when a process is being developed for a new product. We now examine three classes of decisions that affect process development performance: (1) approaches to *integrating* process and product development; (2) the *timing* of technology transfer from R&D into operations; and (3) the degree of *local autonomy* the facilities belonging to multi-unit networks should be given in developing and changing processes.

7.4.1 Integrating Product and Process Development

Process development seldom operates in a vacuum. The most challenging process development projects are those where a new process is being designed for a new product. As discussed earlier, these types of projects subject both product and process development to intense time pressures. In addition, however, when a new process is being developed for a new product, coordinating the design of both creates special organizational and technical challenges. Process engineers must understand the product design specifications, and product designers need to understand the limits of the process.

To make matters even more complicated, neither the product design nor the process design are developed in a static context. The product design parameters typically evolve throughout a project as product designers gain information from product tests and experiments. Specific elements of the product design may change in ways that require substantial changes in process technology. Or, preliminary market feedback may reveal that customer demand will be much different than originally anticipated (this often, in turn, is a function of the product design), which has implications for the capacity of the process. For example, a pharmaceutical company might not know how effective a proposed new drug will be (implying what dosage that will be required in order to achieve the desired effect, and the number of times per day it should be taken) until well along in the clinical testing process—and long after it has to begin building the manufacturing capacity to produce it. Even more disruptive, a competitor may introduce a new product that suddenly creates a much lower price point in the market. Whereas process designers may have started out with a target cost of $10/unit, they may now have to design a process capable of delivering the product at $5/unit.

It is no wonder, then, that one of the greatest sources of tension in new product development projects occurs at the interface of product design and process design. Many outstanding new products and services have failed commercially because of a poor fit with their associated operating processes. These problems are often manifested in poor initial product quality and high warranty costs, and can be just as damaging in service settings.

Consider the advent, in the 1990s, of "global fee" contracting in health care. Under traditional insurance contracts, hospitals billed insurance companies for each service provided to a patient, and physicians billed insurance companies for their services separately. Global fee contracts, in contrast, offered hospitals a fixed lump-sum payment to cover the health care needs of a designated population of patients (e.g., heart patients, patient over the age of 65, etc.), and included physicians' fees. The global fee concept was attractive to hospitals because it enabled them to manage care and costs with less interference from managed care plans. On the other hand, the new contracts also required that they perform new tasks. For example, they now were responsible for managing the risks of medical losses, a function that had previously been performed by insurance companies. They also had to decide how to divide up the lump sum payment across hospital departments (e.g., cardiology, cardiac surgery, nursing, radiology, etc.). Moreover, since they were now responsible for actually reimbursing physicians, they needed mechanisms for processing payments. Finally, in order to manage their costs effectively, hospitals had to develop processes that coordinated care from the time patients entered until they were discharged and recovered. Unfortunately, many hospitals lost significant money on such contracts because they lacked the competencies to develop the operating processes required to perform these new functions effectively.

Companies now utilize three basic approaches to dealing with the integration of product and process development: (1) the creation of integrated development teams in which process development and operations are "core" members; (2) the use of design for manufacturability (DFM) methodologies; and (3) prototyping processes.

Integrated Development Teams

Development teams that include both process developers and operations experts facilitate communication and coordinated decision making, and are now in widespread use. There is strong evidence that integrated cross-functional teams lead to better development performance than more functionally oriented approaches. For instance, a study of twenty-nine automobile development projects found that projects incorporating process engineers and manufacturing personnel into the core development teams had better overall performance in terms of lead time, engineering productivity, and quality.[14] Further discussion of cross-functional teams is contained in Chapter 8 (particularly Section 8.5.2).

Simply having a cross-functional team in place does not, of course, by itself ensure better integration between product and process design. Strong team leadership and adequate resources are essential. In addition, it is almost inevitable that certain product design choices will be in conflict with process goals, and vice versa, as product design always involves trade-offs. To sort through these trade-offs it is necessary at the outset for the project to have a clearly defined strategy that lays out competitive priorities (e.g., functionality will be more important than low costs). In some situations design-for-manufacturability (DFM) methods can provide a useful way to sort through these issues.

Design for Manufacturability

DFM tools and methods became quite popular during the early 1980s as one approach for smoothing the design-manufacturing interface. With DFM, design choices are evaluated not only according to the usual criteria of product functionality and customer requirements, but also in terms of their impact on the manufacturing process. Several different approaches to DFM have been advocated, but all essentially strive to create a decision-making methodology for incorporating manufacturing issues into design choices.[15] In its most basic form, DFM can simply be a list of design rules that must be followed to ensure compatibility with existing operating capabilities (e.g., specifications should require tolerances no smaller than 0.001"). DFM also has been used to reduce the manufacturing complexity of a product design—for instance, designing a product so that it contains fewer parts, or does not need to be turned repeatedly or worked on at awkward angles during manufacturing.

The term design for manufacturability suggests that this approach is useful only for manufactured goods. However, the concept may be even more important in service settings where consumers interact directly with the operating system. A service experience can be utterly ruined if the customer is required to perform a complex and confusing array of tasks (automated call centers with large number of options and sub-options would be an example). The intellectual property embedded in "one-click purchasing" has become a major battleground for Internet retailers precisely because it facilitates consumers' interaction with the service process. Some of the best practitioners of DFM, in fact, are service providers. For example, McDonald's scrutinizes every detail of every item on its menu, from french fries to fajitas, to ensure that it can be prepared in a timely and consistent manner.[16] Providers of professional services, such as accounting, investment banking, and consulting firms, also have adopted aspects of DFM—although they almost never refer to it by that name. Management consulting firms, for instance, often create standardized templates or "PowerPoint slide decks" that capture the firm's methodologies in a way that can be marketed and implemented by less experienced consultants.

Although DFM can be a useful approach, its limits must be recognized. For DFM methods to work, there needs to be a detailed understanding of the linkages between design choices and measures of manufacturing/service performance. For example, if it were known that the costs of a particular assembled product increased exponentially with the number of unique components, then a DFM process could be useful in minimizing the number of component parts. In the case of McDonald's, the company has invested heavily in researching the root causes of certain types of quality problems. For instance, through extensive research and experimentation it learned that potatoes should be cured three weeks before freezing in order to produce consistent fries, and that they needed to have a starch content of 21 percent in order to be cooked to uniform crispness. This level of detailed process knowledge enabled McDonald's to establish detailed product specifications so that it could then concentrate on simplifying the procedures used in producing them.

If the mapping between design choices and operating performance is unclear, however, DFM is of more limited use. In this case, developing a prototype might be a better way to explore their interaction.

Prototyping

Every project aimed at launching a new product or service invariably uses prototypes of some type to gain feedback on technical and marketing aspects of the design. In an automobile development project, for instance, prototypes are built to test the performance characteristics of the vehicle, as well as its ride, its safety, and its overall aesthetics. Prototypes are generally thought of as physical models of products, but today's more advanced computing power has made it possible to create *virtual* prototypes. Automobile companies now test the safety of alternative designs through simulated crashes, and Boeing developed the 767 jetliner without building a single physical prototype.[17] Investment banks similarly model the behavior and performance of complex financial derivatives through computer-simulated markets.

In the vast majority of organizations, prototyping is the province of the engineers and technical experts charged with designing the product. In service organizations, the marketing group often conducts field tests where potential customers evaluate a proposed service concept. The focus of prototyping, however, is generally on identifying problems with *product* design (e.g., a tendency for an automobile to become noisy under certain road conditions). As a result, prototypes often are built in specialized departments using methods, technology, and workers that are vastly differently from those that will ultimately be used when the product is introduced commercially. That is, the product might be hand-built by a highly skilled technician using general-purpose tools (like hammers, chisels, and sandpaper) rather than being produced on a high-speed assembly line using automated tooling.

The problem with this approach to prototyping is that it provides almost no feedback whatsoever about production issues. Very often process design problems, or problems with the manufacturability of a design, are not revealed until later stages of the development cycle, when formal *pilot* production runs are made. Depending on the product and the context, this may be too late and such problems may not be resolved by the time commercial production starts. One way to address this problem is to construct prototypes using a process that more closely resembles the operating environment in which the commercial product will ultimately be produced. In most cases it is extremely difficult and costly to replicate this environment when building a prototype. It is possible, however, that key elements of the final production environment can be employed to provide important feedback about manufacturing issues.

BMW learned the value of using prototyping as a mechanism for integrating product and process design issues in the early 1990s.[18] Up to then it had used highly skilled technicians to fabricate prototype vehicles by hand. To maximize flexibility, only general-purpose tooling was utilized. Materials often were substituted to enable certain parts to be fabricated quickly. For example, the dashboards of prototypes were made out of fiberglass rather than polyvinylchloride (PVC)—the material that ultimately would be used in production vehicles. The advantage of fiberglass in prototyping is that it can be shaped by hand, rather than requiring specialized molds, as is the case for PVC. BMW's prototype builders were so meticulous and highly skilled that they could produce prototypes that were very representative of product designers' intentions. As a result, these prototypes were extremely useful for learning about such important characteristics of the car as its appearance, comfort, handling, performance, and safety.

Unfortunately, this approach to prototyping yielded virtually no feedback about the manufacturability of a given design. This became a competitive issue for BMW in the late 1980s when Toyota and Honda entered the luxury car market with their Lexus and Acura lines of vehicles. Customer surveys revealed that Lexus's new vehicles had significantly lower defect rates and other manufacturing-related problems than did BMW's new models. As they investigated this new competitive threat, BMW senior management learned that its new models tended to experience significant manufacturing problems during their initial manufacturing launch. It was often only during this phase—when the factory was supposed to be increasing production to commercial levels—that design-related manufacturing problems were discovered. A decision was made to conduct an experiment on one of the new models then in development. Rather than building the entire prototype by hand, its interior would be constructed using methods, workers, and tooling that would be similar to those used during commercial production. The experiment worked. During the prototyping process, a significant number of manufacturing-related design problems were uncovered and ultimately corrected, long before the vehicle went into commercial production. When the vehicle was launched it had one of the best quality records in the company's history.

7.4.2 Timing the Transfer of New Process Technologies into Operations

A second major set of issues that must be dealt with in developing a new process technology concerns the timing of its transfer from development into operations.

Deciding when a process technology is "ready" to be transferred is a subject of great debate in most organizations. Proponents of the "get it right the first time" philosophy generally argue that a technology should be largely error free by the time it is transferred. This perspective puts emphasis on minimizing major design changes after the transfer and logically leads to a strategy of keeping the technology in R&D until fairly late in the development cycle. An alternative perspective is that it is simply impossible to anticipate all the problems that may be encountered with a new process and that, in any case, the R&D group is the least well equipped to identify these problems. Proponents of this perspective argue that the operations organization should get its hands on the new process technology as early as possible in order to apply some real-world understanding to its development.

There is no one right answer to this debate. The timing of technology transfer is contingent on several factors, two of which are discussed below: designing a framework for process development experimentation, and balancing the value of learning *by* doing versus learning *before* doing.

A Framework for Process Development Problem Solving and Experimentation

Despite differences in the ways new processes are developed in different industries, the problem-solving approaches used have certain similarities. The starting point for process development is a detailed description of the product, if not a complete product design. Of course, the product design may still be evolving when process development starts. Indeed, as described above it is now quite common for product and process design to occur simultaneously. Likewise, targets for process performance—such as costs, capacity, yield, throughput, quality levels, and tolerances—may only be framed as broad estimates or ranges. The job of process developers is to determine the process design parameters that are most likely to meet the expected performance targets under expected commercial operating conditions. This is essentially a problem-solving process that attempts to narrow the gap between what is known about the process and its likely performance, and what needs to be known in order for the process to perform as desired.

Experimentation lies at the heart of this problem-solving process. Process development experiments can take many forms and be conducted under a variety of conditions. One way to characterize different experiments is the extent to which they are conducted under conditions representative of the final operating environment. Figure 7-3 depicts the continuum of settings in which such experiments can be conducted, from purely theoretical calculations and computer-aided simulation at one extreme to pilot runs conducted under full-scale operating conditions at the other.

While the specific methods of experimentation might vary between service and manufacturing contexts, there are strong analogies between them. For instance, when an online retailer tries to develop a new order-fulfillment process, its operations group may begin with a conceptual exercise to map out the desired flow. This is essentially a "thought experiment" that is analogous to what process engineers do in manufacturing settings when they first begin to conceptualize a process. The

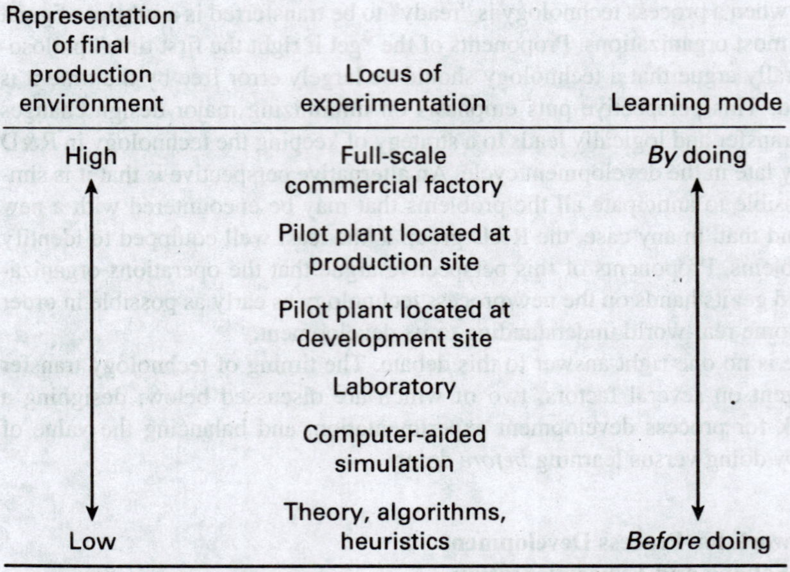

Figure 7-3 The Locus of Experimentation and Representation

retailer's design group may then utilize software models to identify possible bottlenecks and test the impact of intra-day demand variability and uncertainty on capacity utilization. As a next step, they might pilot the new process in a specific operation and modify the process before rolling it out more broadly.

Learning by Doing versus Learning before Doing

Most process development projects utilize experiments that fall in different places along this continuum. The key issue, however, is one of balance and mix. Some companies prefer more "lab-focused" approaches to development because they tend to allocate a greater share of their process R&D budget to laboratory experimentation and/or building capabilities in computer-aided simulation. Such firms also tend to transfer the process to an actual manufacturing facility or service center relatively late in the development cycle, with the expectation that most of the key process problems will have been identified (and resolved) in previous laboratory and pilot scale tests. Since most of the knowledge about the process is acquired before it is transferred into operations, this approach has been referred to as learning *before* doing.[19] Other firms take a more "operations-focused" approach, preferring to transfer process technologies to operations fairly early in the development cycle and allowing most of the experimentation and problem solving to occur within that context. The bulk of resources in these organizations get allocated to process engineering at the operating site, and to building large-scale pilot facilities that are nearly identical to full-scale facilities. Since most of the knowledge about the process is acquired through actual operating experience, this approach can be termed learning *by* doing.

Whether an organization should take a more lab-focused (learning before doing) or operations-focused (learning by doing) approach to process development is an important issue, because experiments conducted in different settings have different cost profiles. Simulations and laboratory experiments typically are far less expensive than experiments conducted at the other end of the spectrum. However, laboratory experiments and simulations do not always provide good predictions of how a process will behave when operating under normal operating conditions, with commercial equipment (as opposed to laboratory equipment or simulated equipment), and with regular operators (as opposed to highly skilled scientists and engineers).

Laboratory experiments can be viewed as highly simplified representations of the future commercial process. A laboratory experiment with a chemical process, for example, is qualitatively very different from the same process carried out in a large-scale chemical plant, yet each element of the experiment has analogies in the factory. The small glass test tubes represent the factory's stainless steel reaction tanks; the thin glass mixing rods used to stir the reaction simulate the forces of automated steel rotors; and the chemist who sets up the experiment and watches over it plays the role of both the factory operators and the computer-based process control system.

The conditions of such an experiment clearly are very different from the future full-scale operation, and these differences can profoundly affect the predictive power of the experimental results. The chemical process may behave differently in a small vessel than in a large one, or in a glass versus a stainless steel vessel. The chemist may stir the process very differently from the way it would be stirred by large, computer-controlled rotors. Thus, the key trade-off between experimental modes is the *cost per experiment* (in both resources and time) versus the *fidelity of the feedback.* The *learn-to-burn* ratio can be thought of as the amount of insight yielded by an experiment relative to its cost. In determining what mix of experimental approaches should be deployed in process development, an organization should seek to maximize the learn-to-burn ratio.

Whether the learn-to-burn ratio is maximized by lab-oriented or by more operations-oriented approaches to process development depends on the knowledge base underlying the technology. Where underlying cause–effect relationships are well known and there is relatively complete knowledge of the future operating environment, one may know enough about the critical variables and their behavior to design highly representative laboratory experiments or simulations that provide reasonably accurate predictions of expected commercial performance. A good example would be where process engineers can utilize software models that simulate process flows and bottlenecks accurately enough to design a facility layout. Given sufficiently deep knowledge of the key variables effecting process performance, the learn-to-burn ratio is generally quite high for lab-focused approaches.

In contrast, when the theoretical or practical knowledge of the effects of scale and other environmental factors is limited, the learn-to-burn ratio of laboratory experiments usually is quite poor. Subtle (and often unknown) differences between the laboratory setting and the commercial operating environment could have major impacts on process performance, so feedback from laboratory experiments will be less predictive of the problems and performance that will be experienced under full-scale commercial operating conditions. Consider the problems that Disney initially experienced when it opened its first theme park outside the United States: EuroDisney in France.[20] The early operating problems experienced there (long lines, lower than expected revenues) were puzzling, given the extensive planning that went into EuroDisney and the company's depth of experience operating similar theme parks elsewhere. When the park actually opened for operations, however, nuances in European consumer behavior (e.g., a tendency to spend more time eating lunch) that were not included in the planning model were major sources of operating problems. If critical variables cannot be modeled accurately ahead of time, whatever is learned in simulations or small-scale pilot experiments might not be very helpful in predicting what will happen when the process is transferred into full-scale commercial operations. Instead, evaluations of the process need to be done under conditions as close to actual operating conditions as possible. The learn-to-burn ratio is higher in the operating setting than in laboratory settings. Transferring a process to an operating unit earlier, when it is still being developed, and refining it there (learning *by* doing) should be a more effective approach.

This discussion suggests a contingent approach to process development strategy based on the depth of knowledge about the process, as summarized in Figure 7-4.

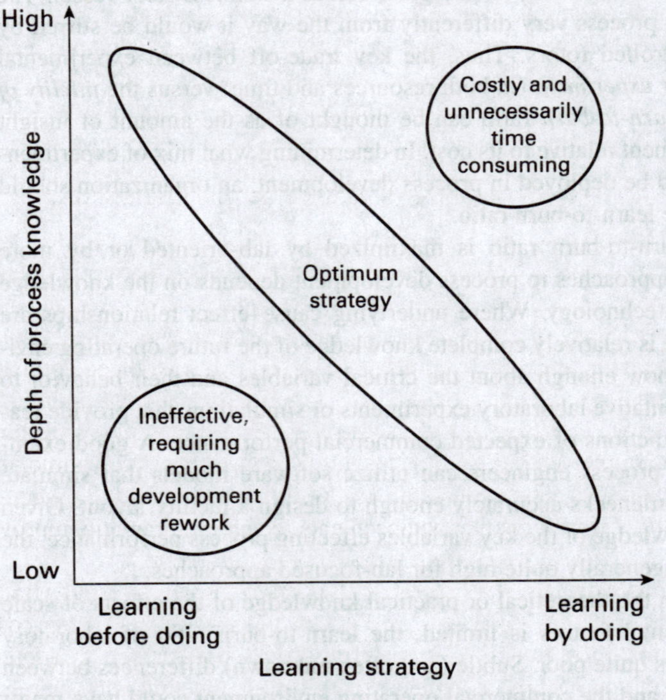

Figure 7-4 The Link between Knowledge and Learning Strategy

7.4.3 Centralized versus Decentralized Process Development and Technology Choices

The final element of an organization's process technology strategy that we will address is analogous to one discussed in Chapter 6: the degree to which process technology choices are centralized versus decentralized. Although this apparently is only an issue for organizations with multi-unit operations networks, if suppliers are considered part of a network it applies to the vast majority of companies. Under an extreme form of the centralized approach, process technologies are selected and developed by a central process technology group. Operating units (plants, service centers, distribution centers) responsible for a given product or service are then essentially mandated to adopt a uniform standard process technology. Discretion to modify the standard technology by one of the operating units, even if this would lead to performance improvement, is limited. As with Intel's Copy-Exact strategy (as described in Chapter 5, Section 5.4.3), modifications must first be approved by the central group before being rolled out across the entire network.

Under the decentralized approach, each operating unit is given a high degree of latitude in developing, choosing, and modifying technologies. At the extreme, each operating unit has its own process development group that is *completely* responsible for the technologies used there. There is little or no coordination or sharing of technologies across sites. As a consequence, different sites producing the same product or service may utilize vastly different processes.

Like the timing of technology transfer, this is an issue of great contention in many organizations. In general, managers responsible for an operating unit strongly prefer to have control over the technologies used on their site. They mistrust a central engineering group's ability to develop process technologies that will work equally well at all sites, and reject the "one size fits all" principle that underlies strongly centralized approaches. They also can feel shackled by the need to clear every process change through the central group.

As we have stressed throughout this book, there is no one approach that works equally well for all organizations under all circumstances. Companies competing in the same industry often take different approaches to process technology, and/or alter them over time to match changes in their competitive environment. Consider the example of ITT-Automotive, a leading manufacturer of anti-lock braking systems (ABS).[21] Prior to the mid-1990s, the company used a fairly decentralized approach to process development. Product engineering was done in Germany, but individual plants (two located in the U.S., one in Belgium, and one in Germany) were responsible for developing, implementing, and improving their own process technologies. One plant in particular, located in Asheville, North Carolina, had nurtured a highly involved and supportive workforce that had been able to achieve dramatic improvements in manufacturing quality and productivity.

Then, facing the challenge of needing to produce a new generation ABS at much high volumes, with a faster rate of ramp-up, and at dramatically lower costs than previous systems, the company's engineering leadership decided to adopt a dramatically different approach: to completely automate production and centralize all development and process technology decisions in its German engineering group.

Almost needless to say, this caused a great deal of friction within the company as it represented a major change in the roles and responsibilities of the non-German plants. Part of the reason for the conflict might have been political (the plant managers justifiably feared a loss of power). A more fundamental problem with the proposal to centralize all process development, however, was that it required the organization to adopt a new set of skills and a different set of criteria for making trade-offs. Under decentralized process development the plants had become quite good at experimenting with, learning about, and improving their processes, but there had been little learning *across* the plant network. Centralization would clearly reduce the scope for "local" plant level experimentation, but it could potentially offer the opportunity to improve learning across the network. Decentralization and centralization represent fundamentally different *learning models,* each of which is appropriate under different circumstances.

Centralized Process/Technology Development

The chief advantages of centralizing the selection and development of process technology are analogous to those of conducting operations in a single location rather than spreading them out over multiple facilities, as described in Chapter 5. A centralized approach can:

- Achieve a critical mass of technical talent in order to stay on the cutting edge of process technology changes. This is likely to be particularly true when process technologies are complex systems requiring large, multidisciplinary teams.
- Eliminate redundant development efforts across sites, and facilitate communication and coordination with outside suppliers of technology and equipment.
- Extract the cumulative experiences of multiple operating units more efficiently. This may enable a company to exploit learning curve economies and improve process performance better than any one unit could have done on its own. A centralized group also can achieve economies in transferring the same technology across multiple sites.
- Act as a conduit for ensuring that best practices are shared across dispersed operating units.
- Enable the implementation of standardized process technologies across multiple units. This may have strategic advantages in markets where customers want the flexibility to source products or services from any site, yet still require a high degree of consistency.

Decentralized Process Technology Development

The chief advantages of a decentralized approach are analogous to those of an operating network of focused facilities:

- "Local" process development and engineering are likely to be more responsive to the needs of its particular environment and customers. For example, a plant in a high-wage area might prefer a more automated process than do plants in low-wage areas.

- Decentralizing process development and technology selection expands the number of process experiments that can be conducted within the network. This may reduce process risks as well as facilitate the creation of better performing processes over time.
- The transfer of technology from R&D to operations is likely to be faster and smoother when they are located at the same site.
- Giving an operating unit "local" autonomy to select its own process technologies usually enables it to experiment with and improve its own technologies at a faster rate than if all process innovations are centrally controlled, since the most innovative units are not constrained by laggards.
- A decentralized approach enables each operating unit to tailor its processes to the specific needs of its particular customer base.

Making the Trade-Off

It should be clear from this discussion that centralized and decentralized approaches each have their advantages and disadvantages. The choice, then, comes down to the organization's specific strategy and competitive priorities. Three sets of issues are relevant to making this choice:

1. *How important are "local" differences in markets or operating conditions?* In some types of markets there is tremendous competitive value in being able to guarantee that the process technology being utilized across multiple operations is exactly the same. This is particularly true for products whose process and product technologies are highly interdependent. The Copy-Exact approach made it possible for Intel to use the same process technology at plants around the world to supply global customers with a highly consistent product. In less interdependent markets, local variation in either customers or markets is significant and important to process design. For example, in regions with high wages and a strong technological infrastructure, the use of highly sophisticated automated processes may be justified. In a low wage, less technologically developed context, it may be better to use a less sophisticated, more labor-intensive process. Differences in culture, work habits, unions, and regulation are also important factors.

   A good principle is to develop centrally those aspects of the process where strong economies are associated with standardization, and allow local choice for others. For example, McDonald's is renowned for its highly consistent product quality, and maintains tight control of many aspects of its franchisee's process technologies. However, its units are allowed—within limits—to adapt McDonald's standard processes to local conditions, and to conduct a reasonable degree of controlled experimentation. In France, for example, McDonald's has found that it pays to spend lavishly on chic interiors and amenities such as music videos; it also provides an expanded product line (including a ham-and-cheese "Croque McDo"). As a result, in 2002 its French customers were spending more than twice as much per visit as in the United States and McDonald's was opening a new unit in France every six days—while closing almost 200 units in other countries that year.[22]

2. *How fully can the process be optimized prior to transfer to operations?* With a centralized process technology strategy, all operating units move in lock step when making changes in a process technology. Having all operating units use the exact same technology, of course, is terrific if the technology in question is reliable, robust, and efficient. However, if the process technology is not optimal, the lock-step approach saddles *all* of the plants with a problematic process. While nothing stops improvements from being implemented later, it is generally cumbersome to coordinate these changes across a multiunit operating network. Because a centralized approach makes it difficult to make significant process changes after the initial transfer, it is better suited to cases where the process technology can be developed right the first time. If significant learning-by-doing is required to work out the bugs and optimize a process, however, autonomous plant-level experimentation is warranted.

   This was Intel's rationale for investing heavily in facilities and capabilities that enabled it to develop optimal processes before launching a new product. Its "Technology Development Fabs" are essentially full-scale replicas of its commercial manufacturing facilities, allowing Intel to fully test out a new process in a setting nearly identical to the commercial production environment, and to identify and resolve problems before transferring it to the plant network.

3. *Do the major improvements in performance generally occur by incrementally improving a particular generation of process technology or by developing completely new generations of process technology?* Because a centralized process technology strategy makes it cumbersome to change a process technology after the initial transfer, "local" improvement opportunities are essentially forgone. Thus, when there are significant opportunities for fine-tuning a process by making multiple improvements in it after transfer, the centralized approach can be quite costly in terms of lost opportunities. However, when major productivity, quality, reliability, or other performance improvements are driven by the implementation of completely new generations of process technology, the centralized approach has the upper hand.

   Consider two examples. In one case, a product's cost has historically been reduced by 40 percent over its ten-year life cycle. In the other, the product life cycle is much shorter—two years, say—and the total cost reduction during that period typically amounts to only 5 percent. In addition, each new product generation creates opportunities for process innovation that reduce cost by 25 percent. In the first case, a centralized process technology strategy would be cumbersome. Instead, it would be better to give one's operating units the freedom to find and exploit improvement opportunities, and provide mechanisms to enable sharing of best practices across facilities. In the second case, the big pay-offs come from introducing new generations of process technology and rolling them out to the network as quickly as possible. Losing opportunities to incrementally improve technologies within a product generation is less important than quickly making the transition to a new generation. When product life cycles are very short, the strategy of "launch now—improve later" will not work, because later is *now.*

7.5 PROCESS DEVELOPMENT IN PERSPECTIVE

Process technology is a hidden source of competitive advantage in many industries. Unfortunately, many companies fail to exploit this advantage because they view process technology superiority as relevant primarily for cost reduction, and thus important strategically only for commodity products. Yet, as we have discussed in this chapter, new process technologies often underpin the launch of successful new products in a variety of both service and manufacturing industries.

Unlocking the potential of process technology, however, requires more than simply recognizing that it "matters." Process development performance is rooted in specific organizational capabilities and choices. In this chapter, we looked at three key drivers of process development performance: 1) the integration of product and process development; 2) the timing of technology transfer from development to operations; and 3) the degree of autonomy granted to operating units to develop, change, and improve process technologies. There is no one right way to manage process development. Superior process development occurs when companies match their strategy for process development to the specifics of the technological and competitive environment in which they operate. In this chapter, we have identified several of the factors that influence the specific approach a company should take to process development.

It is important to reemphasize that most organizations do not operate in a static context. Technology changes. Markets change. Competition changes. Indeed, as an organization gains experience with certain technologies, its own capabilities and knowledge base evolve. Hence, what works today may not be appropriate tomorrow. Matching one's development strategy to one's context is thus a dynamic process. The challenge is to capture learning from each development project and apply that knowledge—possibly even altering one's total approach to project management—on the next. Creating such a capability is an essential contributor to operations excellence in today's competitive environment. We revisit these themes in the next chapter.

NOTES

1. See, for example, Imai et al. (1985), Clark and Fujimoto (1991), Wheelwright and Clark (1992), Wheelwright and Clark (1995), Iansiti (1995), and Ulrich and Eppinger (1995).
2. Abernathy and Utterback (1978), Abernathy (1978).
3. Utterback (1994).

4. See, for example, Abernathy and Clark (1985), Tushman and Anderson (1986), Henderson and Clark (1990), and Christensen (1992).

5. Nevins et al. (1989) and Ulrich and Eppinger (1994).

6. Looking back, closed steel automobile body designs did not become feasible until several manufacturing innovations were developed in the 1920s, including new processes for manufacturing lightweight, high-quality sheet steel and the introduction of automatic welding (Abernathy 1978).

7. See, among others, Imai et al. (1985), Clark and Fujimoto (1991), and Iansiti (1995).

8. See, e.g., Clark and Fujimoto (1991).

9. Clark and Fujimoto (1991), for instance, found that Japanese automobile companies not only tended to overlap product and process engineering to a greater extent than U.S. and European firms, they also had faster process engineering cycles.

10. Appleyard et al. (2000).

11. See "Plus Development Corp. (A) and (B)" (HBS case numbers 9-687-001and 9-688-066).

12. See "How J&J's Foresight Made Contact Lenses Pay," *Business Week,* May 4, 1992, p. 132.

13. See "How a $4 Razor Ends Up Costing $300 Million," *Business Week,* January 29,1990, pg. 62. In 2003, Schick Razor introduced a *four* bladed razor, but was immediately sued by Gillette for patent infringement.

14. Clark and Fujimoto (1990).

15. Ulrich and Eppinger (1995).

16. See "McDonald's Corporation (Abridged)" (HBS case number 9-603-041).

17. See "The Boeing 767: From Concept to Production (A)." (Harvard Business School Case 9-688-040).

18. See "BMW: The 7-Series Project (A)" and its associated "Instructor's Note" (HBS case numbers 9-692-083 and 5-692-094) for additional information about this situation.

19. Pisano (1996).

20. See McGrath and McMillan (1995).

21. See "ITT Automotive: Global Manufacturing Strategy (1994)." (HBS case #9-695-002), and its associated Teaching Note (#5-696-040).

22. See "What's This? The French Love McDonald's?", *Business Week,* January 13, 2003, p. 50, and "Hamburger Hell," *Business Week,* March 3, 2003.

Chapter 8

Creating an Edge through Superior Project Management

8.1 INTRODUCTION

Although project management has long been recognized as a form of operations management, throughout most of the twentieth century, it was regarded as being of rather secondary concern. Most of the projects undertaken by companies, aside from infrequent large construction and defense-related projects, were involved in the development of new products or processes. Until the 1980s, however, product/process life cycles were relatively long and, since these products and processes tended to be designed for mass markets, not only did the time required to develop a new product or process represent just a small proportion of its total lifetime, but the costs of development were only a small proportion of a unit's full cost when spread over a lifetime's output. In this context, most treatments of project management in operations management texts and courses tended to depict it as simply one extreme (and therefore relatively uncommon) of the continuum that proceeds from "one of a kind" to "commodity" products or processes. In recent years, however, an ability to manage projects effectively has become ever more important for operations managers, for a variety of interrelated reasons.

First, as intensifying global competition forced a slow convergence in product costs and quality, competitive success increasingly came to depend on rapid product and process development. Moreover, product life cycles in many industries were shortening, requiring that the costs of development projects be amortized over fewer years and total units. Therefore, faster development had to be achieved with fewer resources and expenses. Relatedly, the globalization of competition introduced more and more companies into established markets. In response, companies increasingly sought to differentiate themselves by focusing attention on ever-smaller market niches (giving rise to the concept of the *micro-niche*), and/or by customizing products according to the needs of specific user groups. The more customized the product, the more its development and production required project management mindsets and approaches. As a result, projects have come to consume a growing chunk of an operations organization's time and resources.

In addition, as described in Chapter 1 (Section 1.3), information-intensive products generally are costly to produce but cheap to reproduce (e.g., software, entertainment, pharmaceuticals, etc.), so their cost structures are dominated by the up-front costs of developing products and processes rather than the variable costs of production and distribution. Moreover, the *network effect* increases the importance of being an early participant in a new market, so fast project completion becomes essential. The same forces are seen even within the operations of traditional Old Economy companies, as IT has become increasingly important and resource consuming (see Chapter 6).

Finally, as described in Chapter 2, toward the end of the twentieth century many companies came to recognize that sustainable competitive success was based more on developing distinctive organizational capabilities than on individual products or attaining a specific market position. One of the best ways to cultivate management talent and develop new capabilities, as well as honing existing ones, they learned, was through carefully selected assignments to project teams. Operations managers therefore found themselves spending an increasing proportion of their time on project teams, not only those devoted to developing new products and processes but also to improving existing processes so as to achieve better quality, productivity, responsiveness, and resource utilization. The increasing number and importance of projects, in fact, has led a number of companies to set up separate project management offices to organize and coordinate them all.[1]

The next section provides a brief historical overview, describing two very different approaches for managing projects that gained wide acceptance over the last half of the twentieth century, and the strengths and limitations of each. We then turn to a discussion of three basic elements of effective project management.

1. *Cultivating,* creating, and selecting the right portfolio of projects (doing the right things)
2. *Executing* projects quickly and efficiently (doing things right)
3. *Learning* from project experience, so that both project execution and project teams and managers steadily improve over time (doing it better next time)

8.2 TWO HISTORICAL APPROACHES TO PROJECT MANAGEMENT

8.2.1 Critical Path Analysis

Victory in World War II was achieved in large part through the successful management of a large number of massive development projects. These ranged from the development of new aircraft and other weapons, to mobilizing and executing major amphibious invasions, to—most famously—the Manhattan Project that produced the atomic bomb. The difficulties associated with managing such large projects, combined with their importance, encouraged a wave of new thinking about how to structure and execute them. One of the resulting new approaches became especially popular with both managers and academics. The *Critical Path Method,* as it was called (although other names were also applied to it), essentially extended the traditional Gantt chart's step-by-step graph into a two-dimensional depiction that allowed one to incorporate a richer set of interactions among a project's individual activities.

To illustrate this approach we will use a hypothetical construction project. After listing each of the major activities required by this project, together with their expected completion times and the prior activities that had to be completed before one could start work on each (see Figure 8-1), the diagram depicted in Figure 8-2 can be drawn of these relationships.[2]

In this diagram, each separate activity is represented by one of the nodes in the network (the bottom number in each node represents the activity's expected completion time), while the lines depict the precedence relationships among activities, showing which must be completed before work on one of the subsequent activities can begin.[3]

Diagramming projects in this way has a number of advantages. First, it forces managers to be precise in their specification of all the individual activities that are necessary to complete a project, the resources and time required to accomplish them, and the order in which they must be undertaken. Second, it helps identify the "choke points" in the project—where a number of preparatory activities must be completed in order for progress to continue. In the above example, activity G ("erect building...") represents such a choke point. Third, it provides a convenient

Job	Job description	Immediately preceding jobs	Normal time
A	Procure materials	Start	3
B	Prepare site	Start	6
C	Prepare request for Engineering Departmental approval	Start	2
D	Prefabricate building and deliver to site	A	5
E	Obtain Engineering Department approval	C	2
F	Install connecting lines to main system	A	7
G	Erect building and equipment on site	B, D, E	4

Figure 8-1 Tasks Required to Complete a Major Construction Project

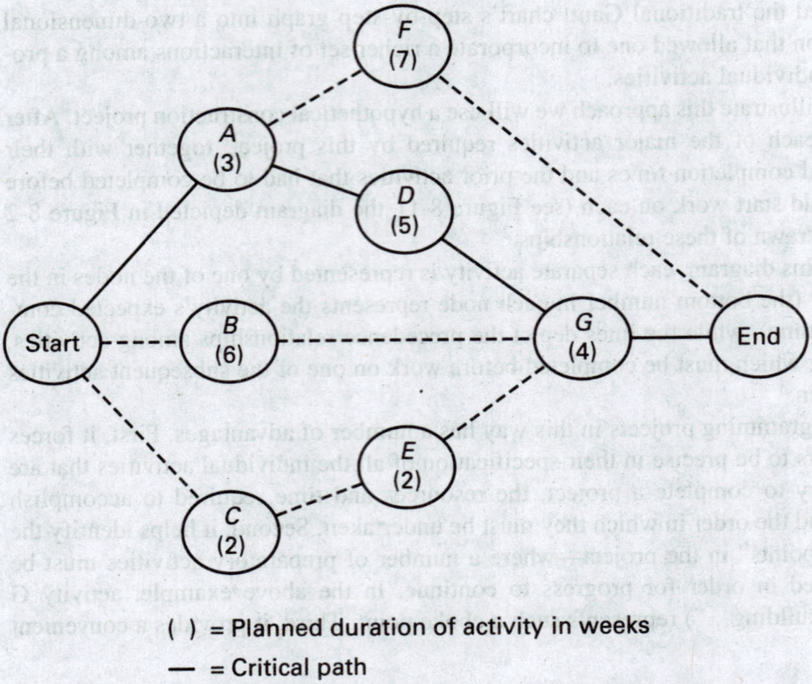

Figure 8-2 Critical Path Diagram for Major Construction Project

framework for monitoring the ongoing work on the project, allowing one to track the progress of individual activities and make decisions whether to add or remove resources from it if progress is slower or faster than expected.

Just because an activity is running behind its expected schedule does not necessarily imply that additional resources ought to be committed to it, however, nor does the fact that an activity is on schedule mean that attempts should not be made to accelerate its completion. Speeding up an activity whose completion time is not likely to affect the completion time for the whole project represents a waste of resources, while speeding up an on-time activity might result in earlier completion of the whole project. The final great advantage of this approach, therefore, is that through the use of a simple algorithm one can identify which pathway through the project diagram represents its *critical path:* the sequence of activities, from the start of the project to its end, that is expected to take the longest time to complete. In this simple example the path (A – D – G), representing a total of twelve weeks, constitutes the critical path.

Reducing the time required by any of the activities on the critical path will reduce the project's total time to completion—unless, of course, that reduction results in the emergence of a new critical path, a different "longest time" pathway of activities on the project diagram. By identifying and monitoring a project's evolving critical path, project managers are able to identify where scarce resources can best be applied, and from where they can be taken without penalty. Through the use of computer simulation they even can conduct simple explorations of the impact of uncertainty about project completion times.

The simplicity and effectiveness of the Critical Path Method, or CPM, led hundreds of companies to attempt to apply it to their large projects in the 1950s and 1960s, and it still is being used today. As useful as this technique proved to be for many project managers, for a variety of reasons it has proven even more attractive for operations management academics. They liked the fact that diagramming a project was analogous to preparing a process flow diagram, so the CPM reinforced project management's connection with one of the "core" operations management techniques they were teaching. Moreover, the CPM's simplicity made it easy for students to learn, and enabled instructors to employ enjoyable pedagogical techniques, such as games and student competitions. These provided students with useful, generalizable, and sometimes counter-intuitive insights. Best of all, it made it possible to apply analytical rigor to a messy problem and even offered the promise of identifying an "optimal" solution to it. As a result, for many years most operations management textbooks and courses confined their treatment of project management to descriptions and elaborations of the CPM. This is still true today, long after companies have recognized its severe limitations and its use has declined.

What are these limitations? First, the CPM assumes that a project can be defined quite precisely before it begins—that is, one proceeds toward a known outcome through a known, and well defined, sequence of interrelated steps that must take place in a prespecified order. Many actual development projects, however, begin with little more than a product or process concept that has to be explored, refined, and possibly altered substantially before actual development takes place. For projects such as these, it is generally impossible to specify up-front all the necessary activities that will be required for development—let alone to make any reasonable estimates of expected time durations. For that reason, they are more like conducting a somewhat erratic search in an unknown terrain rather than choosing paths along an existing system of pathways through it. Such searches are difficult to direct from "on high"; the project team must have considerable authority to change direction as it goes along.

Second, all constraints are assumed to be "hard," in the sense that no part of activity B can begin until all of activity A has been completed. In most projects, however, some overlapping of activities is possible and, as we will shortly see, finding ways to increase these overlaps is one of the keys to speeding up project completion time. Adding this kind of flexibility complicates enormously the application of the CPM approach.

Third, the CPM is essentially numerical and mechanical; people and human issues do not enter into the analysis. No assistance is provided in such areas as project team organization, staffing, cohesion, and commitment, which are now recognized as being critical to product success. Relatedly, although the CPM might be useful in managing a single complicated project (or a small number of them), its usefulness decreases when a company has to manage multiple projects at the same time. Strict application of the approach would require, each time the completion of a project activity or some unexpected change causes a new critical path to emerge, that top management get involved in making resource allocation decisions across projects that are competing for the same corporate resources. Even more important, the CPM approach provides little guidance for dealing with such central issues as selecting the right projects, grooming effective project managers, building the skills and capabilities of team members, "juggling" the mix and priorities of projects as they and the competitive environment evolve, and transferring skills and learning from one team to another.

8.2.2 Stage-Gate Approaches

As companies experienced these problems and issues, they evolved toward a quite different model of project management, one that allowed top managers to withdraw from active involvement in the day-to-day activities and decisions of individual projects but maintained their ability to step in and exercise control at critical points. Instead of attempting to monitor and control each project activity, as with the CPM, project activities are grouped into a few rough sequential chunks, phases, or "stages." A basic set of such stages, for example, might include "concept development," "detailed design," "prototype development," "testing," and "production ramp-up." Indeed, the traditional approach for developing computer software, termed the *Waterfall Model,* is based on five analogous stages: Requirements Analysis, Specifications, Design, Coding, and Integration/Testing.[4] Within each stage the project team has considerable autonomy to explore alternative options, make choices, and deploy resources, but the project cannot move to the following stage until it has gone through the "gate" of a formal management review. There progress is reviewed, a decision is made whether to continue, additional resources are authorized, and general guidance is given as to the direction that the team should take next. Once this review has taken place, work on the previous stage is frozen, and the team cannot iterate back to it. Through this process the project design gradually evolves toward increasing levels of specificity and organizational involvement.[5]

Many companies have sought to increase the degree and frequency of management control by increasing the number of stages (so that each contains fewer activities) and review gates. For example, one large company's "Tollgate Process," depicted in Figure 8-3, incorporated eight separate reviews, breaking both the simple "concept development" and "detailed design" stages into two separable stages. This necessitated separate reviews of the product's Concept, Feasibility, Preliminary Design, and so on.

Similarly, the project management process for developing new products at Philips's worldwide organization in the 1980s incorporated seven reviews, or *milestones.* This process, as implemented by Philips's Taiwan subsidiary when developing a new computer monitor, contained the steps described in Figure 8-4.[6]

Stage-Gate (sometimes called Phase-Gate or Phase-Review) models became very popular during the 1980s. Although labeled in various ways, such models were the mainstay of the product development approaches that most consulting firms advised their clients to adopt. Like the CPM, Stage-Gates had a certain philosophical appeal to operations managers, who were drawn to the idea of bringing discipline to the often-chaotic management of projects. Moreover, the Stage-Gate approach has a number of advantages that should not be underestimated. First, by mandating a

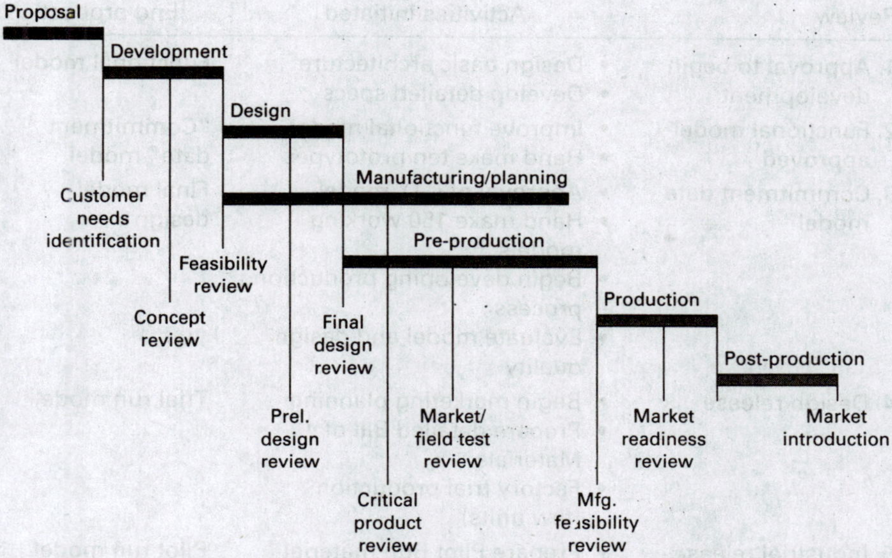

Figure 8-3 One Company's "Tollgate" Development Process

common roadmap, process, and language, it seeks to impose a consistent approach to the development process. Many organizations, prior to adopting a Stage-Gate approach, had no basic template for executing projects. Different groups and departments often employed different processes, without mechanisms to coordinate decisions and technical problem solving. Second, Stage-Gates, as the name suggests, provide a means for making "staged" commitments of resources as a project progresses. Without such gates, project selection often became an "all-or-nothing" proposition: after a project was funded, there were few formal review points to assess its progress and to determine whether it should continue. In this sense, Stage-Gates enable senior managers to commit resources in a fashion similar to that venture capitalists use when funding a new enterprise. Finally, the Stage-Gate approach's formal reviews provide senior managers with a mechanism for monitoring projects and making critical decisions about their scope and direction.

Unfortunately, over time the Stage Gate approach to project management was found to have its own set of limitations. First, it suffers from the quintessential management dilemma: the more one attempts to "control" a set of projects from on high (through more frequent and thorough management reviews), the greater the demands on top management time, the more time projects wait at a gate while awaiting a review, and the less project teams are able to adapt to changing technologies and competitive environments. A method that attempted to conserve scarce resources and reduce risk in a relatively stable environment became increasingly inappropriate for a world that was demanding ever-faster, flexible, and innovative development projects, and it broke down completely when the time required to complete a project exceeded the time required to respond effectively to competitive

Review	Activities initiated	End product
1. Approval to begin development	• Design basic architecture • Develop detailed specs	Functional model
2. Functional model approved	• Improve functional model • Hand make ten prototypes	"Commitment date" model
3. Commitment date model	• Approval of C.D. model • Hand make 150 working models • Begin developing production process • Evaluate model and design quality	Final model design
4. Design release	• Begin marketing planning • Prepare detailed Bill of Materials • Factory trial production (few units)	Trial run model
5. Industrial release	• Prepare Pilot Run material • Pilot Run (several hundred units) • Adapt and debug production process • Production QA check	Pilot run model
6. Commercial release	• Ramp up production • Commercial rollout	Commercial product
7. Release for mass production	• Mass production	

Figure 8-4 Project Reviews for Philip-Taiwan's Development of a New Computer Monitor

assaults. In the early 1990s, for example, many U.S. auto and electronics companies that had adopted the Stage-Gate approach discovered that their Japanese competitors had discovered ways to design and introduce new models in about half the time it took them.[7]

Second, applying the same Stage-Gate process across all projects ignores the contingent nature of product development. As we have emphasized throughout this book, there is no "one best way" to manage anything. Projects with different characteristics—different levels of uncertainty, risk characteristics, technical and market objectives, and complexity—call for different approaches to project conceptualization and execution.

Finally, companies that employ a Stage-Gate approach risk having their development processes ossify to the point where they actually become a barrier to change. There is nothing inherently rigid about a Stage-Gate approach; like any process it can be adapted and changed over time as organizations identify opportunities for improvement. However, in reality, once organizations have gone through the pain of implementing a Stage-Gate process and achieved the necessary buy-in from all the various functions involved in development, it is difficult to revisit the approach's fundamental assumptions. Thus, if not managed carefully, the Stage-Gate process itself can become a barrier to implementing such lead-time-reducing improvements as compressing individual steps, eliminating unnecessary steps, or conducting certain activities in parallel rather than in sequence.

Stage-Gate processes also share some of the same limitations as the CPM. Like CPM, they are mute with respect to such critical organizational issues as project team composition and structure, project leadership, and problem-solving skills. Nor do they provide guidance about project selection or how to foster and implement learning across projects.

We do not mean to imply that Stage-Gate approaches are ineffective, only that they are not as universally applicable as their widespread use might suggest. As with CPM, they are appropriate when the assumptions underlying them fit a given situation. Even then, however, simply adopting either methodology is unlikely to lead to a satisfactory rate of project success over time unless it is supplemented with informed managerial guidance and complementary human resource systems. In the remaining sections of this chapter we outline a strategic framework for project management that incorporates the project selection process, the project execution process, and learning across projects.

8.3 CREATING, SELECTING, AND MANAGING PROJECT PORTFOLIOS

When an organization's projects are routinely late and fail to achieve their objectives, senior managers generally respond with attempts to improve their *execution.* For instance, they might adopt a Stage-Gate approach, increase the training of project managers, or search in an ad hoc fashion for ways to cut time out of individual activities. These are all logical and reasonable approaches to take, but many of the problems encountered during a project's execution start long before the first design decision is made, before the project team is in place, and even before the project leader is picked. Instead, the roots of failure often are located in the process (or the lack thereof) by which projects are selected and the whole *portfolio* of projects is managed. In many organizations, there is no systematic process for identifying project opportunities and then culling those opportunities into an appropriate number and mix of projects.

As a result, organizations are prone to undertake far too many projects relative to the resources they have available. One study found that a company's proposed utilization of engineering resources sometimes exceeded its capacity by 300 percent![8] Our own experience with projects involving product/process development, information technology, and operations improvement suggest that such over-commitment is commonplace. Moreover, when one looks carefully at the purposes and scope of individual projects, it is not unusual to find that these projects are not well-aligned with the company's overall strategy or operating priorities. Thus, even if successfully executed, they would not contribute to the firm's competitive advantage.

In this section we provide some basic principles for assembling, organizing, and managing a portfolio of projects. They involve four processes, which operate sequentially in an individual project but are all going on within a company at the same time:

1. *Seeding.* Encouraging an extensive and rich mix of potential project ideas.
2. *Weeding and Feeding.* Selecting which ideas to turn into formal projects, and providing those projects with the appropriate people, managers, and resources.
3. *Cultivating.* Maintaining an appropriate mix of projects under development, establishing priorities among them, modifying them as new information becomes available, and pushing them through to completion.
4. *Plowing under.* Culling the project portfolio. As markets shift and technologies evolve, many projects lose their competitive attractiveness during their development. Or they require resources that can be applied more profitably elsewhere. Maintaining a healthy portfolio therefore often requires decisions to kill projects that are well along in their development.

A useful way to depict the operation of these four processes is the *development funnel,* as shown in Figure 8-5. The wide mouth of the funnel represents the large number of project ideas that become candidates for selection. The narrow neck captures the fact that only a small proportion of them can be allocated resources and support their development requires. The funnel's tube represents the time required to complete development of the projects so selected, and the outlets at the bottom of the tube represent the exit points for abandoned projects. The following subsections elaborate on the four processes described above.

8.3.1 Seeding: Encouraging a Rich Mix of Alternative Project Ideas

Good project ideas can come from a variety of sources and from many levels in an organization. Far too often, however, companies do not "open the mouth" of the

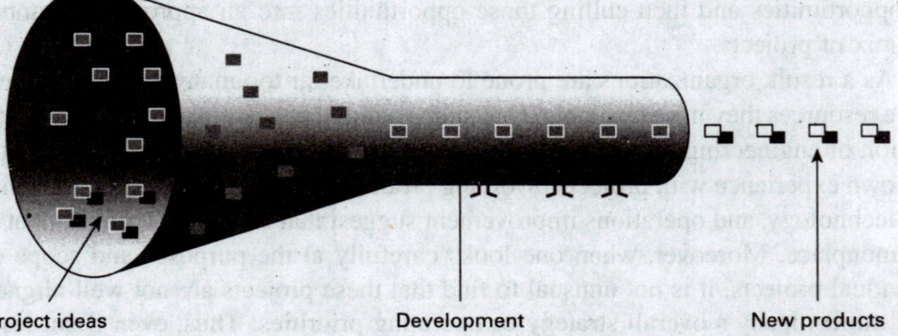

Figure 8-5 The Development Funnel

funnel wide enough to pull in project ideas from multiple sources. If most ideas for projects are generated by the same group of people or functional organization within a company, they tend to be rather similar. Marketing tends to generate ideas for improving existing products, based on their customers' reactions and/or their own experience in trying to market them. Operations tends to generate ideas for simplifying the design of the product or otherwise improving its production and delivery. R&D/engineering tends to seek opportunities to exploit the latest technology. And top management is always on the lookout for other ways to reduce costs (e.g., outsourcing) and for projects that might allow them to enter entirely new markets. If a company relies exclusively on one of these functions to generate project ideas, the results are predictable. Generating a rich mix of alternatives requires that as many people and organizational groups as possible be encouraged to contribute project ideas, and they should be rewarded for doing so.

In addition to providing mechanisms for a variety of internal groups to contribute project ideas, senior management also should create conduits to encourage and solicit project ideas from external sources such as customers, suppliers, partners, and even competitors. Some companies require groups of employees to visit selected customers on a rotating basis so that they can get a better sense of how their products are used and the kinds of problems their customers are attempting to deal with. Others, such as Milliken, invite cross-functional groups to visit trade shows and the labs of equipment providers so that they can gain better perspective on the emerging process technologies that are likely to become available. Many companies "benchmark" their products and processes against those of their best competitors, or against "world class" organizations that utilize similar processes (see Chapter 10).

8.3.2 Weeding and Feeding: Winnowing Project Ideas and Providing Resources

The real goal is not just to pick the best projects, but also to pick the best *portfolio* of projects. This best portfolio is not necessarily the one that incorporates all the best project ideas, since some of these ideas may be in direct competition with one another so that only one among them may eventually be introduced. Furthermore, all projects are in indirect competition in that they consume resources from a relatively fixed pool; therefore, choosing certain ones is likely to undermine the efficacious development of others.

For most organizations the binding resource is skilled people, particularly high performers who have specific technical skills. Unfortunately, many managers who would never agree to scheduling a critical piece of equipment at more than 100 percent of its capacity often attempt to extract the greatest possible value from their highly skilled people by assigning them to several "key" projects at the same time and thereby overcommitting their time. Their intent is to ensure that their best people never find themselves with nothing to do, but the actual consequence is that these people are forced to run from project to project as situations requiring their skills arise. As a result they spend much of their available time "on the fly," learning about each new situation—as well as everything that has transpired since they last worked on that project (and, in the process, forgetting much of what they had been doing on their previous projects)—and fighting fires. Worse, they spend valuable time in a series of unproductive meetings, composed of large numbers of people who are unprepared to contribute because they are spending all their time in other meetings! All this reduces the amount of time the organization's best people can spend utilizing their skills to actually improve the conceptualization and execution of healthy projects. In fact, research suggests that because of this behavior pattern highly skilled people (e.g., R&D engineers) ought not to be assigned to more than two or three projects at the same time.[9]

Overcommitment leads to the sort of *capacity squeeze* that was discussed in Chapter 3 (Sections 3.2.2 and 3.2.3), and the impact of such squeezes is the same when managing projects as it is when managing ongoing operations. As mentioned there, according to "Little's Law," the average time a job spends being processed from the time it enters production to the moment work on it is completed (lead time, LT) is equal to the average number of jobs in process at the same time (WIP), divided by the average rate at which jobs are completed (Rate):

$$LT = WIP/Rate$$

For example, if ten jobs are in process, and one is being completed every two days, on average (implying a daily completion rate of 0.5), the typical job will spend twenty days in process.

As WIP increases, therefore, lead times will also increase unless there is a corresponding increase in the rate of completion. Of course, this relationship only holds *on average*. It is always possible to "expedite" a specific order or a particular batch of production, but this simply delays all of the other orders and batches. The same is true for projects. If we replace WIP with "PIP" (projects in progress), we can see that as the number of projects increases, the average lead time to complete any given project will also expand. Thinking about the problem this way forces managers to recognize that, just as with other processes, a project's lead time depends on their organization's capacity to execute them—which, in turn, is dependent on the resources available and the number of projects simultaneously requiring those resources. Unfortunately, most project schedules are set without taking into account either capacity or the number of other committed projects. The result is that scheduled completion times are often woefully unrealistic.

This kind of dysfunctional situation is made worse if, as is usually the case, in addition to the projects that have received formal management approval the organization is secretly undertaking several bootleg projects that represent a few people's labors of love. Thus, what management thinks is only a modest overcommitment of engineers' time might actually be much worse. The outcome is the worst of both worlds: inefficient utilization of the time of one's best people, as well as projects that are over time and budget, and therefore do not have the competitive impact that was expected of them.

When creating a strategy for designing and organizing a project portfolio, one should recognize that there are several different types of projects, and each type requires a somewhat different approach. There are many ways projects can be categorized. One way that has proven to be useful in many organizations is to characterize projects according to the amount of "newness" they are expected to create or respond to. They can usually be placed into one of the following four categories, ranging from "least" to "most" new:[10]

1. *Support/enhancement.* These projects seek to achieve modest enhancements in an existing product/process, taking advantage of its existing market acceptance, feedback from users and field service, and ongoing improvements in its underlying technology.
2. *Derivative.* Such projects seek either more substantial improvements in performance or features, and/or appeal to a different (or larger) group of users. They also build on the accumulating experience with the core product/process, and may attempt to utilize a recent advance in the basic technology.
3. *Platform/next generation.* Rather than extending an existing basic product/process concept, such projects attempt to create a new platform upon which a new generation of successor products and processes might be based. In their attempt to provide a new set of benefits to users that will have prolonged appeal, they attempt to incorporate the very latest understanding of market trends and user preferences, and to exploit advanced technology. The basic architectures of such products and processes must be sufficiently robust to support future enhancements and derivative models.
4. *Breakthrough.* As their name suggests, these projects attempt to create a radically new product or process, one that may appeal to a totally different market (or to very different needs within the same market) and makes use of state-of-the-art technologies, often including those still unproven or not yet fully developed.

In the case of an operating process, a *derivative* project might aim to improve the yield of a particular process step by "tweaking" process parameters or by making refinements in equipment. In an IT setting, such a project might encompass an upgrade to an existing software system (e.g., going from Time Scheduler 2.4 to version 2.5). A *platform* process development project, on the other hand, typically requires introducing next generation process technology and equipment. An example of such a next generation process development project would be a semiconductor manufacturer's move from 8-inch (200 millimeter) to 12-inch (300 millimeter) wafers. This entails investing in completely new equipment across virtually the entire manufacturing process. *Breakthrough* process projects entail developing and implementing a fundamentally new process technology, such as going from a batch process to a continuous flow process or adopting 24-hour "lights out" fully automated production.

As argued above, a company should not attempt to undertake more projects than it can provide resources for or manage effectively. The most critical resource is good project managers, and good project managers are both in short supply and individually limited—by skills and experience—in the range of the projects they can guide effectively. For example, most organizations have relatively few "heavyweight" project managers (as described in the next section), who have the experience, credibility, and organizational clout to manage the kind of highly skilled and relatively autonomous project teams that can undertake large and complex platform or breakthrough projects. However, they generally have many more "lightweight" managers, who have enough experience to oversee simple product/process enhancements, often operating within the protective confines of their functional groups.

Moreover, as with the development projects themselves, the creation and management of the project portfolio should be linked back to the company's overall competitive context and strategy. It probably does not make sense for a company that competes in a rapidly changing industry to authorize all the incremental projects that it can possibly staff, or for one that seeks to differentiate itself by being flexible and responsive to commit the bulk of its resources to cost reducing products and processes. Similarly, a company that operates in mature markets with products that are built into customers' long-lived equipment probably should not devote more than 5 to 10 percent of its resources to breakthrough projects, as users are unlikely to adopt radically new products very quickly. The bulk of its resources would more profitably be spent on simple enhancements of its basic product(s). However, a company in a fast-moving, high-technology environment with short product life cycles might pursue competitive differentiation primarily through the introduction of new platforms that can then be quickly and efficiently leveraged into a stream of derivatives that serve different customer segments.

Too many companies lack formal processes for sorting out project proposals and linking the selection among them to their overall competitive strategy. As a result, projects get funded for political reasons, or because they appear particularly exciting to key people. In contrast, an effective selection process not only ensures a mix of projects that is doable within the constraints of an organization's resources, as discussed earlier, but (1) is valuable competitively, in that it meets the needs of targeted users and/or builds the strength of one's brand or reputation; (2) makes the best use of existing personnel, prior experience, and other resources; (3) provides appropriate learning experiences so as to expand the managerial resources available for future project assignments; and (4) creates or enhances a path that is projected to lead to organizational distinctiveness and longer-term competitive advantage.

8.3.3 Cultivating the Project Portfolio

The development funnel depicted in Figure 8-5 is simple and logically appealing, but it does not represent actual practice in most organizations. Some companies follow approaches that might be modeled better by a French horn, as projects repeatedly cycle through the same activities because of managerial changes of mind. Others look more like Rube Goldberg devices, with projects entering at peculiar points, proceeding in erratic paths, and exiting the process randomly—only to reappear in disguised form elsewhere. In order for a development funnel to operate as intended, it must be consciously *managed* to operate that way.

Unfortunately, top managers often fundamentally misunderstand what is required to manage a project funnel. Many confine their involvement to one or both of the two *ends* of the funnel: either reviewing project concepts and selecting specific projects, or managing the resulting product's production ramp-up and market roll-out. They implicitly assume that, once started into the funnel's neck, projects will automatically proceed smoothly through it. Or, more disruptively, managers jump in midway through the development process—typically at the point an actual production prototype is available for inspection—and propose changes that undermine much of the previous design work and require costly and time-consuming rework. However, they tend to avoid the tough but essential decisions regarding whether to stop projects, as discussed below.

Top managers also tend to ignore the division of responsibilities between themselves and those assigned to manage a project. Project managers are ultimately responsible for their project's cost, quality, and time to completion. Their success or failure generally is clearly visible, and there usually is fairly little that senior managers can do to affect such issues without constant personal involvement. The best use of their time is to ensure that the project teams maintain a clear sense of purpose and priorities. For example, the Medtronic Corporation achieved a major improvement in its product development performance in the late 1980s when its vice president for Product Development began making his project teams accountable for just four clearly defined measures of performance: speed, cost, quality, and innovativeness. One project manager commented, "We used to spend lots of time debating what we should do. One of [our V.P.'s] greatest achievements was in cleaning up the front end … by articulating very clearly what our strategy was … [and] well-defined criteria [to] guide these decisions."[11]

The most important things that top managers can do to facilitate the work of project managers operate at a higher level. First, they have to provide guidance as to the *scope* of the project. For example, as work proceeds and new information becomes available, should its original scope be maintained or should it be expanded or contracted? Then, as the project proceeds they can facilitate *communication* among project managers, and between them and other groups—both internal and external—that may be able to provide useful information.

One approach for formalizing and structuring such communication is the Quality Function Deployment (QFD) technique, sometimes referred to as the *House of Quality.* In seeking to relate user needs directly—and profitably—to product and process specifications, it employs a series of matrices to link the work done on one aspect of a project with the related work done in connection with other aspects.[12] Such simple paper-based communication tools can become inadequate, however, as the number of separate groups involved in a project increases. This typically occurs when new products/services have to be developed in conjunction with the new processes required to deliver them, and as suppliers and customers increasingly get involved in these development efforts. Fortunately, new information technologies are now available to facilitate communications among multiple parties. For example, a critical part of the process development involved in the production of the new Virginia class of submarines by General Dynamic's Electric Boat division was the creation of common databases and communication links that allowed different components and systems of the submarine to be produced in many locations by different organizations.[13]

Relatedly, managers can serve to facilitate *coordination* among the different groups working on the same project or across projects that have features or resources in common, as well as *resolve disputes* involving the various parties. Finally, and most importantly, they can prepare and mobilize the *human resources* that will staff and manage future projects.

8.3.4 Plowing Under

As mentioned earlier, not every project that receives formal approval and funding ends as expected. Some hit a technological or market barrier that prevents completion. Others are discovered to overlap with other projects to an extent that requires they be combined or selected among. And some simply, through mismanagement or team incompetence, never meet their stated objectives. When this happens, top management has an obligation to stop work on the project and redirect its resources to more profitable activities. This is both difficult and unpleasant because each project usually has become somebody's "baby." Such decisions, therefore, are not only difficult for the same reasons that all resource allocation decisions are difficult, but they tend to be political and personal. It is almost impossible to turn such decisions into "win-win" situations: somebody clearly loses, and they often are friends or people who have done favors for you in the past.

8.4 MAINTAINING DISCIPLINE AND FOCUS IN THE PROJECT PORTFOLIO

One of the biggest challenges senior managers face in managing a portfolio of projects is to keep their development process responsive and dynamic while resisting the ever present pressures to "add just one more project" or to respond to the latest crisis ("if we don't develop a new version of product X, customer Y is going to switch to a competitor"). Otherwise, they usually find themselves at some point forced to go through a gut-wrenching exercise of re-sizing their project portfolio by culling dead-end projects and realigning the remaining projects with their competitive strategy. In the aftermath of these marathon reassessments, there is both a feeling of accomplishment and trepidation. Although painful, there is a sense of relief that tough decisions have been made and that the portfolio has finally been "cleaned up." Nobody, however, is particularly interested in repeating the pain of the exercise, and thus the portfolio becomes a static snapshot, with little or no implications for future resource allocation decisions. Without an ongoing process for managing a project portfolio, it slowly but surely regresses to its previous state through a series of incremental decisions, made by different managers at different places in the organization and at different points in time. Then, after a few more years, the painful exercise has to be repeated.

Managing the project portfolio should be viewed as routine, a process just like capital budgeting and financial reporting. A number of practices help make this process work.

1. *Start with a strategy.* As we have emphasized throughout this book, all elements of an operations strategy should reflect a company's situation and competitive strategy. The same is true for a project portfolio strategy. There is no "optimal" project portfolio. What is best for a given company depends on its overall strategy, and if that strategy does not provide meaningful guidance about the approximate number and mix of projects, the company needs to refine its strategy.

2. *Don't jump too quickly to project selection.* There is a natural tendency for companies to start with an existing set of projects, and cull them based on their available resources and strategy. This temptation must be resisted. Considering only existing projects tends to cause managers to attempt to "shoe-horn" existing projects into the current strategy, rather than considering completely new projects. Only after managers have a clear and meaningful articulation of their strategy should they focus on the appropriate mix of project types. What percent of our resources should go to breakthrough projects? What percent should go to new platforms? To derivative projects? Once there is agreement as to how high-level resources ought to be allocated, managers are in a better position to choose the number of projects that should be undertaken in each category (e.g., "based on our strategy, we should start ten derivative projects this quarter, two platforms, and one breakthrough").
3. *Compare "apples to apples."* As senior managers begin the process of actually selecting projects, they must avoid the temptation to line up all the potential project ideas and pick "the best" ones—and certainly not the ones that promise the highest returns on investment (ROI)! Derivative project ideas must compete with other derivative ideas; platform ideas with other platforms. If your capacity constraints and strategy say you should do ten derivative projects, and you have twenty great derivative project ideas, you still should do only ten derivative projects. If you start comparing derivative projects (which typically have shorter term, more certain pay-offs) to platforms, the derivatives will almost inevitably drive out the platforms. Financial measures like ROI and NPV typically work better for derivatives (where cost and benefits are more certain) than for platform and breakthrough projects. Because platform projects create options for future derivative projects, their option value should be formally or informally taken into account in project evaluations (see Chapter 9).
4. *Create rigorous systems for estimating project resource requirements and tracking available capacity.* The biggest barrier to implementing this kind of portfolio management is a lack of data about project resource requirements and capacity. Managers often lament that it is simply impossible to estimate requirements because "every project is different," and that it is impossible to track who is working on which projects because the organization is working on so many of them. Ironically, these same companies often are able to estimate sales and costs for literally thousands of SKUs; they can estimate costs of materials acquired from hundreds of suppliers scattered around the world; they can estimate earnings per share to the penny. None of these costs are particularly easy to estimate, yet companies have developed and invested in accounting and control systems that enable this to be done quite routinely. It is not inherently more difficult to estimate resource requirements and track resource availability for projects. It just requires investment in project level accounting and control systems. Because projects only recently have begun to play a major role

in operations, however, developing "project accounting" systems has typically not been a high priority for most companies.

5. *Create a closed-loop system.* A well-running company should be spawning lots of great ideas for projects all the time. This puts nearly constant pressure on the portfolio management process. Literally every day, someone, somewhere in the organization, will want to start a new project, but the company is unlikely to have the resources available to start a new project every day. Derivative projects create the most struggles, as they appear to consume the fewest resources, so there is a strong temptation to just squeeze one more in. Very quickly, however, these derivatives can overwhelm the system.

   One organization that struggled with this problem had developed an effective system for dealing with its platform and breakthrough projects, as those required major resources and thus attracted senior management attention. Derivative projects, however, were finding their way onto its project list and devouring far more resources than had been budgeted for such projects. The company dealt with this problem by creating a senior management committee specifically responsible for approving derivative projects, of which thirty to forty typically were underway at any given time. During any one-month period, however, the company generally was finishing only two or three projects. Thus, in order to keep their capacity balanced they only should approve two or three new derivative projects per month. To maintain portfolio discipline, the management committee would meet only once per month and decide which two or three new projects to initiate. If it turned out that no derivative projects had been completed the previous month, then no new project starts were approved. By doing so, the company created a closed-loop system that helped ensure that its total project commitments did not exceed its available resources.

8.5 DESIGNING A STRATEGY FOR PROJECT EXECUTION

A rigorous, well-managed portfolio creation and project selection process will help an organization pursue the right number and mix of projects, but that is only half the battle. Superior performance still requires outstanding *execution* of the individual projects. Earlier in this chapter, we discussed two of the traditional approaches for managing individual projects and their limitations. In this section, we offer a framework for thinking about project management as a system of principles, processes, and organizational structures that must be coherently designed to support broader strategic priorities. Thus, again we do not advocate a single "best practice" approach to project management. Instead, we strive to make the reader aware of the types of choices that must be made when managing projects and the inherent trade-offs those choices pose.

Research on product development highlights the powerful impact of five types of choices on performance:[14] (1) project definition and scope; (2) the organization of project teams; (3) the structure and flow of project tasks and activities; (4) methodologies and technologies for design, prototyping, and testing; and (5) a mechanism for senior management review and control. Each of these is discussed below.

8.5.1 Project Definition

Project definition is one of the most critical determinants of product development performance. Many of the problems encountered when executing projects are rooted in the way the project was defined at the outset. For example, projects that are defined too broadly or ambiguously can easily lead to a situation where different people or functions have made critical project decisions based on different assumptions or expectations. Projects that lack clear definition and boundaries are also vulnerable to "feature creep" and protracted debates over what the capabilities and performance objectives of the product or process ought to be. This, of course, contributes to extended lead times. At the other extreme, a project also can be too tightly prescribed at the outset. The problem with an overly narrow definition is that new information and learning generated during the project is more difficult to incorporate into it, and the resulting product may fail to meet customers' evolving needs.

Companies take different approaches when defining projects. Some rely heavily on information from existing customers ("voice of the customer" processes) to define the specifications that meet their needs. Microsoft, for instance, prepares very detailed specifications for each generation of the Windows Operating System prior to launching it.[15] Others, such as Netscape, have taken a more evolutionary approach. They develop a "quick and dirty" concept of the product and then allow it to evolve through a process of continual interaction with customers during the actual development process. The best way to proceed depends on the type of project, the type of product or process, and the market being served. Projects that build on previous generations or existing platforms (derivative projects) and serve the needs of existing users generally can begin with a more detailed definition. In contrast, it usually is more difficult to fully anticipate customer needs and write detailed specifications up-front for a project whose goal is to create a "breakthrough," such as the first-generation Sony Walkman or the process for producing the first disposable contact lens.

8.5.2 Project Teams

Development projects are complex undertakings. Essentially, they require people, who have various skills and perspectives and come from different groups within the organization, to coordinate and integrate their activities and decisions toward a common goal. Choices about project governance and staffing significantly influence the performance of development projects. While certain types of project governance choices are often very explicit (e.g., "We use fully dedicated project teams"), others are often implicit (e.g., "We think engineering is ultimately responsible for getting the design right"). One encounters a range of project team types in practice. At one extreme are traditional *functional* teams. In such teams each organizational function (e.g., hardware engineering, software engineering, mechanical engineering, production engineering, manufacturing, and marketing) takes responsibility for a different "piece" of the project. Few, if any, organizational mechanisms are provided to integrate problem solving and decisions across the functional groups. The functional approach tends to work best in situations where in-depth functional expertise is the ultimate driver of the project's success. Obviously, such an approach runs into problems for projects where speed of development and/or a high degree of integration and coordination across functions is essential.

To overcome the limitations of a purely functional organization, many companies utilize other types of project teams, vested with greater levels of authority. One step up from the functional team is the so-called *lightweight* team—"lightweight" in the sense that it is vested with relatively few resources and little decision-making authority. Composed of representatives from each functional organization, such a team acts largely as a forum for information exchange across functions. The project manager (who typically is assigned to multiple projects) is responsible for coordinating schedules, organizing meetings, tracking progress, and identifying problems that need resolution. Should a major dispute arise, however, authority to resolve the issue lies with senior functional managers, not with the project team, as does responsibility for most substantive issues involving design, operations, or marketing.

To create a higher degree of integration and coordinated problem solving across functions, and to improve the lead time, efficiency, and quality of certain types of projects, many organizations will vest their project teams with a greater degree of authority. So-called *heavyweight* teams are typically composed of full-time members from various functions, who often are physically co-located. Unlike their counterparts in lightweight teams, members of a heavyweight team do not merely serve as emissaries from their functions, but instead play an active role in shaping project-level decisions. Although some major decisions may still be vested in the functions, within certain limits the project team has authority to make substantive decisions affecting the project. Likewise, the leader of a heavyweight project team is not simply a coordinator, but an active and authoritative manager of both the team and the process. Heavyweight project leaders are akin to general managers. As such, they (as well as most of the other members of their teams) are generally dedicated to just one project and—as with a division general manager—are fully responsible for its overall success.

Heavyweight project teams typically work best in development projects that require a high degree of cross-functional integration. One study of the development of new automobile models[16] found that projects utilizing heavyweight team structures performed significantly better (in terms of lead times, engineering efficiency, and product quality) than those using either functional or lightweight approaches. Pioneered by Toyota and Honda, heavyweight teams now are used extensively by automobile companies throughout the world; Chrysler's "platform teams" are one highly publicized example. They also are widely used in the electronics industry,[17] and are beginning to be used by pharmaceutical companies that are facing increasing pressure for shorter, more efficient drug development. For instance, in the mid-1990s Eli Lilly formed heavyweight project teams for two new drugs—Zyprexa and

Evista—which then were in later stages of development.[18] The results so impressed Lilly management that heavyweight project teams were adopted for other development projects.

In heavyweight project teams, team members who are not "core" still tend to reside and work in their functional groups. That is, the functions are not completely separated from the project, but instead play a critical supporting role. For certain types of projects, however, companies may go a step further and choose to separate the entire team from the existing organization. These are sometimes referred to as *autonomous* teams, and can be viewed as spin-outs. Indeed, the formation of an autonomous project team for the development of a radically new product or process often is the precursor to a new business unit. Autonomous teams are typically most beneficial for projects requiring completely new technical and commercial capabilities for the company. In situations where the project team is asked to "start with a blank slate" and "think outside the box," there can be benefits to preventing the existing organization from "polluting" the thinking of the team with traditional approaches.

8.5.3 Structuring the Flow of Project Tasks and Activities

Development projects typically involve many different activities, which are carried out by many different groups of people. In order to facilitate integration and track progress, it is important to impose some structure on the development process. As discussed earlier (Sections 8.1.1 and 8.1.2), the Critical Path Method and Stage-Gate models both are attempts to organize the tasks and activities of development into a logical structure.

The problem with the standard Stage-Gate approach, as discussed there, is not just that it tends to take too long, but by assuming that all important design issues can be resolved early on, and then freezing that design, it locks project teams into a development path that is difficult to alter as new information about user needs and technological advances becomes available. Accommodating such new information would require that both "concept development" and "detailed design" be allowed to evolve, in effect extending those stages forward along the project's timeline so that they overlap several *subsequent* stages. Just as critical, delaying the testing a new product or process until all its components have been designed and assembled prevents important information, about performance and how users interact with it, from being revealed to the design team. This is particularly important when the product/process is highly innovative and therefore both its operation is unproven and users are unfamiliar with it. Moreover, studies have shown that more than 75 percent of a product's total lifetime costs are essentially determined during the formulation of its basic concept.[19] This implies that production and after-sales service expertise ought to be applied much earlier in its development process than is usually the case under the Stage-Gate approach—that is, that later stages ought to be extended *backward* along the project timeline. This understanding has led to a new model for project development, which we refer to as *Asynchronous*.[20]

An example of this approach is provided in Figure 8-6, which contains a stylized depiction of how Netscape developed its Navigator 3.0 Web browser. Notice

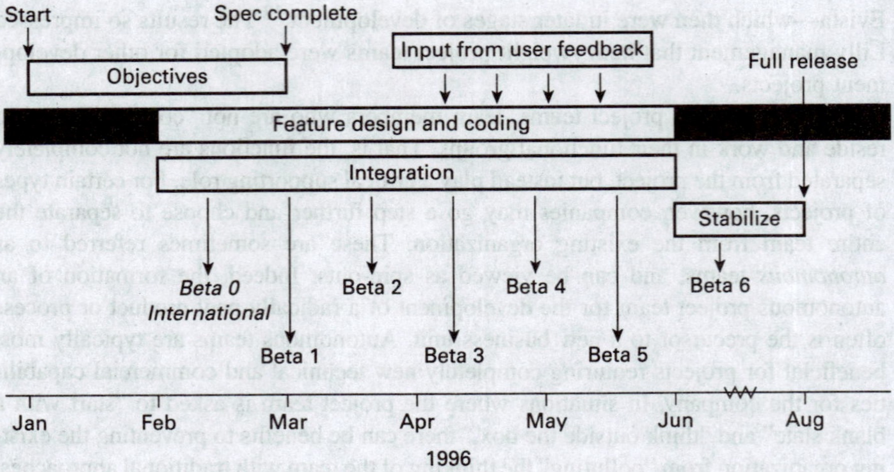

Figure 8-6 Netscape's Asynchronous Development of Navigator 3.0

that Netscape's development of that browser's basic concept and objectives continued well after work had begun on specific features, and even after the new product's first internal test. The design of specific features, and decisions regarding which ones to include in the final product, in turn, continued almost until the product was released, and incorporated repeated feedback from potential customers. This was obtained through a series of Beta tests, where incomplete—but working—versions of the evolving product were distributed to sophisticated users for their testing and reactions. Whereas the Stage-Gate approach is sequential and attempts to integrate separable activities through careful "hand-offs" at each gate, asynchronous development is fluid and ad hoc. Development activities are iterative, and rely heavily on close interaction with users and an extended series of tests that commence very early in the process.

It needs to be reemphasized that this approach, like CPM and Stage-Gates, is not universally applicable. It appears to be particularly appropriate, however, when developing products or processes in dynamic market and technological environments, where their basic concept and architecture are continually evolving, and where it is difficult to predict what the interactions among various features are going to be. Moreover, it is only possible in situations where developing prototypes and making major design changes are not too time-consuming or costly. Software products seem particularly amenable to this approach, but it also has been used for simple consumer and entertainment products. Maintaining control and forward motion in this kind of process requires a small, experienced, and close-knit cross-functional development team, led by a full-time project leader.

In addition, it is critical that the basic architecture of the product or process be structured so that it is flexible enough to accommodate continual change, even if this leads to some degradation in performance. As a manager at Altavista, a Web-based company, explained it: "Architectural design efforts are structured to give priority not to performance, but to independence. We create interfaces [so that] when one module changes the others are … insulated. If we were trying to optimize the size and efficiency [of a design] we would not do this …"[21]

8.5.4 Methodologies for Design, Prototyping, and Testing

At its most basic level, a development project is composed of a series of problem-solving cycles focused on closing the gap between desired and existing product/process capabilities. Each cycle consists of designing a possible solution, building a virtual or physical prototype, and testing that solution. Many people associate prototypes with physical manifestations of a product or process, but it is important to emphasize that a "prototype" is anything designed to represent the product/process in some form. There are many other forms of prototypes, including mathematical formulae, theoretical and empirical models, schematics, spreadsheets, CAD drawings, and computer simulations.

Organizations face many complex choices when executing design-build-test cycles. For instance, as discussed in Chapter 7 sometimes they minimize physical prototypes by undertaking extensive simulations and other design methodologies in an attempt to "get it right the first time." Others, in contrast, engage in extensive building and testing of physical prototypes. Here again, there is no one best way. Different technologies entail different costs for creating and testing physical prototypes and offer different opportunities for learning through simulations of virtual prototypes.[22] As we have seen (section 7.4), Boeing makes extensive use of computer simulation to study aircraft performance and test alternate designs because, given almost 100 years of aircraft design, the underlying parameters are understood well enough to create valid predictive models. In addition, Boeing has a powerful incentive to utilize computer simulation because it is so enormously costly and time consuming to build a physical mock-up of an aircraft. Similarly, automotive companies' use of computer simulation to "crash-test" a vehicle design enables them to build fewer physical prototypes (a significant saving because automobile prototypes can cost $1 million each and take several months to build) and to dramatically accelerate the development cycle. But again, this kind of simulation is only possible because automobile companies have, through many years of experience, developed valid predictive models of how different designs affect crash performance.

There are other environments where physical prototyping may be relatively inexpensive and the ability to learn from simulation low. For instance, in the case of radically new products, allowing customer to interact with a physical prototype is often the only way to really learn about their needs and the problems they experience using it.[23] In other cases, there is simply not enough prior knowledge to create effective simulation models. Despite many recent advances in biomedical know-how, for example, drug discovery continues to require extensive trial-and-error, and it is still virtually impossible to predict how most drugs will perform in humans without thorough testing. As a result, regulatory authorities require that drugs go through extensive clinical trials before they can be sold. A company's strategy for design-prototyping-test needs to be tightly tied to other elements of its development strategy and the constraints and realities of its technological environment.[24]

8.5.5 Senior Management Review and Control

Senior managers influence development projects both directly and indirectly. Different companies adopt different approaches for reviewing projects to ensure that they are meeting expectations and to provide guidance and coaching. They also employ different practices regarding the nature and timing of senior management involvement. As a general principle, getting senior managers involved earlier in projects—at the point of project definition and goal setting—is preferable to late intervention. Often, however, senior managers do not focus their full attention on a project until it gets close to market, at the point costly investments have to be made in tooling, plant and equipment, and product promotion. Unfortunately, by that time, it is generally too late for top management to make any really substantive changes in the actual product or process itself, or at least to do so without causing significant cost or delays.

Senior managers can play various roles during the course of a project and their choice shapes the nature of their interaction with the project team. One role is mentoring. Many senior managers got to be "senior" because they were successful at running projects. Thus, they have experience that may be helpful in coaching less experienced project leaders. A more experienced team may not need as much mentoring, but senior managers' advice and input on critical issues may still be valuable, and project "reviews" take the form of collaborative problem-solving between the project teams and senior managers. Finally, given the cost, risks, and impact of development projects on overall company performance, senior managers play a very legitimate role in their governance and decision making. As projects unfold, they often encounter surprises or problems that require important and difficult decisions. Should the project continue or be terminated? Does it need more resources? Should its scope be altered? Should design A or design B be chosen?

All projects do not require the same level of intensity of senior management review and control, of course. A project entailing low technical and commercial risks that is expected to take only six months to complete requires far less senior management involvement than does a highly expensive, multiyear project aimed at a launching a major new platform in a user environment or employing a technology with which the company has little experience.

8.5.6 A Contingent Model of Project Management

The previous discussion has suggested that for each of the five dimensions of project execution strategy there are a variety of approaches that can be taken, depending on the nature of the project. Figure 8-7 attempts to summarize this discussion by aligning each of the dimensions with the different types of project (derivative, platform, and breakthrough).

8.6 LEARNING FROM PROJECT EXPERIENCE

We conclude this chapter by noting that organizations that are outstanding at project management usually did not start out that way. They developed their project

	Project Type		
Element	Derivative	Platform	Breakthrough
Project definition	Narrow, tightly specified requirements Focus on existing processes or customers/market segments Leverage existing platform	Definition encompasses goals and requirements of an anticipated future stream of derivative projects	Exploratory, high risk nature of project inhibits tightly defined specification Project definition articulates broader concept; definition evolves through early stages
Project Teams	Functional or Lightweight	Heavyweight	Heavyweight or Autonomous
Task Sequence and Structure	Low technical and commercial uncertainty enables tight specification of process Process focuses on ensuring conformance to narrow goals	Development process structured around key milestones Early stages of process focus on systems architecture	High levels of technical and market uncertainty require highly flexible development process Process focuses on experimentation, and adapting the project to new information
Design, Protctype, Test	Leveraging design from an existing platform enables streamlined prototyping	Simulation and prototyping focuses on system integration issues at front-end Testing emphasizes system level integrity	Emphasis on rapid, iterative problem solving through prototyping
Senior management review and control	Front-end senior management to ensure scope and focus Monitor execution and performance of team leader	Frequent senior management reviews throughout Emphasis on ensuring appropriate integration across functions, and approval of major changes	Senior management acts as a project's "board of directors," providing broad oversight and approving major investments Focus on risk management

Figure 8-7 Matching Project Execution Strategies to the Type of Project

execution capabilities over time, and became more successful than others by continually learning from their experience. It is often forgotten that every project—whether aimed at launching a new product, developing a new process technology, implementing a new IT system, and so on—has two outputs. One is the new product, the new process technology, the new IT system, and so on that the project originally was launched to create. This is its most visible outcome, and thus tends to be the major focus of attention. If the product is successful in the market, for instance, the project is generally considered a success. There is, however, a second output from every project, one that generally receives far less attention: learning and skill-building. Projects create opportunities for learning. Sometimes this learning can involve technical issues ("How do we make the product or process more reliable next time?"), but very often the most valuable learning centers on organizational processes ("How can we make the project team *function* better next time?").

Unfortunately, few organizations take full advantage of the opportunities to learn from their project experience. Instead, once a project is completed the people involved scatter, with everyone anxious to get started on something new. This is particularly true if the project experience was less than ideal. In cases where the project was severely late, over budget, or performed poorly in the market, the "stench of failure" becomes all the more reason to move on. Even worse, the fear of being blamed for failure leads those involved to take cover, as nobody is anxious to live through the experience of a project review. Making such reviews even more uncomfortable, many organizations use the unfortunate term *post-mortem* to describe them. Ironically, such so-called "failures" are exactly the projects that provide the most opportunity for learning. As the result of an unwillingness to learn from experience, the same mistakes that plagued one project appear time and again in future ones.

How can companies get around this problem? The topic of organizational learning, of course, has been the subject of endless books, and occupies the concluding two chapters in this one. Although we cannot do full justice to the topic here, we will offer a few basic mechanisms that we've seen organizations use to improve their rate of learning from project experience.

First, post-project reviews need to become a routine part of the development process. Some organizations actually make the project review a formal "sign-off" gate at the end of the project. That is, the project is not considered complete until a formal assessment has been done. Note, however, that adhering to such a process requires senior management commitment to hold teams accountable for conducting such self-assessments. In the case of long development cycles (e.g., three years or more), in fact, it may be useful to conduct *interim* assessments. The problem with such interim reviews, of course, is that in the "heat of battle" the project team might not be particularly focused on the lessons they are learning.

On the other hand, conducting interim assessments has two big advantages. One is that the quality of the information gathered is far better because the project team can tap into its own recent experience. In reviews conducted after a project is completed it can be very difficult, if not impossible, to reassemble critical information about events and problems that arose near its beginning, possibly years earlier. A second advantage of interim reviews is that the lessons learned might be applied during the remainder of the project, and thus offer immediate benefits to the team. For instance, if the team learns early on that it is struggling because of insufficient skill at resolving cross-functional problems, training or facilitation could be implemented immediately to redress this deficiency. Again it needs to be emphasized that ensuring that teams conduct interim reviews requires active senior management encouragement and support.

Second, project assessments, whether conducted afterward or in progress, must be executed with the same degree of rigor as any other development activity. The use of data and problem-solving techniques to identify and address underlying problems is absolutely essential. Techniques such as root-cause analysis, fishbone diagrams, Pareto analyses, and other structured problem-solving approaches (see Chapter 10) can be helpful.

Third, the results from such reviews must be shared broadly with other project teams and throughout the organization. As will be discussed in Chapter 10, companies usually struggle with how best to share learning across projects. Some have invested in sophisticated computer-based "knowledge management" systems. Unfortunately, the barrier to sharing information is rarely technical in nature. Too often, the teams conducting the assessment simply have little incentive to share what they have learned, and future teams have little incentive to learn.

Here again, senior management involvement is critical. If senior managers are involved in reviewing and evaluating project experiences, they can become a powerful conduit for encouraging the transfer of learning. In order for this to become possible, however, senior managers have to make clear what their expectations are regarding the sharing of knowledge and learning. The question they have to pose repeatedly is, "What have we learned from this experience?" If project teams are not asked to share what they have learned, and/or are not rewarded for it, they are unlikely to do so. Similarly, if senior managers tolerate project teams that refuse to consult other teams or ignore the lessons learned from past projects, then it should come as no surprise when teams repeat the mistakes of others, and projects are late, go over budget, and achieve poor results.

Finally, a word about the mechanics of the review process. Some companies have hired consulting firms to conduct their project assessments. Although the use of outside experts to facilitate or to provide input can be useful in some situations, in general the process should not be subcontracted to staff members or to outside consultants. Learning is best achieved first-hand. This means that the project team needs to take ownership of its own learning process. Senior management's role is, first, to push the team to conduct a high-quality assessment. Second, it must avoid doing things that undermine thorough and honest evaluations. The single biggest impediment to getting high-quality assessments and learning from projects is fear. When people are afraid of the ramifications of failure or mistakes, they will be reticent to step forward and be forthright. Through either omission or commission, critical issues, problems, and events will go unreported. In environments lacking a sense of "psychological safety" organizational learning tends to be severely inhibited.[25] It is the responsibility of senior managers to create an environment—through their words, actions, and behaviors—that is conducive to open discourse, information sharing, problem resolution, and learning.

NOTES

1. See, for example, "Office Discipline: Why You Need a Project Management Office," *CIO Magazine* (July 1, 2003), 82–88.

2. This example is drawn from the "Reynolds Construction Company" case contained in Marshall et al. (1975).

3. This description employs the "activities on nodes" approach; see Levy et al. (1963). Another way to diagram projects, with its own set of adherents (see Kelley, 1961), is to have the arrows represent the activities. Each node then represents the completion of all the activities required before the arrows emanating from that node can begin. Both approaches use the same analytical technique and provide the same managerial guidance.

4. See, for example, MacCormack (2001).

5. Ulrich and Eppinger (1995) describe the Stage-Gate approach in greater detail and provide many additional references.

6. See "Philips-Taiwan" (HBS case #9-692-037).

7. Clark and Fujimoto (1991) provides specific information about product development comparisons in the auto industry, while Wheelwright and Clark (1992) provides more general examples and managerial guidance.

8. Wheelwright and Clark (1992).

9. See Wheelwright and Clark (1992).

10. This categorization is drawn from Wheelwright and Clark (1992).

11. See "We've Got Rhythm! Medtronic Corporation's Cardiac Pacemaker Business" (HBS case # 9-698.004).

12. See, for example, Hauser and Clausing (1988).

13. See "The Virginia Class Submarine Program: A Case Study," General Dynamics Electric Boat document, February 2002.

14. This section and the next draw heavily on Clark and Fujimoto (1991) and Wheelwright and Clark (1992).

15. MacCormack (2001).

16. Clark and Fujimoto (1991).

17. Iansiti (1995).

18. See "Eli Lilly: The Evista Project" (HBS case #9-699-016).

19. See "Improving Engineering Design," National Academy of Engineering (1991).

20. See MacCormack et al. (2001). What they call a "Flexible Development Process" we refer to as "Asynchronous."

21. Quoted in MacCormack et al. (2001), p. 145.

22. For more on the issue of experimentation and prototyping strategy, see Thomke (2003).

23. Thomke and von Hippel (2002).

24. Pisano (1996), Thomke (2003).

25. See Edmondson (1999). Similarly, a study of learning behavior in the implementation of a new cardiac surgical technology found that surgical teams with higher levels of psychological safety were more successful than teams with lower levels (Edmondson et al., 2001).

Chapter 9

Evaluating and Justifying Capital Investments

9.1 INTRODUCTION

The success of any organization is measured largely by the effectiveness with which it utilizes the various kinds of assets entrusted to it: facilities, technologies, and people skills. The costs, lifetimes, degrees of liquidity, rates of obsolescence, and riskiness of these assets vary according to their form, scale, and location. Moreover, once in place they often are relatively immobile. Although it is possible to buy buildings and move equipment, it can be much more difficult to move the people, and their support structures, whose capabilities are necessary to make that plant and equipment productive. Finally, the choices made at any point in time affect not only current operations, but also the environment within which future decisions will be made. Hence major changes and additions to operating assets have to be made carefully and patiently.

In the preceding chapters, we focused our attention on specific kinds of facilities/technology decisions and strategies. Underlying those discussions, however, was the notion that a change in a firm's strategy entails more than simply changing one or more individual decisions; instead, the *pattern over time* of those decisions must be altered. To achieve that kind of change in an historical pattern of behavior, an organization usually has to make substantial changes in the decision-making *procedures* it follows when making investments. In this chapter we focus specifically on those procedures, for three reasons:

1. Major proposals to alter or expand operations generally involve substantial amounts of capital investment, so top management usually requires that they be subjected to a number of tests and evaluation techniques that are primarily financial in nature. Learning to use such techniques skillfully and wisely enhances the likelihood that the appropriate decisions will be made.
2. Most companies have a well-developed capital authorization process that must be followed when requesting funds. Developing skill in shepherding proposals through the corporate labyrinth is essential if an operations

organization is to assemble, over time, the resources it needs to achieve competitively superior performance.

3. Investment proposals provide excellent opportunities for operations managers to inform top managers about their operations organization's strengths, opportunities, and strategic direction.

Before outlining this chapter, let us briefly describe the typical scenario that companies follow when they evaluate major facilities projects. As summarized in Table 9-1, it is narrow in scope, limits attention to established alternatives, deals only with a single business or facility and a specific problem(s), and is dominated by purely financial considerations.

Given the complexity and importance of decisions regarding an operation's structure and infrastructure, it is not surprising that most firms tend to approach them *individually* and *sequentially*—as a series of discrete projects that can be analyzed, evaluated, and implemented one by one as needs and opportunities arise. Such a project-by-project approach simplifies the analysis and reduces the likelihood that important details will be overlooked. Over time, however, this kind of process is likely to deflect corporate attention away from longer-term competitive issues, and the decisions regarding different kinds of investments might not fit together well. As a result, truly innovative proposals are only generated and considered in response to unusual pressure—at which point it is often almost impossible to do much more than simply "manage the damage." Because of its focus on specific problems and financial considerations, moreover, this kind of process can lead to inadequate investment in building an operations organization's strategic capabilities over time (see Chapter 2).

Table 9-1 Typical Scenario for a Major Investment Project

1. The project is formulated as a "capital investment proposal" that is targeted toward meeting the needs of a specific facility, product line, and/or business/market.
2. To simplify its evaluation, the project is treated as if it would not have any impact on other facilities or businesses.
3. The proposal generally is triggered either by growth in demand or by unsatisfactory performance in an existing business or facility (the assumption being that this unsatisfactory performance is due to structural inadequacies).
4. A team of managers and specialists is given responsibility for defining and evaluating various options for overcoming these deficiencies, and is expected to recommend one of these alternatives and guide it through the approval process.
5. While the assessments and preferences of key managers are given consideration, the bulk of the project team's efforts is spent performing financial analyses of the preferred alternative(s) to ensure that it meets required investment hurdles and can withstand the scrutiny of the corporate financial staff and top management.
6. The team's recommendation adheres to the pattern of previous decisions (unless key managers have left), and deals largely with the specific near-term problem(s).

This chapter suggests ways to avoid these types of problems, and to encourage the formulation and execution of coherent investment strategies. In Section 9.2, we address issues related to staffing and managing the project team entrusted with the generation and evaluation of an investment proposal. Section 9.3 describes the mechanics of some of the more common approaches used in evaluating the financial impact of such proposals. Finally, Section 9.4 briefly describes the approach one company followed in attempting to make its investment decisions consistent with its operations strategy.

9.2 MANAGING THE INVESTMENT PLANNING PROCESS

Managing the investment planning process involves three basic activities. The first is *organizational*—determining who will participate in formulating and evaluating specific plans and project proposals. This involves deciding what level(s) in the organization should be involved in such planning, as well as the number, qualifications, and skills of the people assigned to the project team. The second has to do with *problem definition*—the assumptions to be made, the objectives to be satisfied, and the alternatives to be explored. This entails defining the scope of the project, the motivation for it, and the perspective to be taken by the project team. The third concerns the tools to be used and the *procedures to be followed* in evaluating alternatives and making a persuasive case to top management for the one recommended.

Before looking at the sequence of steps that investment projects typically follow, it is useful to consider the usual motivations that impel companies to initiate such activities. Increasing demand is the most common motive; few companies are willing to forgo opportunities to grow with their markets, and therefore (as described in Chapter 3) a projected increase in demand almost invariably triggers a capacity review and the development of proposals for meeting any projected shortfall. Other motivations for making facilities and technology investments, however, can be equally, if not more, important. A long-term decline in demand, for example, also may trigger a capacity review. This review usually is not conducted under the same degree of organizational pressure as is the case with increases in demand, as the company may be able to shift products from more crowded facilities to underutilized ones. But when its facilities are highly specialized, or inappropriate for other reasons, a company might be forced to consider closing one of them. The question is, "Which one?" Generally, this decision cannot be made on a decentralized basis or following a democratic process.

Another trigger is the opportunity to add, replace, or upgrade a facility, piece of equipment, or system that incorporates a new or enhanced technology. If the organization's managers have been kept abreast of their operation's competitive needs and the way technologies are evolving, such upgrades can be planned and implemented smoothly and systematically. If they lack this perspective, however, when caught by surprise they might react precipitously by closing down one facility or system and starting up an entirely new one.

Investment projects also may be triggered by events in the firm's competitive or regulatory environment. Increasingly tough environmental controls, for example, have forced thousands of process investments. Unfortunately, these kind of requirements often are viewed only in negative terms, rather than being seen as opportunities that, when combined with other changes, might together actually enhance an operations' competitiveness.[1]

An even more compelling motivation—but, unfortunately, one observed only infrequently in practice—is the opportunity to make a significant improvement in the firm's competitive position through a *linked sequence* of investments. An example of this more proactive approach is provided in Section 9.4.

There are eight steps commonly followed when formulating, selecting, and monitoring investment proposals. For each step, we will discuss its basic purpose, the issues raised in carrying it out, and the approaches that are typically adopted:

1. Evaluate the existing operation's structure and infrastructure.
2. Forecast that operation's capacity and competitive needs.
3. Define alternatives for meeting those likely needs.
4. Perform financial analyses of each alternative.
5. Assess key qualitative issues for each alternative.
6. Select and defend the alternative to be pursued.
7. Implement the chosen alternative.
8. Audit actual results.

9.2.1 Evaluate Existing Operations

The major objective of this step is to define and apply appropriate measures of the effectiveness of a specific operating unit or system, and its impact on other parts of the business. The companies that stumble over this step typically do so because they define the problem too narrowly. As noted in Chapter 3 (Section 3.2), for example, there are a number of different ways to measure capacity, and each may suggest a different expansion proposal. Unfortunately, Step 1 is passed over rather quickly in most firms, and only one or two fairly narrow measures of an operation unit/system's effectiveness are addressed. Although this might facilitate the movement of a proposal through subsequent steps, it often severely limits the range of the alternatives considered in Step 3, and locks the organization into a limited set of objectives for the investment. Thus, it might lead to less creative solutions to particular situations.

9.2.2 Forecast Capacity and Competitive Requirements

Step 2 requires that forecasts be developed of the business's future requirements by technology, product/market, and geographic area. In making these forecasts, one should include external (competitive) as well as internal factors, and use different approaches so as to cross-check the estimates that result.[2] In addition, it is useful to develop forecasts of the *cost structure* that is likely to be required for the firm to be competitive at some future point in time.

Before this can be done, however, there must be agreement on the project's time horizon. Firms typically employ horizons that reflect the time required to both implement the project and achieve a desired level of sales or profitability, or they use "industry norms" as their guideline. It is important to avoid being constrained by past practice, however, and to consider alternative (usually longer!) horizons. Managers should be asked to consider the *sequence* of expansions that might follow the initial one—or, at a minimum, "the plant after next."[3]

Managers also need to relate their long-term, strategic planning to shorter-term operating plans and systems. Figure 9-1 suggests how this might be done in the context of capacity planning, where four different time frames are likely to interact: long-range planning (more than one year), annual planning, short-term scheduling (up to three months), and, finally, dispatching (generally less than one month). Each type of planning in Figure 9-1 is linked to those having longer- and shorter-term duration. For example, the annual capacity plan constitutes one portion of the long-range capacity plan, but it also establishes the framework within which schedules are developed and modified as the firm proceeds through the year.

The level of the managers involved in planning also depends on the investment time horizon, as indicated at the left in Figure 9-1. Although top management is likely to be directly concerned with long range planning, operating level managers typically handle work order scheduling and dispatching. Annual capacity planning (often referred to as aggregate planning or master scheduling) usually involves senior operations or facilities managers and their functional counterparts in marketing, engineering, and product development.

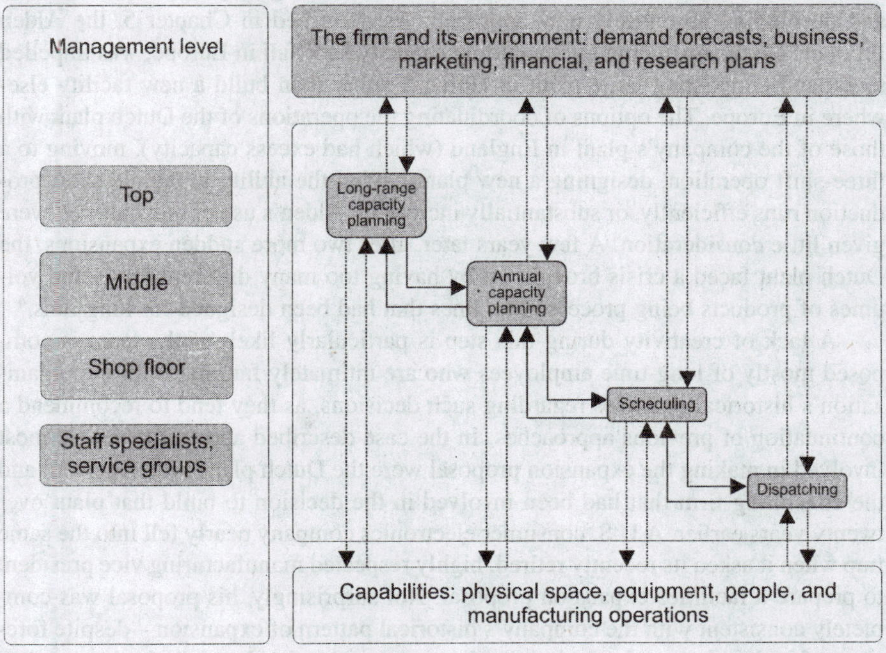

Figure 9-1 Capacity Planning Time Horizons in Operations

Dividing the time horizon into manageable subsegments makes it easier to identify all the major factors that interact to affect an operation's effectiveness. Most long-term planning procedures, unfortunately, deal only with facilities and equipment decisions, implying that they are the most critical decisions. Human resource and logistics issues are at least as important in our view, as they provide many of the crucial linkages between strategy and tactics.

9.2.3 Define Alternatives for Meeting Requirements

In spite of the obvious need to consider a variety of alternative ways for meeting projected requirements, many firms react to projected shortfalls by thinking simply in terms of expanding an existing operation: more floor space, another shift, or a new machine. Planning systems that respond to such shortfalls by occasionally triggering a comprehensive review of the available alternatives, however, are much more likely to generate proposals that have the potential to make a significant improvement in a company's competitive position.

One reason managers tend to consider only obvious options is that they wait too long before deciding to act. This places the team responsible for proposing a solution under severe time pressure. Unless it can come up with a quick alternative, it is likely to restrict its attention to approaches that have been followed in the past, or those known to be favored by key managers. This tendency is reinforced by the realization that doing "more of the same" almost always appears to require less investment and be faster to implement than would conducting a comprehensive review and developing an entirely new approach. As described in Chapter 5, the Alden Products Company, facing an impending capacity shortfall in Europe, was impelled to expand an existing large plant in Holland rather than build a new facility elsewhere in Europe. The options of coordinating the operations of the Dutch plant with those of the company's plant in England (which had excess capacity), moving to a three-shift operation, designing a new plant having the ability to handle short production runs efficiently, or substantially increasing Alden's use of outsourcing, were given little consideration. A few years later, after two more sudden expansions, the Dutch plant faced a crisis brought on by having too many different kinds and volumes of products being processed on lines that had been designed for long runs.[4]

A lack of creativity during this step is particularly likely if the team is composed mostly of long-time employees who are intimately familiar with the organization's historical practices regarding such decisions, as they tend to recommend a continuation of previous approaches. In the case described above, the people most involved in making the expansion proposal were the Dutch plant's management and the consulting firm that had been involved in the decision to build that plant over twenty years earlier. A U.S. consumer electronics company nearly fell into the same trap when it asked its recently retired, highly respected manufacturing vice president to prepare a facilities expansion proposal. Not surprisingly, his proposal was completely consistent with the company's historical pattern of expansion—despite forecasts of major changes in the industry's market and technology. At the last minute, the company brought in an outside consultant in order to develop the "new approach" that was subsequently adopted.

In addition to encouraging the consideration of new alternatives, adopting a longer time horizon also makes it possible to consider changing the way a company's facility *network* is organized, focused, and coordinated. Creative approaches can be encouraged by asking people to think in terms of the network and systems they would *like to have* at some comfortably distant point in the future, and how each should be focused. This makes it possible to evaluate alternative expansion proposals in the context of the "ideal" structure and infrastructure. As discussed in Chapter 5, specifying in advance a facility's maximum size and degree of specialization makes it easier to identify the number of facilities that are eventually likely to be needed to supply one's market, and encourages thinking about the sequence in which they might be added.

9.2.4 Perform Financial Analyses of Each Alternative

Once the alternatives have been clearly defined, their financial attractiveness must be assessed. Section 9.3 outlines several techniques that can be used in conducting this evaluation, but it is important to emphasize that each alternative considered should be evaluated using a common set of assumptions. Using a computer spreadsheet program aids in estimating the sensitivity of important financial summary measures to changes in key assumptions.

Before evaluating different options, one must choose a basis for comparing them. Any project can be made to look attractive if it is compared against something sufficiently unattractive. Since the whole purpose of a financial evaluation is to determine the relative attractiveness of various investments, the appropriate place to begin is to determine the financial value of making the *most effective* use of existing resources; this becomes the *base case*. Notice that this base case may involve substantial changes in operations; *it does not mean doing nothing*. (Most projects, particularly those that support expansion and growth, look excellent when compared with doing nothing!) Defining the base case properly allows one to disentangle the cost savings associated with *expanding* operations from those resulting from simply *improving* them. We have seen many cases where the apparent savings associated with investing in a new, highly efficient facility disappear after taking into account the possibility of improving existing facilities.[5] Once an appropriate base case has been established, each option can be compared in terms of the cash flows and other benefits/drawbacks that result from changes from that base.

9.2.5 Assess Key Qualitative Issues for Each Alternative

In this step, the *qualitative* issues relevant to each alternative are assessed. These include factors that cannot be quantified because the data required to do so are unavailable, as well as those for which no good quantitative measures exist—such as short-term versus long-term considerations, the ease of implementation and operation, and the fit with the firm's competitive environment and business strategy.

One company, for example, experienced continuing, unexpected problems as a result of a previous, poorly conceived facilities plan, so it incorporated several new qualitative concerns when developing its next plan a few years later. Various managers were asked to assess the possible outcomes for several different courses of action, and those assessments were combined to develop consensus measures of their financial impact. Considerations included the market share loss that might be expected to result from each option due to start-up and quality/reliability problems, the impact of possible labor disruptions, and the possible *diseconomies* of increasing the size of existing facilities (as discussed in Section 3.2).

9.2.6 Select and Defend the Alternative to Be Pursued

Deciding which of the alternative proposals to recommend is not the end of the job; one must then guide the chosen proposal through the capital approval process. Since the project team assigned to this task plays an important role in ensuring that all important considerations have been taken into account and analyzed objectively, careful thought should go into how it is composed. In one company the project team was composed entirely of engineering and production managers, and conspicuously lacked representatives from human resources/labor relations, marketing, or international operations—even though the proposal involved supplying overseas divisions as well as domestic ones. The alternative recommended by this project team later was described as "what one might expect when engineers talk to engineers." During its implementation, several major problems arose that could be attributed directly to perspectives that were missing in the original project team. Eventually these problems torpedoed the project.

The organizational level and composition of the project team also influences the political process through which the project's approval is achieved and the degree to which various constituencies within the firm support its implementation. A project team that includes a wide range of perspectives and develops a rich set of alternatives when addressing a given situation is less likely to adopt a standard approach that overlooks important factors. Some companies even assign two different teams to the same project, so as to introduce an element of competition into the development of innovative alternatives, and to provide an incentive to thoroughly investigate common ones. A similar approach sometimes is used during new product development, as when Apple developed its original Macintosh computer.

Finally, a project initiated at a lower level in the organization must be "sold" to top management. Understanding the requirements (and biases) of the corporate approval process can help ensure that the project team's recommendation surmounts the procedural hurdles at higher organizational levels.

9.2.7 Implement the Chosen Alternative

Once an alternative has been approved, two other important issues must be addressed. The first has to do with the performance measures to be used in monitoring the project after its implementation. If a major expansion or modification of an existing facility is involved, it probably will be necessary to redefine the facility's charter (as discussed in Chapter 5) before developing such measures. Not only should time- and budget-related milestones be established, but also one should check to make sure that the project is fostering the basic capabilities, and creating the types of competitive advantage, that it was expected to provide.

The second issue involves identifying the actions and resources that will have the greatest impact on the overall success of the project. The firm must make certain that these resources are provided and applied in a timely and effective manner. In the case of one oilfield equipment manufacturer, for example, this required identifying the major tasks required to support a sequence of capacity/facilities decisions over a five-year period, estimating the skills that would be required at each step along the way, and developing a plan for obtaining those skills and capabilities, either internally or from outside sources.

9.2.8 Audit Actual Results

Few organizations audit the results of approved projects in any systematic fashion, although such audits can serve a very useful purpose. As with development projects (discussed in Chapter 8), audits provide feedback for improving the procedures the firm uses when developing future proposals. The results of any major facilities, technology, or systems investment should be reviewed both against its implementation plan and against how effective it has been in dealing with the problems that triggered it. In addition, some firms' reviews include a requirement that a second approval be obtained for any capital that was *not* spent during the year for which it was authorized. This helps ensure that expenditures are not being postponed just in the interest of boosting some group's short-term profits, and that the rationale that originally justified the expenditure is still valid.

It is critical to establish in advance the measures to be used in a project's evaluation, because (as we shall see in Section 9.3.3) some of the traditional measures that companies use to report financial results are likely to be different from those that were used to justify the project, *even though it is delivering exactly the results predicted.* As a result, the project might appear to be more or less successful than anticipated. Companies that have carried out this kind of audit generally find that it is most useful when, in addition to the usual financial review, it also checks whether the project is providing the intended support for their competitive strategy. Not only do such reviews ensure that capital has been spent on approved uses, they also may suggest improvements in the investment evaluation process.

9.3 FINANCIAL ANALYSIS OF PROPOSED INVESTMENTS

Since most of a company's capital is invested in its operations organization, senior managers see a lot of proposals for major new investments in operations and tend to scrutinize them very carefully. Whereas people rightly are regarded as its heart and mind, and equipment its nerves and muscles, cash is its lifeblood. Unless the company is able to cover its expenses, replenish its resources, and pay back those who have provided it with capital, it cannot long survive. As a result, despite protests about "bean counters" with "green eye shade" mentalities who don't properly appreciate beautiful technology, inviting markets, and elegant systems, operations managers seldom can avoid having the financial implications of their investment proposals subjected to a detailed review by their company's financial staff.

Therefore, a project team must prepare a thorough and persuasive financial justification, even if the numbers by themselves are not what finally "sells" the project to corporate management. Often, in fact, the team is required to follow a rather rigid format that seeks to ensure the proposed investment will meet or surpass the firm's stated financial objectives. This section provides an overall framework for thinking about different ways for evaluating proposed investments, and describes some of the specific techniques that are commonly used.

Although we have emphasized the necessity of maintaining a long-term perspective when developing and evaluating major investments in operations, we recognize that it often is difficult to maintain such a perspective in the face of short-term needs and opportunities, career aspirations, and organizational politics. Therefore, toughness, persuasiveness, and commitment are probably more important to an operations manager's success than detailed knowledge of the latest financial technique. However, these techniques must be thoroughly understood in order to defend one's proposals before those who understand only numbers. If a proposed investment does not meet a company's stated financial goals, the amount of persuasion required to get it approved, in preference to other proposals that apparently do, rises by an order of magnitude.

9.3.1 A Framework for Assessing the Financial Attractiveness of Proposed Investments

Before examining specific financial analysis techniques, it is useful to sketch out a simple framework for organizing them. Most business organizations—as with most people—have four major concerns in mind when they contemplate a proposed major investment:

1. *Security*—How safe is my money? How soon will I be able to get it back?
2. *Recompense*—How much more will I get back than I invested?
3. *Predictability*—How sure can I be about the anticipated returns from this investment?
4. *Option Value*—What future opportunities will this investment open up to me?

Since the security and predictability criteria both embody concerns about an investment's "riskiness," they sometimes are lumped together into a single criterion. However, it is useful to separate them since they describe two different kinds of risk. The predictability of an investment's return generally refers to its *internal* uncertainty (such as the amount of the initial investment, its returns, their timing, and the project's lifetime). Security is more concerned with uncertainties *external* to the investment that might, for example, cause one to want to discontinue the project and invest in something else if unanticipated problems or opportunities present themselves. Thus it is related more to the desire for liquidity, with "wanting your money back" in your own hands, than with knowing exactly what the investment's returns will be. The investment's option value, on the other hand, attempts to capture the value of the opportunities (foreseen or not when the investment was considered) to invest in other profitable activities that could present themselves in the future *only* if the investment is made. It is related to both of the other types of risk, but its evaluation requires a very different kind of analysis, as we will see in Section 9.3.6.

Believing that stockholders and lenders prefer smooth earnings growth over time, senior financial managers often express concern about a fifth aspect of a proposed capital investment: the "smoothness" of its annual cash flows. A major part of their job is ensuring that the firm has sufficient funds on hand each year to meet its capital charges (both debt payments and stockholder dividends), to finance the investments that it is likely to want to make, and to meet unexpected financial demands. Large investments whose returns are highly variable from year to year (even if relatively predictable) can complicate this task considerably.

9.3.2 Measures of Security

The most commonly used measure of the security of a proposed investment is its *payback,* defined as the length of time until one gets one's money back. This is determined simply by adding up the project's anticipated cash flows, positive or negative, and determining the month or year when that cumulative cash flow finally becomes positive for good. We say "for good," because certain types of projects might require both an initial investment and a follow-up investment at some later date. In such situations, the cumulative cash flow will start off negative, grow to be positive over time (the "initial payback"), then go negative again, and finally turn positive again for the remainder of the project's lifetime. A simple way to estimate this payback period is to divide the initial investment by its *average* annual cash flow over the project's lifetime:

$$\text{Est. Payback} = \frac{\text{initial investment}}{\text{avg. after tax cash flow}} \tag{9-1}$$

where the after-tax cash flow is equal to the project's profit before depreciation and income tax, less the tax paid (or, equivalently, its profit after tax plus depreciation). This estimate will vary from the true payback to the extent that the project's average cash flow is different than the actual flows in its early years (which are the only ones that determine the true payback). In Section 9.3.4, we will describe another approach to calculating payback, which takes into account the time value of money.

Despite its imperfections, an estimate of payback is one of the most widely used measures of an investment's attractiveness. Several studies of the capital investment process used by a number of companies—including some of the most sophisticated ones—suggest that over two-thirds of them take an estimate of payback into consideration.[6] Many companies, in fact, require that a proposed investment meet a given payback criterion before they even look at any other measures of its attractiveness. This hurdle may be rather arbitrary, reflecting the firm's capital constraints, the degree of risk to which it is willing to expose itself, and the type of investment being considered. The industry context is also a factor, as it provides information about the likely risks and rates of change in technologies and markets.

In particular, small companies that lack adequate financing and have to scramble periodically to meet financial obligations often require that each investment be recouped before the next financial emergency is likely to arise.

Many high-tech companies, for example, require paybacks of less than two years on new investments. This reflects both the rapidity of product and process obsolescence in such industries and the shortage of capital—due to their high growth rates and typically heavy reliance on internal financing. The dependence on internally generated funds, in turn, often stems from the reluctance of outsiders to lend money to firms that are exposed to such risks, and from the unwillingness of the firms themselves to take on the burden of large interest charges and capital repayment schedules, given their volatile earnings prospects.

A Numerical Example

To facilitate our exposition we will use a simple numerical example: a hypothetical proposal to completely renovate and modernize a facility devoted to a product line that is likely to be rendered obsolete by a new and potentially superior technology in a few years. The existing facility is increasingly unreliable and costly, and its continued use cannot be justified economically. The decision, therefore, is either to make the investment or exit that business. Once out, it will be almost impossible to reenter the business in the future because of the loss of critical people, organizational capabilities, market relationships, and damage to the firm's reputation as "a reliable supplier"; in that sense the investment decision is irreversible. The costs and returns of this project are summarized as follows:

1. The investment required consists of \$8.0 million in depreciable purchased equipment, plus \$2.0 million in installation and start-up costs that are to be expensed as incurred. Starting in year 6, \$500,000 will have to be spent each year in maintaining, refurbishing, and updating this equipment.
2. Depreciation is calculated on a straight-line basis over the equipment's expected eight-year lifetime.
3. Operating Margins are projected to increase gradually as projected sales and production levels rise to the facility's capacity limit in year 4.
4. Income taxes are calculated assuming a 40 percent combined (federal plus state) tax rate.
5. Cash flow is equal to the actual cash transactions during the year: operating margin less equipment-related costs less income taxes. Therefore, in year 1, the plant's operating profit before taxes is equal to its Operating Margin *less* equipment installation costs *less* depreciation = \$2.0 – 2.0 – 1.0 million, implying a loss of \$1.0 million. This will reduce the taxes paid by the corporation by \$400,000 (assuming the firm's other businesses are profitable). Therefore the net cash flow after tax is \$2.0 – 2.0 + 0.40 million = \$400,000.
6. The end of the equipment's useful life occurs at the end of year 8; it is assumed not to have any salvage value, since the product it produces is likely to become obsolete.

Table 9-2 Proposal to Renovate a Facility (All Numbers in $000)

End of Year	Equip. related costs	Depreciation	Operating margin	Taxes on op. prof.	Profit after tax	After tax cash flow	Cumul. cash flow
0	8,000						−8,000
1	2,000	1,000	2,000	−400	−600	400	−7,600.0
2	0	1,000	2,400	560	840	1,840	−5,760.0
3	0	1,000	2,800	720	1,080	2,080	−3,680.0
4	0	1,000	3,000	800	1,200	2,200	−1,480.0
5	0	1,000	3,000	800	1,200	2,200	720.0
6	500	1,000	3,000	600	900	1,900	2,620.0
7	500	1,000	3,000	600	900	1,900	4,520.0
8	500	1,000	3,000	600	900	1,900	6,420.0
Totals	11,500	8,000	22,200	4,280	6,420	14,420	
Averages	1,437.5	1,000	2,775.0	535	802.5	1,802.5	

In this example, the payback for the $8.0 million investment occurs about two-thirds of the way through year 4, at the point the cumulative cash flow, which began the year at a negative $1,480,000, passes through 0 on its way to a positive $720,000 at the end of the year: 1,480/(1,480 + 720) = 0.67. The estimated payback, calculated using equation (9-1) and the *average* after tax cash flow of $1,802,500, is 8,000/1,802.5 = 4.44 years.

9.3.3 Measures of Recompense

Assuming that the project's payback is acceptable, most firms next want to measure its expected earnings generating ability: How much more cash will the project return than was invested in it? Several measures of recompense are used in practice; three are described below:

$$\frac{\text{average annual profit after tax}}{\text{average beginning-of-year investment book value}} \qquad (9\text{-}2A)$$

$$\frac{\text{average annual net cash flow}}{\text{initial investment}} \qquad (9\text{-}2B)$$

$$\text{average annual cash inflow} - \text{cost of the capital invested} \qquad (9\text{-}3)$$

The approach summarized in equation (9-2A) attempts to duplicate the *book return on investment* (*ROI*), which is a common accounting measure of a company's overall profitability. Approach (9-2B) is an "improvement" used by some companies to reflect the actual cash flow, including depreciation, arising from the investment. Since using book value in the denominator would, in effect, double count the impact of depreciation, the entire initial investment is used. Approach (9-3) is usually referred to as the "residual income" of the investment, as it represents the amount of cash generated by the project in excess of the full cost of borrowing the funds for it, and/or redirecting those funds from other projects. Various other names have been attached to it, such as "residual value added" and "Economic Value Added", and different methods of calculating a project's cash flows have been proposed, but the basic concept is the same.[7]

It would be convenient if payback and return on investment (based on the average net cash flow) were complimentary concepts—the first measuring the *quickness* of return ("security") and the second the *total* return ("recompense"). If true, the use of both measures would provide a balanced approach to evaluating an investment. Unfortunately, the great majority of the investments one sees in practice, like our numerical example, involve an initial cash outflow followed by a sequence of inflows. In this situation the return on investment as calculated by (9-2B) is essentially the *reciprocal* of the estimated payback period calculated by (9-1). In other words, these two calculations are just variants of the same calculation. In our example, the estimated P/B is 8,000/1,802.5 = 4.44 years (as calculated earlier), while the average ROI is 1,802.5/8,000 = 22.5 percent = 1/4.44.

Approaches (9-2A) and (9-2B) both are easy to calculate and, for lifetimes in the range of 5–15 years, they usually lead to similar values. In our example, 802.5/4,000 = 20.1 percent, and 1,802.5/8,000 = 22.5 percent. They can diverge widely, however, depending on the investment's lifetime, the growth rate of earnings, the depreciation method used, etc. We return to this issue in section 9.3.4. Not only can they result in conflicting estimates, but also both approaches are based on average cash flows and do not take into account the *timing* of those cash flows.

Finally, assuming the company's average cost of capital (or, alternatively, what it could earn on other investments) is 15 percent, the residual income of the project (equation 9-3) is:

$$\text{residual income} = \text{avg. net cash flow} - 15\text{ percent} \times (\text{initial investment})$$
$$= \$1{,}802{,}500 - 0.15 \times \$8{,}000{,}000 = \$602{,}500$$

9.3.4 Recompense—The Accumulated Cash Balance

All the measures described up to now suggest that the investment depicted in Table 9-2 will yield a return on investment in excess of the firm's 15 percent opportunity rate. But these calculations were based on *averages* over the lifetime of the investment, and did not take into account the "time value of money" for the firm considering the investment. That is to say, most managers would prefer to receive the after tax cash flow of $2.2 million in year 1 and the $400,000 in year 4 in that example, rather than the other way around—even though either sequence leads to the same estimated payback, accounting rate of return, and residual income. What would be the value of such a speedup in receipts? That depends essentially on what the firm could do with that extra money between year 1 and year 4.

If, for example, our hypothetical firm is able to invest any spare funds in other investments that have roughly the same degree of risk and promise a 15 percent rate of return on investment, then a dollar received now is equivalent to $1.15 received a year from now, to $1.3225 = (1.15 × 1.15) received two years from now, and so on. These equivalences assume that every unused dollar can be invested in those "other investments," and that nothing else would cause the company to prefer receiving the cash in a given year. Taking the time value of money into account provides another way to determine our project's payback: calculate the length of time until its inflows, in effect, "pay down the loan" represented by the initial investment at a bank that is charging interest at a rate of 15 percent per year.[8] This calculation for our hypothetical project is detailed in Table 9-3. It shows, somewhat surprisingly, that instead of the 4.44 year payback period calculated in Section 9.3.2, taking into account the time value of money suggests that the project *never* reaches payback during its eight-year life; at the end of year 8 it still "owes the bank" $1,177,000.

9.3.5 Recompense—The Net Present Value

Another way to account for the time value of money is to reverse the process described above: rather than calculate the *future* value of a cash flow received today, calculate the *current* value of each future cash flow. For example, $1.00 received two years from now is equivalent to $0.7561 (= 1/1.3225) received today if it can be invested at the same 15 percent rate of return. This allows us to "discount" the cash flows (whether positive or negative) that the proposed investment is expected to generate at various times in the future back to their equivalent value today (that is, their *present* value). If one then subtracts the cost of the proposed investment (or its present value, if that investment takes place over several years) from the sum of the present values of the ongoing cash inflows, one obtains the *net* present value (NPV) of the investment. This provides another measure for comparing alternative investment proposals. This calculation for our hypothetical company is contained in Table 9-4, and shows that the projected investment in modernizing its facility has a *negative* present value of ($384,800).

The same result can be obtained from the Accumulated Cash Balance, whose value (as shown in Table 9-3) at the end of year 8 is –$1,177. Multiplying this figure by the discount rate for the end of year 8 (0.3269 in Table 9-4), so as to translate that future value into its value at the beginning of year 1, gives $–384.8.

In other words, even though our earlier estimates of the project's accounting rate of return and residual income (which both were based on average cash flows over its entire life rather than the actual timing of those cash flows) both suggested that it would provide a rate of return greater than 15 percent, the project actually will not be as profitable to the firm as would investing the same amount of money in other projects that would provide a 15 percent rate of return. This is why our calculation of the project's time-adjusted payback period in Table 9-3 indicated that payback would not take place during the project's lifetime.

A few experiments quickly show that the resulting NPV is fairly sensitive to the choice of the desired rate of return. Unfortunately, choosing the rate at which to discount future cash flows is not an easy one, and there is a continuing fierce debate as to how it should be done. The crux of the difficulty is the implied assumption that

Table 9-3 Proposal to Renovate a Facility (All Numbers in $000)

Cost of Capital/Req'd Rate of Return = 15%

End of year	Equip. related costs	Depreciation	Operating margin	Taxes on oper. prof.	Profit after tax	After tax cash flow	Implied int. on acct.	Value of account before CF	Value of account after CF
0	8,000							–8,000.0	–8,000.0
1	2,000	1,000	2,000	–400	–600	400	–1,200.0	–9,200.0	–8,800.0
2	0	1,000	2,400	560	840	1,840	–1,320.0	–10,120.0	–8,280.0
3	0	1,000	2,800	720	1,080	2,080	–1,242.0	–9,522.0	–7,442.0
4	0	1,000	3,000	800	1,200	2,200	–1,116.3	–8,558.3	–6,358.3
5	0	1,000	3,000	800	1,200	2,200	–953.7	–7,312.0	–5,112.0
6	500	1,000	3,000	600	900	1,900	–766.8	–5,878.9	–3,978.9
7	500	1,000	3,000	600	900	1,900	–596.8	–4,575.7	–2,675.7
8	500	1,000	3,000	600	900	1,900	–401.4	–3,077.0	–1,177.0
Totals	11,500	8,000	22,200	4,280	6,420	14,420			
Averages	1,437.5	1,000	2,775	535	802.5	1,802.5			

Table 9-4 Proposal to Renovate a Facility (All Numbers in $000)

Cost of Capital/Req'd Rate of Return = 15%

End of year	Equip. related costs	Depreciation	Operating margin	Taxes on oper. prof.	Profit after tax	After tax cash flow	Discount factor	Present value	Cumul. P.V.
0	8,000						1.0000	–8,000.0	–8,000.0
1	2,000	1,000	2,000	–400	–600	400	0.8696	347.8	–7,652.2
2	0	1,000	2,400	560	840	1,840	0.7561	1,391.3	–6,260.9
3	0	1,000	2,800	720	1,080	2,080	0.6575	1,367.6	–4,893.2
4	0	1,000	3,000	800	1,200	2,200	0.5718	1,257.9	–3,635.4
5	0	1,000	3,000	800	1,200	2,200	0.4972	1,093.8	–2,541.6
6	500	1,000	3,000	600	900	1,900	0.4323	821.4	–1,720.2
7	500	1,000	3,000	600	900	1,900	0.3759	714.3	–1,005.9
8	500	1,000	3,000	600	900	1,900	0.3269	621.1	–384.8
Totals	11,500	8,000	22,200	4,280	6,420	14,420			–384.8
Averages	1,437.5	1,000	2,775.0	535	802.5	1,802.5			

the rate of return the firm can expect to receive from its investments is the same as the cost of the capital required to finance these investments. If one is willing, in effect, to assume that all investments should be expected to generate the *same* rate of return, the company's *weighted average cost of capital* is recommended. This is obtained by estimating, separately, the cost of its debt capital and the cost of its equity capital, and then calculating the weighted average based on the proportions of each in its total assets. However, if one prefers to assume that different kinds of investment should be expected to generate different rates of return, then each investment should be broken up into its components and the discount rate for each component should be applied in calculating its present value (see Section 9.3.7).

9.3.6 Recompense—The Internal Rate of Return

Because the NPV is measured in monetary units (e.g., dollars), it does not provide a good measure of the *efficiency* of invested capital, that is, how "profitable" the investment is *per dollar* invested. This makes it difficult to compare projects requiring different amounts of initial investment. One often-used measure of efficiency is the project's "profitability index:" the ratio of its NPV to the initial investment, which attempts to translate the NPV into a per-dollar basis. In our example, since the NPV is negative (assuming that the required rate of return is 15 percent), the profitability index is –0.048 (= –384.8/8,000).

Another common measure of efficiency is the project's "internal rate of return" (IRR), sometimes called its *internal yield.* It is defined as the interest rate that causes the project's net present value to equal zero, and is equivalent to the *yield to maturity* of a bond. For our hypothetical project the IRR is about 13.7 percent, as shown in Table 9-5.

Although net present value and internal rate of return both take the time value of money into account when comparing different investments (as, in a sense, does the project's residual income),[10] neither of them reliably indicates which subset from among a group of proposed projects will yield the highest total present value to the firm if there is a constraint on the investment funds available. Nor are the two measures internally consistent; it is entirely possible that one proposed investment has a higher NPV (and a higher present value per dollar invested) than another, for a given discount rate, but has a lower internal rate of return.

Another problem that arises when trying to compare a series of investments is that (as mentioned earlier) a project's accounting return on assets described earlier, whether calculated using equation 9-2A or 9-2B, can be quite different from its internal rate of return. This disparity is distressing because a project's accounting ROA (which is analogous to the firm's average return on assets) often is calculated periodically as part of the firm's reporting and control processes. Hence a project's "observed" ROA (or the ROA of a group of assets all of which were approved on the basis of a NPV or IRR criterion) may bear little resemblance to the measures calculated when deciding to adopt that project. That is, the project's promised IRR will be one number, but the return on assets measure used in assessing its ongoing performance may be some very different number—even though all cash flows turned out to be exactly as predicted. Exactly how much they differ turns out to

Table 9-5 Proposal to Renovate a Facility (All Numbers in $000)

Cost of Capital/Req'd Rate of Return = 13.7%

End of year	Equip. related costs	Depreciation	Operating margin	Taxes on oper. prof.	Profit after tax	After tax cash flow	Discount factor	Present value	Cumul. P.V.
0	8,000						1.0000	–8,000.0	–8,000.0
1	2,000	1,000	2,000	–400	–600	400	0.8795	351.8	–7,648.2
2	0	1,000	2,400	560	840	1,840	0.7735	1,423.3	–6,224.9
3	0	1,000	2,800	720	1,080	2,080	0.6803	1,415.1	–4,809.8
4	0	1,000	3,000	800	1,200	2,200	0.5984	1,316.4	–3,493.4
5	0	1,000	3,000	800	1,200	2,200	0.5263	1,157.8	–2,335.7
6	500	1,000	3,000	600	900	1,900	0.4628	879.4	–1,456.3
7	500	1,000	3,000	600	900	1,900	0.4071	773.4	–682.8
8	500	1,000	3,000	600	900	1,900	0.3580	680.3	–2.6
									~0

depend on a variety of factors, including the life of the asset; the depreciation method used, and the growth rate of demand.[11]

Finally, an increasing number of academics and business practitioners have expressed additional, more qualitative concerns about the kinds of approaches to evaluating capital investment proposals described above.[12] One is that the apparent objectivity and mathematical logic of these approaches can delude managers into thinking that they are being precise and objective when, in fact, the results obtained depend largely on a number of assumptions and estimates that have been arrived at very subjectively. Another concern is that many companies tend to evaluate investments on a project-by-project basis, rather than taking into consideration their interrelationships and the competitive implications of *not* making an investment. Third, such approaches tend to understate the value of investments that have high "option value" (to be discussed in Section 9.3.8), such as those that embrace new technology, R&D, process improvement, and human skill development.

Finally, they worry about the subtle dangers of any approach that is based on systematically discounting the future when choosing among alternative investments—the essence of the present value calculation. There are two primary shortcomings of discounting:

1. Companies tend to pick hurdle/interest rates that are too high (and therefore discount future cash flows too heavily), in comparison both with their historical returns on investment and with their average cost of capital, which biases them against making investments that would increase their total value. (However, hurdle rates that are higher than justified by a company's cost of capital also may reflect constraints other than the desire to use limited capital most effectively, such as the limited availability of key managerial resources or other organizational capabilities.)
2. Traditional present value calculations make the implicit assumption that an investment decision is *reversible,* in the sense that if it is not made today it can be made later (that is, the only penalty from delaying the investment is contained in the discount factor). Yet delaying certain kinds of investments may lead a company into a position of strategic vulnerability from which it can be very difficult to extract itself.

9.3.7 Measures of Predictability

The third dimension of concern about a proposed investment is the predictability of its anticipated costs and returns, which requires measures of the uncertainty associated with them. Uncertainty about the amount of investment required, the project's annual cash flows, the timing of major external events, and the project's useful life all fall into this category. Although a variety of approaches can be used to measure the predictability of a proposed investment, we will touch on only three. The first seeks to assess the *knowable* uncertainty associated with the investment. The second alters the evaluation procedure to reflect the different kinds of risk associated with a project. The third suggests ways to assess the impact of one specific cause of uncertainty—inflation—on the attractiveness of an investment.

Predictability—Explicitly Measuring the Impact of Uncertainty

A number of approaches for characterizing and measuring the uncertainty associated with a proposed investment have been advocated and tested. Most begin with the computation of one or more measures of security and recompense, as described earlier, based on the *expected* values of the project's investment, cash flows, rate of obsolescence, and so on. If those expected values lead to acceptable summary measures, then an attempt is made to assess the investment's overall predictability. The simplest way to do this is to conduct a "sensitivity analysis" of the likely variation in these measures due to changes in the principal variables. Each variable is changed by some amount (plus or minus 20 percent, say, or plus or minus the amount whose probability of being exceeded in either direction is 25 percent), and a simple computer spreadsheet is used to calculate the resulting impact on the project's payback, present value, and other measures. Having identified those variables that appear to have the greatest impact on the project's valuation, one can then determine how big a change is required in order to cause the project's summary measures to fall outside the acceptable range.

A more formal way to measure the uncertainty/predictability of a proposed investment is to assess subjectively the probability distributions of all the key variables, and use these probability distributions to determine (through Monte Carlo simulation) the resulting profitability distribution of the overall measure. Although a number of companies experimented with this approach, commonly called *risk analysis,* in the 1970s and 1980s, relatively few companies use it today.[13] This is largely because of the problems involved in assessing all the required probability distributions—particularly those describing the joint behavior of two or more variables. Some companies, therefore, have adopted an intermediate step in which only three levels are assessed for each variable ("optimistic," "most likely," and "pessimistic," say) and are used to estimate the likely range of each summary measure.

Predictability—Adjusting the Financial Review Procedures

In an attempt to incorporate the impact of a project's uncertainty into their evaluations, companies sometimes modify their financial evaluation procedures in one of two ways. One approach (suggested earlier in our discussion of the discount rate to be used in calculating an investment's net present value) is to require that different types of projects meet *different* hurdle rates. The justification for this approach is that different types of investment projects usually require different forms of financing. Indeed, the *same* type of investment made in different countries could have different levels of risk or importance to the firm. Therefore, goes the argument, the same benchmark rate of return should not be used for all of them.[14] The multiple hurdle rates used by one company are summarized in Table 9-6.

Using different hurdle rates for different types of investments, however, can have the effect of channeling an increased percentage of the firm's available funds into certain types of activities and away from others. Hence, apparently innocuous changes in hurdle rates can have important long-term effects on a firm's competitive position, unless its managers exercise careful discipline over their whole portfolio

Table 9-6 Illustration of Multiple Hurdle Rates

		Effect of proposed investment on					
Purpose of investment	Examples	Cost	Volume	Technology	Business risk		Hurdle rate
Maintain Existing Business	Replace/rebuild existing facilities, Meet government requirements for environment, safety, health, etc.	NC*	NC*	NC*	NC*	→	0 percent
Reduce costs/ improve process	Rationalization, New equipment to replace labor or improve quality	Decrease	NC*	Small change	Small increase	→	15 percent
Maintain process/ increase volume	Plant expansion, equipment purchase, increase working capital	Small decrease	Increase	NC*	Small increase	→	15 percent
New product or process		?	?	?	Increase	→	25 percent

*NC = No change.

of investments. The existence of multiple hurdle rates also might shed light on a common complaint of business managers: "Why is our ROA only 10 percent when all major new projects over the past several years have promised at least a 20 percent return?" Other than the previously mentioned disparity between the value of the internal yield that is projected for an investment and the ROA that is actually observed, it might reflect the fact that a high proportion of the firm's investments is being directed toward preserving or replacing existing facilities—which in many companies are required to provide a smaller rate of return—rather than into investments in new products or processes that are riskier and therefore must surpass a higher hurdle rate.

Another modification in financial reviews that is often made is to require that higher levels of management be involved in the review process as the amount of money at stake increases. In the case of very large investments, the board of directors usually gets involved.

Predictability—Adjusting for the Effects of Inflation

These paragraphs differ from the preceding ones in that, instead of describing a technique for incorporating the impact of uncertainty on a proposed project, we deal here with one of the major sources of such uncertainty in many countries: inflation. The impact of inflation on all four of our measures—security, recompense, predictability, and option value—is so important that it should be addressed directly, if only briefly.

For most of the period after World War II, the United States and other developed countries generally were able to keep inflation under control. As a result, the financial evaluation procedures that most firms employed either excluded completely the impact of inflation or gave it little consideration. Occasionally, however, as when sudden increases in energy prices triggered sharply higher rates of inflation (10 to 25 percent), business executives were forced to understand and deal with this pervasive and pernicious phenomenon. By the end of the 1990s, inflation had been largely tamed in most of the developed countries of the world. In fact, as discussed in Chapter 1, because of the widespread overcapacity in many basic industries there was growing concern (particularly in Japan and Germany) about the opposite problem: deflation. In contrast, the financial turmoil that led many developing countries in Asia and Latin America to devalue their currencies had caused their own rates of inflation to go up. As a result, today's managers of multinational companies still must take into consideration the possible impact of unpredictable changes in inflation rates as they evaluate specific investments in different parts of the world.

Most companies' attempts to incorporate inflation's impact into their investment analyses are rather simplistic: The costs and revenues associated with a project are "adjusted for inflation" by increasing them by the estimated rate of inflation before calculating their NPV and/or IRR. Scaling up both costs and revenues by the same ratio to reflect inflation, however, usually makes proposed investments appear *more* attractive than they actually are, since this causes their profit margins to increase, as well. The truth is much more complex. Inflation causes a variety of changes in the values of different variables associated with an investment project. These changes take place over different periods of time and are affected by different aspects of both the investment project and the inflationary pressure.

First, costs tend to increase. This, after all, is the operative definition of inflation. Usually material costs increase first and then, after some lag, labor and overhead costs go up. This causes operating margins to fall, together with the rate of return on existing assets.

Second, over a period of time the company attempts to raise the prices of its products and services. The time it takes to restore its previous profit margin depends on how fast the impact of rising costs gets translated into profit declines, the competitive situation, and the extent to which the government seeks to control prices.

Third, these increases necessitate more working capital. Accounts Receivable tend to go up in tandem with sales revenue (driven by price increases), while inventories increase with the cost of goods sold (a combination of material costs and labor costs), offset by an increase in Accounts Payable due to higher material costs. Each component, therefore, is subject to a different rate of inflation. As a result, even though the company's investment in fixed assets may be unaffected (until they are replaced with new assets), its total assets will go up.

Fourth, over time, the cost of capital rises. Potential purchasers of both debt and equity demand higher rates of return to compensate for the loss of their money's purchasing power.

Fifth, after awhile the company will either expand its capacity or replace old equipment. At this point, it is affected by the inflation rate prevailing in the capital equipment industry.

Sixth, if its profitability is still depressed, the company might have to take on more debt to finance the increase in working capital and the need for new, higher-priced equipment.

In short, inflation has a number of complex and interacting effects that are not captured by most companies' measures of financial performance (ROA measures, in particular, tend to overstate actual profitability during high inflation) or their procedures for evaluating proposed investments.[15] In many cases, it is possible to model these effects, and test their impact through the use of a computer simulation or spreadsheet analysis, as described earlier. Our intent here, however, is simply to warn against the use of simplistic assumptions and approaches.

9.3.8 Assessing a Proposed Investment's Option Value

Up to now we have been considering investments that are "traditional" in the sense that they involve familiar technology, utilize familiar inputs and existing organizational capabilities, and produce familiar products and services. Therefore, their costs (both initial and ongoing) and returns are relatively predictable, and their "value" can be assessed largely in terms of their financial benefits. Many investments, however, generate returns other than financial results. They may provide valuable information, open up new opportunities, cultivate expertise in new technologies, foster new capabilities, or provide access to new markets.

Consider, for example, a pharmaceutical company that is confronted with three proposals, each of which would require a major investment. The first, from the company's manufacturing organization, would enable the replacement and modernization of some existing equipment at one of its chemical plants. This will both reduce that plant's operating costs and increase its capacity and flexibility. The cost of operating this new equipment and the revenues expected from its operation both are based on considerable experience, and the capabilities required to operate it are already in place. Investing in this equipment is unlikely to require anything from the company other than the money required for its purchase and installation, and its operation is unlikely to provide anything beyond the profits it generates.

The second proposal is a request from the company's R&D lab to initiate a major study of a recently identified disease pathway, which might eventually lead to the discovery of new therapeutic treatments. The third is a request from the vice president for Information Technology to replace the company's existing hodgepodge of personal computers, which have different architectures and are connected to several internal networks that cannot exchange information easily. She proposes to develop a new integrated worldwide computer network that communicates through the Internet. This will lead to some cost savings, as well as faster sharing of information about products, markets, competitors, financial results, and so on.

These three investments clearly impose different demands on, provide different opportunities to, and create value for the company in different ways. The new chemical equipment essentially replicates existing operations and promises improved profitability in a well-established business. It fits the traditional facilities investment model that we have discussed up to now. The R&D investment, by contrast, is intended to generate new scientific knowledge, but what that knowledge will be or how—if at all—it can be employed is unclear. It is not likely to generate any cash flows, and the risks associated with it are almost impossible to assess in advance, so it would be meaningless to try to evaluate this proposal using a traditional investment analysis. It must be defended on the basis of a strategic evaluation of its costs, risks, and potential benefits.

Finally, the investment in a new computer network—like many facilities investments today—falls somewhere between those two extremes, containing elements of both. Its evaluation, therefore, should combine a pure financial analysis, based on the investment's identifiable costs and savings, with a strategic assessment of the new organizational capabilities it will foster. In particular, these new or enhanced capabilities will create options for future activities that the company may (or may not) decide to engage in. In assessing this investment's overall attractiveness, the company will somehow have to augment the value of its financial characteristics with the "value" of such options.[16]

The option value of a proposed investment represents the value of the future opportunities that would be made available only if the investment were made. Like the ante in a poker game, the investment may promise no return other than the opportunity to look at the cards to be dealt, at which point one can either fold or "exercise the option" by making additional investments in an attempt to win the pot. Any measurement of an investment's option value, therefore, has to be based on assessments of what future opportunities might be created by it, as well as of the likelihood that each of these opportunities will arise and the possible returns to the investor if they do. This is a heroic undertaking in most cases, and this kind of quantification normally can be carried out only if very simplifying assumptions are made.

The simplest and most familiar types of options are those for financial securities. Financial options have become increasingly popular over the past two decades—to the point where markets for them (and the "derivatives" based on them) often are larger than the markets for the underlying assets themselves. Consider, for example, the simple "Call Option": you buy the option (i.e., make an investment) to purchase a certain asset (a common stock, bond, or commodity) at a specified price (called the *strike price*) within some prespecified time period. If during that period the asset's price never exceeds the strike price, you would not exercise the option and would lose the amount of your investment. The option becomes increasingly attractive, however, as the asset's price increases beyond the strike price. The option's value is based both on its initial cost and the probabilities that the price of the underlying asset will take on specific values in the future.

Calculating the value of this kind of option is relatively simple for European Options, which can be exercised only at a specified time in the future, since then one simply needs to estimate the probability distribution for the asset's price at that single point in time. Figure 9-2 depicts the profit function and probability distribution associated with such an option.

The problem becomes considerably more complex for an American Option, which can be exercised at any time prior to the termination date, as one then has to

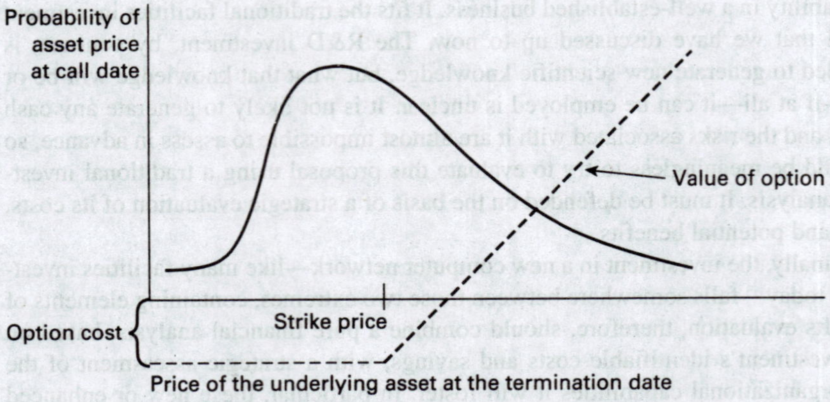

Figure 9-2 Value of a European Option

specify the probability distribution of the option at each point in time between "now" and the termination date, as well as a decision rule describing when it will be exercised. The solution for, and analysis of the implications of, this more common type of option (whose nonfinancial version is now often referred to as a "real option") won Nobel Prizes for their creators.[17]

Despite the difficulty of calculating most options (other than those involving financial instruments), we want to draw attention to one of their most important characteristics. Usually one assumes that an increase in the uncertainty of a project causes its value to decrease. This decrease in value typically is called a *risk discount* and is the reason people are willing to pay higher prices for government-backed securities than for *junk bonds* that promise the same stream of interest payments. It also is the rationale behind adopting different discount rates to evaluate different kinds of investment projects (as described in Section 9.3.7). But options are different: their value *increases* as the uncertainty surrounding them goes up. This is because, as can be seen in Figure 9-2, the investor does not have to exercise that Call Option if the price goes down. On one hand, the investor's exposure is limited to the cost of buying the option. On the other hand, the greater the upside uncertainty, the more profitable the option becomes.

Just because the calculation of an option's exact value is difficult (and, in fact, often impossible unless one makes greatly simplifying assumptions) doesn't imply that one should ignore it. Many investments—like those our pharmaceutical company was considering in R&D or the adoption of a new IT/process technology, as well as those for entering a new market or geographic region—are only attractive if one takes into account their option value. Rough approximations in such cases usually are better than nothing.[18]

For a highly simplified example of how such analyses might be carried out, consider how the evaluation of the hypothetical project described in Table 9-2 might change if, instead of certain abandonment after eight years, there was about one chance in three that the new technology that was expected to render it obsolete would turn out not to be viable because of environmental and/or health concerns. In this case, after year 8 the company could choose to renovate its facility for about $2.0 million and continue on as before. Its operating margins would be expected to stay about the same as before, and the annual cost to maintain and repair the equipment would continue at a rate of $500,000 per year for another eight years.

The calculation of the value of this option (since the company doesn't have to make the follow-on investment until it finds out whether or not the old technology will be displaced by the new one) is provided in Table 9-7. It shows that if the anticipated replacement technology is not introduced after all, the follow-on investment of $2.0 million required to continue utilizing the old technology becomes highly attractive: its present value as of the beginning of the project (i.e., the beginning of year 1) is $1,693,300.

When that amount is combined with the negative $384,800 NPV of the initial $8.0 million investment, the present value of the combined project is $1,308,500. Since there is only one chance in three that the failure of the new technology will allow a profitable follow-on investment, the project's *expected* present value (which assigns a one-third probability to the more favorable outcome) is equal to:

$$(1/3)(1308.5) + (2/3)(-384.8) = \$179,600$$

Therefore, the option to continue running the facility after year 8 makes the initial investment attractive, after all. The value of that option is calculated by subtracting the present value of the project without the option from its present value with the option:

$$179.6 - (-384.8) = \$564,400$$

9.3.9 Caveat Calculator!

This section has provided a brief overview of some of the commonly used methods that companies employ in attempting to incorporate a variety of considerations into their analyses of major investment proposals. There is considerable evidence that over time large companies are using more and more "sophisticated" approaches, in the sense that they are taking an increasing number of considerations into account and assessing the impact of the uncertainty associated with them. One recent survey, for example, found that whereas in 1980 only 35 percent of *Fortune* magazine's list of the 1,000 largest U.S. companies utilized cost of capital (e.g., NPV or IRR) techniques in their analyses, by 1997 that percent had doubled. In addition, by then about three-quarters also were using different hurdle rates for different kinds of investments.[19]

The picture was somewhat different, however, for *real-option analysis,* the most "modern" (and intellectually exciting) analytical technique. Despite the substantial academic literature that grew up around the idea that many investments can be thought of as a collection of different types of options, and that these options can be evaluated using techniques similar to those used in valuing financial options, companies appeared to be disillusioned by their experiences trying to apply that idea in practice. One study in 2000, for example, found that less than 10 percent of companies were

Table 9-7 Follow-On Investment in a Renovated Facility (All Numbers in $000)

Cost of Capital/Req'd Rate of Return = 15%

End of year	Equip. related costs	Depreciation	Operating margin	Taxes on oper. prof.	Profit after tax	After tax cash flow	Discount factor	Present value	Cumul. P.V.
8	2,000						0.3269	–653.8	–653.8
9	500	250	3,000	900	1,350	1,600	0.2843	454.8	–199.0
10	500	250	3,000	900	1,350	1,600	0.2472	395.5	196.5
11	500	250	3,000	900	1,350	1,600	0.2149	343.9	540.4
12	500	250	3,000	900	1,350	1,600	0.1869	299.0	839.5
13	500	250	3,000	900	1,350	1,600	0.1625	260.0	1,099.5
14	500	250	3,000	900	1,350	1,600	0.1413	226.1	1,325.6
15	500	250	3,000	900	1,350	1,600	0.1229	196.6	1,522.3
16	500	250	3,000	900	1,350	1,600	0.1069	171.0	1,693.3
Totals	6,000	2,000	24,000	7,200	10,800	12,800			1,693.3
Averages	750	250	3,000	900.0	1,350	1,600			

employing real option analysis in their investment evaluations, and that 32 percent of those that had experimented with it had abandoned that approach during the year. Its lack of attractiveness appeared to be due primarily to the complexity, and resulting lack of "transparency," of the calculations required, and (paradoxically) that its implementation required assumptions that were unrealistically oversimplified.[20]

It should be noted, however, that several other surveys over a rather long period of time have shown little relationship between the degree of sophistication of the methodologies employed by companies and their overall financial performance.[21] This suggests that, while perhaps useful in helping managers disentangle and think about various aspects of a proposed investment, putting too much effort into incorporating more and more considerations, and performing increasingly complex analytical procedures, in evaluating potential investments is unlikely to be worth the extra effort. One is better off spending time addressing the substantive issues covered in this book's other chapters than on playing around with different interest rates and option values. An understanding of financial techniques, therefore, has value for an operations manager largely to the extent that it enables her to respond effectively to questions and requests from those who lack a deep understanding of the technical and strategic issues involved. It also allows her to ascertain in advance the likely weaknesses in an investment's financial justification, and prepare appropriate responses to challenges.

9.4 INTEGRATING INVESTMENT PROPOSALS INTO LONG-TERM STRATEGIES

The preceding sections of this chapter dealt with a number of the specific tasks that ought to be addressed by an investment planning process. These ranged from assigning the team that prepares the proposal, to selecting specific techniques for evaluating its financial attractiveness. Table 9-1 summarized the typical scenario that many firms follow when faced with a major investment project, and we commented on some of its weaknesses. We now contrast that scenario with a process, summarized in Table 9-8, that facilitates the formulation, approval, and successful implementation of investments that reinforce an operations strategy.

The most important distinction between the approaches summarized in Tables 9-1 and 9-8 lies in their underlying philosophy. The strategy-driven process, in contrast with the problem-driven process, views investments as providing a specific desired long-term operations structure, infrastructure, and capabilities, rather than simply providing additional resources for existing products in existing markets. As a result, a sequence of such decisions is connected by their adherence to the firm's overall strategy. Moreover, the decision-making procedures used place relatively less emphasis on financial analyses and more on qualitative factors, long-term effects, and the overall health of individual and combined facilities.

As an illustration of how such a process might look in practice, consider the approach followed by one company. It decided that an expansion of capacity would be required to meet a projected increase in demand, and a project team was formed consisting of the marketing vice president, the operations vice president, the product manager responsible for the products in question, and an outside consultant. The

Table 9-8 A Strategy-Driven Investment Decision Process

1. Individual projects arise not just in response to immediate business needs or operating problems, but are designed proactively in an attempt to provide the full set of capabilities needed to support the company's desired competitive advantage. They relate directly to major aspects of the company's competitive strategy and environment.
2. Alternatives are defined creatively, and represent a broad array of options compared with the company's past practice (as well as that of its industry).
3. The impact of an investment is evaluated in terms of its impact on the performances of both the new (or modified) facility or business and the firm's other facilities.
4. Specific recommendations are placed into the context of a logical sequence of decisions, although they might also reflect directional changes that are supportive of the business's long-term competitive strategy.
5. Recognizing that operating units, technologies, and systems last over several product/market generations, decision-making procedures take into account the future transitions and roles likely to be required.

team eventually recommended (among other things) building a new facility and moving some existing operations to other, more appropriate facilities. As a result, this project provided an opportunity to review and rationalize the company's three existing facilities while adding a fourth. Moreover, the new facility was given a detailed "charter" that specified its capabilities and performance expectations.

Since this company made major investments in expansion fairly infrequently, its top management sought confirmation from its finance staff. Anticipating this, the project team had developed a computer model that could perform a range of calculations, consider various options, and conduct sensitivity analyses. This detailed financial review took more time, but it also led to a broader base of support for the project during its implementation.

Because of the careful work that had been done in advance, approval by the board of directors was fairly rapid. Given the finance staff's careful evaluation of the project proposal, top management decided it should be assigned responsibility for auditing the project's implementation in accordance with the detailed implementation plan included in the proposal. To facilitate this financial audit, criteria were specified for evaluating the performance of the new facility, as well as those of the other facilities affected. This helped focus each facility's attention on specific activities that were critical to both its success and that of the entire facility network.

Three aspects of this process are worth emphasizing. First, the team assigned to the project was consciously provided with the skills and capabilities that allowed it to propose and evaluate substantial changes in operating structure and systems. Second, senior managers recognized that their real objective was not to project the past into the future, but to treat the proposed project as the first step toward a *desired* future. Finally, these managers involved the rest of their organizations in the preparation of the new facilities plan, which helped ensure its effective implementation once approved.

NOTES

1. See, for example, Reinhardt (2000).

2. Wheelwright et al. (1983), for example, provides a number of different approaches for preparing such forecasts.

3. See Malpas (1983).

4. See "Alden Products, Inc.—European Manufacturing" (HBS case 9-667-099).

5. See, for example, the case "American Connector Co. (A)" (HBS Case #9-693–035), discussed in Chapter 2.

6. See "Survey and Analysis of Capital Budgeting Methods Used by Multinationals," Oblak and Helm (1980).

7. Solomons (1965) provided one of the earliest descriptions of the Residual Income concept, which he reported was then in use at the General Electric Company. Sheked et al. (1997) provides a more recent analysis.

8. An estimate of this time-weighted payback period also can be obtained by calculating the project's *duration:* the weighted average term to maturity of its cash flow stream. The concept of duration was developed originally to measure the effective lifetime of a bond whose coupon rate is different than the current interest rate on similar bonds. It is equal to $\Sigma[tCF_t/(1 + r)^t]/ \Sigma[CF_t/(1 + r)^t]$, where CF_t is the cash flow in year t, and r is the rate of return required to make the denominator equal to the bond's current price. See Blocher and Stickney (1979). This measure is seldom used in evaluating capital investment projects, however, since it is just as easy to calculate the actual time-weighted payback period as in Table 9-4 below.

9. For further explanation of this issue, as well as others raised in this section, see Brealey and Myers (1995) and Luehrman (1997).

10. It can be shown that, if the project's residual income is defined properly, its NPV (as calculated in Table 9-5) is equal to the present value of its year-by-year residual incomes; see Ohlson (1995). Moreover, Anctil et al. (1997) have shown that if a firm uses "maximum short-term residual income" as its criterion in making a series of investments over time, it will achieve roughly the same result as if it had chosen those providing the highest NPVs.

11. About the only easy relationship between the three occurs for investments having very long lifetimes. In those cases the accounting ROA, as calculated by equation (9-2B), will be about the same as the internal rate of return. Unfortunately, that common value will be roughly *half* the value calculated by equation (6-2A)! For additional information about alternative ways of evaluating investment opportunities, and the circumstances under which they may differ, see Brealey & Myers (1996), Solomon (1966), van Breda (1981), and Wilkes (1977).

12. See Hayes and Garvin (1982); Hayes and Jaikumar (1988); Myers (1983); and Dixit and Pindyck (1995).

13. The Risk Analysis approach is described in Hertz (1968); for an example of its recent use see Nichols (1994).

14. See, for example Brigham (1975).

15. For a perspective on the impact of inflation on the value of a whole company, not just on a specific investment project, see Modigliani and Cohen (1979).

16. For additional insight on these issues, see Myers (1983) and Hayes and Jaikumar (1988).

17. For a detailed history of the development of the theory of option pricing, as well as many of the seminal articles that influenced its progress, see Merton (1990).

18. For descriptions of the calculations required, see Dixit and Pindyck (1995) and Luehrman (1998). Examples of how different companies are attempting to incorporate the option value of proposed investments into their financial justifications are contained in Miller and Park (2002).

19. Gitman and Vanderberg (2000). See also Bierman (1993) and Farragher et al.(1999).

20. See Teach (2003).

21. For example, Farragher et al. (2001), measured "sophistication" according to the degree to which a firm incorporates strategic considerations, multidimensional objectives, a wide set of alternatives, forecasts of a multiple variables, risk assessment, and the time value of money into its analysis, and could "not support the hypothesis that firms with higher performance employ more sophisticated capital budgeting processes."

Chapter 10

Sharpening the Edge: Driving Operations Improvement

The rate at which individuals and organizations learn may become the only sustainable competitive advantage, especially in knowledge-intensive industries.

—Ray Stata[1]

10.1 INTRODUCTION

Up to this point our discussions of different ways to improve operating effectiveness have been based primarily on the notions of fit and focus. *Fit* refers to the need for an operation's structure—specifically, its decisions regarding capacity, facilities, sourcing, and process/information technologies that were discussed in previous chapters—to fit both with its infrastructure (internal coherence) and with its business unit's competitive strategy (strategic consistency). The closely related concept of *focus* refers to the establishment of clear priorities for the operations organization so that it can concentrate its limited resources on a restricted set of activities and thereby seek competitive superiority along the most critical competitive dimensions.

As a consequence of this logical thread, we have directed our attention primarily to major strategic initiatives that could be developed and managed as large projects: restructuring (and possibly either pruning or outsourcing) operations that are unfocused and/or inconsistent with an organization's competitive strategy, and investing in new facilities, technologies, and activities that will create and support a more effective structure. However, simply having a coherent operations structure and infrastructure that meshes with a chosen strategic direction does not by itself ensure competitive success. If it could, how can one explain the outcomes of Formula One car races? Or consider the familiar sight of a group of identical sailboats that approach the starting line together. All are of the same size and shape, each is similarly equipped and crewed, and they follow the same course, driven by the same wind and currents, with the same objective. All, in short, have the same competitive strategy and have matched it with the same operating system. Yet, at the end of the race some boats are in front while others are far behind. And usually, if one watches the same group of boats race again and again, the same ones end up in front a disproportionate number of times.

In the short term, an appropriately structured and focused organization is likely to do very well against unfocused, inefficient competitors. But, over time, competitive forces will either require those competitors to restructure themselves so as to improve their operating effectiveness, or cause them to fall by the wayside—to be replaced by new, hungrier, more focused and innovative companies. In a competitive environment, therefore, Darwinian survival lies not just in an organization's adoption of an appropriate operations structure and infrastructure, but in its ability to adapt to changing conditions and improve its performance over time.

There are different ways to pursue improvement, however, and each approach requires different organizational capabilities and associated management skills and activities. Moreover, different competitive and technological environments favor different approaches. In this chapter we will attempt to describe some of the basic approaches to organizational improvement and their implications for operations managers. In Chapter 11, we will continue this discussion by describing various ways that top management can facilitate—or impede—organizational improvement.

10.2 A FRAMEWORK FOR ANALYZING ORGANIZATIONAL IMPROVEMENT

The behavior over time of operating effectiveness, particularly labor productivity, has been one of the most studied phenomena in business, economics, and organizational behavior. Attempts to explain the rate and causes of observed improvements, and predict future levels, have fostered multiple theories of economic growth, industry structure, and competitive advantage.

10.2.1 A Macro Perspective: Learning and Experience Curves

One of the most ubiquitous—and somewhat puzzling—findings about organizational improvement at the macro level has been the widely observed tendency of many products' labor content and/or unit cost (adjusted for inflation) to fall by a roughly constant percentage every time their cumulative production volume doubles.[2] Thus, for a 75 percent "learning curve," say, the labor hours required to produce the two-thousandth unit would be 75 percent of those required to make the one thousandth unit.

This type of relationship suggests that direct hours per unit can be approximated by some negative power of cumulative units: hours/unit ~ n_t^{-b}, where n_t represents the cumulative number of items produced at any point in time t, and b reflects the rate of cost decreases.[3] This implies that when labor hours per unit are plotted against cumulative volume on log-log paper they should cluster around a straight line with slope $-b$. Such relationships have been observed in industries ranging from simple, stable commodity-like products like crushed gravel, to such highly complex ones as aircraft and cardiac surgery,[4] to fast-moving ones like semiconductors, although each tends to follow a different (and usually unpredictable, a priori) rate of learning.

Note that the *rate of learning,* as defined here, is not the same as the *rate of growth in labor productivity.* To translate a learning rate into its implied rate of productivity growth one must specify the length of time it takes to double cumulative output. For example, if it took only one year to double the cumulative output of a product that followed an 80 percent learning curve, then only 8/10 as much labor would be required for the last unit produced that year as compared with the last unit produced during the preceding year. In productivity terms, this would be stated as a 20 percent improvement in labor productivity. However, if the product's cumulative production volume was increasing at a rate of only 41.4 percent over the year (implying that it would take two years for cumulative output to double), the observed rate of productivity growth would be only about 10 percent.

The early attempts to estimate learning curves initially only attempted to track and predict direct labor hours per unit. Later the concept was broadened to encompass *total cost* per unit (or, alternatively, value added per unit), and the relationship between such measures of performance and the cumulative number of units produced was termed the "experience" curve. As with learning curves, experience curves also have been observed to track along a straight line when plotted on log-log paper. Either depiction of organizational improvement exemplifies the "dynamic economies of scale" that were introduced and contrasted with the more familiar "static" economies of scale in Chapter 3.

Learning/experience curves have been applied to a variety of organizational levels, from a department within an operating unit, to the whole unit, business or company, and even to entire industries and national economies. Although similar computational techniques are used at each level, collecting and interpreting actual data and determining their implications for management action can differ greatly depending on the level in question. Although the mathematics of learning curves may appear exact, their actual estimation usually is based on quite messy empirical data. Even the mathematics is suspect, since it is not grounded on any natural laws. In addition, an organization's experience curve is highly dependent on management decisions and behavior, so considerable judgment is required when applying such a curve to a specific situation. A brief discussion of how learning curves can be estimated is contained in this chapter's Appendix.

10.2.2 Different Mechanisms for Driving Organizational Improvement

In order to dig beneath the macro view of organizational improvement, as depicted in learning/experience curves, and understand the actual processes through which it takes place within an organization, it is useful to differentiate among various types of learning and consider the different mechanisms that facilitate each. For example, how a person learns to do something better is different from how a group of people gets better. Similarly, how a group gets better at doing something it already is doing is different from how it learns to do something it has never done before. And for an organization composed of many groups to improve its performance requires still different approaches. In most organizations, of course, all these types of learning are going on, often simultaneously, and they interrelate in complex ways—affecting *who* is doing the learning and *where* and *how* it is taking place. The following questions may help clarify the basic mechanisms at work:

1. Does the learning take place within a single group, or in an organization composed of several groups?
2. Is most of the anticipated improvement expected to come from analyses performed by "experts" (e.g., industrial engineers, scientists, or corporate staff) or from experimentation and suggestions at the operating level? (In Chapter 7 this dichotomy was characterized as "learning *before* doing" versus "learning *by* doing.")
3. Is most of the improvement expected to come discontinuously, from a few major changes, or more continuously, from multiple small steps?
4. Is most of the improvement expected to come from doing familiar things better or from incorporating new ideas and practices from outside the organization?

We address various aspects of each of these approaches to improvement in Sections 10.3 through 10.6, then organize them into a rough framework in Section 10.7. Finally, in Section 10.8 we provide detailed examples of two common, but very different, improvement approaches and discuss some of their implications for management practice. In the next chapter, we discuss alternative strategies for organizing and managing a company's improvement efforts.

10.3 "WITHIN" VS. "ACROSS" GROUP IMPROVEMENT

When most people consider improving something, they think in terms of "*within* group" learning. That is, how does a group of people get better at doing something? The second type, "*across* group" learning, is quite different and concerns the way an organization composed of different groups (e.g., functions, product groups, geographic entities) can combine their efforts to achieve greater improvement than would be possible if each individual group worked by itself.

10.3.1 Enablers of, and Constraints on, "Within" Group Improvement

As a starting point to our discussion of "within group" improvement, it is important to differentiate between *individual learning*—the improvement over time in the performance of a given person—and *organizational improvement.* A simple example using the game of golf highlights several of the key aspects that frame our discussion of those two phenomena.

"Individual Learning"

People just starting to play golf usually need lots of strokes to get through 18 holes, but over time, as they continue to play, their scores tend to get better—up to a point. After that point their performance tends to level off (the score at which it levels off determines whether they end up as weekend golfers or on the professional tour). Why do they get better, and then why, beyond some point, do they stop getting better?

Table 10-1 summarizes some of the physical and mental causes of improvement in an individual's golf game. First, over time playing golf strengthens certain critical muscles and gives you better control over them. Moreover, constant repetition causes conscious actions to become internalized in the subconscious; for example, being able to hold the club and swing it properly without thinking frees up your mind so that you can focus on the specifics of each shot. Feedback from observing the results of previous decisions in certain situations leads you to avoid error-producing and/or ineffective actions and reinforces effective ones. Reading books, watching videos, and getting advice from more experienced players helps you incorporate the techniques and "tricks" that time has shown to be most successful. Finally, as you get better, you find that you can begin to exploit the capabilities of better (and usually vastly more expensive!) equipment.

Why would a person be willing to spend all this time and money learning to play golf, and endure the aggravation and frustration—not to mention the slings and arrows of outraged partners—that go with it? Because they *want* to! Some people, in fact, seem to want to almost to the exclusion of almost everything else. So why don't they continue to get better indefinitely, as the learning curve would suggest?

The reason is that almost every one of the factors that enable individual improvement has a flip side that impedes it beyond some point. Different people have different degrees of muscular strength and coordination, and reach their individual limits after awhile. If there are long intervals between the times you play golf, you tend to "forget" some of what you have learned. Actions that you internalized into your subconscious because they helped you when you first started playing may actually hamper performance after you have become a better player (i.e., bad habits). Imitating the techniques that have worked for superior players might not be appropriate for people who have different levels of strength and coordination. And even the best golf clubs have limits; ultimately, they are no better than the person

Table 10-1 Actions that Affect Individual "Learning" (e.g., Golf)

Factors that *enable* improvement	Factors that *impede* improvement
Strengthening critical muscles	Reaching physical limits
Feedback: learning to avoid errors and reinforcing effective approaches	Interruptions that lead to forgetting
Practice (which translates conscious into unconscious behavior)	Internalizing bad habits
Studying and coaching: transferal of others' proven techniques	Adopting practices that are inappropriate, given one's personal constraints or attributes
Using better tools and equipment	Constraints imposed by equipment and the rules of the game
Motivation and incentives	Frustration, boredom, loss of motivation

who swings them. But the main reason most people stop getting better at some point is that they simply lose the motivation to improve further. It just isn't "worth it" for them to devote the time, spend the money, and endure the aggravation associated with playing golf every day in the attempt to get better. They rest on their oars—satisfied with the level of performance they've already achieved.

Group/Organization Improvement

Given this analysis of the causes of and constraints on individual learning, why are business organizations apparently able to get better *indefinitely,* as suggested by the learning curve? As summarized in Table 10-2, although individual learning contributes to it, group learning is a very different phenomenon.[5] The left-hand column of Table 10-2 indicates that groups can exploit far more mechanisms for achieving improvement than can individuals. For example, even though the people who make up a group are subject to the same leveling off of improvement described above, that group has the added option of dividing up a complete task and assigning various pieces of it to sub-groups that specialize in each task segment.[6] One of the problems when playing golf is that you have to do everything yourself. If a group of people decided to play golf in a highly competitive environment, however, rather than relying on a single individual's capabilities for the entire game, they probably would assign different kinds of shots to people who were especially selected and trained

Table 10-2 "Within Group" Organizational Learning (e.g., the "Learning Curve")

Factors that *enable* improvement	Factors that *impede* improvement
Individual learning	Slowdown in individual improvement
Division of labor, specialization	Poor organization and communication
Designing and adopting improved products and processes	Resistance to changing products and methods: the "not invented here" (NIH) syndrome
Selecting and training new members (and eliminating poorer performers)	Constraints imposed by: work rules, labor contracts, and loyalty to long time associates
Substituting materials and/or capital for labor	Materials shortages Capital limitations
Exploiting economies of scale	Encountering the diseconomies of scale
Acquiring better equipment, incorporating new technologies	Technological constraints (e.g., the "sound barrier," the speed of electrons)
Changing the rules of the game	Government regulations or societal restrictions
Motivation, incentives	Inertia or preference for the status quo reduce the incentive to improve
Leadership	Lack of leadership

for each: one person for tee shots, another for approach shots, another for sand traps, another for putting, and so on.

Like individuals, organizations can study their performance and try to develop better ways to do their work. Moreover, they usually have far more resources at their disposal. To begin, they can assign many more than two eyes and one brain to the task of identifying opportunities and providing suggestions for improvement. They can hire and train process engineers and other specialists to develop superior methods. They can replace resources that are expensive or in short supply (skilled labor, say) with better alternatives (e.g., computerized equipment and purchased materials or parts)—while individuals must live with their own physical and mental constraints. They can send teams to study the best practices of other organizations. And if all else fails, they can do something individuals can't do: replace themselves—that is, replace poorer performing members with better performing ones!

Business organizations not only can acquire better equipment, but also they are not as limited in terms of the technologies incorporated in that equipment. Nor are they constrained by the regulations that, in effect, limit ordinary golfers. They don't, for example, have to use traditional "golf clubs" (pieces of wood or metal attached to the end of a stick). Instead, they might be able to develop small gas-propelled cannons, say, to replace drivers, and computer controlled hole-seeking robots to replace putters—just as airplanes have largely replaced trains and ships as long distance passenger transporters. In business, the rules of the game, and its implements, are constantly being redesigned. The coming of the Internet, for example, has given small organizations the ability to reach potential customers directly and thereby reduced the competitive advantage of larger companies' more extensive sales organizations.

Moreover, as organizations get larger they can create and exploit economies of scale, which (as outlined in Chapter 3) can be obtained through a variety of management actions, including the use of higher volume facilities that require less labor and have lower capital cost per unit of capacity. This permits increased throughput without a proportional increase in people and capital, and/or reduced changeover costs if specific facilities are dedicated to certain high-volume products or services. In highly capital-intensive industries, such activities can be some of the most important sources of continued cost improvement.

Unlike individuals, who often find themselves trapped in a system they do not have the abilities or resources to change, moreover, business organizations sometimes are able to "change the game" by adopting new competitive strategies and introducing entirely different products or services. When Federal Express entered the package delivery business, for example, it didn't play the same game as the entrenched players. Instead it was able to offer guaranteed overnight delivery by setting up a whole new system based on a hub-and-spoke transportation network and ownership of all components of the pickup and delivery process. Similarly, in the 1980s and 1990s, Toyota and other Japanese auto manufacturers ignored the competitive strategy of their entrenched, and much larger, U.S. competitors—which emphasized surface appearance and planned obsolescence—and took a third of the U.S. passenger car market by offering low defect rates and superior product reliability. This was equivalent, in a sense, to changing the way golf is scored: seeking to reduce the number of missed shots (or lost balls!) rather than the total number of shots played.

As one reviews the various approaches to organizational improvement in Table 10-2, it can be seen that most can be categorized as attempts to eliminate one or more of the barriers that impede individual improvement: providing the organization with better people, methods, tools, products, and strategies. But such approaches merely *enable* improvement; they do not *drive* it. Why do business organizations drive themselves to improve their performance using all these approaches? Because they are motivated to do so, directly by their managers, and indirectly—but powerfully—by the need to survive against the attacks of competitors who *are* continually improving their performance. Individuals can decide to relax about their golf game; a company that relaxes will eventually find itself out of business.

These various sources of improvement, it should be noted, operate over different time frames. Most of the improvements that are possible in the near term—within a period of a few months, say—generally arise out of individual learning and training, methods improvements, and the introduction of new materials and equipment that allow the same work to be done more efficiently. Over an intermediate time frame, on the order of one to three years, an organization can recruit more effective people, put them to work identifying problems and proposing solutions, conducting process R&D, reorganizing work flows, and designing new products.[7] Building and exploiting scale advantages, introducing a wholly different product or process technology, or redefining the game, by contrast, generally require several years of effort. Analog Devices, which designs and manufactures specialized I.C.s, came to the conclusion that the time required by an organization to achieve a given amount of improvement is largely a function of the elapsed time it takes it to identify and eliminate problems. The speed of these improvement cycles, it asserts, is more a function of organizational complexity and bureaucracy than it is of cumulative volume, as the traditional learning curve suggests.[8]

Moreover, the path to improvement is not always a straight one. Some of these activities (the introduction of new people, say, or the adoption of a new incentive system) may require a gestation period before real improvement is realized. Others may even cause a decrease in performance before the status quo is regained and superior performance becomes possible. For example, in a study of one company's attempt to improve its overall manufacturing efficiency by introducing the same major piece of equipment in several of its plants,[9] it was found that some of these plants experienced a *decline* in their total factor productivity for up to a year after the renovation was completed. At one plant the imputed cost of that decline in performance was almost twice as great as the cost of the equipment itself. Since that plant was barely able to regain its original performance level, it never was able to recoup that loss. Another plant, however, was able to overcome the disruption caused by the same upgrade rather quickly, and soon thereafter achieved the operating improvements that had been anticipated.

This phenomenon is often even more pronounced when a company introduces a substantially different technology into its operation. For example, the 5.25-inch hard disk drive was rejected by the manufacturers of minicomputers when first introduced, because its storage capacity, access time, and cost per bit all were worse than the 8-inch drives then in widespread use.[10] Making the improvements that allowed the new drive to meet and eventually surpass the performance of the 8-inch incumbent took almost ten years, but it resulted in the smaller drive becoming the technology of choice—only to be similarly displaced by 3.5-inch disk drives a few years later! As a result, the pattern of improvement over long periods of time seldom reflects the elegant simplicity and continuity suggested by the learning curve. Rather, more often it exhibits a series of "scallops" and "toe-ups," often interlaced with periods of fluctuating performance around a constant value. Over a long period of time, however, the cumulative effect of all these discontinuities often generates a pattern that—when plotted on log-log paper and looked at from a sufficient distance—looks roughly like a straight line.

The Barriers to Organizational Improvement

Just as a variety of factors can cause a slowdown in individual learning, organizational improvement also has natural impediments (summarized in the right hand column of Table 10-2). For example, companies face their own external constraints, including government regulations and restrictions imposed by labor contracts. In addition, as organizations divide up work and assign it to specialists, they tend to create complex, often bureaucratic organizations in which communications are indirect and awkward, decisions slow, and changes difficult to implement.[11] Moreover, if such changes are allowed to become codified into formal policies and procedures, organizations often find it difficult to "unlearn" them when an environmental or strategy change requires different approaches.

Finally, people who are asked to limit their attention to a small part of a complete product or service tend to lose understanding of the product as a whole and how it relates to the needs of users. As a result, some companies have found that it is possible to achieve both significant improvements in labor productivity and improved customer satisfaction by *reducing* the division of labor. For example, one U.S. supplier of auto parts replaced several of its large assembly lines with a much greater number of small workstations, where individual workers performed multiple tasks. This both reduced the inventories and floor space required and allowed workers to redesign their own jobs. As a result, double-digit improvements in productivity were obtained.[12]

10.3.2 Transferring Improvement *Across* Groups

Once one group within an organization learns how to do something well, how does it pass that learning on to other groups? Again and again, one sees examples of companies that make the same mistakes again and again as different groups, such as the project teams discussed in Chapter 8, plunge ahead unaware of the experience of previous groups. Similarly, different groups within a company (even within the same division) often exhibit widely differing levels of performance in carrying out similar activities. Studies of operating units producing similar products or services within the same company reveal cases where the performance (as measured by total factor productivity, defect levels, on time deliveries, inventories, etc.) of the best group was two to three times that of the worst group.[13] Within the same *industry* (four-digit SIC code) the disparities are even greater: the average value added per employee-hour of plants at the 90th percentile is four times that of those at the 10th percentile.[14] Despite such findings, transferring superior practices within a company appears to be surprisingly difficult. Why don't the worst groups learn from the best groups? Why don't the best groups teach the worst groups? What can companies do to encourage learning *across* units?

There are many reasons why good performers don't pass on their expertise to bad ones, but most boil down to that familiar problem, lack of motivation. Transferring learning requires time and effort on the part of both the giver and the receiver. The well-performing unit pays much of the cost, direct or indirect, of this effort, but the poorly performing unit gets all the benefit. In fact, if the company allocates rewards on the basis of *relative* performance, the "good" unit's altruistic efforts may actually cause its rewards to decrease if the "bad" unit improves sufficiently.

Given this apparent asymmetry of rewards, why don't the "bad" units eagerly seek out the help of better-performing sister units? One reason is pride: for a group to accept help from another is akin to acknowledging that it is deficient.[15] Another reason reflects the tradeoff between short and long term: accepting the services of a teacher requires that the poorly performing group reassign employees from producing goods and services to learning new approaches. This often leads to a short-term decrease in organizational performance—which is hard to justify when one's performance is already the subject of concern.

Still another common justification for not accepting assistance is that "our situation is different," the implication being that the "good" unit is operating in an environment that provides it with some form of advantage that is not available to the "bad" unit, and/or that its methods are not effective outside that favorable environment. In many cases, of course, there is some truth to such reasoning: wage rates, skill levels, and material and energy costs all differ from region to region. Also, few groups perform *exactly* the same operations as their sister groups. Products, volumes, product mixes, and customer requirements often vary rather widely across operating units. (This was the reason, as discussed in Chapter 7, that some companies allow process development to be decentralized.) In most cases, however, rejecting offers of assistance for this reason is simply an excuse for avoiding the effort required to learn new methods and make the necessary changes in operations. It generally indicates that the unit is buffered in some way from the pressure of the competitive environment. Later in this chapter we will describe various ways through which top management can facilitate across group improvement.

10.4 LEARNING BY DOING VS. LEARNING BEFORE DOING

As described in Chapter 7, one's understanding of any activity can range through several levels. At one end of the spectrum, it is primarily *tacit.* That is, one can learn how to perform the activity—or perform it better—only by actually doing it. Over time, as you gain experience, you can experiment with different ways of doing it to see if your performance improves. We usually refer to such tacit knowledge as a *skill.* That's how, for example, we typically learn to play golf or tennis, drive an automobile, and make or sell something. This kind of knowledge is both slow to acquire and difficult to pass on to others, except by watching them as they try their hand and "coaching" them along.

At the other extreme is *explicit* knowledge: one understands fully the causes and mechanisms at work in the activity and can prepare an instruction sheet or computer program for carrying it out. This kind of knowledge can also be difficult to acquire (we still don't fully understand, for example, how to control many biochemical reactions), but once acquired is relatively easy to pass on to others. To the extent that the tasks an organization performs are based on explicit knowledge, it is justified in hiring "experts" whose primary responsibility is to study and find better ways to do things. Manufacturing engineers, for instance, are trained to study production processes and identify ways for improving them.

Most activities, of course, fall somewhere between these two extremes. One understands some of the principles and mechanisms, but not all. Where along that spectrum a given activity lies influences how one should go about trying to improve it. If, for example, the activity is based primarily on tacit knowledge, you are not likely to be able to make substantial progress through analysis and detailed "improvement plans," no matter how many experts you hire. Instead, you probably will achieve progress faster by asking a lot of people to offer suggestions for improving the particular activities they are engaged in, trying them out in controlled experiments, and encouraging others to adopt the improved methods. Alternatively, if the chemistry of a certain drug is well understood, it probably is better to ask a group of expert chemical engineers to design a process for producing it than to attempt to develop a process through trial and error.

10.5 TRANSFERRING LEARNING IN FROM OUTSIDE THE ORGANIZATION

Both within group and across group learning are based on internal sources of improvement. Increasingly, however, companies are discovering that keeping up with world-class competitors in today's ferocious competitive markets requires that they also look outside themselves for improvement ideas. Because of the difficulties of transferring tacit knowledge, this approach to organizational improvement tends to emphasize explicit knowledge, and many of the requirements of "learning before doing" apply.

One obvious source of suggestions for improvement is one's customers. Many companies now seek feedback from their customers, and build the "voice of the customer" into their operating plans and new product development. For example, companies such as Worthington Steel routinely encourage their production workers to visit nearby customers to learn how the products they produce are used, and to ask for suggestions regarding how they could be improved.

Suppliers can be another source of ideas for improvement, as they often can provide insight into how your competitors are utilizing their products or services.

They also are likely to have better information than you do about some of the new materials, equipment, and technologies that are under development and that might influence your operations in the future. In the attempt to better evaluate the new approaches and technologies developed by their equipment suppliers, for example, companies like Milliken & Co. routinely ask production workers to join the delegations of manufacturing engineers and financial analysts sent to equipment trade shows. They have found that those who actually work with machines often provide a different, and very valuable, perspective when assessing a new piece of equipment.

A third source is companies in the same industry that do not compete directly with you—either because of geographical separation or because they produce different products and/or serve different customers. A final source is companies operating in different businesses, but which carry out certain operations that are similar to your own, such as warehousing/distribution, customer service, customer billing, and account management. This approach, called "Competitive Benchmarking," can be carried out either informally, through one-on-one relationships, or through consortia of a number of companies that agree to share data on common processes with one another. The nonprofit American Productivity and Quality Center, for example, has organized one of the largest of these consortia. Another source of examples and expertise are the winners of the National Malcolm Baldrige Award—U.S. companies (and divisions within companies) that are judged to have demonstrated exceptional improvements in quality and productivity. These winners are required to share their expertise with others.

Finally, some companies seek to import improvements by buying, leasing, or hiring expertise or technology. Unfortunately, even though such imported systems, methodologies, or technologies may be vastly superior to their own, companies often find them difficult to assimilate, and even sometimes "reject" them—just as the human body attempts to reject an organ transplant that may be essential to its survival. Moreover, even though transferring explicit knowledge may be relatively easy, it is often extraordinarily difficult to transfer the tacit skills required to exploit it properly. As a result, companies typically encounter problems when they attempt to import *best practices* (or simply *better* practices) from other organizations that have developed those practices largely through a "learning by doing" approach, as their effective implementation requires a substantial amount of (almost invisible) tacit knowledge. This is the one of the main reasons why so few companies have been able to implement Toyota's justly famous Toyota Production System (TPS) with any degree of success, despite the many careful descriptions of the practices embedded within it that are available today.[16]

As another example, during the mid-1990s, two shipyards in Korea produced similar types of cargo ships within a few miles of each other.[17] One, owned by Daewoo, emphasized worker training and internal process development. By 1994 (after starting from far behind), it had caught up with the performance of world-class Japanese shipyards. The other, owned by Samsung, designed new process technologies in a separate facility, or purchased them from outside vendors, and then attempted to introduce them into its shipyard. Although Samsung also made remarkable improvements in its performance, it often experienced multiple problems and delays in these transfers.

Just as in the case of across-group learning, organizations instinctively tend to shy away from "*into* group" learning, as it calls into question their (and, more specifically, their managers') basic competence. Moreover, the difficulties encountered when transferring new practices from another company in the same industry and country pale compared with those associated with transfers across countries and cultures. As described in Chapter 1, even though hundreds of U.S. companies have been trying to assimilate Japanese approaches to quality improvement and inventory reduction since the early 1980s, most have yet to achieve similar levels of performance.

10.6 BREAKTHROUGH VS. INCREMENTAL IMPROVEMENT

As we observed in the introduction to this chapter, in a competitive environment a company's *competitive effectiveness* (lower cost, better quality, more features, longer product life, etc.) must improve over time. If it does not, it will soon find itself replaced by competitors that do. A combination of two very different approaches can be employed in advancing a firm's effectiveness, shown graphically in Figures 10-1a and 10-1b.

One extreme approach is through a series of *strategic leaps:* a few major steps forward at critical points in time, as depicted in Figure 10-1a. These "leaps" might take a variety of forms: totally reconceptualizing the design and/or content of a product or service, moving to another location that promises major improvements in skill levels or wage rates/labor relations, purchasing a major component or service instead of making it internally, adopting an entirely new process technology, or modernizing and/or completely "reengineering" an existing process (see discussion below). Between these giant steps, only incidental improvements

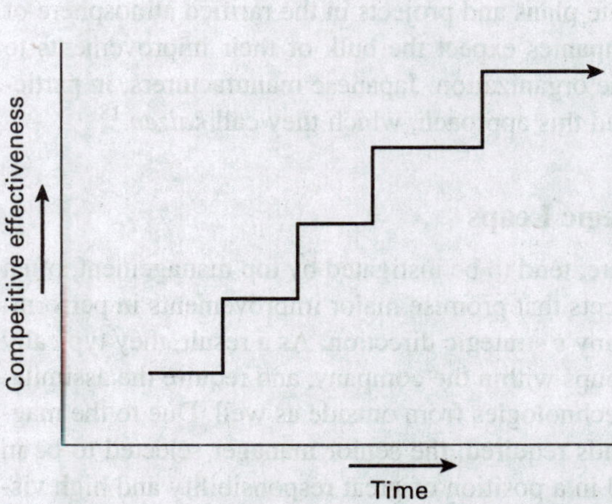

(a) "strategic leaps"

Figure 10-1a Competitive Effectiveness over Time: Progress through "Strategic Leaps"

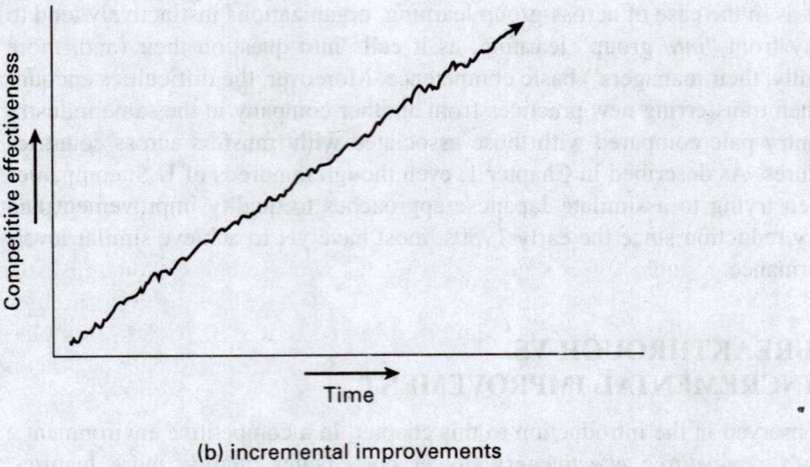

Figure 10-1b Competitive Effectiveness over Time: Progress through Incremental Improvements

in competitive effectiveness are sought, as the company digests its last step and contemplates the next.

At the opposite extreme, a company can seek progress through a series of relatively small steps whose cumulative impact is just as great. Instead of relying on a few major discontinuities, it continually strives to strengthen its competitive position through a variety of incremental improvements, as depicted in Figure 10-1b. These might include methods improvements, defect reduction, improving product reliability, and speeding up set-up, production cycle, and delivery times. Few of these steps are likely to be very visible or risky. Rather than putting massive resources into developing elaborate plans and projects in the rarified atmosphere of a remote headquarters, such companies expect the bulk of their improvements to bubble up from lower levels in the organization. Japanese manufacturers, in particular, have adopted and popularized this approach, which they call *kaizen.*[18]

10.6.1 Implementing Strategic Leaps

Strategic leaps, by their very nature, tend to be instigated by top management, often even the CEO, and focus on projects that promise major improvements in performance and/or changes in the company's strategic direction. As a result, they typically involve several organizational groups within the company, and require the assimilation of expertise, practices, and technologies from outside as well. Due to the magnitude of both the efforts and funds required, the senior manager selected to be in charge of such a project is placed in a position of great responsibility and high visibility. In fact, being associated with a successful project typically is regarded as a stepping stone to top management. Because of the magnitude and complexity of the changes involved, as well as the need to incorporate external/explicit knowledge, "learning *before* doing" is essential. As a result, a long period of study and analysis is usually necessary before taking any action. The project leader, therefore, usually selects a team—often drawn from several organizational groups and incorporating outside experts—to help conduct analyses, propose alternative solutions, and implement the one selected.

Implementing a strategic leap, therefore, usually involves the conceptualization and management of a major project, as discussed in Chapter 8, as well as many of the same steps and activities as those associated with the major capital investments described in Chapter 9 (particularly Section 9.2). Given those previous discussions, and our description of process reengineering in Section 10.7.1 (an example of a strategic leap approach), we will refrain from going into more detail at this point about the implementation of strategic leaps.

10.6.2 Implementing Incremental Improvement

There usually are multiple causes of problems in an organization—ranging from poor product designs to poor worker training to dysfunctional incentive/compensation systems to malfunctioning equipment to erratic and defective deliveries from suppliers. As a result, a given problem usually cannot be eliminated through a single corrective action. Individual causes must be identified, prioritized, and eliminated one by one by various groups working throughout the company. Through this relentless, multipronged attack (the analogy to "jungle fighting" is sometimes used), the company gradually strips away the contributing causes until the *root* cause(s) of the problem is revealed.

Incremental improvement also tends to emphasize tacit knowledge (and therefore "learning *by* doing"), since the availability of explicit knowledge would enable one to implement directed improvements that were larger than those achievable by simply feeling one's way along. Although such improvement programs are often undertaken by several groups within a company at the same time, each is likely to be self directed and so may take quite a different path from the others. All these paths, however, generally incorporate five interrelated steps:

1. Problem identification
2. Problem prioritization
3. Waste removal
4. Problem analysis
5. Controlled experimentation

Problem Identification

You cannot begin to reduce or eliminate a problem until you know that the problem exists. In order to be able to see a problem clearly, of course, the operating process in which it is encountered has to be under sufficient control that the problem can be recognized as an anomaly, rather than as simply a manifestation of normal process variation. To use an extreme example, if a machine only works 10 percent of the time, the natural question that arises when it stops working is, "How can we get it working again?" rather than, "Why did it stop working?" Therefore, before attempting to improve a process, it should be clearly defined and characterized, including the nature and magnitude of its observed variation as well as the primary causes of that variation, and the major problems/weaknesses it experiences. Standards and procedures must be established and documented.

Once an operating problem has been identified, management must ensure that the people affected by it communicate their awareness of the problem to those who might be able to help resolve it. This is more difficult that one might expect, because in an operating environment people tend not to see the problem itself but rather its *symptoms.* Such symptoms may be relatively innocuous—an occasional "jam" in the machine, say, or a customer who leaves the waiting line before being served. Moreover, the operators who experience a problem/symptom often instinctively resist reporting it to superiors who would be in a better position to identify and correct its underlying cause, because they worry that they—the "messengers who carry bad news"—will be thought responsible (and penalized) for causing the problem. Finally, under the relentless pressure to serve customers and meet output schedules, the usual response when a problem is encountered is to apply a "quick fix"—a simple attempt to bypass it or take a compensatory action that reduces its immediate impact. The implicit assumption is that somebody, sometime in the future, will address the underlying cause. When that time arrives (if it ever does), unfortunately, so many other problems will have been experienced that—unless careful records were kept—it becomes difficult to recreate the conditions under which that specific problem occurred with sufficient accuracy to study it properly.

Therefore, successful continuous improvement programs seek ways to encourage people at all levels in the organization to get involved in identifying, describing, and communicating problems. This won't happen, of course, unless people are rewarded, rather than punished, for pointing them out.[19] Problem communication sometimes is as informal as having operators and/or their supervisors post simple written summaries of problems on bulletin boards that are visible to fellow operators, other shifts, process engineers, and managers. The Toyota Production System, in addition, makes extensive use of "Jidoka" devices and techniques that seek to make problems instantly self-evident, and "Andon" cords that, when pulled, allow assembly line operators to call attention to a problem by both halting the production line (or at least part of it) and triggering a call for assistance.[20] This not only makes a problem immediately visible, but it also puts tremendous pressure on the organization to fix it immediately, before too much output is lost. In order for such an approach to work properly, of course, the process has to be under sufficient control that problems arise relatively infrequently. Otherwise, their occurrence would overwhelm the organization's capacity to solve them, and the cost of line stoppages would be prohibitive. For that reason, the introduction of Andon devices represents more the *result* of a successful improvement effort than the *vehicle* for achieving it.

Problem Prioritization

A committed effort to improve operations that has been going on for a number of years should have identified and removed the underlying causes of most major operating problems, to the point where (as for the Toyota Production System) the organization can address new problems as they arise. Until this point is reached, however, the number of problems encountered in a given period of time is likely to exceed the capacity of the organization to deal with them. In this more typical situation the organization needs to develop policies for evaluating and prioritizing problems—which should be addressed first, which next, etc.—so that people can make most effective use of their limited time and problem solving capacity.

This kind of prioritization is sometimes handled informally, by the operators themselves or their supervisors, on the basis of the perceived costs, lost time, and disruptive effects associated with various problems. Alternatively, a variety of more formal approaches may be employed, including *Pareto analyses* of the relative incidence of different kinds of problems, and *Fishbone analyses* to ascertain the underlying common causes of a set of related problems.[21] Whatever approach is chosen is less important than the fact that some attempt is made to organize the problem-solving effort. If this is not done, an organization can too easily fall into a *fire fighting* mode of behavior.

The problem with fire fighting is not only that it is unlikely to identify and remove the root causes of the observed problems, but also it actually can cause new problems to emerge. This is because problems tend to increase as an operation approaches its capacity. Under pressure to maintain the rate of output the natural reaction when a problem is encountered (or, more often, a symptom of an underlying problem) is to address it quickly and superficially, using a "band-aid solution." As a result, the problem does not go away but instead reappears again, perhaps in a different place and with a somewhat different set of symptoms. As people frantically turn their attention from one such "fire" to the next, they soon find themselves pushed to the limits of their capacity.[22] As we saw in Chapter 3 (Section 3.2), this causes the "work in process" (in this case, the list of problems waiting to be addressed) to increase rapidly—which heightens the pressure on the organization and further encourages the adoption of quick fixes.

Reinforcing this kind of behavior is the fact that many people *enjoy* fire fighting! They regard it as more exciting than idly monitoring a smooth running operation, and they get a sense of accomplishment when they appear to have corrected a problem. Some organizations even encourage such fire fighting by recognizing and rewarding those who are regarded as unusually energetic and effective crisis managers. The contributions of those who prevent problems from occurring in the first place, however, are almost invisible.

Waste Removal

In its fullest sense, waste is anything that consumes resources but does not add value to a product or service. Therefore, it can take many forms,[23] the most obvious of which is a defective product that is discovered during processing or is returned by a dissatisfied customer. In addition to the wasted resources consumed in producing a defective product, even more waste accrues from having to create and manage a system for dealing with a high incidence of defects: assigning inspectors to make checks at various points along the process in the attempt to catch the defects before they progress too far, providing rework stations to correct those defects, and scheduling the production of more items than are really required in the expectation that some will be defective. Finally, if the product or service results in unhappy users, people must be assigned to deal with their complaints. In the attempt to retain their business, they may have to provide them with special treatment (including substitute—and sometimes, more expensive—products at the same price).

Other forms of waste include unnecessary process steps, such as compiling information that is never used,[24] duplicate efforts (as when one person or group is asked to verify the work done by another group), and errors in market forecasting, inventory measurement, and production planning/scheduling that lead to the production of the wrong items or amounts. Idle people and equipment are equally wasteful. Less obvious, but just as wasteful, are idle goods—work in progress that is waiting to be worked on. A related type of waste is unnecessary or needlessly long transport distances. Not only do movements of goods or people require labor and equipment time, they also cause WIP and throughput times to increase. Moreover, they complicate record keeping, scheduling, and supervision, all of which consume time and resources.

Waste fosters more waste. For example, more WIP means longer throughput times. As the time required to get through a process increases there is more opportunity for products to deteriorate and/or disappear (or, in service operations, for potential customers to defect), and it takes longer to identify the existence of processing problems and their contributory causes. Thus, defects tend to accumulate. Longer production lead times also make demand forecasting more difficult, further increasing the likelihood that excess or insufficient products will be produced.

Problem Analysis

Once a process is well understood and much of the waste removed, it becomes possible to identify, define, and document problems more accurately. The next step is to identify their underlying causes. Typically a team of people with different kinds of training and perspectives on the problem—from process engineers to quality assurance to line operators—are involved in this effort. A variety of techniques have been developed for isolating, characterizing, and getting to the root causes of problems, ranging from statistical to laboratory analyses. One of the best-known procedures is called "Asking the 5 Why's."[25] One starts with an observed symptom and asks why it arose. Once its immediate cause has been identified, one asks why that cause existed, and so on until—five levels down—the root causes of the problem are usually revealed.

Controlled Experimentation

After a problem has been identified, prioritized, and analyzed, people must decide on an appropriate corrective action. A number of possible ways to eliminate the problem or otherwise improve the process may be suggested, depending on the depth of the analysis and the number of people involved, and it may not be clear which is best. Identifying the best solution therefore often involves conducting a series of controlled experiments, using a Plan-Do-Check-Adjust[26] process. That is, a proposal for improving the process and an experiment for verifying its effectiveness are formulated (Plan), the experiment is carried out (Do), the actual result of the experiment is compared with the expected outcome (Check), and in light of this new information the problem is redefined and a new action proposed (Adjust). Over a series of such PDCA cycles, the cause(s) of the problem are slowly revealed and removed.

10.7 A FRAMEWORK FOR IMPROVEMENT ACTIVITIES, WITH TWO EXAMPLES

Returning to the description of different forms of learning outlined in Section 10.2.2, Table 10-3 attempts to place the different approaches we have discussed into a simple framework. It should be emphasized that the lines between the different sectors of this table are not "hard" ones. *Individual learning,* for example, could involve considerable study prior to trying something new, and *across group improvement* could conceivably result in a performance breakthrough. The table does attempt to capture, however, the following general contentions:

1. *Incremental improvements* are generally achieved through changes in—and by—what we referred to in Chapter 2 as an organization's infrastructure: its people, their values and behavior, and the systems and policies that affect their work.
2. *Breakthrough improvements* generally require (or at least emphasize) major structural changes, including equipment, facilities, sourcing, and

Table 10-3 Nature of Improvements Sought

Nature of knowledge base	Incremental/infrastructural	Breakthrough/structural
Tacit: Learning *by* Doing	(I) • Individual Learning • Within Group Improvement (e.g., *kaizen,* PDCA experiments, Total Quality Management, JIT)	(IV) Toyota Production System, Long-term "stretch" goals (e.g., Six Sigma improvement)
Explicit Learning *before* Doing	(II) *Across* Group Improvements; Benchmarking/best practices	(III) *Into* Group Improvements: Process reengineering, introducing an ERP system, World-class practices

organizational structure. In the long term, of course, consistent application of a powerful coherent philosophy, such as that embodied by the Toyota Production System or Six Sigma Quality, may over time lead to changes in structure as well as similar dramatic improvements.

3. *Learning by doing* generally is associated with incremental, within-group improvements, while transfers of improvements across groups generally require a substantial amount of explicit knowledge.
4. *Attempts to impose radically new approaches*—either following those learned from observing the practices of "World Class" companies, or from outside consultants and external providers of systems or technology—generally are formulated in advance of implementation (and so require explicit knowledge) and imposed on the organization with the expectation of a breakthrough improvement in performance.

With this classification in mind (which we will revisit in Chapter 11), we now turn to examine in detail two of the most prominent—and diametrically opposed—performance improvement approaches in use today: business process reengineering and total quality management.

10.7.1 Example A: Business Process Reengineering

One of the most widely adopted and publicized examples of the breakthrough approach has been *business process reengineering* (BPR). Although the idea of looking at a complex operating task as a whole and redesigning it "from scratch" dates back at least a hundred years to Frederick Taylor (and the application of the same concept to larger systems was inherent in the "systems analysis" that gained popularity during the 1960s), the term itself first became widely used only in the early 1990s.[27] By defining a "business process" as a collection of related activities that combine to create value, the application of this approach was expanded from traditional manufacturing and logistic processes to both services and clerical processes such as customer billing, accounts payable, and the scheduling of maintenance and repairs.

BPR proponents argued that most existing organizational structures and processes were designed at a time when critical business information was relatively difficult to obtain and slow to communicate throughout a large company. Such constraints induced companies to divide up complex, information-intensive activities into a series of specialized stages, each of which required only limited amounts of specific types of information and was assigned to a separate organizational entity. The result was an intricate and cumbersome collection of business subprocesses whose multiple steps often necessitated repeated transfers of information and materials from one organizational group to another. A hierarchical *command and control* management structure was then required to oversee and coordinate all these organizations and their activities. Only the top layers of management, as a result, had access to all information, which they tended to guard carefully.

As computer and communications technology evolved, however, information became relatively easy to obtain and transfer. BPR proponents asserted that this has made traditional organizational structures and the processes they engendered obsolete. They were inefficient, slow, unresponsive to shifts in customer needs, and resistant to change. BPR proponents suggested, therefore, that huge gains in performance—at least 25 percent and sometimes more than 100 percent—could be achieved if firms looked at their business processes afresh and redesigned them starting with a clean slate, combining "out of the box" thinking with a deep understanding of the sophisticated capabilities of modern information technology.[28] BPR, therefore, inherently seeks breakthrough improvements. Moreover, it assumes that the process being reengineered is understood well enough (enabling learning *before* doing) to be completely redesigned, and it encompasses all the organizational groups that participate in carrying out the whole process.

The Steps in a Reengineering Project

Different authors propose that somewhat different procedures be followed in a process reengineering project, but most include the following steps.

1. *Prioritization.* Identify one or more critical, high-impact organizational processes that offer the highest potential for substantial improvement and competitive impact. If low cost is the key to the company's strategy, then the processes selected should have a major impact on delivered cost; if fast delivery is key, then one should focus on processes that offer the highest potential for reducing throughput and delivery times. High priority also should be placed on eliminating the impediments to the process imposed by the company's existing organizational structure—which often represents the ossified vestiges of decisions made years before when the company's technology, strategy, and competitive context were very different. As described above, other prime candidates for reengineering are processes whose existing design is largely the result of the limitations of outdated information technologies. Vastly increasing the accessibility of information and the speed with which it can be transmitted from one step to the next often may allow one to completely restructure the process.
2. *Cross-organizational initiatives.* Since looking at a business process as a whole—from the initiation of a request to the delivery of the desired product or service to the ultimate customer—usually cuts across functional or other organizational boundaries, BPR requires across-group improvements. Therefore, it is essential that senior managers provide their full commitment and support. Not only must they authorize the often-substantial resources (including key people's time) required to carry out extensive studies and implement the reengineered process, they must be willing to deal with the organizational pain associated with moving selected activities out from under the control of existing organizational units and placing them under the direction of a new "process owner."
3. *Broad-based teams.* Although outside advisers and specialists in various aspects of the process may be included as needed, the core of a process improvement team ought to be company employees who not only are

actively involved with the process but cover its entire scope. If possible, the "customer" of the process—the person or group that receives the process output, whether internal or external to the company—should be included on the team. In addition to having the skills and time necessary to carry out the project, the team needs to have the authority (or the ability to secure that authority from top management in a timely manner) to make decisions and allocate resources.

4. *Process measurement and analysis.* Having decided, in consultation with customers and top management, which aspects of the process are most in need of improvement, the team needs to develop quantitative measures of the most critical dimensions of process performance. Such measures depend on the situation, but generally include not only the process's *efficacy* (that is, its ability to accomplish the required task) and the *efficiency* with which it utilizes resources, but also its *speed, quality, flexibility,* and *dependability.* Some of these measures may already be available through internal company reports—although the adequacy of such measures needs to be carefully checked—while others may have to be developed from scratch. Then the process should be thoroughly analyzed and a process flow diagram created to chart the sequence of activities that currently comprise it.
5. *Identification and removal of waste.* Step 5, along with Steps 3 and 4, have much in common with the corresponding steps in the incremental improvement process described in Section 10.6.2.
6. *Think "outside the box."* Once the waste in an existing process has been stripped away, so that its core activities are clearly revealed, the team is asked to "step outside" the existing process and imagine how it could be accomplished if one sat down and tried to design it with a fresh piece of paper and access to the latest information technology. The goal should be radical change leading to significant improvements in the most critical performance measures, so this step requires lots of time, and imagination. Data about possible alternative processes must be collected and analyzed, the problems associated with each must be identified and resolved, and issues of implementation must be surfaced.
7. *Plan of action.* A cohesive action plan must be developed and presented effectively to top management, and approval secured for the resources necessary to implement it.

Reengineering Failures

The logic and eloquence of its initial proponents, the early examples of its apparently successful application in several well-known companies, and the enthusiastic support of the management consulting industry (which saw in it the potential for a profitable new line of business), fostered a bandwagon effect that swept through U.S. industry in the early 1990s. Hundreds of companies initiated attempts at process reengineering, driven by top managers and enlisting the assistance of thousands of consultants, experts in information technology, and change facilitators. Many of these efforts appear to have been successful in achieving the kind of results that were anticipated. However, one study of more than a 100 reengineering projects reported an overall failure rate of about two-thirds, and that "most process reengineering efforts have in fact had little measurable impact on the overall business unit";[29] another study of 150 companies reported no "compensatory long-term benefits" from all the turmoil such efforts caused.[30]

Almost all reengineering projects, moreover, have experienced substantial—and sometimes fatal—organizational resistance. Companies often found that they did not really have sufficient understanding of their business processes to apply the "learning before doing" approach, and that a more experimental approach was more appropriate. In addition, employees complained that they essentially were being asked to critique their own jobs and possibly, as a result, put themselves out of work. Making things worse, they were being observed, interrogated, and "assisted" by droves of outsiders (many of them young and inexperienced, even though they often were paid more than the company's own people), who then took credit for any performance improvements that resulted—sometimes over the employees' eliminated bodies. This resistance and its associated decline in employee morale, coupled with inflated top management expectations, led to the dramatic failure of many process engineering efforts.[31] US West, for example, reportedly spent almost $300 million on a reengineering project that took longer and produced less improvement than anticipated. This disappointing result led to the departure of a number of high-ranking managers as well as other organizational changes.[32]

These numerous and well-publicized failures provided the incentive for reengineering proponents to engage in a period of soul searching, followed by another series of books and articles explaining why the failures had occurred and proposing the changes that should be made when attempting to implement BPR.[33] In the meantime, the business press and corporate management had shifted their attention to a *new* "big idea" for completely restructuring a company's operations: Enterprise Resource Planning. ERP, as described in Chapter 6, seeks to establish a common database for all of a company's worldwide information (e.g., product codes, customers, employees, suppliers, etc.) and prescribe standard procedures for financial reporting, billing customers, scheduling production, and so on. This turned out to be an even more expensive undertaking, and an even bigger business opportunity for consulting firms. The long-term effectiveness of these ERPs is still unclear, and several disastrous experiences have been widely reported. For example, Dell Computer reportedly pulled the plug on its purchased ERP system after spending two years and $200 million on it.[34] A study of more than 100 large-scale ERP initiatives published in 2000 by one consulting firm (BCG) indicated that only about a third were considered successful.[35]

10.7.2 Example B: Total Quality Management (TQM)

The total quality management movement gained impetus in the U.S. and other countries in the early 1980s as managers came to realize that the success of Japanese-made products was based to a large extent on their reliability and freedom from defects. These competitively significant differences could not (as first thought) be attributed to the supposed advantages associated with operating in Japan, such as low labor and interest costs, government subsidies, and societal attitudes and modes of behavior. Nor were they due to the adoption of a few simple practices, such as quality circles. Instead, the Japanese quality advantage appeared to be the result of a complex, interrelated set of practices, attitudes, and techniques that had largely been learned from U.S. managers and consultants in the 1950s and then adapted, refined, and improved over the following three decades.[36] Moreover, the philosophy and methodologies underlying TQM could be transplanted to other countries. The essence of the TQM philosophy was that major improvements in process effectiveness could result from a continuous series of incremental efforts, largely undertaken within individual operating groups, directed towards identifying and removing all sources of process variation.

As this realization spread, and quality became recognized as an increasingly important basis of competition, hundreds of companies jumped on the quality bandwagon. This movement was given further credibility and support by the institution of official quality awards in various countries, such as The Deming Prize (by Japan's Union of Scientists & Engineers), The Malcolm Baldrige Quality Award (by the U.S. Department of Commerce), and The European Quality Award. Similar awards have been created by a number of other countries, as well as several state governments in the United States. In addition, the International Standards Organization instituted its ISO 9000 standards, with the initial aim of identifying reliable suppliers by establishing clear quality standards and requiring detailed documentation of their processes and procedures.

As with process reengineering, various authors provide different lists of the key "steps" in a TQM program, which largely overlap those described in Section 10.6.2 in connection with Incremental Improvement. In addition, organizations are advised to:

Focus on the Long-term

Changing attitudes and practices takes a long time, as does integrating all the programs that attack different sources of quality problems (including work practices, equipment, suppliers, product designs, and operating complexity and confusion) into a cohesive whole. Not only must the organization address these problems directly, it also must support TQM initiatives indirectly through training programs, measurement and incentive systems, organizational structures, and managerial styles. The ultimate goal is the elimination of all defects, which some companies have operationalized as "Six Sigma" quality: reducing the percentage of defects to under 3.4 per million (which represents the probability that a Normally distributed random variable falls more than three standard deviations above or below its mean value).

Base Decisions on Facts and Analyses

Nothing can be improved until it is measured. Identifying problems and their magnitudes, assessing the impact of various possible sources of process problems and/or variation, and estimating the effect of possible countermeasures all require careful data collection and analysis. To this end, as mentioned earlier, a number of quantitative tools are available, including Pareto and Fishbone diagrams, statistical analyses, process control charts, and robust experimental designs.[37]

Listen to the Voice of the Customer

Quality must be defined in terms of what customers truly need, and it must reflect *all* aspects of the company's interaction with its customers. This means that delivering a defect-free product or service is not enough. One must deliver it when the customer wants it, furnish adequate instruction and support in using it, provide accurate and timely bills, and offer satisfactory after sale services.

Involve the Entire Company

The people who know most about a process are the people who work with it on a daily basis. They should be given "ownership" over it, which includes not only operating it effectively but also the responsibility for identifying the sources of the major problems being experienced and proposing corrective actions. To carry out these responsibilities, they must be given appropriate training, sufficient time to perform them properly, supportive systems and managers, and adequate resources (including specialized assistance).

Senior managers need to support all these initiatives, as well as encourage the application of TQM principles in all corporate functions and activities. Moreover, they must "walk the talk"—applying the same principles to their own work and consistently reinforcing the idea that quality improvement is the company's top priority.

TQM Failures

Unfortunately, as with reengineering, TQM has engendered considerable controversy and apparently failed to meet the expectations of the majority of the western companies that have embraced it. Surveys by several consulting firms suggest that only about one-third of all TQM efforts have been successful.[38] One study suggests, in fact, that TQM programs have had little impact on operating performance, even though they do seem to lead to improved customer satisfaction (probably because of their emphasis on getting direct feedback and suggestions from customers).[39] On the other hand, other studies concluded that companies that "have made serious efforts to implement TQM system" and/or won quality awards tended to achieve somewhat better financial performance and higher increases in stock prices than companies that didn't.[40] Still another study of more than a thousand Australian and New Zealand manufacturing facilities suggested that, while TQM programs did seem to improve operating performance, most of this improvement apparently came from the "soft" elements just described: top management leadership, listening to the voice of the customer, and employee involvement. The "harder" elements, such as process analysis, fact-based analysis, and continuous improvement appeared to have less effect on ultimate performance.[41] Similar controversies surround other types of incremental improvement programs, from reducing inventories to improving new product development processes.

10.7.3 Comparing Business Process Reengineering and TQM

As one examines the steps involved in both process reengineering and TQM programs, they appear to have much in common. They both, for example, focus on process improvement and emphasize the importance of top management support, getting the perspective of customers, setting priorities, and basing measurement and analysis on quantitative data. The spirit of TQM is much different, however, particularly in its emphasis on delegating primary responsibility to the people who work with a process (not outside consultants), on improving existing processes rather than replacing them with entirely new processes, and on pursuing long-term goals through small steps rather than major leaps. Finally, while both approaches seek improvement efforts that span functional/organizational boundaries, process reengineering attempts to achieve this integration through a "grand plan" (learning before doing), while TQM typically employs learning by doing to encourage improvement—often self-directed—throughout the organization. These fundamental differences in philosophies and approaches often have resulted in warring camps at organizations that chose to undertake both types of programs at the same time. At American Express, for example, it is reported that the debate was paralyzing the organization until the senior executive in charge of reengineering redefined it using quality terminology.[42]

Our discussions of these two different approaches to organizational improvement have another important common thread: both approaches have experienced high failure rates. Sometimes they fail quickly; more often they appear to succeed at first but then experience diminishing results. By contrast, both approaches have been successfully applied in many companies. In the next chapter we will step back and examine some of the basic causes of failures in operations improvement efforts—many of which operate, to various degrees, no matter which kind of approach to improvement is followed. We then discuss how these reasons for failure can be overcome through the adoption of an effective strategy for improvement by a management group that is committed to its implementation.

10.8 ORGANIZATIONAL IMPLICATIONS OF DIFFERENT APPROACHES

In the previous section, we proposed a simple 2 × 2 framework (Table 10-3) for thinking about the different mechanisms that drive organizational improvement. Theoretically, initiating activities in any of the four quadrants of Table 10-3 will lead to a higher level of operating performance over time, so on what basis should a company decide to emphasize one or another? One might think that, rather than having to make such a choice, a company ought to make use of all of them simultaneously. Each, however, places different demands on an organization and exposes it to different kinds of issues. As a result, a company's choice of any one of them as its preferred approach to improvement can have dramatic implications for the kind of systems, people, and organization needed to support that choice, as described in the following sections, and these different organizational mechanisms can come into conflict.

10.8.1 *Quadrants I & IV:* Incremental Improvement/Learning *By* Doing

Activities in these two quadrants are very much in the spirit of the *kaizen* approach pioneered by Japanese companies. Although such improvement activities may appear haphazard and uncoordinated to an outside observer, they often demonstrate a remarkable coherence and effectiveness. The most successful ones are marked by a common philosophy of improvement, and driven by continual management pressure. Sustained pressure, by itself, is not sufficient, however. Real sustainability requires that management surround such improvement activities with the kind of supporting activities and policies described in Section 10.6.2.

10.8.2 *Quadrant II:* Transferring Incremental Improvement Across Organizations

We discussed in Section 10.3.2 the difficulties associated with transferring superior methods developed by one group to other parts of an organization. Unfortunately, as described in Chapter 7, encouraging each group to develop and implement its own improvement projects actually can make such transfers even more difficult, because groups then tend to take pride of ownership in the methods they develop. If they then are asked to adopt the methods developed by another group, their own efforts, in effect, are disparaged. Companies that have been successful in making such transfers generally appear to use variants and combinations of three integrative approaches:

1. Transferring people
2. Communicating information about best practices
3. Establishing centers of excellence

Transferring People

People often are moved from one group to another as part of their training or professional development program, or because one group's workload is decreasing while another needs more people. In either case, the movement of people is unlikely to have much impact on the receiving group's performance. But sometimes people are moved (usually temporarily) with the specific intent of facilitating performance improvement. Either people are transferred from better performing units as teachers (one hopes, of course, that the performance of *both* units doesn't improve as a result!), or into better performing units so that they can learn from the best.

Unfortunately, if too extensive, such transfers can conflict with the maintenance of the stable human resources that facilitate within group improvement.

Japanese companies are often cited for their ability to balance these somewhat competing needs. When setting up a factory in another country, they often train their new workers by bringing them back to Japan to work in sister factories.[43] Other companies, in contrast, rely on a particularly powerful functional group to transfer ideas for improvement. For example, the corporate accounting group at Molex, Inc. (a company that produces electronic connectors in more than thirty countries) routinely rotates young accountants through several of its international subsidiaries as part of its training program. These people, who must measure and report performance results, are in a good position to identify practices that lead to superior results.

Communicating Information about Best Practices

Some companies carefully seek out and study their best performing units in an attempt to identify the practices that led to their success. Then they orchestrate corporate seminars or group visits from other units in the attempt to encourage them to adopt these methods. A few companies have set up in-house consulting groups to facilitate the process of identifying and transferring best practices to units that request their assistance. Other companies, rather than specifically drawing attention to their best units, simply organize regular meetings of representatives from similar groups (e.g., quality assurance, manufacturing engineering, human resource management) across the company to meet and compare notes.

Establishing Centers of Excellence

Other companies have sought to encourage the development of superior practices by asking different operating units to assume responsibility for becoming the corporate leader for a specific activity. For example, one plant might be asked to become the corporate *Center of Excellence (CoE)* for plastic molding, another to become the CoE for just-in-time scheduling, and so on. By getting each unit to focus its energies on a limited set of tasks, the hope is that it will both be able to make more progress than it would if it attempted to improve all of its operations simultaneously, and also avoid reinventing the wheel. Each CoE then has the responsibility for reporting its results to the other units within its group and helping them adopt the improvements it has pioneered.

10.8.3 *Quadrant III:* Breakthrough Improvement through Strategic Leaps

As described earlier, breakthrough improvements are likely to require major expenditures of funds and people's time. A great deal of staff involvement is required, and the expertise of many highly specialized people—financial analysts, strategic planners, legal experts, scientists, outside consultants, and/or public relations personnel—may have to be tapped. Because of the magnitude of the funds required to implement a strategic leap, the timing of such changes becomes important. A decline in profits, an increase in interest rates, an unexpectedly attractive alternative use of funds (such as a potential acquisition), the sudden departure of a key project champion or expert, or a sudden surge of orders that pushes the whole organization to the limit of its resources—all can delay the project or "put it on hold."

On one hand, being highly visible, the people or groups proposing and/or leading such efforts tend to be exposed to a considerable amount of risk. On the other hand, those who succeed become heroes. As a result, the people who rise to the top of companies that rely primarily on strategic leaps tend to be one of two very different types. Some are those who successfully conceived and/or implemented two or three of these major leaps during their careers (the "lucky gamblers"), and who thus have an exaggerated sense of their skill and ability to control events. This tends to make them instinctively supportive of new proposals for radical change. Many of the others are those (primarily corporate staff) who were able to avoid being associated with any major failures—and are therefore highly averse to change in general.

Such leaps require great top management involvement, but they do not usually require outstanding, highly trained people lower down in the organization. Their job is simply to operate the structure that top management and its staff specialists have created for them. Training and upgrading workers or lower-level managers is not particularly useful because their newly developed skills may be made obsolete by the next strategic leap (to a new location, market, or technology, say). Nor are personnel policies that reward employee longevity particularly desirable. They are felt to reduce the company's flexibility—its ability to pull up stakes and move to a new location, to sell the business, or to make a significant reduction in employment because of a major automation or reengineering program.

Similarly, it is not necessary for operators or lower-level managers to have a detailed understanding of how their own operation affects, and is affected by, other parts of the organization, because these relationships may change entirely during the next major transition. Employee suggestion programs are not particularly useful for the same reason: line workers cannot possibly understand how their proposed changes would support, or possibly undermine, the company's overall strategy (much less the next major leap it is contemplating), and they lack the skills or expertise required to develop ideas for meaningful changes.

Finally, strong process engineering skills, especially at the facility level, are not essential since the major changes in processing technology that occur are likely to be acquired from the outside. As a result, such improvements often are associated with the introduction of major new products or lines of business that necessitate *replacing* substantial portions of the existing process (requiring a major investment of corporate funds) rather than *upgrading* an existing process. Since ongoing improvements are not expected, the only local engineering inputs required are largely of a maintenance or sustaining nature.

10.8.4 *Quadrant IV:* Breakthrough Improvement through Sustained Incremental Efforts

Most companies sooner or later encounter substantial problems when attempting to follow an improvement strategy that seeks major advances in performance primarily through incremental steps. Some of the reasons for this will be discussed in Chapter 11, where we focus on the organizational implications of this approach, but another is primarily psychological in nature. Baldly put, incremental progress is regarded as *boring* by many people. It requires the mentality of marathoners or long distance swimmers: one must keep concentrating on doing relatively simple things over and over for long periods of time. *Forever,* in fact, because (as a famous Nike advertisement put it) "There is no finish line."

This makes it difficult for many companies to maintain ongoing commitment to incremental improvement throughout their organizations. It is particularly difficult to maintain the enthusiasm and energy of top managers, because this kind of improvement strategy does not create *heroes*—and the visibility, admiration, and financial rewards that go along with being a hero. In a fundamental sense, then, pursuing incremental improvement runs counter to the basic mentality of western managers who have been raised in cultures that revere heroes, leaders able to snatch victory from the jaws of apparent defeat—through end runs (such as General McArthur's famous landing at Inchon during the Korean War), ninth inning home runs, and goals made just as the clock runs out. Business journalists (as well as business school casewriters) glorify such heroics, just as sports journalists glorified Joe DiMaggio and Michael Jordan. Stories about marathon winners, by comparison, usually receive relatively little visibility.

Moreover, incremental improvement requires lots of low-level expertise—that is, expertise *at* low levels in the operations organization, not low levels *of* expertise. Developing this kind of expertise is a long process. Great effort must be spent on recruiting workers and managers who are both loyal and amenable to long periods of training. Once hired, these people's capabilities must continually be improved and expanded, through both formal education programs and job assignments that provide a broad understanding of the company's products, processes, and competitive environment. Top management must work to augment this understanding and keep it current by disseminating information about customers, market trends, new technologies, current financial results, and the activities of competitors. Firms that adopt a focused, long-term incremental improvement approach must therefore develop the kind of managers who can stimulate and facilitate this kind of progress, resource allocation systems that support it, compensation and promotion systems that encourage it, and measurement systems that can track it. The great advantage of such systems, as discussed in Chapter 2, is that since home-grown capabilities take a long time to develop, and are therefore difficult to imitate, they can provide a sustained competitive advantage.

Finally, once this investment in low-level expertise has been made, it is important to retain within the company the people who possess it. Long-time employees have another advantage: over time, through their multiple job assignments they develop personal relationships with people in different parts of the organization. These relationships make it easier to implement small changes that require close communication between, and the cooperation of, several different groups. This is important because such changes are typically so small and require so little capital that senior managers and their staffs seldom get involved in implementing or coordinating them. Line managers tend to be more supportive of such efforts if they are intimately familiar with their processes and people, so can understand the value of such changes and anticipate enjoying their benefits over time. Similarly, operators, engineers, and lower-level managers are more likely to support and participate in suggestion programs, quality circles, and the like, if they can equate the organization's long term success with their own.

10.8.5 The Risks of Different Approaches

BPR and TQM illustrate two highly contrasting approaches to improvement. Few companies confine their efforts to either extreme, of course; most prefer to adopt different approaches along the broad spectrum between them in different situations. However, as alluded to earlier, the "get rich quick" mentality that characterized the end of the twentieth century, together with the financial rewards and visibility that accrue to managers who are able to achieve major advances in performance, subtly encourages most companies to focus on strategic leaps. The business press has contributed to this glorification of breakthroughs, to the point where western companies today appear to place relatively little emphasis on seeking incremental improvements within their existing structures and technologies.

That may help explain why a nation that was capable of putting a man on the moon and inventing genetic engineering is seemingly incapable of producing a more defect-free car than Toyota. The reason most U.S. companies don't try to make a more defect-free car than Toyota is because we *can* put a man on the moon! The same skills and managerial psychology that enable an organization to conceive and carry out breakthrough projects may hamper it in a competitive environment where success is based more on a series of small steps than on a few dramatic breakthroughs.

Unlike the hare in Aesop's fable, however, the companies competing in the New World Economy find themselves pitted against not one, but dozens of tortoises. In that fable, of course, the tortoise won the race. Is this likely to happen to business hares as well? To answer that question, let us examine the risks of each approach. The great risk of the incremental approach is being leapfrogged (to mix our metaphors) by a competitor that abandons its traditional technology, location, or corporate strategy and adopts a new and more successful one. The folklore of business is full of such examples: vacuum tubes being replaced by transistors, traditional cameras by digital cameras, general-purpose department stores by *category killers* (e.g., Toys 'R' Us, Home Depot, and Staples) that target specific markets; the list goes on and on.

Conversely, the great risk of the strategic leap approach is that a new breakthrough may not be available exactly when it is needed. That is, after seizing a major competitive advantage, a company may see it nibbled away by competitors that gradually adapt themselves to the new technology or strategy and then push it beyond the limits the first company was able to achieve. This happened, for example, to the U.S. producers of DRAMs and videotape recorders in the 1980s, and is apparently what UPS is doing to Federal Express in the package delivery business today.[44] That is when the company would like to take another major leap forward. But what if its laboratories and strategy departments cannot provide a breakthrough on demand?

An obvious response in such an eventuality is for the company to adopt an incremental approach until a breakthrough does become possible. But this is not easy for a firm that has configured itself around the expectation of repeated breakthroughs, as it bears little resemblance to one that takes the incremental approach. Managers and workers have different skills, instincts, and psychological mind-sets.

The reverse, however, is not true. Companies that adopt an incremental approach are not precluded from eventually accommodating themselves to a major change. Many of the skills and resources required to implement strategic leaps can be acquired from outside experts and organizations. Whereas it might take a decade or more to build a loyal, experienced, and broadly trained workforce, one can hire a consulting firm in a day and license a new technology in a matter of weeks. In other words, the ability to make progress through incremental change does not preclude a firm's ability to master a major change, although it may slow it down.

This, then, provides another, and somewhat sobering, perspective on the problems that many firms are facing in today's unforgiving competitive world. In the fable, the tortoise won the race simply because the hare fell asleep, just as many U.S. companies and industries fell asleep prior to the onslaught of foreign competitors in the 1980s. Today the nature of the problem is somewhat different: in most mature "Old Economy" industries the development of markets and technologies tends to move forward in a steady, almost predictable manner, along established trajectories—what Thomas Kuhn referred to as "normal science."[45] Even in such high-technology industries as semiconductors, computers, and biotech, the progress of the early 2000s is taking place within technological frameworks that essentially were established decades earlier. Consider, for example, "Moore's Law," which states that I.C. density and speed should double roughly every 18–24 months. First proposed by Intel's Gordon Moore in the mid-1960s, it still (in slightly modified form) operates today. In a world where dozens of hungry competitors from around the world are contesting mature markets, the opportunities for dramatic breakthroughs may be fewer than before.[46]

Situations still arise, of course, where a strategic leap is called for. For example, in the last two decades of the twentieth century huge new labor pools and potential markets in China, Eastern Europe, and Latin America became available to Western companies. Satellite communications and the Internet opened up new ways to communicate with suppliers, customers, and partners, as well as with one's own employees. Genetic engineering, the sequencing of the human genome (as well as those of related organisms), and new approaches for analyzing proteins, opened up a new world of possibilities for diagnosing and treating disease.

Yet even in the presence of such discontinuities, strategic "end runs" are not easy to make—as witnessed by the disappointingly slow results experienced by companies that made major investments in Russia and China, and the failures of many "dot-com" companies that sought to radically restructure markets and supply chains. Today's sophisticated multinational companies have been quick to exploit the emerging new markets and pools of low cost labor in the world, as well as the astonishing new developments in biotech and IT. In a world where opportunities for major leaps are fleeting, companies probably are going to have to rely on incremental methods for the bulk of their improvement. In today's competitive swamp, a hare's leaping ability may not help it win races against a bunch of tortoises.

NOTES

1. Stata (1989), written when he was CEO of Analog Devices, Inc.

2. The first systematic studies of the dynamic nature of manufacturing costs occurred in the 1920s (see Rohrbach, 1927; and Wright, 1936). Analyses of the hours required to assemble a given airframe for the Army Air Corps over several years revealed significant reductions in the amount of labor required. Comparing direct labor hours required per unit of production to cumulative units revealed a relationship that was called first the "manufacturing progress function" and later the "learning curve." For more information about the history of learning curves, see Dutton et al. (1984), which also contains a set of references up through about 1982; more recent references can be found in Sinclair et al. (1996). See also Hirschmann (1964).

3. For example, when b =.152, unit cost falls by 10 percent with each doubling of cumulative production; for b = .322 it falls by 20 percent, and for b = .515 it falls by 30 percent. See the appendix to this chapter.

4. Pisano et al. (2001).

5. For another perspective on this issue, see Kim (1993).

6. Although the benefits of such specialization (usually referred to as "the division of labor") were known long before Adam Smith's time, his assertion that a group of workers, each of whom specialized in one step in the manufacture of pins, could produce far more pins in a day than could the same number of workers who each made the whole pin, is the starting point for much economic theorizing about the phenomenon. Although Smith's assertion has been accepted almost without question for over two centuries, recent evidence, as discussed later, suggests that if the division of labor is carried too far it can actually *reduce* productivity.

7. Sinclair et al. (1996), for example, studied the cost reductions achieved over a 30-month period in 221 products produced by one major specialty chemical manufacturer, and found that the primary factor influencing their rates of improvement over that period was the amount of process R&D conducted.

8. Stata (1989).

9. See "The high performance factory," chapter 6 in Hayes et al. (1988).

10. Christensen (1998) provides a history of the evolution of disk drive technology, as well as examples of similar behavior in other industries.

11. As Grover and Malhotra (1997) eloquently phrased it: "Traditional organizational forms reflect [the division of labor], whether … applied to processing insurance forms or to manufacturing a product. With time, functions, positions and specialists proliferated, as did bureaucracy and the rules to handle increasing contingencies. Along with growth in rules, tasks and complexity was the pyramid management structure needed to put all the pieces together. The problem is that many companies are paying more for the glue than for the real work."

12. Ibid.

13. See Hayes et al. (1988); also, Chew et al. (1990).

14. Bartelsman and Doms (2000) provide a summary of these studies.

15. The well-known "Not Invented Here" syndrome is explored further in Katz and Allen (1982).

16. See Spear and Bowen (1999), who refer to these practices as "artifacts" of TPS's underlying philosophy.

17. See "Daewoo Shipbuilding and Heavy Machinery," and "Samsung Heavy Industries: The Koje Shipyard," case studies 21 and 22 in Upton (1998).

18. A book by the same name (Imai, 1986), has become the standard reference.

19. Edmondson (1999), for example, has measured the effect of team members' sense of "psychological safety" on team learning.

20. See "Toyota Motor Manufacturing, U.S.A., Inc." (HBS case #9-693-019).

21. Imai (1986) and Mizuno (1988) describe these techniques in more detail.

22. Bohn (2000) provides a fuller description of the mentalities and dangers of the fire fighting syndrome.

23. Shigeo Shingo lists the "classic seven wastes" as overproduction, waiting, transportation, unnecessary processing steps, inventory, motion, and defects; see Hall (1987).

24. As Peter Drucker (1988) put it, "There is nothing more useless than to do efficiently that which doesn't have to be done at all!"

25. "Asking 'Why' 5 Times" describe the process somewhat more accurately.

26. The final A usually denotes "Act," but this is sometimes confused with "Do," while "Adjust" captures the actual meaning somewhat better.

27. One of the earliest and most influential publications was "Reengineering Work: Don't Automate, Obliterate" by Hammer (1990); a similar message was conveyed in "The new industrial engineering: information technology and business process redesign" by Davenport and Short (1990), which appeared about the same time.

28. The following definition, proposed by a leading practitioner, captures the essence of process reengineering: "A methodological process that uses information technology to radically overhaul business process and thereby attain major business goals." See Grover et al. (1993).

29. Hall et al. (1993).

30. Thiagarajan and Balachandran (1999).

31. See, for example, Hall et al. (1993).

32. See "Reengineering Repercussions" by J. King (1993).

33. With titles such as *Reengineering Management: The Mandate for New Leadership* (Champy, 1995), and *Beyond Reengineering* (Hammer, 1996).

34. Similarly, Nike's CEO, Phil Knight, upon reviewing the results of its new Supply Chain Management system is reported to have asked incredulously, "Is This What I Get for My $400 million?" See "Return on Investment," *CIO Magazine* (August 15, 2002): 75–76.

35. "Boston Consulting Group (BCG) Study Finds Widespread Dissatisfaction Among Decision-making Executives," March 21, 2000; see BCG's Web site: www.bcg.com.

36. For different perspectives on the evolution and characteristics of the quality movements in the United States and Japan, see Cole (1998), Garvin (1988), and Hayes et al. (1988, chapter 2).

37. See Imai (1986), Juran (1988), Mizuno (1988), and Ryan (1989).

38. See Ernst & Young et. al (1992) and Burrows (1992). Cole (1998) and "The Cracks In Quality," *The Economist* (April 18, 1992): 67–68, summarize several of these studies and the conclusions to be drawn from them.

39. See Choi and Eboch (1998).

40. See Easton and Jarrell (1998) and Hendricks and Singhal (2001).

41. See Dow et al. (1999).

42. See Caldwell (1994).

43. Also described in "Toyota Motor Manufacturing, U.S.A., Inc." (HBS case # 9-693-019).

44. See "Ground Wars: UPS's rapid ascent leaves FedEx scrambling," *BusinessWeek* (May 21, 2000): 64–68.

45. In his seminal book (1956) *The Structure of Scientific Revolutions.*

46. For another perspective on this issue, see Christensen (1998). He argues that many industries are vulnerable to "disruptive technologies," which he differentiates from major improvements to an industry's current dominant technology. A disruptive technology appears initially to offer no (indeed, often negative) benefits to existing customers but finds a market among a different set of users, and is able to sustain improvements in performance that allow it, over time, to rise to match or surpass the capabilities of the current dominant technology.

Appendix

10A.1 CALCULATING LEARNING CURVES

As described in Section 10.2.1, the mathematical equation describing the classical learning curve is:

$$h(n) = an^{-b} \quad \text{(10A-1)}$$

where

n = cumulative production count, beginning with the first unit

$h(n)$ = direct labor hours required to product the nth unit

a = a parameter representing the labor hours required to produce the "first" unit

b = a parameter that measures the rate at which $h(n)$ decreases as n increases.

Because learning curves are frequently stated in terms of the percent reduction in labor associated with each *doubling* of cumulative volume, it is useful to consider a specific form of the learning curve relationship:

$$h(2n)/h(n) = a(2n)^{-b}/an^{-b} = (2)^{-b} \quad \text{(10A-2)}$$

where n again is the number of units produced up to some *prior* point in time, and $2n$ is the number of units produced up to the *current* point in time. This demonstrates that the exponent b in equations (10A-1) and (10A-2) can be directly related to the rate of learning that characterizes each doubling of production. Representative values of the exponent b and the corresponding rate of learning are listed in Table 10A-1.

When the labor hours for a specific unit of production are not easy to measure, the *average* unit labor hours can be used instead. This is due to the fact that as n increases, the average number of labor hours required to produce n units asymptotically approaches

$$h_{avg}(n) \cong \Sigma\, h(n)/n = an^{-b}/(1 - b) \quad \text{(10A-3)}$$

Notice that the exponent of n in this equation (which again equals the slope of the curve when plotted on log-log paper) is the same value as in Equation (10A-1), which describes the labor hours required to produce an incremental unit.

Predicting the future labor hours (or cost) of a given product usually is done by estimating the slope of the curve that most closely fits its historical cost behavior over time. There are two commonly used methods for estimating the rate of learning. The first is simply an informal graphical method: visually fitting a straight line through the actual data plotted on log-log paper. In many instances, the approximate

Table 10A-1 The Exponent *b* and the Rate of Learning

b (Exponent value)	Rate of learning (Labor hours for item 2*n,* as a percent of those for item *n*)
0.000	100
0.074	95
0.152	90
0.235	85
0.322	80
0.415	75
0.515	70
0.623	65
0.738	60

For example, in an 80 percent learning curve, $h(2n)/h(n) = 0.8$, which equals $2.0^{-.322}$.

results so obtained are sufficiently accurate for management planning. In other cases, the amount of data available and the need for greater accuracy may dictate the use of a more formal statistical line-fitting technique, such as regression analysis.

This estimated curve can then be used to plan future labor requirements, given anticipated volumes of production. Such forecasts may be based, in part, on an analysis of the learning curves observed in connection with other related products. They also, however, require considerable subjective judgment. A description of the wide range in learning rates observed in studies of different industries is provided in Dutton and Thomas (1984).

10A.2 USING EXPERIENCE CURVES IN DEVELOPING A COMPETITIVE STRATEGY

Although many companies have successfully pursued a learning curve-based strategy of cost-reduction, to be effective such a strategy must be buttressed with other elements. These include:

1. *Aggressive pricing,* often in *anticipation* of expected cost reductions; this both encourages the growth of the market and seeks to discourage new companies from entering—enabling one to move down the learning curve faster than competitors;
2. *Relentless process improvement*—faster than competitors; and
3. *Sufficient financial resources* to support the negative cash flows during the early years, during which the company needs to expand production well in advance of demand while investing aggressively in process improvements.

Most companies, however, reject learning curve-based strategies. Those in mature industries seldom see sufficient opportunities for dramatic cost improvement through increasing cumulative volume faster than their competitors. Others simply decide, for one or both of two reasons, that total dedication to moving down the learning curve is not the primary means through which they wish to seek a competitive advantage. The first reason is that pursuit of competitive advantage through aggressive cost reduction requires a market environment that allows one to maintain a dominant position (and therefore a continuing cost advantage) once it is achieved. Small specialized firms that focus all their attention on specific market segments, however, may be able to take sales away from a firm that is pursuing a high-volume strategy. Often they are just as profitable as large, broad-product-line firms. Second, they may prefer to attract customers by establishing superiority on a competitive dimension other than cost (the approach adopted by General Motors when it successfully attacked Ford's Model T, as described in Chapter 11).

Two of the most frequently cited examples of companies that have followed an innovation (as opposed to an efficiency) strategy with reasonable success are Apple Computer and Sony. Both have chosen to seek their primary competitive advantage through developing innovative, top-of-the-line products. Such a strategy requires that one's manufacturing organization be highly flexible, since one is likely to change or replace products sooner than would a company that pursues a cost minimization strategy. In addition, it tends to put more emphasis on new product R&D and pursues an umbrella pricing strategy in the early stages of a product's life cycle. Rather than continually lowering prices simply to build volume, an innovation strategy seeks a substantial return on the product's initial investment early in its life so that funds will be available for developing new products. A cost minimization strategy, in contrast, tends to require longer paybacks on investments, with benefits coming after the product matures and after the firm has a dominant market and cost position in the industry. As pointed out in Chapter 2, whether a firm follows a strategy based on efficiency, innovation, or some other criterion, it needs to tailor the key tasks and skills of its people to the express needs of that strategy.

Chapter 11

Guiding the Pursuit of an Operations Edge

11.1 INTRODUCTION

In today's increasingly cutthroat and rapidly changing world, relentless competitive pressures require ever-higher levels of performance. Healthy survivors know that they must continually strive to sharpen their operating edge—in costs, quality, delivery, speed, or flexibility. In this environment, the key to *sustainable* success lies not just in how good an organization is, but in how fast it is getting better. In the previous chapter (Section 10.3.1) we summarized some of the various ways through which a business organization can surpass the physical and mental limitations of any single human being, as well as those apparently imposed by existing personnel, technologies, materials, competitors, and regulations. These include increasing the scale of their operations and exploiting the resulting static and dynamic economies, designing more effective facility networks, adopting and making the most of new product, process, and information technologies, managing projects faster and more effectively, and institutionalizing a program of operating improvements. All these various activities—the subject of previous chapters—must be given coherence and direction by an overarching strategy for operations. Given the obviousness of this challenge, and the availability of proven solutions, why should any company lose momentum and fall off the learning curve?

Consider, for example, the following companies, representing a variety of industries, and ask what they all have in common: A&P Stores, Apple Computer, Cincinnati Milacron, Ford Motor, IBM, Lotus Development, Pan American Airways, Philips Electronics, RCA, Sears Roebuck, Texas Instruments, US Steel, and Westinghouse. The common thread is that each, at one point in time, was the world leader in its industry, and then lost its lead. Indeed, some no longer operate in the businesses in which they used to be preeminent, and others have ceased even to exist. Why, given all the advantages of size and market leadership that the learning curve promises, did they lose their leading positions? Why were other companies, often initially much smaller and more constrained, able to surmount similar technological, market, and regulatory obstacles and surpass them?

11.2 WHY DO COMPANIES LOSE THEIR COMPETITIVE ADVANTAGE?

We have discussed in earlier chapters some of the reasons for such performance plateaus—and even, sometimes, declines. In Chapter 2, for example, we described how some small companies have been able to overtake and surpass their larger competitors, and in Chapter 10 we sketched out some of the reasons different kinds of improvement programs have failed. There are a variety of explanations for these more comprehensive competitive failures. They include:

1. Being leapfrogged by a radically new technology or competitive strategy (as described in Section 10-6)
2. Failing to make the sometimes subtle adaptations in organization and management required by apparently straightforward changes in strategy and/or product/process technologies (as happened, for example, when the dominant producers of photolithography equipment for semiconductor manufacturing were unable to make the transition to "stepper" techniques)[1]
3. Continuing to restrict one's attention to serving the needs of powerful existing customers, and thereby neglecting the needs of new market segments that are more attracted to a new technology that has little appeal for existing customers (as when the dominant producers of mechanical excavators failed to respond to the threats and opportunities presented by small hydraulic units)[2]
4. Simply being unable to keep up the pace of operating improvements established by competitors

Although they differ in important ways, the underlying culprit in all the "failure modes" mentioned above is a management group that is unable—or, more often, unwilling—to make the effort and/or the sacrifices required to keep driving ahead. Apparently secure in their market leadership and "first mover advantage," they ignore the powerful advantages of an adept follower, which can study the leader's successes and failures before investing in a new market or technology using the latest equipment, product designs, and approaches. As one considers the various factors that support or hinder organizational improvement, as summarized in Table 10-2, it becomes clear that complacency is the single biggest cause of slowdowns in organizational improvement.

If allowed, organizations—like people—tend to become resistant to doing new things. Why change something that has worked successfully in the past? Or, expressed more colloquially, "If it ain't broke, don't fix it." Allowing such complacency to develop and prevail reflects primarily a failure of management—both the lack of pressure for further improvement and the lack of a strategy for achieving it. It reflects an implicit decision that the benefits of such additional improvements are no longer worth the cost and effort required. Henry Ford's comment almost a hundred years ago about the power of improvement and why it often stagnates still applies today: "The competitor to be feared is one who never bothers about you at all, but goes on making his own business better all the time … when a business ceases to be creative, when it believes it has reached perfection and needs to do nothing but produce … it is done."[3]

Since organizational adaptation and improvement are essential to ongoing competitiveness, they necessarily are a central responsibility of top management. This responsibility cannot be ignored, deferred, or delegated. Attention to, measures of, and rewards for operating improvements should occupy as much management time as that devoted to growth in sales and profitability. When organizations fail to improve their performance as fast as competitive pressures require it is usually, unfortunately, because their managers simply did not understand the depth of commitment and sacrifice required to get such programs started and keep them moving forward. "One-minute" solutions and exhortations to be more accepting of change simply are not sufficient.

Some companies are able to maintain steady improvement, and adapt quickly to major innovations over many years, while others fail—despite what appears from the outside, at least, to be a similar degree of top management support. Still other companies appear to thrive in an atmosphere of almost benign neglect from top management. Why, when ongoing improvement is so essential to success, so conspicuous in the business press, and so talked about by top management, do improvement efforts fail? What is it that other management groups do that cultivates ongoing success?

11.2.1 The False Promise of Simplistic Solutions

People generally like to take part in improvement activities. They relish the challenge, they like working together to solve problems, and they enjoy seeing their efforts lead to successful outcomes. Over time, however, as discussed below, they tend to grow weary and long to sit back and savor the fruits of their past successes. Overcoming this natural organizational fatigue, and maintaining the momentum of improvement efforts is a major challenge for management. Unfortunately, too many managers seem to act as if maintaining organizational momentum can be overcome with magic bullets or simple tools—that, for example, "teams" of "empowered" people will automatically rise to the challenge and deal with the mundane issues of improvement while they devote themselves to more strategic issues.

Teams Are Not a Panacea

One of the most overused and least understood words in the current management vocabulary today is "team."[4] In companies today a team often is proposed as the answer to almost any managerial ailment—almost to the point of being a mantra. A problem is recognized, a team is assigned to deal with it, and management turns its attention elsewhere, assuming that the problem is being taken care of.

Those who have lived in the city of Boston for many years know, however, that simply having a team doesn't mean you'll win the most important games (or even the majority of them). We therefore would like to offer some cautionary comments about teams. Teams are not the answer to every problem. There probably are more bad, dysfunctional teams than there are good ones. Effective teams, to begin, must be composed of competent members—and preferably star players. We all have seen sports teams that are dominated by one or two outstanding players, surrounded by several mediocre players whose primary role is to "feed the ball" to the stars and stay out of their way. Those teams don't tend to win a lot of games.

Many corporate teams are similar in that one of two of their most capable, committed, and respected people can carry out the assigned task faster and more effectively by themselves, unencumbered by meetings and the suggestions offered by the other, less capable, team members. Not only that, but some people prefer to work on their own. Forcing them onto a team may cause the performance of those individuals to decline, as well as that of the team as a whole. Many workers in Levi Strauss' U.S. factories, for example, objected to the company's 1992 directive to abandon their previous individual piecework system and work in groups of 10 to 35. The expected increase in productivity did not materialize, and morale suffered.[5]

Not only do effective teams require competent members, those members must be unselfish and respect each other's special capabilities. If a supposed star doesn't trust the ability—or respect the judgment—of her teammates, she is unlikely to pass the ball to them at critical moments and will try to do everything by herself. The best teams not only pass the ball back and forth, but know each other well enough that they pass the ball where they know their teammates are *going* to be. Indeed, some studies have shown that the most effective product development teams have worked together for three to five years. After that, however, their effectiveness appears to decrease—probably due to people's unconscious inclination, when confronted with problems similar to those encountered in the past, to rely on previous solutions that had proven satisfactory rather than try to develop new ones.[6]

As mentioned in Chapters 7 and 8, a growing body of evidence also suggests that, in the case of major projects, small, dedicated teams are more effective than larger ones whose members each work on several other projects at the same time. Simply getting team members together becomes exponentially more difficult as their number increases. And when they do meet, if team members are each spending only a small portion of their time on a project (so their minds are filled with the problems and issues associated with their other assignments) a substantial portion of each meeting must be devoted to bringing everybody up to date; they must be reminded about what the situation was the last time they met and what has transpired since then. Again, research in several industries has suggested that a team's effectiveness is greatest if its members are engaged in only one or two other team projects, and it falls off rapidly as additional team assignments are added.[7] Moreover, if all team members are dedicated to a single project, they can co-locate. This both simplifies communications and, by facilitating meetings, speeds up decision making.

Finally, effective teams require capable leaders, people who not only command the respect of other team members but whose credibility with groups outside the team allows them to represent their team's concerns and needs effectively. Even more important, when teams are entrusted with critical tasks in which speed and innovativeness are essential, their leaders must have the ability to attract and allocate the necessary corporate resources. Finding, developing, and rewarding such leaders is a critical—as well as difficult and time consuming—job for top management.

Empowerment Is Not a Panacea

Worker empowerment is another ubiquitous management buzz-phrase that often is advocated, without careful scrutiny, as the solution to myriad problems. The basic concept behind empowerment (which is related to, but not the same as, worker autonomy)—giving employees more freedom to make the decisions that affect their jobs and working environments—is an enlightened one, and serves as a foundation for such other admirable concepts as *job enrichment* and *self-motivated work teams.* Its careless application, however, can quickly lead an organization into dangerous waters.

Before diving head first into a program of worker empowerment, for example, an organization should first address such basic questions as *which* of its people should be empowered, and what *limits* should be placed on their empowerment. At one level, for example, operators may be empowered to inspect their own output for defects and set up and perform routine maintenance on their own equipment. At another level, they might be empowered to create their own work schedules and job assignments, and to resolve internal personal conflicts. At still a higher level it might include hiring, training, and compensating new people. At each level, empowering one group inevitably implies that another group is *dis*empowered. Often this group is the one immediately superior to the newly empowered group; that is, supervisors and middle managers. To the extent that this provides an opportunity for operators to take over simple tasks that they are perfectly capable of handling, it facilitates faster responses and more informed decision making. Empowerment also adds variety to people's jobs and reduces communication delays and other sources of frustration, making work more interesting.

But many companies are discovering anew that experience and specialized skills also are important, and that removing whole layers of middle management from an organization can rob it of important capabilities. For example, giving more power to autonomous product development teams, as discussed in Chapter 8, almost inevitably reduces the power and, over time, the expertise, of functional groups. Before taking anything away from an organization it is necessary to ask why it was there in the first place. Simply removing it without eliminating the reasons for its existence can quickly lead to problems. Analogously, even though inventory in a manufacturing process is generally characterized as waste, reducing that inventory without first reducing the variability in demand, supplier deliveries, and processing times that made it necessary can create even greater waste.

Similarly, one must decide at what level in the organization to permit empowerment. Individual operators? Work teams? Whole departments? The more an operating task is interdependent, requiring that a number of interrelated tasks be performed in a specific sequence, the less sense it makes to empower individual operators or small groups. Some organizations, for example, have created internal conflicts by trying to combine worker empowerment (which requires a certain amount of employee discretion) with a tightly coupled just-in-time production system that seeks to respond rapidly to downstream demands.[8] Also, empowerment carries with it increased responsibilities and, often, more work. As a result, many companies have found that their people are increasingly resistant to empowerment's demands as it is pushed down into lower levels of the organization.

Third, *how much* empowerment/autonomy should be allowed? In a sense, this question is at the core of the perennial organization question of centralization versus decentralization. Its appropriate resolution for an individual organization lies somewhere in the wide gray area between absolute monarchy and mob rule. Clearly, some constraints on empowerment are required: service personnel should not be allowed to make impossible promises to customers, and operators should not be free to employ methods that do not lead consistently to high quality parts. Once an organization has trumpeted its belief in worker empowerment, however, it soon finds that it has stepped out on a slippery slope. Any attempt to rein in or constrict that empowerment is likely to be seen as hypocritical—new evidence that management does not really trust its employees, and is therefore not to be trusted itself. As a result of these and other factors, according to one noted authority on the subject: "there has been little growth in empowerment over the last 30 years … [because the] change programs and practices [employed] are full of inner contradictions that cripple innovation, motivation, and drive."[9]

11.2.2 The Dynamics of Organizational Stagnation

Organizational improvement stagnates for a variety of reasons. Managers who think that maintaining momentum simply requires that they apply continual pressure are underestimating the challenge. Unless they understand the forces and dynamics that drive stagnation, efforts to apply pressure can backfire and lead to lower commitment, morale, and performance.

Frustration and Boredom

In the previous chapter (Section 10.8.4), for example, we mentioned that organizations, like people, tend to tire of doing the same things over and over. Improvement efforts carry an added challenge, however, in that the rate of improvement inherently becomes more difficult to sustain over time. This is due to the gradual elimination of the "low-hanging fruit"—the obvious constraints on operating performance that are relatively easy to identify and remove. These are likely to be things like inadequate or error-prone tools and equipment, faulty or late information, a lack of adequate training, expertise, or assistance, or simply not being given the time to address and eliminate problems as they arise. As these immediate constraints on improvement are removed, progress tends to be quite rapid.

After a series of such early, easy, and morale boosting victories, however, many companies decide to raise the bar by establishing higher goals, or expanding the organizational scope of the improvement efforts. Not only does this appear, in effect, to penalize those responsible for the previous success, but also it often occurs at about the same time most of the obvious problems have been identified and dealt with. The remaining constraints—the *causes of the earlier problems*—are soon found to be more difficult to ferret out and correct. They may be embedded in the complexities of one's technologies or markets, or (worse!) in the complexities of the organization's own systems, policies, and traditions—even its essential culture. This is one of the reasons that many companies have found that it is easier to institute improved methods in a new facility, even one in a supposedly "developing" country, than in an existing facility in its home country.

Not only are these subtler and more complex constraints more difficult to isolate, understand, and create corrective actions for, their organizational roots often make them more difficult to tamper with. The commitment of even top managers may be shaken, as they come to understand the impact such changes are likely to have on other groups within the company, as well as on their own activities and opportunities. One firm, for example, found that a successful effort to improve its direct operating costs over time had a major impact on its cost structure. Altering the ratio of variable to fixed costs required changes in both its accounting system and overhead structure.[10] Such unexpected (and sometimes unwanted) consequences are likely to cause the people further down in the organization—who are growing more frustrated as they see further improvement becoming harder rather than easier over time—to test their managers' resolve by slackening their efforts. This brings us to the second major cause of stagnation.

A Failure to Internalize Improvement

Those who have embarked on an activity for which they have little enthusiasm, no matter how "good it is" for them (examples include losing weight and learning another language), know that their resolve is likely to diminish fairly quickly. Developing the kind of long-term commitment that leads to eventual success requires *internal* motivation—"wanting" it yourself rather than doing it because other people want you to do it.

Organizations behave the same way. As a result, no matter how much pressure top management applies, and how much excitement is created initially, the resulting rate of improvement is highly dependent on management's direct involvement and determination. As management attention flags, or is distracted by other problems, improvement tends to slow. Such slowdowns can become precipitous when, as often happens, the management "champions" of these efforts lose credibility and/or decide to move on. Long-term, continuing improvement, therefore, requires that the whole organization internalize the improvement efforts' motivation and goals. This implies that ongoing pursuit of an operations edge has to be based on a coordinated program of training, rewards, and self-reinforcing feedback. At a minimum one has to guard against creating negative feedback, as discussed next.

Punishing Success

People want to be rewarded for doing the right thing. One of the problems with finding ways to improve a task is that it is likely to mean that less people are required to perform it. At a minimum, the people doing that task are probably going to have to change what they are doing, no matter how much they enjoy doing it. Many companies' improvement efforts have ground to a halt when this ultimately led to layoffs because the rate of improvement was greater than the growth rate of sales.[11] This possibility should be taken into consideration early on, therefore, either by reducing the goals and scope of the improvement efforts so that they can accommodate the expected growth in sales or by providing attractive employee separation packages. At a minimum, top management has to provide convincing evidence to their people that the consequences to all of them from *not* achieving a certain rate of improvement are likely to be worse than the consequences to some of them if it is successful.

These three dynamics, as well as others not mentioned here, can wrestle improvement efforts to a standstill. Overcoming them and continuing to sharpen one's operations edge, therefore, requires a *strategy* for improvement, not simply a generalized "feel good" commitment. There is no "one best way" for a given organization to improve, any more than there is a best way to compete or to configure an operations organization. Because of different competitive strategies, business environments, and organizational capabilities and weaknesses, an improvement effort that proves highly effective in one company may be ineffective at—or even rejected by—another.

11.3 CREATING AN IMPROVEMENT STRATEGY

Most managers, at every level, understand the need to improve, and are constantly assaulted by suggestions as to how to do so. In Chapter 10 we discussed two of the most popular improvement programs, BPR and TQM, but there are dozens of others: ERP, JIT, QFD, lean manufacturing, benchmarking "best practice," total preventive maintenance, concurrent design, and so on, many of which have been mentioned in earlier chapters. Each has its own disciples, books, seminars, and consulting firms offering assistance. In addition, operating improvement can be achieved in a variety of ways: by improving the use of existing resources on existing products and services; by designing new products or services that use fewer resources and/or offer better quality, performance, or profitability; and by selectively applying the capabilities of new and more effective people and technology. Each approach tends to have its own advocates within an organization (operations managers, for example, tend to prefer the first, while marketing people and product designers prefer the second, and process engineers the third).

How can top managers rise above the onslaught of well-meaning suggestions from their friends and colleagues, who arrive back fresh from attending seminars, listening to speeches or reading books by proselytizers, or simply talking to a recent convert during a long airplane trip? Where should they start? How many different programs should they engage in at the same time? What should they say no to, or terminate?

The answers to such questions must be based on a company's improvement strategy, which is an essential part of any operations strategy. Initiating a simple project or approach (e.g., TQM, cross functional teams, or ERP) is *not* a strategy. Like any other strategy, an improvement strategy must include five basic aspects:[12]

1. *A direction in which the organization should focus its efforts:* Different types of improvement programs attack different aspects of performance: costs, reject levels, delivery speed, product development, and so on. Given that most organizations have limited resources, so can't improve along all

dimensions at the same time for very long, which dimension(s) are *most* in need of improvement? Such decisions must take into consideration the organization's competitive strategy, industry position, resources, and market environment.

2. *Establishing and cultivating expectations and goals:* In order to provide their wholehearted support to an improvement effort an organization's people have to believe both in the necessity for improvement and that the amount of improvement being sought is realistic—that is, within their capabilities. Some organizations have to react quickly to a sudden recognition of competitive vulnerability, having fallen far behind in cost, quality, and so on. Others need to have a sense of the rate at which they have to improve in order to keep up with the normal rate of progress in their industry. Others need "stretch goals" to force them to stop thinking only about ways to improve current practices and begin considering entirely new ways for performing the required tasks. Still others, in order to convince themselves that a goal is realistic simply need to be informed about the rate of improvement they have been able to achieve in the past. Analog Devices (discussed in Chapter 10), for example, found that the rate of improvement (as measured by the "improvement half life": the time required to achieve an improvement of 50 percent in some measure) that it had been able to achieve in certain kinds of improvement activities had been remarkably consistent over time.[13] Finally, management should communicate a sense of what would constitute "success." Ideally, the goals established also should lead to improvements that are clearly visible—both within the company and externally to customers.
3. *Organizing for implementation:* Long-term improvement requires a series of interlinked activities, all of which support the chosen performance dimensions. How should these activities be organized, who within the organization should be their "champions," and what role should top management play in them?
4. *Providing appropriate resources:* Different kinds of improvement programs require different resources and "tool kits." Some require highly trained workers, good cross-functional relationships, and substantial organizational trust. Others require lots of capital, specific technologies or expertise, and/or extensive support from external consultants. Before embarking on an improvement program, therefore, management has to marshal sufficient amounts of the required financial and human resources to implement it effectively.
5. *Developing contingency plans:* An improvement strategy is not static; it should adjust as a company's competitive environment and operations strategy evolve. Moreover, different types of improvement programs cultivate very different capabilities over time. These capabilities enable an organization to do certain things more easily, but they also can make it harder to do other things.[14] As a result, not only do they have important strategic implications, but they often make it possible for a company to deviate from its strategy if the future evolves in unexpected ways.

Implementing such a strategy requires constant, coherent communication—about priorities, goals, organizational resources and their constraints, and changes in plans, as well as about the progress being made and the lessons being learned. If a management group is really committed to making an improvement strategy work, it will talk about and reinforce that strategy at every opportunity. But sermons and exhortations alone are insufficient. Ongoing progress requires a consistent focus, driven by clear metrics and closely linked to the expressed needs of customers/users, all operating within a disciplined organizational structure

In addition to these "strategy basics," however, an improvement strategy requires decisions about the principle approaches and methodologies to be used in pursuing improvement. For example, should it be tightly focused on a single performance dimension or seek simultaneous improvements on several? Should it emphasize the activities encompassed by only one or two of the four quadrants depicted in Table 10-3, or pursue activities in all of them? Should it be driven and directly controlled by top management, or diffused throughout the organization with a "let a hundred flowers bloom" philosophy? We will now describe three of the most common ways companies have chosen to design and implement improvement strategies.

11.3.1 Tightly Focused, Top Management-Driven Improvement Programs

Single Performance Measure, Dominant Quadrant

Many companies focus all their energies on improving a single measure of performance, following one or both of two rationales:

1. Improving that measure is thought to provide a key foundation for the company's competitive strategy (and/or shore up a critical competitive weakness).
2. Improving that performance dimension is considered a prerequisite to improving others.

Moreover, either explicitly or implicitly (that is, as revealed by their actual behavior over time), they tend to emphasize activities in only one or two of the quadrants in Table 10-3 (reproduced on the next page).

The confining of attention to a limited set of alternatives usually is due to senior managers' biases and beliefs, based either on what has worked for them in the past, on their unthinking acceptance of industry practice, or simply on their belief that it is easier to initiate, communicate, and control a limited set of activities than a broader mix. Such tightly focused improvement efforts usually also reflect the personal vision of one or two top executives, and so exhibit both the strengths and weaknesses (discussed later in this section) inherent in this form of top management support.

An example of this kind of improvement strategy is the classic learning curve-based strategy that has been followed by many capital intensive, mass production industries such as chemicals and auto production. Directed almost entirely toward cost reduction, it is driven by top management and implemented through a sequence

Table 10-3 Nature of Improvements Sought

Nature of knowledge base	Incremental/infrastructural	Breakthrough/structural
Tacit: Learning *by* Doing	(I) • Individual Learning • Within Group Improvement (e.g., *kaizen*, PDCA experiments, Total Quality Management, JIT)	(IV) Toyota Production System, Long-term "stretch" goals (e.g., Six Sigma improvement)
Explicit: Learning *before* Doing	(II) *Across* Group Improvements; Benchmarking/best practices	(III) *Into* Group Improvements: Process reengineering, introducing an ERP system, World-class practices

of structural changes over time that seek to exploit all the various economies of scale described in Chapter 3. In a sense, it epitomizes the Strategic Leap approach to improvement and thus falls primarily within quadrants III and IV in Table 10-3. The classic example of this strategy was Henry Ford's attempt to minimize the manufacturing cost and maximize the unit sales of his Model T, and its consequences illustrate both its power and its potential weaknesses.

There were five major elements in Ford's implementation of the learning curve strategy:

1. *Product standardization and stability.* Parts were simplified and standardized, only minor changes were made in the car's basic design, and customers were given few options (e.g., "any color you want as long as it's black"). Moreover, as experience was gained, parts that had been "over designed" because of technical conservatism were redesigned for lower cost.
2. *Process rationalization and labor specialization.* Process rationalization, accompanied by increased division of labor, led to greater specialization in labor skills and increasing substitution of capital (equipment) for labor. The production throughput time was reduced as more narrowly skilled workers performed shorter tasks, enabling the development of the moving assembly line. As the amount of direct labor fell, support functions, such as materials handling, grew in importance.
3. *Scale economies.* Spreading overhead over larger production volumes reduced unit costs. Moreover, the production process was reorganized to exploit longer-term scale economies. Activities (such as engine plants) with high scale economies were centralized as volume increased, while those that did not offer substantial economies (such as assembly plants) were dispersed to trim transportation costs.
4. *Equipment specialization and backward integration.* Processing equipment and facilities were specialized, both for the specific design of the Model T and for individual processing steps. When production volumes increased to the point where Ford could produce its own materials and parts more cheaply than suppliers, it backward integrated.
5. *Materials specialization.* The costs of raw materials and parts were reduced, both through backward integration and the increasing power Ford had over suppliers—who were required to develop parts and materials that would reduce Ford's overall costs.

Ford's approach encompassed all the elements of strategy described at the beginning of this section, except one. Its *direction* was a single-minded focus on cost with the *expectation* of reducing costs to the point where a middle class person could afford to buy a car. It was implemented through structural changes, *organized* and directly controlled by top management. The required *resources* were provided. The only element lacking was a consideration of possible contingencies, and this was its fatal weakness. Henry Ford pursued the learning curve to such a degree that when General Motors introduced more comfortable closed-body vehicles, which steadily became more popular in the early 1920s, it was impossible for Ford to respond incrementally. By 1926 Ford's production process had become so focused and inflexible that all vehicle production had to stop for almost a full year in order to reorganize and retool for the production of its new closed-body Model A. Although Ford recovered market leadership briefly afterwards, its years of domination of the U.S. auto market essentially came to an end with that shutdown.

General Motors soon countered with another series of improved designs and gradually moved ahead of Ford.

As pointed out in Chapter 2, the danger of committing oneself to a strategy based entirely on a single criterion, such as cost reduction, usually tends to limit one's performance along other performance dimensions. In this case, as the cost of the Model T was driven steadily down Ford lost its flexibility and innovative capabilities.[15] As we saw in Chapter 2, low cost is just one of the criteria around which a competitive strategy can be crafted, implying that it should be possible for a competitor to design an effective counter-strategy around one of the other criteria, such as product line breadth (as did GM) or the ability to customize products.

A more recent example of this approach is Oracle Corporation's adoption, mandated by its CEO Larry Ellison, of an ERP system that affected all aspects of its operations. This system established centralized worldwide databases for all of Oracle's major functions—accounting, human resource management, customer billing and service, etc.—and standard processes for handling them. According to Ellison, "When we started this effort last year, I thought we could save $500 million. We ended up saving $1 billion, and I'm convinced we can save $1 billion, maybe $2 billion more."[16] Time will tell if the adoption of this system will similarly impair Oracle's flexibility and ability to further improve its performance.

Single Performance Measure, Multiple Quadrants

Although learning curve strategies tend to restrict their attention to both a single measure and emphasize activities in one or two quadrants, other companies utilize activities in all four quadrants while still focusing relentlessly on improving a single performance measure. Some, for example, regard quality improvement as a driver of improvement along a variety of dimensions, while others focus on inventory and throughput time reduction, and still others on new product innovation. Dell Computer, in contrast, has single-mindedly pursued market share through low prices, achieved through a variety of innovations in product design, manufacturing, distribution, and marketing.[17] This focus on driving costs down and grabbing market share has caused its founder, Michael Dell, to be called "the Henry Ford of the twenty-first century." And, like Ford, there are concerns that by doing so he has reduced his company's—in fact, the whole PC industry's—ability, and willingness, to innovate.

One of the most interesting and effective programs of this type was initiated at Alcoa when Paul O'Neill became CEO in 1987. Even though Alcoa's safety record at that time was considerably better than that of the average U.S. company, the single measure that O'Neill focused on was "time lost to employee injuries." His rationale was that improving safety not only was viewed as important by his workers (and their unions), it also required and underpinned a variety of additional activities that ultimately drove improvements in other performance dimensions. Over the next fourteen years, under a relentless assault that combined employee training, new equipment, changes in policies, suggestion programs, and small group initiatives, Alcoa's time lost due to employee injuries fell from one-third the U.S. average to one-twentieth. During that same period the reduction in this measure was accompanied by steady improvements in labor productivity and profitability. By the end of year 2000, Alcoa's profits had grown by a factor of six, and its market value by a factor of ten.[18]

Another example was introduced in Chapter 7: Nypro's relentless pursuit of improved molding precision in order to make the Vistakon disposable lens a reality. Although its sales were less than $50 million in 1983, Nypro already was recognized as one of the world's most sophisticated manufacturers of customized injection molded plastic parts. That reputation led J & J's Vistakon division to approach Nypro with an extraordinary challenge. Could it make a plastic injection mold that was accurate to within ±0.02mm—a level of precision that represented a *ten-fold* reduction in dimensional variability over the tightest that had ever been achieved by plastic injection molders up to that time.[19] If achieved, however, this would enable Vistakon to eliminate enough costly steps in its production process to allow it to sell a pair of lenses for $8 or less, effectively making them disposable.

Nypro established a team of engineers and technicians that interacted with a corresponding team at Vistakon. Over a period of three years, employing countless iterations of a P-D-C-A cycle based on carefully designed experiments, the Nypro team gradually identified the sources of variation in its lens molds and defined the optimal settings of key process parameters. In early 1986, after having achieved the desired ±0.02mm accuracy in its molds, Nypro discovered that even this level of precision would not allow Vistakon to produce lenses with the required consistency. After further study the Nypro team came to the agonizing conclusion that in order to achieve the precision and reliability required for a truly disposable final product, it would have to increase the accuracy of its molds to within ±0.005mm—*four times* that originally demanded. After more months of experimentation and further improvements, its efforts were successful.

Other examples of this approach include General Electric's *Six-Sigma* quality improvement program, driven by its CEO Jack Welch; Cummins Engine's *Lean Manufacturing* initiative; and AT&T's Universal Card Services' dogged pursuit of improvement in the quality of customer service. The latter case raises some of the problems with this approach.

The Dangers of Tightly-Focused, Top Management-Driven Programs

The dangers of such a relentless, top-down driven strategy have been described in Section 11.2.2. Companies usually experience diminishing returns as employees grow weary of a continual focus on a single aspect of performance. Maintaining momentum as the low-hanging fruit is removed requires constant pressure from top management. Moreover, such programs usually are dependent on the power and personality of one or two leaders, making them highly vulnerable after those champions depart. The experience of AT&T Universal Card Services (UCS) provides examples of all three problems.[20] In 1992, after three years of intense effort, it won the Baldrige National Quality Award. By the end of that year, however, its performance improvement appeared to be leveling off, so management "raised the bar" by increasing the performance standards that were used to calculate employee bonuses. Bonus awards fell immediately afterward, and employees accused management of seeking to increase corporate profitability at their expense. Although adjustments were made that reestablished organizational harmony, shortly thereafter two of the architects and charismatic champions of the quality improvement program (its CEO and its executive V.P. for Customer Services) left the company. In 1997, with the quality of its customer service no longer regarded as vastly superior to those of other credit card companies, and its profitability only marginal, UCS was sold.

One final cautionary point: "Top management support" can easily be carried to extremes. In a sense, it represents a kind of subsidy—a willingness to allocate more attention and effort to one set of activities than to others. Any organization that has sought subsidies or other support—from a government agency, say—soon finds that such subsidies eventually trigger investigations to ensure that the subsidy is being used for the intended purpose. Their investigations usually lead to subtle attempts to interfere with—or, worse, micromanage—those activities that receive subsidies.

Too often, top managers fall into this trap. Having authorized an improvement program, as well as the funds required to train employees, and otherwise provided support to an improvement effort, they soon become concerned as to whether the operating groups are engaging in the "right" activities. Their efforts to designate project priorities, obtain progress reports, and involve themselves in evaluating alternative approaches to improvement often have the effect of frustrating and alienating the operating level employees entrusted with proposing and implementing specific improvements.

11.3.2 Broadly Based, Diffused Improvement Programs

At the other extreme are companies that diffuse their improvement efforts broadly, with little general guidance or oversight. As a result, they often pursue improvements along different dimensions in different parts of the organization, and in all four quadrants, at the same time. In a sense, this is the spirit of the *kaizen* approach pioneered by Japanese companies. Although such improvement programs might appear haphazard and uncoordinated to an outside observer, they often demonstrate a remarkable coherence and effectiveness. The most successful ones are built around a common philosophy of improvement and an environment that fosters activities such as the following:

- Examining the organization's own past experience in the attempt to extract useful information and ideas
- Seeking out and learning from the experiences and best practices of other companies
- Experimenting systematically with new ideas and approaches
- Communicating important information throughout the organization (across functional, business, and geographic lines)

Although management pressure for ongoing improvement is necessary, simple pressure is not enough. Real sustainability requires that management surround the improvement activities described above with a web of supporting activities and policies.[21]

Create a Climate that Encourages and Sustains Improvement

Although creating this kind of conducive environment clearly must start at the top of the organization, the ongoing success of such an approach requires support and reinforcement from all levels. Therefore, these companies work hard to create a set of organizational attitudes and mechanisms that encourage and sustain organizational improvement *without* continual top management attention or involvement. This begins with the cultivation of an organizational "climate" that fosters the kinds of within group, across group, and into group learning that were discussed in Chapter 10.

Irrespective of the exhortations of top management, the people throughout an organization (including lower level managers) are unlikely to invest much time or energy in improvement activities unless there is strong evidence that they are really important to the company, and that their activities will be supported, noticed, and rewarded. Such a supportive environment, which seeks to involve people at all levels in the improvement process, places as much attention on operating *improvements,* and the people or groups involved in them, as it does on current operating *results.* In addition to providing management encouragement and resources, it also establishes a common language and philosophy for implementing improvement throughout the organization, thereby legitimizing the crossing of functional and geographic boundaries. Finally, it encourages people at all levels to identify and define problems, and empowers them to take corrective action, following specified procedures.

Measure and Reward Improvement Efforts

A supportive environment also provides clear measures for tracking desired improvements, publicizes the progress being made, and honors those responsible for it. As the old saying goes, "People don't do what you *expect;* they do what you *inspect.*" For example, Milliken & Co. (another winner of the National Baldrige Award) adopted the practice of asking each of its departments—from production lines to accounting offices to Human Resource managers—to select its own measures of performance and, through large charts on nearby walls, to display the improvements achieved in those measures over time. Top management was less interested in the actual measures chosen (as long as they were felt important and indicative of performance by the people themselves) than that they were displayed for all to see—the people working in that department, those in nearby departments, and managers or customers who were just passing through. To further reinforce the importance of continuous improvement, slogans such as "'best' is the enemy of 'ever better'" are prominently displayed throughout its facilities.

Provide Supportive and Stable Human Resources

A program that emphasizes continuous incremental improvement is highly dependent on the quality and stability of the organization's employees. Anticipated improvements can evaporate quickly if a company creates a working environment that leads to excessive labor turnover, or makes it difficult to attract people with the required skills. One way to ensure that people value improvement is to consciously hire those who are likely to be compatible with such efforts—people who are naturally flexible, curious, and comfortable working together. Once hired, they need to be trained in a broad range of tasks, as well as in problem-solving techniques. They should be encouraged to both look for problems and communicate them to others in an effort to identify and eliminate their root causes. People at all levels are given opportunities to interact with customers or ultimate users (as at Worthington Steel and Intuit), parts suppliers (as at Ford Motor), and equipment suppliers (as at Milliken). Successful efforts are rewarded, in some case with actual financial rewards. Many companies have found, however, that simple recognition—or "celebrations" of achievements—is the most valued reward.

Reduce "Background Noise"

Another way to encourage a conducive climate is to consciously set about eliminating things and activities that *impede* improvement. As described earlier, if a process is not "in control"—that is, if it has a high and unstable level of variability—one is unlikely to be able to achieve a sustainable improvement in any measure of performance. Continual problems create a chaotic environment that makes it difficult to relate observed problems to their causes and restricts the time available to do so because of the need for continual fire fighting. One cannot even learn effectively from making experimental changes in a process if the background noise obscures their effects. Reducing work in process often can facilitate efforts to reduce such noise, since WIP creates delays between the time a problem first appears and when it becomes visible.

Share Information

In addition to bringing processes under control, sustained improvement requires employee training (at all levels), process documentation, problem-solving teams, cross-functional integration, and ongoing measurement of progress. Information needs to be communicated widely throughout the organization—through post-audit reports that review past initiatives and extract the lessons that can be learned from them, by assigning cross-functional teams to address major problems, by moving people around in the organization so that they develop broader perspectives on issues and master new problem solving approaches, and by fostering cross-organizational training programs in which they are given opportunities to train others.

Organize and Manage the Improvement Efforts

The danger of this kind of laissez-faire approach, of course, is that it can lead to organizational schizophrenia—with different groups pursuing different kinds of improvement in different ways. Moreover, the resources required for each group's improvement activities might be in short supply. Employee generated improvement initiatives require management oversight and phasing to ensure that that they do not interfere with one another, that the organization does not take on too much at one time, and that specific resources (key people, say) are not overburdened. Therefore, rather than pursuing projects in the order they are proposed, a rich set of possible projects must be identified so that management can choose among them and combine them in imaginative ways. One way to accomplish this is to establish and maintain a "portfolio" of potential projects at four stages of development:

1. *Committed.* Projects that are fully defined and included in current operating plans
2. *Defined.* Projects that are fully approved and in the process of being scheduled, but are not yet being implemented
3. *Under study.* Projects that require additional engineering, operator, and/or financial analyses
4. *Maybes.* Opportunities that have been identified, but no specific projects for exploiting them have been formally proposed

Separating projects in this manner, and monitoring their flow upward through the various stages, facilitates the management of an organization's improvement efforts. Resources can be allocated among specific projects, and managers can maintain control over the mix of activities being pursued. The project classifications described in Chapter 8, such as *enhancements, platforms,* and *breakthroughs,* also apply to improvement projects, and the organizational techniques discussed there are similarly effective. Through trial and error an organization can develop its own guidelines as to the desired size of this project portfolio. A backlog of projects that together had the potential to achieve three times its annual improvement plan seemed to work at one company we have observed.

11.3.3 Top Management Directed, *Staged* Improvement Programs

Over time, an organization in a competitive environment has to improve along *all* competitive dimensions. However, it also needs to establish priorities that reflect its particular competitive strategy and position. It must balance the contradictory dangers of basing an improvement strategy on a single performance dimension over a long period of time, against those of fragmenting resources and creating confusion by trying to improve in too many directions at once. One way to attack this dilemma is to pursue multidimensional improvements through a sequence of stages over time. The rationale is that improvements in one direction provide the basis for later improvements in others. Moreover, different types of improvement create organizational capabilities that facilitate different competitive initiatives.

Although it does not appear that it consciously adopted this approach at the outset, Toyota Motor provides the classic example of its implementation. Toyota began its quality improvement efforts in the 1950s. At first it simply sought to bring its quality levels up to acceptable domestic standards, and later to international standards, but by the 1960s it had expanded its improvement efforts to include JIT and the reduction of all forms of "waste." Over time the continual reduction in defect and inventory levels not only led to increased productivity, it also allowed Toyota to reduce the amount of capital invested in inventory and facilities. These improvements enabled Toyota to build on its cost and quality advantages by reducing its production throughput and product changeover times. The increased flexibility that resulted led it to introduce *mixed model assembly* (assembling several models simultaneously on the same assembly line), making it possible for Toyota to vastly expand its product line in the 1980s. The natural next step was to attack the product development cycle, allowing Toyota in the 1990s to begin competing on the basis of product innovation.

Observing a similar progression in other companies' improvement efforts, some authors have proposed that a specific sequence of improvements should be adopted. For example, one Japanese observer asserts, "In general, if some [Japanese] companies want to offer 'flexibility' … it is necessary that at least they have already qualified for a minimum level of abilities on quality, dependability and cost improvement. If … not, they get … chaos …."[22] This observation, as well as others, has fostered the proposal that companies attempting to improve operating performance should adopt what has been termed a *Sand Cone* model of improvement. Although the preferred sequence might differ according to circumstance, one recommended order is, first, defect reduction, then dependability, then flexibility, and finally cost efficiency.[23] More recently, there have been attempts to elaborate on this framework by relating specific operating improvements to the development of strategic capabilities.[24]

Such attempts to describe general patterns, however, do not necessary provide useful advice to a company that already has developed certain capabilities and faces a specific competitive environment. For example, should it seek to improve labor productivity through BPR or TQM (our two polar extremes)? Each requires different skills and provides a different path to improvement. BPR requires top management to decide which aspects of performance are most important and set ambitious goals for the improvement effort. Advocates for TQM and the Sand Cone model, on the other hand, contend that reducing defects (or, equivalently, all forms of variation in a process) underlies improvement in *all* dimensions. Addressing issues regarding the appropriate pathway to improvement that should be followed requires that we reprise our earlier (Chapter 2) discussion of capabilities-based strategies.

11.4 STEPPING BACK: THE CONCEPT OF "IMPROVEMENT PATHWAYS"[25]

Different paths to improvement foster different organizational capabilities. Consider, for example, a facility that has established the long-term goal of substantially reducing its lead times and inventories. It could choose to proceed toward this goal in either of two directions. One is the adoption of a JIT-pull production system, which will create strong incentives to reduce set-up times and defect rates, as well as cultivate other JIT-related skills, and institute an ethic of continuous improvement in the organization.

An alternative approach would be to begin with an MRP system—a computerized production scheduling system (described in Chapter 6) that is based on forecasts of future demand and production lead times, as well as on real time data from the shop floor. The initial results might not be very close to JIT. Lead times, in fact, might even increase temporarily, since MRP systems tend to be rather clumsy in handling schedule changes and rush orders. On the other hand, MRP exerts pressure to improve shop floor data and computer expertise, which facilitates better production scheduling and a possible eventual transition to CIM (computer-integrated-manufacturing). Once MRP control and discipline has been established, the organization is in position to reduce the lead times in the system until they approach those of a JIT system.

Note that both paths promise a reduction in inventories and faster response to customer requests. Each, however, cultivates very different capabilities over time, and these capabilities have important strategic implications. On one hand, adopting an MRP-type system fosters skills in using computers and managing databases, neither of which are central to a JIT approach. Pull systems, on the other hand, encourage skills in factory floor problem-solving, incremental process improvement, and fast response. Each approach, in short, tends to leave the organization with a different set of skills and thus a different set of strategic options in the future. A decision about which approach to pursue should not be made without considering which set of capabilities will be most valuable to the company in the future.

Complicating an organization's efforts is the fact that capabilities are ephemeral—they atrophy if not used, and become obsolete if not continually nourished and updated. Moreover, even if it makes the appropriate trade-off between, say, cost and delivery performance, the company will not prevail against competitors that are able to achieve higher performance along *both* dimensions. This suggests that a strategy for operations improvement needs to incorporate the notion of *paths* of learning, or "improvement trajectories."[26]

Consider two competitors, both of which are well managed and extracting the maximum performance from the resources available to them. One competes by offering a broader and more flexible product range than its competitors. As depicted in Figure 11-1, this strategy has required certain operating choices, such as adopting more flexible production equipment, that have caused its costs to be higher than

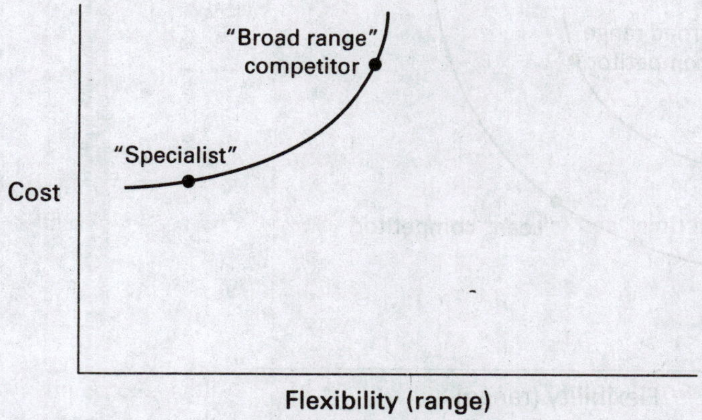

Figure 11-1 Two Competitors: Different Positions on Same Production Frontier

those of one competitor (which we will refer to as the *specialist*) that offers a narrower range of lower-priced products. The two firms are not direct competitors because each offers its customers a different bundle of attributes and has configured itself appropriately in support of its chosen competitive strategy.

Assume now that a new competitor enters the market, bringing with it a very different approach to operations (such as *lean manufacturing*). This new approach gives it advantages in *both* cost and flexibility. In effect, it is operating on on a better production frontier than either the "specialist" or the "broad range" firm (Figure 11-2). This "lean" competitor clearly provides a serious threat because it can offer both the product variety of the "broad range" firm and the low costs of the "specialist."

In this situation our broad range firm will probably find it impossible to compete effectively with its two competitors simply by repositioning itself along its current performance frontier. To survive it must move to the frontier established by its new competitor. The question is, how? One way (arrow 1 in Figure 11-3) would be to reconfigure its operations using its new competitor's innovative approaches as a model, which is likely to necessitate the adoption of an entirely different operations infrastucture. Once it has made the transition to the new frontier, it could then decide how it wanted to position itself along it and adopt an operations strategy supportive of that specific position. For example, it might choose to be a broader range (but slightly more costly) supplier than the new entrant (arrow 2). Conversely, it might move to a lower cost, but less flexible position. In either case, it would have to make the specific structural choices that provided the desired balance between cost and flexibility.

A second possible path is essentially the reverse of the first (Figure 11-4): The broad range firm would first reduce its product range and simplify its operations — in effect, repositioning itself along its current frontier. Once that transition was accomplished, it would make the "lean" infrastructural changes that would give it more flexibility without increasing costs. This sequence would also get it eventually to its desired position on the new frontier. Both approaches would end up at the same place, but they would arrive there via very different paths. Advocates of *lean*

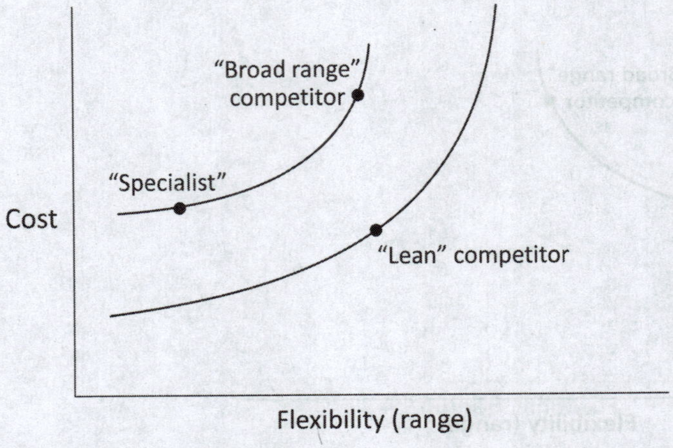

Figure 11-2 Third Competitor Enters on New Production Frontier

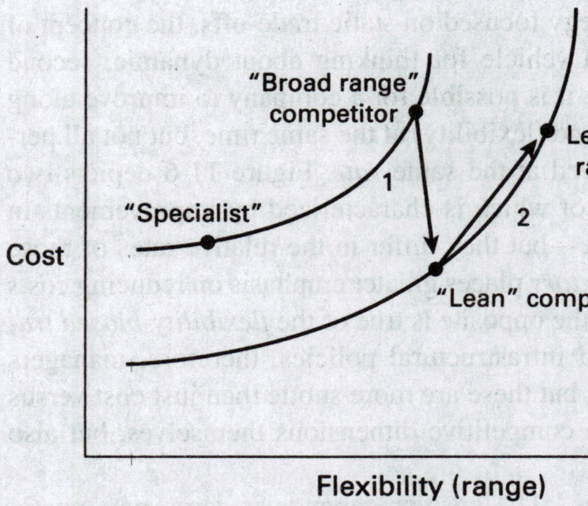

Figure 11-3 Improvement Path A: First Move to New Frontier

manufacturing tend to argue that the major challenge is making the transition to the new frontier, and that adjusting one's position along that frontier is just icing on the cake. Those who are somewhat intimidated by the magnitude of the changes required by a very different approach to operations might see the second approach as being much easier to implement.

Trade-offs and Focus: A Reprise

This perspective also stimulates an alternative way of thinking about some of the questions raised in Chapter 2. First, are trade-offs necessary? Whereas much of the

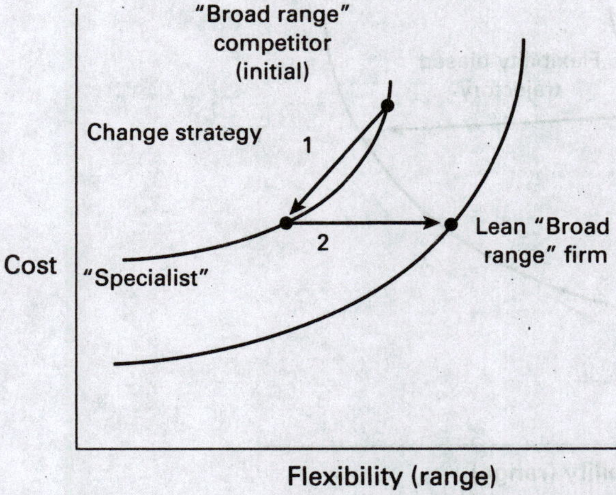

Figure 11-4 Improvement Path B: First Move along Current Frontier

early thinking about operations strategy focused on static trade-offs, the concept of improvement trajectories provides a vehicle for thinking about dynamic, second order trade-offs. As discussed above, it is possible for a company to improve along more than one dimension (e.g., cost and flexibility) at the same time, but not all performance dimensions can be improved at the same *rate*. Figure 11-6 depicts two possible operating trajectories, each of which is characterized by improvements in *both* cost and flexibility performance—but they differ in the relative rates of those improvements. The *cost-biased trajectory* places greater emphasis on reducing costs (but flexibility still improves), while the opposite is true of the *flexibility-biased trajectory*. Through their structural and infrastructural policies, therefore, managers still are faced with critical trade-offs, but these are more subtle than just cost versus flexibility: they involve not only the competitive dimensions themselves, but also their rates of improvement.

Second, how important is focus? The answer depends in large part on the company's improvement trajectory and where it is on that trajectory. Consider the two trajectories depicted in Figure 11-5. A company following either trajectory will become more flexible over time, and may therefore find itself better able to manage operating complexity. This makes tight focus less critical, so it may decide to broaden the focus of its facilities without sacrificing their performance. A company progressing along the flexibility-biased trajectory, however, should be able to operate facilities that are less focused than a company moving along the cost-biased trajectory.

As we have seen, the improvement pathway chosen can have subtle but important effects on how a facility network is organized, the operating capabilities and expertise that are embedded in it, and how well one's organization can perform along various competitive dimensions. In short, the pathway has profound strategic implications. Whether these implications will be recognized, understood, and

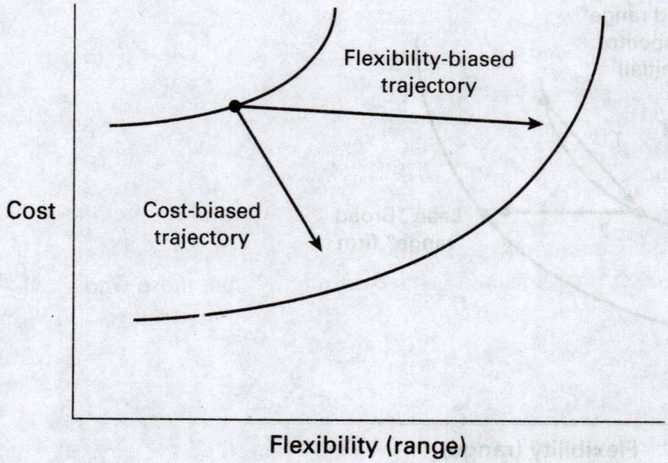

Figure 11-5 Contrasting "Cost-Biased" vs. "Flexibility-Biased" Paths

exploited by the company as a whole depends largely on the *role* that the operations organization is expected to play.

11.5 OPERATIONS ROLE: FROM REACTIVE TO PROACTIVE

Individuals often switch among several roles in the course of a day: dutiful daughter or son, supportive spouse, strict parent, obedient subordinate, demanding boss, etc. How they behave—how much freedom or discretion they have, how assertive they are, and how they interact with others—is fundamentally affected by the particular role they are playing (and are expected to play) at a given time. Similarly, two operations organizations are likely to behave very differently, even though they operate in the same industry and are similarly equipped and staffed, depending on how they perceive their roles and/or are perceived by other groups within the company. Therefore, another critical task of top management is changing the way the operations organization thinks about itself and is regarded by others. If it sees its role as being simply a "good corporate citizen" or "team player," and is therefore willing to wait for requests and directions from others, it never will become a proactive force within the company no matter how much this is desired.

Many managers appear to assume that the proper role for an operations organization is essentially *supportive* in nature—that it should confine itself simply to implementing the company's competitive strategy and marketing objectives as effectively as possible. The consequence of restricting operations' role in this way, however, is that it is forced to wait for others to give it direction and take the lead. Worse, as a result, operations often is expected to compensate somehow for the delays and deficiencies resulting from the incomplete or flawed activities of these other groups. As might be expected, when companies experience competitive difficulties one often finds that the neutral/reactive role played by operations is a cause of many of their problems.

However, an attempt by an operations organization to play a more forceful role when other groups expect it to be reactive (or even submissive) tends to lead to continual friction and infighting. If, for example, it resists their direction (or is simply unable to deal effectively with the crises they create), the situation sometimes deteriorates to the point where the operations organization begins to play an *adversarial* role within the company. This forces the organization to redirect time and energy away from external competitors to dealing with a recurring series of internal conflicts. Usually such bickering is ascribed to poor communications or the natural friction between different personality types. (People engaged in sales or accounting, it is argued, tend to approach problems and behave differently than those who gravitate to being engineers or operations managers.) We argue that another reason is that the different functional groups are likely to be either pursuing different goals and strategies or/and perceiving their roles differently.

As one examines the best companies in the world, it becomes apparent that their operations functions generally play a much stronger role than those of implementer and "fixer." They do not stop once they have configured operations to implement their chosen competitive strategies. Rather than simply carrying out their assigned mission, these operations organizations appear to have the authority to help redefine that mission. Their companies challenge and support them to become so proficient that they are able to generate new opportunities for other functional groups. In the process of identifying and exploiting such opportunities, these elite operations groups are able to participate in—even instigate—the reformulation of the company's competitive strategy and pressure other functions to react to its initiatives. In an attempt to define this larger role, and put it into the context of the other kinds of roles that operations could be asked to play, it has been proposed that the various roles that companies ask their operations organizations to play can be arrayed along a continuum, ranging from purely reactive to competitively proactive. This continuum can be divided into four rough stages of operations proactiveness, ranging from internally focused and reactive (Stage I) to externally (i.e., competitively) focused and proactive (Stage IV).[27]

Implications of Moving from a Reactive to a Proactive Role

Common sense suggests that a company that seeks competitive advantage only through one or two of its functions will not be as formidable as one that pursues advantages in all of them—just as an internal combustion engine loses power when one of its pistons stops firing. Moreover, the interaction of these functions should be both interactive and proactive. In order for this to happen, operations managers need to be fully informed about the major issues facing the business, the strategies being proposed by other functional heads, and the possible implications for operations. In addition, the status, capabilities, remuneration, and credibility of the firm's operations managers should be roughly equal to those of other functional managers. This may require changes in how potential operations managers are selected and trained, the career paths they follow, and the way their performance is measured and evaluated.

To see the impact of this shift in roles, recall that top management tends to focus most of its attention on structural decisions, such as how much operating capacity to provide, what kind of facilities to build and where to build them, the type of process technology to adopt, and vertical integration/sourcing decisions. In a sense, this focus on (an implicitly somewhat static) operations *structure* mirrors the emphasis that the traditional competitive strategy paradigm places on industry position. An expanded concept of operations competitiveness, by emphasizing the importance of capabilities and role, suggests that the operations *infrastructure* (the policies and systems governing capital budgeting, human resources, quality/process control, material flows, and performance measurement) employed to select and control the performance of its physical assets is at least as important as its structure. Moreover, these systems need to be designed so as to encourage the continual adaptation and improvement of an organization's skill base rather than to achieve some "optimal" strategic fit.

The essence of this philosophy is captured in a slogan seen throughout Milliken & Co., one of the leaders in the application of TQM in the United States: "The hard stuff is easy. The soft stuff is hard. And the soft stuff is more important than the hard stuff." The importance of organizational software helps explain why many observers of world class companies in Japan and other countries have returned to report that their facilities and equipment are generally no better than those of their western competitors.[28] Apparently, their superior infrastructures simply allowed them to extract better performance from these hard assets.

11.6 MANAGEMENT: THE ULTIMATE SOURCE OF SUSTAINABLE ADVANTAGE

Throughout this book we repeatedly have stressed the critical role that managers play in achieving a competitive edge through operations. We would like to end it by reemphasizing the power—verging on magic—of what is often more prosaically referred to as "good management." Managers not only make a difference, they can make the *defining* difference in corporate performance. Again and again one sees learned analyses of business data by economists and other social scientists who attempt to ascertain the importance to business success of certain types of decisions or factors: market share, industry structure, the rate of capital investment, R&D spending, and so on. Almost invariably the effect they seek either can't be found or is quite small, a faint signal hidden amidst the general "noise" of many other unknown factors—one of which they sometimes characterize as *management skill.*

We propose that what such studies dismiss as the statistical *residual*—the unexplained effects due to variables they don't understand or know how to measure—is the *real* signal, and it consists largely of management skill, determination, and leadership. The rest is the noise. This is apparent to anyone who studies successful turnarounds, cases where a new management team enters a deteriorating situation (often on the verge of collapse) and, with most of the same employees, the same facilities and equipment, and the same products serving the same markets, is able to effect a dramatic improvement in performance. It is reinforced by comparisons of companies that operate in the same industry, which usually find that the performance of the average company in the top quartile is more than twice (and sometimes more than four times) that of the average company in the bottom quartile. In earlier chapters we reported a similar finding when comparing the performance of factories that belonged to the same company and produced the same, or very similar, products for the same customers.[29] The dramatic impact that a good manager can have on an organization usually swamps the differences resulting from specific environments, decisions, even different countries.

The importance of outstanding management to sustained high performance has become even greater in today's global economy. While global markets are by no means fully integrated (i.e., geographic differences, national boundaries, and cultures still matter), competitors in most industries can easily access the same factors of production anywhere in the world. Moreover, no longer do the United States, Europe, and Japan have a monopoly on highly skilled engineering talent. Today companies around the world can make use of the skills of world-class software engineers in India and electrical engineers in China at a fraction of the wage rates paid to comparable talent in the developed countries. Thus, in a world where the playing field is becoming more level, the management of a company's intellectual, physical, and human resources has become ever more critical to sustained success.

While there may be no general "one best way" or timeless recipe for sustained success, throughout this book we have identified and discussed various management behaviors, attitudes, and philosophies that appear to be critical to sustaining a competitive advantage. Let us close by reflecting on these. First, effective senior managers need to thoroughly understand the complex nature of their organizations. They can not focus just on marketing, or on R&D, or on operations, but must comprehend how all the organization's functions and capabilities fit together as a *system.*

Moreover, this comprehension extends beyond the boundaries of their own enterprise. Every firm is imbedded in a broader network of suppliers, customers, and so on, so it is important to manage across boundaries and to understand that traditional levers of control do not necessarily apply. One senior manager at an electronics systems producer we have studied reported that he spends as much time with critical suppliers of technology as with customers, because he realizes that both are equally critical to his company's success.

The second behavior is a focus on action over analysis. The world is complex. Major decisions are risky and uncertain. Faced with these circumstances, some managers prefer the comfort of elegant analyses and collecting additional data. The more effective ones, however, tend to employ what we have earlier termed *learning by doing:* they grope for answers by running experiments and learning as they go. Their philosophy can be captured by the phrase: "make a little, sell a little, learn a lot." Few companies establish formal measurement and control systems to foster learning. Indeed, despite much discussion about the potential value of sophisticated knowledge management systems, we do not believe the answer lies in more technology or better systems. It resides in management. Learning can only be fostered by management attention and supportive action.

Finally, we have stressed throughout the critical need for managers to focus on improvement. It is relatively easy to muster energy and resources for improvement when a company is struggling, losing a competitive battle, or facing bankruptcy. As mentioned above, there are many stories of corporate turnarounds (e.g., IBM, Intel, and Chrysler to name a few) when the only alternative was bankruptcy. It appears to be much harder, however, to achieve consistent performance improvement when things are going well. Complacency is the biggest enemy of sustained operating performance.

How can complacency be guarded against? Again, while incentive systems and other business processes can channel attention and energy, complacency is ultimately an organizational attitude that reflects the attitudes and actions of management. Perhaps the single biggest fact that successful managers recognize is that competitive battles, unlike sports events or military conflicts, are *never* completely won. Markets change, competitors adapt (or new ones emerge), and technologies evolve, so the pursuit of business success is never-ending. Indeed, longitudinal studies of the financial performance of companies clearly indicate that it is extremely difficult for any firm to sustain returns significantly greater than its industry's average over a 10-year period.[30]

Any illusions about the permanence of business leadership should be put to rest by reviewing the story of the world watch-making industry, which over a 350-year period has been dominated by a succession of seven different countries. In each case the challenging country and companies employed similar tactics, and the dethroned champions made the same mistake: they failed to adapt to changes in the market, in product technology, or in manufacturing methods.[31] As the *Edinburgh Review* observed in 1843: "In the pure and in the Physical Sciences, each generation inherits the conquests made by its predecessors. But in the Moral Sciences ... particularly the arts of administration ... the ground seems never to be incontestably won." That, after all is said, is perhaps the most important (and timeless) secret of business success.

NOTES

1. See Henderson and Clark (1990); stepping back from this single industry example, Langlois (2003) provides many examples of failures that were attributable to technological change that occurred faster than institutions and organizational structures could adapt.

2. See Christensen (1998).

3. As quoted in *Strategy & Business,* Booz-Allen and Hamilton, Issue 18, pg. 155.

4. One of the reasons the word *team* is so ubiquitous, we are convinced, is that the word *committee* has fallen into disfavor, and *workgroup* sounds too impersonal.

5. See "Levi's Factory Workers are Assigned to Teams, And Morale Takes a Hit," *The Wall Street Journal* (May 20, 1998), pp. A1, 13. Similar vignettes are contained in a broader study of teams in the auto industry by Parker (1993) and Tudor et al. (1996). See also Hackman (1994).

6. Seminal work in this field was done by Katz (1982a and b) and Katz and Allen (1982). More recently, Iansiti (1995) found that the performance of teams developing new integrated circuits was highest when they had worked together on two product generations (about five years)—but no longer. A similar pattern of behavior is often observed in sports teams, but there the deterioration in performance is more likely to be due to the natural aging process than to people's inclination to rely on "proven" solutions to familiar problems.

7. Argyris (1998).

8. Wheelwright and Clark (1992).

9. See, for example, Klein (1991).

10. This example is discussed in Keating et al. (1999).

11. Augmented by the "natural" rate of employee attrition, if this is substantial. See Keating et al. (1999).

12. Upton, in "Mechanisms for Building and Sustaining Operations Improvement," (chapter 33 in Hayes et al. 1996), provides additional perspectives on improvement strategies.

13. Stata (1988).

14. Leonard (1994) uses the term *core rigidities* in referring to this "other side of the coin" regarding capabilities.

15. See Abernathy and Wayne (1976) for a fuller description of this famous battle for supremacy.

16. Quote in Serwer (2000).

17. Park and Burrows (2001).

18. For further information, see *Workplace Safety at Alcoa* (Harvard Business School Case #9-692-042), and Arndt (2001).

19. See *Molding the Impossible: The NYPRO/Vistakon Disposable Contact Lens Project,* (Harvard Business School Case #1-694-062).

20. See "A Measure of Delight: The Pursuit of Quality at AT&T Universal Card Services (*A*)" (Harvard Business School Case #9-694-047).

21. For additional insight into these issues, see Evans and Lindsay (2002).

22. Nakane (1986).

23. See Ferdows and De Meyer (1990).

24. For example, Narasimhan et al. (2001) analyzed the performance of 58 of "America's Best Plants" and suggested that they appeared to build their operating capabilities in the following sequence. As in the Sand Cone model, they began by seeking improvements in such "Foundation" capabilities as quality, dependability, speed and cost. Then they focused on labor productivity and process flexibility. These "internal" capabilities provided the basis for improvements that had more visibility to external customers: new product development, and customer satisfaction. Only then were they able to focus attention on profitability and market share growth.

25. Much of this section is based on Hayes and Pisano (1996).

26. See also Clark (1996).

27. Wheelwright and Hayes (1984).

28. See, for example, Garvin (1988).

29. Reported in Hayes et al. (1988), chapter 6.

30. See Ghemawat (1991), and Foster and Kaplan (2001).

31. Those who would like to explore this history further should read Landes (1979).

Bibliography

A

Abernathy, W. (1978), *The Productivity Dilemma,* Baltimore, MD: The Johns Hopkins University Press.

Abernathy, W. and K. Clark (1985), "Mapping the Winds of Creative Destruction," *Research Policy* 14, no. 3.

Abernathy, W., and J. Corcoran (1983). "Relearning from the Old Masters; Lessons of the American System of Manufacturing." *Journal of Operations Management* 3 (4): 155–167.

Abernathy, W., and J. Utterback (1978). "Patterns of Industrial Innovation." *Technology Review* 80, no. 7 (June–July 1978): 2–9.

Abernathy, W., and K. Wayne (1974). "Limits of the Learning Curve." *Harvard Business Review* (September–October): 109–119.

Adler, P. and K. Clark (1991). "Behind the Learning Curve." *Management Science* 37, no. 3 (March): 267–281.

Alexander, C., S. Ishikawa, and M. Silverstein (1977). *A Pattern Language.* New York: Oxford University Press.

Ambrose, S. (1996). *Undaunted Courage.* New York: Simon & Schuster.

Anctil, R., J. Jordan, and A. Mukherji (1997). "The Asymptotic Optimality of Residual Income Maximization." *Review of Accounting Studies* 2 (3).

Andrews, K. (1971). *The Concept of Corporate Strategy,* Dow Jones-Irwin: Homewood, IL.

Argyris, C. (1998). "Empowerment: The Emperor's New Clothes." *Harvard Business Review* (May–June): 98.

Arndt, M. (2001). "How O'Neill Got Alcoa Shining," *BusinessWeek* (February 5, 2001): 39.

Atkeson, A., and P. Kehoe (2001). "Measuring Organizational Capital." Federal Reserve Bank of Minneapolis Staff Report 291.

B

Barabasi, A. (2002). *Linked: the New Science of Networks.* Cambridge, MA: Perseus Publishing.

Bartelsman, E., and M. Doms (2000). "Understanding Productivity: Lessons from Longitudinal Microdata." *Journal of Economic Literature* 38 (3): 569–595.

Bean, J., J. Higle, and R.Smith (1992). "Capacity Expansion Under Stochastic Demands." *Operations Research* 40, S210–S216.

Berger, L., G. Nast, and C. Raubach (2002). "Fixing Asia's Bad-Debt Mess." *The McKinsey Quarterly* 4: 139–149.

Berinato, S. (2003). "A Day in the Life of Celanese's Big ERP ROL." *CIO Magazine* (January 15): 54–63.

Bernstein, P. (1998). "What Did We Gain from Zapping the Deficit?" *Challenge* (May–June): 5–10.

Bierman, H. (1993). "Capital Budgeting in 1992: A Survey." *Financial Management* (Autumn): 24.

Blocher, E., and C. Stickney (1979). "Duration and Risk Assessment in Capital Budgeting." *The Accounting Review* (January): 50–54.

Bohn, R. (2000). "Stop Fighting Fires." *Harvard Business Review* (July–August): 82–91.

Brandenburger, A., and B. Nalebuff (1996). *Co-opetition.* New York: Currency/Doubleday.

Brealey, R., and S. Myers (1996). *Principles of Corporate Finance.* New York: McGraw-Hill.

Brigham, E. (1975). "Hurdle Rates for Screening Capital Expenditure Proposals." *Financial Management* (Autumn): 18–26.

Brown, J., S. Durchslag, and J. Hagel (2002). "Loosening Up: How Process Networks Unlock the Power of Specialization." *The McKinsey Quarterly, Special Edition: Risk and Resilience,* 59–69.

Burrows, P. (1992). "TQM Reality Check: It Works, But It's Not Cheap or Easy." *Electronic Business* 18: 47–54.

C

Caldwell, B. (1994). "Missteps, Miscues." *Information Week* 20 (June): 50–60.

Carr, N. (2003). "IT Doesn't Matter." *Harvard Business Review* (May 2003): 41–51.

Carroll, D. (1997). "Saving the Chief Executive." *Strategy & Business,* Third Quarter, New York: Booz-Allen & Hamilton, 66–73.

Champy, J (1995). *Reengineering Management: The Mandate for New Leadership.* London: Harper Collins.

Champy, J. (1995). *Reengineering Management: The Mandate for New Leadership.* New York: HarperBusiness.

Chandler, A. (1991). *Scale and Scope: The Dynamics of Industrial Capitalism.* Cambridge, MA: Harvard University Press.

Chesbrough, H. (1998). "Towards a More Contingent View of 'Japanese' Supplier Relations: An Empirical Study of Hard Disk Drive Sourcing Decisions in Japanese Notebook Computers." unpublished manuscript, Harvard Business School, June.

Chesbrough, H., and D. Teece (1996). "When Is Virtual Virtuous: Organizing for Innovation." *Harvard Business Review* 74 (1) (January–February).

Chew, W., T. Bresnahan, and K. Clark (1990). "Measurement, Coordination, and Learning in a Multiplant Network." In *Measures for Manufacturing Excellence,* Robert S. Kaplan (ed.), Boston: Harvard Business School Press.

Choi, T., and K. Eboch (1998). "The TQM Paradox: Relations among TQM practices, plant performance, and customer satisfaction." *Journal of Operations Management* 17: 59–73.

Christensen, C. (1992). *The Innovator's Dilemma.* Boston, MA: Harvard Business School Press.

Christensen, C. (1997). *The Innovator's Dilemma.* Boston, MA: Harvard Business School Press.

Christensen, C. (1998). *The Innovator's Dilemma—Why Great Companies Fail.* Boston: The Harvard Business School Press.

Christensen, C., M. Verlinden, and G. Westerman (1998)."Product Modularity, Vertical Disintegration and the Diffusion of Competence," unpublished manuscript, Harvard Business School, October.

Clark, K. (1985). "The Interaction of Design Hierarchies and Market Concepts in Technological Evolution." *Research Policy* 14, no. 5 (October): pp. 235–251.

Clark, K. (1996). "Competing through Manufacturing and the New Manufacturing Paradigm: Is Manufacturing Strategy Passé?" *Production and Operations Management* 5(1): Spring, 42–58.

Clark. K., and T. Fujimoto (1991). *Product Development Performance: Strategy, Organization, and Management in the World Auto Industry.* Boston: Harvard Business School Press.

Cole, R. (1998). "Learning from the Quality Movement: What Did and Didn't Happen and Why?" *California Management Review* 41 (1): 43–73.

Collins, J. (2001), *Good to Great: Why Some Companies Make the Leap … and Others Don't.* New York: HarperBusiness.

Collins, J., and J. Porras (1994). *Built to Last: Successful Habits of Visionary Companies.* New York: HarperBusiness.

Crawford, M. (1992). "The Hidden Costs of Accelerated Product Development." *Journal of Product Innovation Management* 8: 283–294.

Cusumano, M. (1994). "The Limits of 'Lean'." *Sloan Management Review* (Summer): 27–32.

Cusumano, M., and A. Gawer (2002). *How Intel, Microsoft, and Cisco Drive Industry Innovation,* Boston: HBS Press.

D

Davenport, T. (1995). "Business Process Reengineering: Where It's Been, Where It's Going." In *Business Process Change: Concepts, Methods, and Technologies.* V. Grover and W. Kettinger (eds.). Harrisburg, Penn.: Idea Publishing.

Davenport, T. (1995). *Process Innovation: Reengineering Work through Information Technology.* Boston: Harvard Business School Press.

Davenport, T. (2003). "The New Work Order: A Measurable Proposal." *CIO* (June 1): 46–48.

Davenport, T., and J. Short (1990). "The New Industrial Engineering: Information Technology and Business Process Redesign." *Sloan Management Review* (Summer): 11–27.

Das, A., and R. Narasimhan (2001). "Process-Technology Fit and Its Implications for Manufacturing Performance." *Journal of Operations Management* (19): 521–540.

Day, G., and A. Fein (2002). "Shakeouts in Digital Markets: Lessons from B2B Exchanges." The Wharton School Working Paper, Philadelphia, PA.

Dixit, A., and R. Pindyck (1994). *Investment Under Uncertainty.* Princeton, N.J.: Princeton University Press.

Dixit, A., and R. Pindyck (1995). "The Options Approach to Capital Investment." *Harvard Business Review* (May–June): 105–115.

Dow, D., D. Samson, and S. Ford (1999). "Exploding the Myth: Do All Quality Management Practices Contribute to Superior Quality Performance?" *Production and Operations Management* 8 (1) (Spring): 1–27.

Drucker, P. (1990). "The Emerging Theory of Manufacturing." *Harvard Business Review* (May-June): 98.

Drucker, P. (1994). "Knowledge Work and Knowledge Society: The Social Transformations of This Century." The 1994 Edwin L. Godkin Lecture, Harvard University (unpublished).

Drucker, P. (1988). "The Coming of the New Organization." *Harvard Business Review* (January–February).

Dutton, J., and A. Thomas (1984). "Treating Progress Functions as a Managerial Opportunity." *Academy of Management Review* 9: 235–247.

Dutton, J., A. Thomas and J. Butler (1984). "The History of Progress Functions as a Managerial Technology." *Business History Review* 58 (Summer): 204–233.

E

Ealey, L., and G. Mercer (1992). "Assembly as Design." *The McKinsey Quarterly* 3: 113.

Easton, G., and S. Jarrell (1998). "The Effects of Total Quality Management on Corporate Performance: An Empirical Investigation." *Journal of Business* 71: 253–307.

Easton, G., and S. Jarrell (1998). "The Emerging Academic Research on the Link Between Total Quality Management and Corporate Financial Performance." Chapter 2 in M. Stahl, ed., *Topics on Total Quality Management.* Blackwell Publishers.

Edmondson, A. (1999). "Psychological Safety and Learning Behavior in Work Teams." *Administrative Science Quarterly,* 44: 350–383.

Edmondson, A., R. Bohmer, and G. Pisano (2001). "Disrupted Routines: Team Learning and New Technology Implementation in Hospitals." *Administrative Science Quarterly* 46: 685–716.

Ernst & Young and American Quality Foundation (1992). International Quality Study: The Definitive Study of the Best International Quality Management Practices; Top-Line Findings. Cleveland: Ernst & Young.

Evans, J., and W. Lindsay (2002). *The Management and Control of Quality,* 5th ed. Mason, Ohio: Southwestern Publishing Co.

F

Farragher, E., R. Kleiman, and A. Sahu (1999). "Current Capital Budgeting Practices." *The Engineering Economist* 44 (2): 137–151.

Ferdows, K., and A. DeMeyer (1990). "Lasting Improvements in Manufacturing Performance: In Search of a New Theory." *Journal of Operations Management* 9 (2): 168–184.

Fisher, M., J. Hammond, W. Obermeyer, and A. Raman (1994). "Making Supply Meet Demand in an Uncertain World." *Harvard Business Review* (May–June): 83–93.

Foster, R., and S. Kaplan (2001). *Creative Distruction.* New York: Currency–Doubleday.

Freidenfelds, J. (1980). *Capacity Expansion: Analysis of Simple Models with Applications.* New York: Elsevier-North Holland.

Frohlich, M., and J. Dixon (2001). "A Taxonomy of Manufacturing Strategies Revisited." *Journal of Operations Management,* 19: 541–558.

G

Garvin, D. (1988). *Managing Quality.* New York: Free Press.

Ghemawat, P. (1991). *Commitment: The Dynamic of Strategy.* New York: Free Press.

Ghemawat, P. (2002). "Competition and Business Strategy in Historical Perspective." *Business History Review* 76 (Spring): 37–74.

Gitman, L., and P. Vanderberg (2000). "Cost of Capital Techniques Used by Major U.S. Firms: 1997 vs. 1980." *Financial Practice and Education* (Fall/Winter): 53–68.

Gittell, J. (1995). "Cost/Quality Trade-Offs in the Departure Process? Evidence from the Major U.S. Airlines." *Transporation Research Record* 1480.

Godard, J. (2001). "High Performance and The Transformation of Work? The Implications of Alternative Work Practices for the Experience and Outcomes of Work." *Industrial and Labor Relations,* vol. 54, no. 4 (July): 776–805.

Gooding, R., and J. Wagner III (1985). "A Meta-analytic Review of the Relationship between Size and Performance: The Productivity and Efficiency of Organizations and Their Subunits." *Administrative Science Quarterly* 30: 462–481.

Green, H. (2003). "The Web Smart 50." *BusinessWeek* (November 24): 82–106.

Gross, D., and C.M. Harris (1968). *Fundamentals of Queuing Theory.* New York: Wiley-Interscience.

Grossman. S., and O. Hart (1986). "The Costs and Benefits of Ownership: A Theory of Vertical and Lateral Integration." *Journal of Political Economy* 94 (4): 691–719.

Grover, V., and M. Malhotra (1997). "Business Process Reengineering: A Tutorial on the Concept, Evolution, Methodology and Application." *Journal of Operations Management* 15: 193–213.

Grover, V., J. Teng, and K. Fiedler (1993). "Information Technology Enabled Business Process Redesign: An Integrated Planning Framework." *Omega* 21 (4): 433–447.

Gruber, W. (1986). "Chief Information Officer: A Management Concept Whose Time Has Come." IBM Bulletin (February).

H

Hackman, R., and R. Wageman (1995). "Total Quality Management: Empirical, Conceptual, and Practical Issues." *Administrative Science Quarterly* 40: 309.

Hagel, J. and M. Singer (1999). "Unbundling the Corporation." *Harvard Business Review* (March–April): 133–141.

Hall, G., J. Rosenthal, and J. Wade (1993). "How to Make Reengineering Really Work." *Harvard Business Review* (November–December):119–131.

Hall, R. (1987). *Attaining Manufacturing Excellence.* Homewood, IL: Dow Jones-Irwin.

Hammer, M. (1990). "Reengineering Work: Don't Automate, Obliterate." *Harvard Business Review* (July–August): 104–112.

Hammer, M. (1996). *Beyond Reengineering.* New York: Harper Business.

Hammer, M., and J. Champy (1993). *Reengineering the Corporation: A Manifesto for Business Revolution.* London: HarperCollins.

Hammer, M., and J. Champy (1993). *Reengineering the Corporation.* New York: Harper Business.

Hansson, T., J. Ringbeck, and M. Franke (2002). "A New Business Model for the Airline Industry." *Strategy and Business* (Winter; reprint no. 03208): 78–85.

Harmon, R. (1992). *Reinventing the Factory II: Managing the World Class Factory.* New York: The Free Press.

Hauser, J , and D. Clausing (1988). "The House of Quality." *Harvard Business Review* (May–June): 63–73.

Hayes, R. (1985). "Strategic Planning: Forward in Reverse?" *Harvard Business Review* (November–December): 111–119.

Hayes, R. (2002). "Challenges Posed to Operations Management by the 'New Economy'." *Production and Operations Management* 11 (1), (Spring): 21–32.

Hayes, R. and K. Clark (1985). "Exploring the Sources of Productivity Differences at the Factory Level." In *The Uneasy Alliance: Managing the Productivity-Technology Dilemma,* edited by K. Clark, R. Hayes, and C. Lorenz. Boston, MA: Harvard Business School Press.

Hayes, R., and D. Garvin (1982). "Managing as if Tomorrow Mattered." *Harvard Business Review* (May–June): 70–79.

Hayes, R., and R. Jaikumar (1988). "Manufacturing's Crisis: New Technologies, Obsolete Organizations." *Harvard Business Review* (September–October): 77–85.

Hayes, R., and G. Pisano (1996). "Manufacturing Strategy: At the Intersection of Two Paradigm Shifts." *Production and Operations Management* 5, no. 1 (Spring): 25–41.

Hayes, R., G. Pisano, and D. Upton (1996). *Strategic Operations: Competing Through Capabilities.* New York: The Free Press.

Hayes, R., and R. Schmenner (1978). "How Should You Organize Manufacturing?" *Harvard Business Review* (January–February).

Hayes, R., and D. Upton (1998). "Operations-Based Strategy." *California Management Review* 40, no. 4 (Summer): 8–25.

Hayes, R., and S. Wheelwright (1979a). "Link Manufacturing Process and Product Life Cycles." *Harvard Business Review* (January–February): 133–140.

Hayes, R., and S. Wheelwright (1979b). "The Dynamics of Product-Process Life Cycles." *Harvard Business Review* (March–April): 127–136.

Hayes, R., and S. Wheelwright (1984). *Restoring Our Competitive Edge: Competing Through Manufacturing,* New York: Wiley..

Hayes, R., S. Wheelwright, and K. Clark (1988). *Dynamic Manufacturing: Creating the Learning Organization,* New York: Free Press.

Henderson, R., and K. Clark (1990). "Architectural Innovation: The Reconfiguration of Existing Systems and the Failure of Established Firms." *Administrative Science Quarterly* 35, no. 1 (March): 9–30.

Hendricks, K., and V. Singhal (2001). "Firm Characteristics, Total Quality Management, and Financial Performance." *Journal of Operations Management* 19 (3): 269–286.

Hertz, D. (1968). "Investment Policies That Pay Off." *Harvard Business Review* (January—February): 96–108.

Hill, T. (1989). *Manufacturing Strategy: Text and Cases.* Homewood, IL: Irwin.

Hirschmann, W. (1964). "Profit from the Learning Curve." *Harvard Business Review* (January–February): 125–139.

I

Iansiti, M. (1995) "Technology Integration: Managing Technological Evolution in a Complex Environment." *Research Policy* 24: pp. 521–542.

Iansiti, M., and R. Levien (2003). "Keystones and Dominators: Framing the Operational Dynamics of Business Ecosystems." HBS Working Paper: 1/23/03.

Imai, M. (1986). *Kaizen: The Key to Japan's Competitive Success.* New York: Random House.

Imai, K., I. Nonaka, and H. Takeuchi (1985). "Managing the New Product Development Process: How Japanese Companies Learn and Unlearn." In *The Uneasy Alliance: Managing the Productivity-Technology Dilemma,* edited by K. Clark, R. Hayes, and C. Lorenz. Boston, MA: Harvard Business School Press.

J

Jarmin, R. (1994). "Learning by doing and competition in the early rayon industry." *Rand Journal of Economics,* 25: 441–454.

Johnson, T., and R. Kaplan (1987). *Relevance Lost: The Rise and Fall of Management Accounting.* Boston: Harvard Business School Press.

Johnson, D., and U. Wemmerlov (1996). "On the Relative Performance of Functional Cellular Layouts—An Analysis of the Model-Based Comparative Studies Literature." *Production and Operations Management* vol. 5, no. 4 (Winter): 309–330.

Jorgenson, D., and K. Stiroh (2000). "Raising the Speed Limit: U.S. Economic Growth in the Information Age." Harvard University Working Paper (unpublished).

Joskow, P. (1987). "Contract Duration and Relationship-Specific Investments: Empirical Evidence from Coal Markets." *American Economic Review* 77 (1): 168–185.

Juran, J. (1988). *Juran's Quality Control Handbook,* 4th ed. New York: McGraw-Hill.

K

Katz, R. (1982a). "The Effects of Group Longevity on Project Communication and Performance." *Administrative Science Quarterly* 27: 81–104.

Katz, R (1982b). "Managing Careers: The Influence of Job and Group Longevity." In *Career Issues in Human Resource Management,* R. Katz (ed.), Englewood Cliffs, NJ: Prentice-Hall.

Katz, R., and T. Allen (1982). "Investigating the Not Invented Here (NIH) Syndrome: A Look at the Performance, Tenure, and Communication Patterns of 50 R&D Project Groups." *R&D Management,* 7–19.

Keating E., R. Oliva, N. Repenning, S. Rockart, and J. Sterman (1999). "Overcoming the Improvement Paradox." *European Management Journal* 17 (2): 120–134.

Kelley, J. E., Jr. (1961). "Critical-Path Planning and Scheduling: Mathematical Issues." *Operations Research* (May–June): 296–320.

King, J. (1995). "U.S. West's failed restructuring spells IS overhaul." *Computerworld* 29(9): 6.

Kim, D. (1993). "The Link between Individual and Organizational Learning." *Sloan Management Review* (Fall): 37–50.

Klein, J (1989). "The Human Costs of Manufacturing Reform." *Harvard Business Review* (March–April): 60.

Klein, J. (1991). "A Reexamination of Autonomy in Light of New Manufacturing Practices." *Human Relations* 44: 21–37.

Koch, C. (2001). "ERP Integration: Why Your Integration Efforts End Up Looking Like This…" *CIO Magazine* (November 1): 50.

Kolesar, P., and E. Blum (1973). "Square Root Laws for Fire Engine Response Distances," *Management Science* 19 (12).

Koufteros, X., M. Vonderembse, and W. Doll (2001). "Concurrent Engineering and Its Consequences." *Journal of Operations Management* 19: 97–115.

Krugman, P. (1998). "America the Boastful." *Foreign Affairs* (May–June): 32–45.

Kuhn, T. (1956). *The Structure of Scientific Revolutions.* Chicago: University of Chicago Press.

L

Langlois, R. (2003). "The Vanishing Hand: The Changing Dynamics of Industrial Capitalism." *Industrial and Corporate Change* 12(2): 351–385.

Landes, D. (1979). "Watchmaking: A Case Study of Enterprise and Change." *Business History Review* (Spring).

Lawler, E., and S. Mohrman (1985). "Quality Circles after the Fad." *Harvard Business Review* (January–February): 64.

Lee, H., V. Padmanabhan, and S. Whang (1997). "The Bullwhip Effect in Supply Chains." *Sloan Management Review* (Spring): 93–102.

Leiberman, M. (1987). "Strategies for Capacity Expansion." *Sloan Management Review,* Summer: 19–27.

Leiberman, M. (1989). "Capacity Utilization: Theoretical Models and Empirical Tests." *European Journal of Operations Research* 40: 155–168.

Leonard, D. (1994). "Core Capabilities and Core Rigidities," *The Perpetual Enterprise Machine.* K. Bowen, K. Clark, C. Holloway, and S. Wheelwright (eds.), New York: Oxford University Press.

Levy, F., G. Thompson, and J. Wiest (1963). "The ABCs of the Critical Path Method." *Harvard Business Review* (September–October): 98–108.

Lohmeyer, R., J. McCrory, and S. Pogreb (2002). "Biopharma's Capacity Crunch." *The McKinsey Quarterly, 2002 Special Edition, Risk and Resilience,* 9–15.

Luehrman, T. (1997). "What's It Worth?—A General Manager's Guide to Valuation." *Harvard Business Review* (May–June): 132–141.

Luehrman, T. (1998). "Investment Opportunities as Real Options: Getting Started on the Numbers." *Harvard Business Review* (July–August): 3–15.

Luss, H. (1982). "Operational Research and Capacity Expansion Problems: A Survey." *Operations Research* 30: 907–947.

M

MacCormack, A. (2001). "How Internet Companies Build Software." MIT *Sloan Management Review* (Winter): 75–84.

MacCormack, A., R. Verganti, and M. Iansiti (2001). "Developing Products on 'Internet Time': The Anatomy of the Flexible Development Process." *Management Science* 47, no. 1 (January).

Malpas, R. (1983). "The Plant After Next." *Harvard Business Review* (July–August): 122–130.

Manne, A. (1967). *Investments for Capacity Expansion: Size, Location, and Time-Phasing.* Cambridge, Mass.: M.I.T. Press.

Margulis, S. (1994). "Bad News, Good News about Downsizing." *Managing Office Technology* (April): 23.

Marshall, P., W. Abernathy, R. Olsen, R. Rosenbloom, and D. Wyckoff (1975). *Operations Management: Text and Cases.* Homewood, IL: Richard D. Irwin.

McAfee, A (2003a). "Managing Information Technology: Extra-Enterprise Module Note for Instructors." Harvard Business School case 5-603-028.

McAfee, A. (2003b). "Managing Information Technology: Process-Enabling Information Technology Implementation Model Note for Instructors." Harvard Business School case 5-603-029.

McDonagh, J. (2001). "Not for the Faint Hearted: Social and Organizational Challenges in IT-Enabled Change." *Journal of Organizational Development* 19 (1): 11.

McGrath, R. and I. MacMillan (1995), "Discovery Driven Planning," *Harvard Business Review* 73 (July–August): 44–54.

Merton, R. (1990). *Continuous Time Finance.* Cambridge, Mass.: Basil Blackwell Inc.

Meyer, M., and J. Utterback (1995). "Product Development Cycle Time and Commercial Success." *IEEE Transactions-Engineering Management,* 42 (4): 297–304.

Miller, J., and A. Roth (1994). "A Taxonomy of Manufacturing Strategies." *Management Science,* 40 (3): 285–304.

Miller, L., and C. Park (2002). "Decision Making Under Uncertainty—Real Options to the Rescue?" *The Engineering Economist* 47 (2): 105–150.

Mizuno, S. (1988). *Management for Quality Improvement: The 7 New QC Tools.* Cambridge, Mass.: Productivity Press.

Modigliani, F., and R. Cohen (1979). "Inflation, Rational Valuation, and the Market." *Financial Analysts Journal* (March–April): 24.

Monteverde, K., and D. Teece (1982). "Vertical Integration and Supplier Switching Costs." *Bell Journal of Economics,* 13 (1): 206–213.

Mukherhee, A., W. Mitchell, and F. Talbot (2000). "The Impact of New Manufacturing Requirements on Production Line Productivity and Quality at a Focused Factory." *Journal of Operations Management* (June 2000).

Mulligan, P., and A. Nanni, Jr. (2001). "Operations Strategy: A Response to Market Dynamics." Unpublished Working Paper, Babson College.

Myers, S. (1983). "Finance Theory and Financial Strategy." *Interfaces* (Winter).

N

Nakane, J. (1986). *Manufacturing Futures Survey in Japan, A Comparative Survey 1983–1986.* Tokyo: Waseda University System Science Institute.

Narashimhan, R., M. Swink, and S. Kim (2001). "Strategic Capability Progression Paradigm of Operations Strategy: Evidence from America's Best Plants." Dept. of Marketing and Supply Chain Management Working Paper, Michigan State University.

Nevins, J., D. Whitney, and T. DeFazio (1989). *Concurrent Design of Products and Processes: A Strategy for the Next Generation in Manufacturing.* NY: McGraw-Hill.

Nichols, N. (1994). "Scientific Management at Merck: An Interview with CFO Judy Lewent." *Harvard Business Review* (January–February): 89–99.

O

Oblak, D., and R. Helm (1980). "Survey and Analysis of Capital Budgeting Methods Used by Multinationals." *Financial Management* (Winter): 37–41.

Ohlson, J. (1995). "Earnings, Book Value and Dividends in Security Valuation." *Contemporary Accounting Research* 11(2): 661–687.

Oliner, S. D., and D. E. Sichel (2000). "The Resurgence of Growth in the Late 1990s: Is Information Technology the Story?" Federal Reserve Board Working Paper (unpublished).

Ono, H., and M. Rebick (2003). "Constraints on the Level and Efficient Use of Labor in Japan," National Bureau of Economic Research Working Paper 9484.

P

Park, A., and P. Burrows (2001).)."Dell, The Conqueror," *BusinessWeek* (September 24, 2001): 92–102.

Parker M. (1993). "Industrial Relations Myth and Shop-Floor Reality: The Team Concept in the Auto Industry." In *Industrial Democracy in America: The Ambiguous Promise,* N. Lichtenstein and H. Harris, eds., pp. 249–256.

Penrose, E. (1959). *The Theory of the Growth of the Firm.* Basil Blackwell: London.

Pisano, G.(1989). "Using Equity Participation to Support Exchange." *Journal of Law, Economics, and Organization,* 5 (1) (Spring): 109–126.

Pisano, G. (1990). "The R & D Boundaries of the Firm: An Empirical Analysis." *Administrative Science Quarterly* 35 (1): 153–176.

Pisano, G. (1994). "Knowledge, Integration, and the Locus of Learning: An Empirical Analysis of Process Development." *Strategic Management Journal,* 15: 85–100.

Pisano, G. (1996). *The Development Factory.* Boston: Harvard Business School Press.

Pisano, G. (1997). *The Development Factory.* Boston: HBS Press.

Pisano, G., R. Bohmer, and A. Edmondson (2001). "Organizational Differences in Rates of Learning: Evidence from the Adoption of Minimally Invasive Cardiac Surgery." *Management Science* 47 (6): 752.

Porter, M. (1980). *Competitive Strategy.* New York: Free Press..

Porter, M. (1985). *Competitive Advantage: Creating and Sustaining Superior Performance.* N.Y.: Free Press.

Porter, M. (1996). "What Is Strategy?" *Harvard Business Review* (November–December): 61–78.

Prahalad, C. K., and G. Hamel (1990). "The Core Competence of the Corporation." *Harvard Business Review* (May–June): 79–91.

Prais, S. (1973). "The Strike Proneness of Large Plants in Britain." *Journal of the Royal Statistical Society* (A), 141 (3): 368–384.

R

Raymond, E. (1999). "The Cathedral and the Bazaar: Musings on Linux and Open Source by an Accidental Revolutionary." O'Reilly & Associates.

Reinhardt, F. (2000). *Down to Earth: Applying Business Principles to Environmental Management.* Boston: Harvard Business School Press.

Rohrbach, A. (1927). "Economical Production of All-Metal Airplanes and Sea Planes." *Journal of the Society ofAutomotive Engineers* 20: 57–66.

Rommel, G., J. Kluge, R. Chimps, R. Diederich, and F. Bruck (1995). *Simplicity Wins: How Germany's Mid-sized Industrial Companies Succeed.* Boston: HBS Press.

Ruwe, D., and W. Skinner (1987). "Reviving a Rust Belt Factory." *Harvard Business Review* (May–June): 70–76.

Ryan, T. P. (1989). *Statistical Methods for Quality Improvement.* New York: John Wiley.

S

Safizadeh, M., L. Ritzman, L. Sharma, and D. Wood (1996). "An Empirical Analysis of the Product Process Matrix." *Management Science* 42 (11): 1576–1591.

Sanderson, S., and V. Uzumeri (1991). "Cost Models for Evaluating Virtual Design Strategies in Multicycle Product Families." *Engineering and Technology Management* 8 (3, 4): 339–359.

Scherer, F., A. Beckenstein, E. Kaufer, R. Dennis Murphy, and F. Bougeon-Maassen (1975). *The Economics of Multiplant Operation.* Cambridge, MA: Harvard University Press.

Schmenner, R. (1982). *Making Business Location Decisions.* Englewood Cliffs, NJ: Prentice-Hall.

Schmenner, R. (1976). "Before You Build a Big Factory." *Harvard Business Review* (July–August): 77–81.

Schmenner, R., and M. Swink (1998). "On Theory in Operations Management." *Journal of Operations Management* 17 (1): 97–113.

Schultz, K., J. McCain, and L. J. Thomas (2003). "Overcoming the Dark Side of Worker Flexibility." *Journal of Operations Management* 21: 81–92.

Schumpeter, J. (1942). *Capitalism, Socialism, and Democracy.* New York: Harper.

Schneiderman, A. (1998). "Are There Limits to Total Quality Management?" *Strategy & Business, Booz-Allen & Hamilton,* Third Quarter, 35–45.

Serwer, A. (2000), "The Next Richest Man in the World," *Fortune* (November 13): pg. 98–120.

Shaked, I., A. Michel, and P. Leroy (1997). "Creating Value through E.V.A.—Myth or Reality?" *Strategy and Management* 9 (Fourth Quarter): 41–52.

Shorey, J. (1975). "The Size of the Work Unit and Strikę Incidence." *Journal of Industrial Economy* 23 (3): 175–188.

Sinclair, G., S. Klepper, and W. Cohen (1996). "Piercing the Veil of the Learning Curve." Carnegie Mellon University Working Paper.

Skinner, W. (1969). "Manufacturing—Missing Link in Corporate Strategy." *Harvard Business Review* (May–June): 136–145.

Skinner, W. (1974). "The Focused Factory." *Harvard Business Review* (May–June): 113–121.

Smith, R. (1980). "Optimal Expansion Policies for the Deterministic Capacity Problem." *Engineering Economist* 25: 149–160.

Solomon, E. (1966). "Return on Investment: The Relation of Book-Yield to True Yield." In R. Jaedicke, Y. Ijiri, and O. Nielsen, eds., *Research in Accounting Measurement.* Sarasota, FL: American Accounting Association.

Solomons, D. (1965). "Divisional Performance: Measurement and Control." Financial Executives Institute Research Foundation, Inc., New York.

Sousa, R. (2003). "Linking Quality Management to Manufacturing Strategy: An Empirical Investigation of Customer Focus Practices." *Journal of Operations Management* 21: 1–18.

Spear, S. and K. Bowen. "Decoding the DNA of the Toyota Production System." *Harvard Business Review* (September–October): 97–106.

Stalk, G. Jr. (1988). "Time—The Next Source of Competitive Advantage." *Harvard Business Review* (July–August).

Stalk, G. Jr., and A. Webber (1993). "Japan's Dark Side of Time." *Harvard Business Review* (July–August): 93–103.

Stalk, G., Jr., and A. Webber (1993), *Harvard Business Review*, July–August, pp. 93–103.

Stata, R. (1989). "Organizational Learning—The Key to Management Innovation." *Sloan Management Review* (Spring): 63–74.

Stobaugh, R., and P. Townsend (1975). "Price Forecasting and Strategic Planning: The Case of Petrochemicals." *Journal of Marketing Research* (February): 19–29.

T

Teach, E. (2003). "Will Real Options Take Root?: Why companies have been slow to adopt the valuation technique." *CFO Magazine* (July): 73–76

Teece, David (1982). "Toward an Economic Theory of the Multi-Product Firm." *Journal of Economic Behavior and Organization* 3: 39–63.

Teece, D. (1986). "Profiting From Technological Innovation: Implications for Integrating, Collaborating, Licensing, and Public Policy." *Research Policy* 15 (6): 285–305.

Teece, David J. (1996). *The Multinational Corporation and the Resource Cost of International Technology Transfer.* Cambridge, MA: Ballinger, 1976.

Teece D., and G. Pisano (1994). "The Dynamic Capabilities of Firms: An Introduction." *Industrial and Corporate Change* 3 (3): 537–556.

Thiagarajan, S., and B. Balachandran (1999). *Reengingeering Revisited,* Morristown, NJ: Financial Executives Research Foundation, Inc.

Thomke, S. (2003). *Experimentation Matters.* Boston: HBS Press.

Thomke, S., and E. von Hippel (2002). "Customers as Innovators: A New Way to Create Value." *Harvard Business Review* (April): 74–81.

Tilton, J. (1971). *International Diffusion of Technology: The Case of Semiconductors.* Washington, DC: Brookings Institution.

Tu, Y. (2000). "How Robust Is the Internet?" *Nature* 406 (27 July): 353–354.

Tudor, T., R. Trumble, and J. Diaz (1996). "Work-teams: Why Do They Often Fail?" S.A.M. *Advanced Management Journal* (Autumn): 31–39.

Tushman, M. and P. Anderson (1986. "Technological Discontinuities and Organizational Environments." *Administrative Science Quarterly* 31 (1): 439–465.

U

Ulrich, K. and S. Eppinger (1995). *Product Design and Development.* NY: McGraw-Hill.

Upton, D. (1998). *Designing, Managing, and Improving Operations.* Upper Saddle River, NJ: Prentice Hall.

Utterback, J. (1994). *Mastering the Dynamics of Innovations.* Boston, MA: Harvard Business School Press.

V

Van Ark, B., and D. Pilat (1993). "Productivity Levels in Germany, Japan, and the United States: Differences and Causes." Brookings Papers in *Microeconomics* 2: 1–69.

Van Breda, M. (1981). "Accounting Rates of Return Under Inflation." *Sloan Management Review* (Summer): 15–28.

Verity, J. (2003). "The Urge to Merge." *CFO Magazine* (August): 25.

W

Wagner, H. (1975). *Principles of Operations Research* (2nd edition). Englewood Cliffs: Prentice-Hall.

Ward, P., and R. Duray (2000). "Manufacturing Strategy in Context: Environment, Competitive Strategy and Manufacturing Strategy." *Journal of Operations Management* 18: 123–138.

Ward, P., J. McCreery, L. Ritzman, and D. Sharma (1998). "Competitive Priorities in Operations Management." *Decision Sciences* 29 (4): 1037–1048.

Ware, L. (2003). "By the Numbers. CRM: Desperately Seeking Success." *CIO Magazine* (August 1): 20.

Weiss, L. (1975). "Optimal Plant Size and Extent of Suboptimal Capacity." In *Essays on Industrial Organization in Honor of Joe S. Bain,* R. Masson and P. Quall, eds. Cambridge, Mass.: Ballinger.

Wernerfelt, B. (1984). "A Resource-Based View of the Firm." *Strategic Management Journal* 5: 171–180.

West, J., and M. Iansiti. "Experience, Experimentation, and the Accumulation of Knowledge: An Empirical Study of the Evolution of R & D in the Semiconductor Industry." *Research Policy* (in press).

Wheelwright, S. and K. Clark (1992). *Revolutionizing Product Development.* New York: The Free Press.

Wheelwright, S., and R. Hayes (1985). "Competing through Manufacturing." *Harvard Business Review* (January–February): 99–109.

Wheelwright, S., S. Makridakis, and V. McGee (1983). *Forecasting: Methods and Applications,* 2nd ed. New York: John Wiley & Sons.

Wilkes, F. (1977). *Capital Budgeting Techniques.* New York: John Wiley & Sons.

Williamson, O. (1975). *Markets and Hierarchies.* New York: Free Press.

Williamson, O. (1985). *The Economic Institutions of Capitalism.* New York: Free Press.

Womack, J., D. Jones, and D. Roos (1990). *The Machine that Changed the World.* New York: Macmillan.

Wright, T. (1936). "Factors Affecting the Cost of Airplanes." *Journal of Aeronautical Science,* vol. 3: 122–128.

Index

J

K

L

M